CANADIAN CINEMA
in the NEW MILLENNIUM

CANADIAN CINEMA
in the NEW MILLENNIUM

EDITED BY
Lee Carruthers
and Charles Tepperman

McGill-Queen's University Press
Montreal & Kingston • London • Chicago

© McGill-Queen's University Press 2023

ISBN 978-0-2280-1398-3 (cloth)
ISBN 978-0-2280-1594-9 (paper)
ISBN 978-0-2280-1492-8 (ePDF)

Legal deposit first quarter 2023
Bibliothèque nationale du Québec

Printed in Canada on acid-free paper that is 100% ancient forest free (100% post-consumer recycled), processed chlorine free

This book has been published with the help of a grant from the Canadian Federation for the Humanities and Social Sciences, through the Awards to Scholarly Publications Program, using funds provided by the Social Sciences and Humanities Research Council of Canada.

Funded by the Government of Canada   Financé par le gouvernement du Canada   Canada   Canada Council for the Arts   Conseil des arts du Canada

We acknowledge the support of the Canada Council for the Arts.

Nous remercions le Conseil des arts du Canada de son soutien.

Library and Archives Canada Cataloguing in Publication

Title: Canadian cinema in the new millennium / edited by Lee Carruthers and Charles Tepperman.

Names: Carruthers, Lee, 1971– editor. | Tepperman, Charles, 1974– editor.

Description: Includes bibliographical references and index.

Identifiers: Canadiana (print) 20220400393 | Canadiana (ebook) 20220400474 | ISBN 9780228015949 (softcover) | ISBN 9780228013983 (hardcover) | ISBN 9780228014928 (PDF)

Subjects: LCSH: Motion pictures – Canada – History – 21st century.

Classification: LCC PN1993.5.C3 C36 2023 | DDC 791.430971/0905 – dc23

This book was designed and typeset by Peggy & Co. Design in 10.5/13 Sabon.

Contents

Tables and Figures ix

Acknowledgments xiii

Introduction: Towards a Renewed Critical Optics for Contemporary Canadian Cinema 3
Charles Tepperman and Lee Carruthers

PART ONE: FEATURE FILMS AND FILMMAKERS

1 Speaking across Borders: Xavier Dolan and the Transnationalism of Contemporary Auteur Cinema in Quebec 25
Ian Robinson

2 An Equivocal Auteur: Gauging Style and Substance in the Films of Denis Villeneuve 42
Lee Carruthers

3 A "Momentary Melancholy": Female Desire and the Promise of Happiness in the Cinema of Sarah Polley 67
Tanya Horeck

4 Indigenous Women's Cinema in Quebec: The Works and Words of Mohawk Filmmaker Sonia Bonspille Boileau 87
Karine Bertrand

5 *Le cinéma à l'estomac*: Denis Côté and the New Wave of Quebec Cinema (2004–19)   104
   Jean-Pierre Sirois-Trahan

6 Fluid Privilege: Reading "Canadian" Water in *Wet Bum* (2014) and *Sleeping Giant* (2015)   120
   Jennifer VanderBurgh

7 Toronto's New DIY Filmmakers   134
   David Davidson

8 Northern Frights: Canadian Horror in the Twenty-First Century   150
   Murray Leeder

PART TWO: DOCUMENTARY AND EXPERIMENTAL FILMMAKING

9 *Beauty Day* and the Crises of Self-Directed Work   169
   Mike Meneghetti

10 Mythologizing Manitoba: The Negated Truth of *My Winnipeg*   186
   Miriam Siegel and Charlie Keil

11 Indigenizing the Archive: *Souvenir* and the NFB   203
   Gillian Roberts

12 I-doc and My-doc: *Bear 71* and *Highrise* as Canadian Documentaries   217
   Seth Feldman

13 Diasporic Sights: Trauma and Representation in Recent Canadian Poetic Cinema   234
   Dan Browne

14 dominique t. skoltz and New States of Cinematic Matter   256
   Melanie Wilmink

PART THREE: CANADIAN FILM CONTEXTS, FESTIVALS, AND INDUSTRIES

15 A Taxing Culture: Reconsidering the Service Production   275
   Charles R. Acland

16 Collective *Action!* Unions in the Canadian Film and
    Television Industry   298
    Amanda Coles

17 Making *Room*: International Co-productions and Canadian
    National Cinema   321
    Peter Lester

18 Troubling Toronto Queer Festivals: Transgressions in and of
    Queer Counterpublics   340
    Aimée Mitchell

19 From Showcase to Lightbox: Programming the National on the
    Festival Circuit   370
    Diane Burgess

    Contributors   395
    Index   401

Tables and Figures

Tables

2.1 Formal and conceptual trends in the films of Denis Villeneuve. 48

17.1 International co-productions by language of project (film, television, digital media), 2006–20. 327

Figures

1.1 The scene is flooded with excessive emotion as a waterfall suddenly descends upon Fred's living room. *Laurence Anyways* (Xavier Dolan, 2012). Screen capture. 29

1.2 Steve rides his skateboard in a sequence set to Counting Crows' "Colorblind." *Mommy* (Xavier Dolan, 2014). Screen capture. 39

2.1 *Breathing Light* (2013) serves as a model for the alien interview room in *Arrival* (Denis Villeneuve, 2016). 52

2.2 Symmetrical composition in *Maelström* (Denis Villeneuve, 2000). Screen capture. 53

3.1 Tessa as filmmaker in *I Shout Love* (Sarah Polley, 2001). Screen capture. 72

3.2 Margot and Daniel on the Scrambler in *Take This Waltz* (Sarah Polley, 2011). Screen capture. 80

4.1 Sonia Bonspille Boileau with Eve Ringuette and Charles Buckell-Robertson on the set of *Le Dep* (2014). Photograph by Randy Kelly, courtesy of Sonia Bonspille Boileau. 89

4.2 Sonia Bonspille Boileau with actresses Carmen Moore and Lake Delisle on the set of *Rustic Oracle* (2019). Photograph by Randy Kelly, courtesy of Sonia Bonspille Boileau. 97
5.1 Denis Côté. Photograph by Lou Scamble, courtesy of Denis Côté. 105
5.2 Emmanuel Bilodeau in *Curling* (Denis Côté, 2010). Photograph courtesy of Denis Côté. 110
5.3 The zoo as a prison in *Bestiary* (Denis Côté, 2012). Photograph courtesy of Denis Côté. 115
6.1 Water as metaphor in *Wet Bum* (Lindsay MacKay, 2014). Screen capture. 124
6.2 The Sleeping Giant framed in the distance. *Sleeping Giant* (Andrew Cividino, 2015). Screen capture. 128
7.1 Matt Johnson, Matt Greyson, Andy Appelle, Matthew Miller, Jared Raab, and Owen Williams on the set of *Operation Avalanche* (July 2014). Photograph by Colin Medley, courtesy of Zapruder Films Inc. 137
7.2 Dan Montgomery and Kazik Radwanski. Photograph courtesy of MDFF. 142
8.1 Wilderness defeats Alex in *Backcountry* (Adam MacDonald, 2014). Screen capture. 155
8.2 The process of cultural assimilation is represented through a body horror idiom in *File Under Miscellaneous* (Jeff Barnaby, 2010). Screen capture. 156
9.1 Poster for *Beauty Day* (Jay Cheel, 2011), reproduced courtesy of Jay Cheel. 172
9.2 Ralph Zavadil at his video editing suite in *Beauty Day* (Jay Cheel, 2011). Screen capture. 181
10.1 A fancifully fictionalized shot of a sleepy figure inside a train carriage in *My Winnipeg* (Guy Maddin, 2007). Screen capture. 190
10.2 Mother is imbued with the fantastic power of the buffalo in *My Winnipeg* (Guy Maddin, 2007). Screen capture. 195
11.1 Superimposition of children and buffalo in *Sisters & Brothers* (Kent Monkman, 2015). Screen capture. 207
11.2 Separation of birch bark from the trunk in *Mobilize* (Caroline Monnet, 2015). Screen capture. 209
12.1 Poster for *Bear 71* (Leanne Allison and Jeremy Mendes, 2012), courtesy of the National Film Board of Canada. 222
12.2 Production still from *Highrise* (Katerina Cizek, 2010), courtesy of the National Film Board of Canada. 227

Tables and Figures

13.1 *Stone Time Touch* (Gariné Torossian, 2007, 72 minutes, digital video). Reproduced with permission from the artist. 239
13.2 *Echo* (Izabella Pruska-Oldenhof, 2007, 10 minutes, 16mm). Reproduced with permission from the artist. 243
13.3 *perhaps/We* (Solomon Nagler, 2003, 11 minutes, 16mm). Reproduced with permission from the artist. 245
13.4 *What Comes Between* (Cecilia Araneda, 2009, 6 minutes, 16mm/digital video). Reproduced with permission from the artist. 247
13.5 *Retrato Oficial (Official Portrait)* (Francisca Duran, 2003, 1 min, 16mm). Reproduced with permission from the artist. 247
13.6 *her silent life* (Lindsay McIntyre, 2011, 31 minutes, 16mm/digital video). Reproduced with permission from the artist. 250
14.1 *y20 dualités_* at Arsenal Toronto (dominique t. skoltz, 2015). Photo by dominique t. skoltz. 260
14.2 *y20 Huis clos* (2015) at Arsenal Montreal (dominique t. skoltz, 2016). Photo by dominique t. skoltz. 262
14.3 *y20 single channel* (dominique t. skoltz, 2015) at Arsenal Montreal (2016). Photo by Melanie Wilmink. 264
15.1 Poster for *Resident Evil: Afterlife* (2010). Constantine Film. 279
15.2 Poster for *The Shape of Water* (2014). Searchlight Pictures. 279
16.1 Film and television production in Canada by subsector, 2018/19. 305
16.2 Direct FTE jobs in the Canadian independent film and television production industry, by subsector, 2009–19. 306
16.3 FLS total number of projects and expenditure, 2009–19. 307
16.4 Canadian theatrical feature and television, total number of projects and expenditure, 2009–19. 307
16.5 Production distribution by subsector, major production centres, 2018/19. 309
17.1 International co-productions (film) in Canada, 2006–20. 326
18.1 Toronto Queer Film Festival 2017 poster, designed by Gardenia Flores. 344
19.1 Top Ten Film Festival promotional tweet from TIFF. Screen capture. 381
19.2 A promotional banner for National Canadian Film Day, @canfilmday, Instagram, 8 February, 2017. 385

Acknowledgments

The preparation of this book has been a lengthy process, extended in the final phases by an ongoing global pandemic. But it remains a project that was fuelled by the contributors' passion for Canadian films and their commitment to being part of a renewed dialogue about this work. We thank the contributors for their patience and responsiveness, and for sharing their ideas in the first place; it really has been a pleasure to work with this group of scholars. We also thank the filmmakers, programmers, critics, and other advocates of Canadian cinema who make our research possible.

In addition to our wonderful contributors, we wish to acknowledge the support of the Social Sciences and Humanities Research Council. The volume's origins date back to a research project about Canadian film producers. The book benefitted from research funded by that project, and from the contributions of some wonderful research assistants: Mary Arnatt, Neha Bhatia, Joel Sutherland, and Katie Wackett. The editors also convened a workshop about contemporary Canadian cinema at the 2018 SCMS Conference in Toronto – thanks to the participants Magali Simard, Seth Feldman, Peter Urquhart, and Aimée Mitchell, as well as the workshop attendees for their incisive comments, questions, and critiques.

The editors have had numerous enriching conversations with students, colleagues, and visitors to Calgary including Jim Ellis, Matt Croombs, Ryan Pierson, Leah Vonderheide, Andrew Watts, Greg Taylor, Annie Rudd, Trevor Stark, Brian Rusted, George Melnyk, Donna Brunsdale, Gary Burns, Mary Graham, Jarret Twoyoungmen, Deepa Mehta,

Nettie Wild, Phil Hoffman, and Guy Maddin. We also thank Jesse Wente for visiting Calgary to present an incisive CanWest Global Lecture, "Building Narrative Sovereignty: From Philosophy to Implementation," which has shaped our thinking in powerful ways. Beyond Calgary, we sincerely value the friends and colleagues who have been especially supportive of this project: Gillian Roberts, Theresa Scandiffio, Charlie Keil, and Alison Whitney.

Thanks also to the excellent team at McGill-Queen's, especially Jonathan Crago for his keen eye and unwavering support, and the folks there who facilitated every phase of the publication process: Elli Stylianou, Kathleen Fraser, Scott Howard, and Filomena Falocco. We'd also like to acknowledge the anonymous peer reviewers whose generous and detailed feedback shaped the final manuscript in valuable ways.

Thanks, finally, to our families: in particular, Heather, Scott, and Tanya have been supportive at key moments in this process. During the pandemic, friendship has been more crucial than ever: thanks to Jon Mee and Christie Hurrell for visits and good cheer on the stoop, and to Dawn Johnston and Lisa Stowe for all their hospitality and kind commiseration. Last, but definitely not least, thanks to Laurel for enduring long conversations about Canadian film – we hope she becomes an avid viewer!

CANADIAN CINEMA
in the NEW MILLENNIUM

INTRODUCTION

Towards a Renewed Critical Optics for Contemporary Canadian Cinema

Charles Tepperman and Lee Carruthers

At the turn of the last millennium, Canadian cinema seemed at the apex of aesthetic and commercial transformation, fuelled by the emergence of new and critically acclaimed directors across three decades. Building on the success of established auteurs like David Cronenberg, Denys Arcand, and others, new figures such as Atom Egoyan, Deepa Mehta, and Patricia Rozema began to claim international recognition, signalling the arrival of Canadian cinema to the global scene. At the same time, Canadian film institutions underwent parallel metamorphoses, as the Toronto International Film Festival (TIFF) grew into one of the preeminent festivals in the world. Tax credit policy drove similar transformations of scale, recasting what had been a relatively small industry into a major hub for global film production, located primarily in Vancouver, Toronto, and Montreal. With vibrant independent films from English and French Canada, as well as the breakout success of the Inuktitut-language film *Atanarjuat: The Fast Runner* (Zacharais Kunuk, Inuk) at Cannes in 2001, Canadian film appeared set for tremendous growth in the new century.

Yet two decades on, we find ourselves with a very different picture of Canadian cinema's status. The promise of international recognition and imminent expansion, so plausible in the early 2000s, has faltered, leaving Canada's industry with a reduced cultural footprint. While Quebec filmmaking retains a popular dimension, the sense of celebrity associated with Canadian indie directors has receded from everyday discourse. Academic discussion of Canadian cinema has waned as well, corresponding to paradigm shifts in the field: in large part, film scholars have moved away from the concepts and methodological practices that once facilitated our understanding of Canadian filmmaking, setting aside broad notions of "nation" and the auteur, as well as tasks of close textual reading. Recalling (and deepening) the long-standing dilemma of national distinctiveness, such changes effect a compound problem of visibility: Canadian productions of the last twenty years have not only endured a sharp decline in commercial and cultural status, they also lack the explanatory frameworks that once gave them legibility.

This problem also relates to the divergent trajectories that Canadian filmmaking has pursued in the past twenty years, moving towards scales of production at once too big and too small. On one side, policymakers in the early 2000s supported the production of bigger-budget films, in hopes that these would reach larger audiences.[1] This ambitious focus on the global, however, has tended to efface local markers: while made in Canada, such big-budget productions (including co-productions, and so-called runaway productions) are not always recognizable as Canadian films at all. At the other end of the spectrum, Telefilm and the NFB have promoted microbudget film production, striving to nurture new talent and creative experimentation in the Canadian film context. Yet this strategy has not been broadly impactful: such initiatives, while supportive, tend not to produce work that is seen beyond the film festival circuit. To complicate matters, the power of film festivals themselves to provide a platform for the work has also diminished in recent years: TIFF's Perspective Canada program, which played a crucial role in elevating the status of a generation of new Canadian directors in the 1990s, was discontinued in 2004.[2] There are certainly exceptions to this trend – including a somewhat more robust domestic market for Quebec films, and the rise of Indigenous directors – but in general, Canadian cinema has been winnowed by divergent impulses, unable to harmonize the competing claims of commercial and creative imperatives.

This volume is a considered response to this situation, aiming to revitalize scholarly attention to Canadian cinema through focused case studies of films, filmmakers, and film contexts in Canada since 2000. Specifically, we hope to highlight the particularities of Canadian cinema *now*, tracing its eclectic energies across local and global forms. The chapters assembled here spend time with large-scale commercial works and at the margins of film production, finding in these diverse practices a certain resistance to received ideas. Through varied critical and analytical approaches, these studies speak to the diversity of Canada's population; the transnational nature of contemporary film culture; and the hybrid film styles that filmmakers deploy today. Taken individually, the chapters are often granular in their mode of observation, remarking on the characteristic look and feel of recent films, even while rethinking the extent to which they constitute a shared media terrain. In this way, the book negotiates a productive tension between analysis and theory, or between the twinned scholarly tasks of investigation and extrapolation, testing the explanatory power of each. It strives to convey the richness of Canadian cinema coherently, capturing specificities and larger trends, while acknowledging remarkable contrasts of scale and prolific diversities. From an editorial standpoint, the temptation is to propose a unifying concept for both Canadian industry and practice that claims to contain its multitudes, somehow explaining complex processes without reduction. This book does not promise such a concept, or endorse one: instead, we try to hold open a space a little adjacent to theory, but receptive to the dialogue that it potentially creates. As a collection, this volume proposes a *renewed critical optics*, reading recent Canadian films in ways that are open-ended and energizing for future research.

A renewed critical optics seeks to provide fresh perspectives on new and neglected films and filmmakers within the recent Canadian scene. While certain directors – Denis Villeneuve, Xavier Dolan, Sarah Polley, Guy Maddin, and Zacharias Kunuk, most prominently – have received considerable critical acclaim, this recognition has not always sparked a proportionate response among film scholars, nor yielded a decisive research framework to situate their distinctive contributions to cinema.[3] Even less attention has been paid to the creators of small-budget independent films, documentaries, and experimental works in the past two decades, though these texts likewise deserve our attention. The authors contributing to this volume redress this issue in thoughtful ways, introducing readers to lesser-known films and filmmakers while making a compelling case for their relevance, or alternately, by reading celebrated directors and films innovatively, to invite a reconsideration of their relationship to Canadian film practice. What unifies these discussions is an appreciable critical energy that derives from a close engagement with the films themselves; a desire to forge new scholarly approaches for analyzing individual works, categories, and contexts; and above all, a commitment to keeping the conversation about Canadian film going.

Most recently, Canadian cinema has faced a host of new challenges, as filmmakers, producers, institutions, funding agencies, and festivals grapple with pressing issues of diversity and technological transformation. Government film agencies have newly established policies and offices to stimulate opportunities for groups that have long been marginalized in Canadian film production: to this end, new gender parity goals were established by the NFB and Telefilm in 2016; the Indigenous Screen Office was established in 2018; and the Black Screen Office was established in 2020. At the same time, Canadian producers struggled to adjust to the changing media distribution model posed by streaming services like Netflix: in 2020, the federal government initiated the process of bringing these non-Canadian companies under the jurisdiction of the Canadian Broadcasting Act. It is hoped that these changes will result in more government support for the production and distribution of Canadian content.

In the past two years, Canadian cinema has also reckoned with the realities of a global health crisis. The unprecedented conditions created by the COVID-19 pandemic threatened to extinguish the theatrical exhibition of Canadian films altogether, pushing both cinema and festival programming online. The Canadian production sector was adversely affected by these sudden circumstances, with filming halted or delayed due to health concerns; fortunately, the industry quickly developed safety protocols, increasing the likelihood that production will fully rebound in the post-pandemic context. Writing in 2022, it is still too soon to say how Canadian film will emerge from this global crisis: while Canadian cinema may be profoundly altered by these developments, this book will help us to envision the scale and significance of such transformations.

Renewing the Conversation about Canadian Cinema

Because the last wave of publications about Canadian cinema appeared over a decade ago, our book provides a more proximate assessment, speaking to the latest films and evolving contexts of production. Reviewing the most recent crop of scholarly studies, one immediately observes their critical range and value, but also the extent to which this literature leaves open important opportunities for investigation. This volume is strongly motivated by the stylistic features of individual works, and in particular, the way these specificities discernibly mediate both proximate and transnational influences. In other words, this collection is keenly interested in the way that such influences flow across borders and circulate within filmic texts, leaving traces for fruitful interpretation.

Several publications appearing in the early 2000s sought to trace Canadian cinema's historical trajectory while responding to major advances in its development through the 1980s and 1990s. For example,

Jim Leach's *Film in Canada* (2006, second edition 2011) stands as the most comprehensive overview of Canadian film to date, but as a general survey of historical and contemporary material, its scope does not lend itself to in-depth examination of recent films.[4] With a different approach to historical overview, Jerry White's edited collection *The Cinema of Canada* (2006) presents essays on twenty-four films, covering English-, French-, and Indigenous-language filmmaking from the 1940s up to 2001, but with a major focus on films from the 1980s and 90s.[5] Three other volumes have scrutinized Canadian cinema's more recent development. In their 2002 collection, *North of Everything: English-Canadian Cinema since 1980*, Bill Beard and Jerry White assembled essays examining different aspects of Indigenous and English-language Canadian cinema, tracing a host of Canadian film contexts before focusing on particular directors of feature and avant-garde films in Canada.[6] Our collection shares Beard and White's goal of being wide ranging while speaking to individual works, but in this volume, we have grouped studies of English-, French-, and Indigenous-language filmmaking together to foreground potential interconnections across divergent titles produced and circulating in Canada since 2000.

Taking a more narrowly focused approach, Tom McSorley and André Loiselle's 2006 volume, *Self-Portraits*, surveys production in select regions of Canada from the 1990s to the early 2000s.[7] Finally, David Pike's *Canadian Cinema since the 1980s: At the Heart of the World* (2012) addresses the successes of the art cinemas in Quebec and Ontario during the 1980s and '90s, as well as Quebec's popular output, linking them to the rising status of the Toronto International Film Festival.[8] A handful of other studies have explored Canadian cinema from different vantage points, addressing Asian-Canadian cinemas, Canada's cultural industries, and Canada's urban imaginary, but the chronology of these texts is chiefly constrained to the early 2000s.[9] The essays in our collection extend some of the critical trajectories initiated in this scholarship, but with a marked commitment to the increasingly cosmopolitan, diverse, and transnational nature of cinema in Canada.

In the interim, only one study has examined contemporary Canadian film and film culture in any detail. Will Straw and Janine Marchessault's recent collection of essays, *The Oxford Handbook of Canadian Cinema* (2019), provides a broad overview of the field while also advancing new conceptual and theoretical frames.[10] Their volume, more than any before, seeks to dismantle the scaffolding of "national identity" in Canadian film studies so as to examine the topic from new vantage points. On one hand, this emphasis invites a more capacious understanding of

Canadian cinema that includes media art installations and video games, as well as conventional modes of film production and consumption. On the other, it identifies linkages between films and political solidarities, especially with respect to feminist, Indigenous, and LGBTQ+ communities. We share the editors' commitment to identifying new connections across disparate topics while also seeking renewed methods and critical frameworks for Canadian cinema and its contexts.[11] But in our collection, these priorities are recalibrated to assume a different form: rather than presenting wide-ranging explorations of different Canadian cinema topics, our authors advance their insights in a more concentrated fashion, examining select films and filmmakers intensively, as though held in close-up. While there are genuine affinities with Straw and Marchessault's volume, the studies collected here speak concretely to the themes and stylistic strategies that have catalyzed individual works over the past two decades. These detailed case studies are designed to promote lively discussion about particular films and the contexts that nourish them, serving as appealing models of analysis for emerging scholars and seasoned researchers alike.

Another recent and essential development in Canadian cinema is the marked expansion of Indigenous filmmaking in Canada since 2000, which has seen both increased production and a widening of critical attention. As noted at the outset, *Atanarjuat: The Fast Runner*, the first feature film released in the Inuktitut language, was released in 2001 to global acclaim, premiering at Cannes and receiving the Camera d'Or award. This widespread recognition prompted discussion about the ways Indigenous filmmaking is supported in Canada; since the film's release, there have been meaningful efforts to expand training and production opportunities for Indigenous filmmakers. Looking to the literature, Marchessault and Straw's collection helpfully situates these shifts, especially in Karine Bertrand's overview of Indigenous filmmaking and MacKenzie and Westerståhl Stenport's discussion of Inuit cinemas. Likewise, a special issue of the *Canadian Journal of Film Studies* on "Indigenous Cinema and Media in the Americas: Storytelling, Communities, and Sovereignties" has further extended the scholarly examination of recent Indigenous filmmaking.[12] Once again, our volume's contribution to this growing body of work lies in its focus on individual filmmakers and films, featuring chapters on First Nations filmmaker Sonia Bonspille Boileau, for example, and the NFB's *Souvenir* film project. Within this collection, these essays participate in the vital process of nuancing accounts of Indigenous filmmakers in relation to Canadian institutions and shared production contexts, mobilizing new and profound pathways of research.

This volume also charts another kind of shift related to Canadian cinema that concerns its broader conceptualization. Critiques of "national cinema" necessarily alter the way filmmaking in Canada is conceived and have featured prominently in film studies scholarship for over two decades.[13] Some of these critiques are motivated by the cultural and economic globalization that took form in the 1980s and 90s and has since accelerated, fuelled by the internet, social media, and digital distribution. As many scholars have noted, these developments have tended to erode the autonomy of nations as distinct economic and cultural formations.[14] Nevertheless, an idea of nation still provides a facilitative category for understanding flows of global populations, capital, and culture – though one that requires ongoing problematization. Research in film studies has identified *transnational cinema* as a valuable framework for examining the relationship between the economic forces and cultural affinities within borders and the movement and exchange of these across the globe.[15] This transnational approach is an informing principle for this volume, deployed explicitly by a number of our contributors, recognizing the permeability of national borders and the complex flows of commerce and culture that inflect Canada's cinema.

Re-evaluations of Canadian nationhood gained additional force in 2015 when the Truth and Reconciliation Commission brought the historical effects of residential schools, colonization, and systemic racism against Indigenous people to the centre of Canadian media discourse. If the dualities of French- and English-language cinemas in Canada had already unsettled the idea of nation as a unifying category, the recognition of Indigenous nations and territories within Canada has further dismantled it, insisting on the plurality of Canadian cinema as comprising multiple nations and creative practices. The discussions collected here share this insistence, making an acknowledgment of Canada's troubling history of colonization part of what nation means in our assessment of institutional policies and cultural networks. We have sought to make the visibility of Indigenous experience and Canada's colonial past an essential part of this book's contemporary critical optics, aiming to reveal Canadian cinema and questions of national identity with new clarity.

Writing Canadian Cinema in a Time of Change

This book comes together at a moment of flux within Canadian film scholarship and film practice, and therefore reflects recent modulations in scholarly language and priorities as well as new ways of conceiving aesthetics and politics at a dynamic interface. This conceptual realignment introduces fresh complexities and affords some excellent scholarly opportunities: our collection highlights the growing number of films made by women, LGBTQ+, and Indigenous people, for example, and acutely assesses both the international and local valences of Canadian film production. Representing the remarkable range of film production in Canada over the past two decades, however, is a daunting task for any publication. Canadian film includes a large English-language industry (largely based in Toronto and Vancouver); a robust French-language film industry (primarily in Montreal); and an increasingly acclaimed sector of Indigenous filmmaking (occurring across Canada). In addition to these major segments, there are significant communities of filmmakers from other regions and marginalized groups who contribute to the multifaceted nature of Canadian film practice. At the federal level, agencies such as Telefilm Canada and the National Film Board support film production under the oversight and regulation of the federal government. But significant differences in institutional, cultural, and creative contexts exist when we examine these sites of production and circulation according to provincial, regional, linguistic, and local logics.

The chapters in this collection touch on aspects of these different contexts, but not all of them in equal measure. While our volume's greater focus on English-language film production reflects the economic division of film production in Canada, it does not fully convey the cultural significance of Quebec and Indigenous cinemas or their justified critical acclaim. With these diverse contexts in mind, it is valuable to briefly sketch the general terrain of film production and circulation in Canada. Overall, commercial film production in Canada includes both Canadian content production and foreign and location service (runaway) production.[16] The latter category is significantly larger than the former: in 2019/20, 112 Canadian theatrical feature films were made, but Canadians worked on 166 runaway feature film productions, often with much larger budgets than the Canadian films. While foreign service production has increased significantly over the past decade, Canadian independent production has stagnated.[17] Most of this production activity takes place in Ontario (38 per cent) and BC (30 per cent), with a slightly smaller share in Quebec (25 per cent). Only a very small share of the total Canadian film production is Indigenous, but this is certainly growing.[18]

Approximately three-quarters of domestic Canadian film production is in English, but as we have noted, these films struggle to attain visibility within the pop cultural landscape. Since Canada is considered part of the domestic market for the American film industry, English-language

Canadian films compete against American films with much larger production budgets (typically more than ten times that of a Canadian film), and which benefit from enormous promotion and distribution budgets as well. Because of these factors, films from English Canada struggle to gain large theatrical releases that could reach wide audiences; given these constraints, it's unsurprising that Canadian films are far less prominent than American titles within our cultural discourse. While the increase in overall production (domestic and foreign service production) can have some positive effects on the English-language production ecosystem, key creative roles for foreign productions shot in Canada often aren't available to Canadians. As director of the Writers Guild of Canada Maureen Parker notes, "[Foreign location service production] has taken over our industry ... Canadian tax dollars are being used to support U.S. production. Canadians are making shows that they have no ownership in, and which lack a Canadian voice."[19] Because the writing teams for US productions are typically based in Hollywood, Canadian writers need to move to the US to find these opportunities, even if the film is eventually shot in Canada. So while the English-language Canadian film industry has grown significantly over the past two decades and created new roles and opportunities for technical and craft professionals, there is not necessarily a corresponding growth in opportunity for Canadian creative voices, especially writers and directors.

The film scene in Quebec, however, differs from other parts of the country. While it also includes some foreign service production, it is notable that domestic film production has been a substantial part of the province's culture for decades. Overall, approximately 25 per cent of Canadian film and TV production in Canada takes place in Quebec, but it assumes much greater prominence in that context: its enhanced status within the province relates to the characteristics of the French-language industry and the extent to which domestically produced films sometimes receive a robust cultural reception. Across the Canadian English-language market, domestically produced films typically capture less than 2 per cent of the theatrical box office revenue; in the French-language market (primarily in Quebec) local productions have averaged about 12 per cent of the theatrical box office over the past decade.[20] We can identify three broad categories of domestic production in Quebec: genre films that find a large domestic audience in the province but have very little popular success internationally (*Séraphin* and the *Les Boys* franchise, for example); a strong tradition of art cinema filmmaking that finds critical success on the international festival circuit, but a relatively small audience domestically (Denis Côté, Sophie Deraspe, Kim Nguyen); and a handful of prestige filmmakers whose global success, sometimes in the form of Oscar nominations, has resulted in strong commercial and critical success both in Quebec and abroad (Arcand, Dolan, Villeneuve, Vallée). The cultural significance of domestic filmmaking in Quebec is reflected in the prominent role played by the Société de développement des entreprises culturelles (SODEC). While other provinces have provincial agencies dedicated to administering tax credit programs and promoting filmmaking in their jurisdictions, SODEC's mandate is much more expansive and focuses on supporting Quebec culture (not just industry) in film and other arts. The work of SODEC extends from Quebec's Loi sur le cinéma legislation, which specifically creates supports for film production and culture in the province.[21] In this important respect, film policy in Quebec has been more squarely devoted to accomplishing cultural objectives via production, where other provinces have prioritized economic aims.

Concerning the expansion of Indigenous filmmaking in Canada in recent years, programmer and Indigenous film advocate Jesse Wente (Ojibwe) has characterized the phase following *Atanarjuat: The Fast Runner* as a "New Wave" of Indigenous filmmaking.[22] In 2018, Wente was named first director of the Indigenous Screen Office, an agency established to "provide narrative sovereignty and to help make resources become available to accomplish that goal."[23] He writes, "Not only do Indigenous peoples need a vibrant screen sector, one that employs them, and allows for the telling of our own stories; such a sector is also deeply important for non-Indigenous peoples – so that they may hear our stories from us, so that we may learn together, so that we may build a better future for us all."[24] The past few years evidence the kind of proliferation that Wente describes, heralding a number of critically acclaimed films by Indigenous filmmakers: these include new works by established directors Kunuk and Alanis Obomsawin (Abenaki), and a new generation of emergent filmmakers such as Tasha Hubbard (Cree), Jeff Barnaby (Mi'kmaq), Tracey Deer (Mohawk), Elle-Máijá Tailfeathers (Blackfoot and Sámi), Lisa Jackson (Anishinaabe), and Sonia Bonspille Boileau (Mohawk), among others. Indeed, Indigenous films have raised the profile of Canadian cinema both domestically and abroad. Within Canada, the imagineNATIVE Film + Media Arts Festival has served as an important venue for launching Indigenous films since 1998; in recent years new works have also premiered at TIFF and other major international festivals. Thus the scale and significance of Indigenous filmmaking in Canada has grown very quickly.

While this collection cannot speak to all of Canada's film production cultures and contexts, its case studies serve as useful points of access to

… a range of milieu, inviting further research. We have also sought to highlight the varied scholarly approaches that can be brought to Canadian cinema topics: for example, a discernible through line for this volume is its effort to revive methods of close textual analysis, arguing for the continued utility of this approach as it reveals the aesthetic complexity of individual works and the ways Canadian filmmakers respond creatively to the medium.[25] Another connective thread concerns the increasingly transnational nature of film production and circulation: several of the essays featured here interrogate the place of Canadian cinema in a multi-ethnic and globalized context. This volume also addresses the ways that recent Canadian films mediate issues of reconciliation between the settler state and Indigenous people. Foregoing any single critical framework for these complex issues, our contributors engage them through generative modes of inquiry, initiating rich conversations with filmmakers and detailed examinations of filmic texts. Finally, this book considers the extent to which the past two decades are conditioned by vast changes in media technology, including the proliferation of digital production and distribution and the decline of theatrical moviegoing and network television.

As these different emphases attest, the discussions featured here vary widely in subject matter and approach. Nevertheless, recurring critical foci can be distinguished across the chapters, locating strong alignments: this volume considers Canadian film in a transnational frame (global audiences and industries); re-evaluates previous critical categories (auteur, documentary, and experimental film); examines creative and cultural networks (young cinema in Toronto and Quebec, festivals and community-building); and illuminates geographies of cultural and climate disaster (wilderness spaces, Indigenous cultures). In addition, it provides new scholarship on key developments in Canadian cinema of the past twenty years, including the *renouveau* or Quebec New Wave, the Toronto DIY film scene, i-docs, and diasporic experimental filmmaking. Alongside its case studies of films and filmmakers, contextual studies are featured here that break new ground by bringing the methods of media industry studies to examinations of Canadian film policy, labour, and film festivals. Finally, this book provides introductions to important but unheralded media artists and filmmakers, centring figures that deserve a larger place in our cultural and scholarly discourse.

The book is organized into three thematic sections: Feature Films and Filmmakers; Documentary, Experimental, and Hybrid Forms; and Canadian Film Contexts, Festivals, and Industries. The first section explores some of the key feature-length fiction films and filmmakers of the past two decades. Ian Robinson opens the collection with a discussion of one of the most internationally successful Canadian directors of recent years, Xavier Dolan. Through an examination of Dolan's six features, with a special focus on *Mommy* (2014), Robinson outlines the international appeal of the young filmmaker and his films about queer coming of age. Rejecting an emphasis on national allegories, Robinson argues that Dolan's success rests on his ability to connect with both transnational art film culture (Cannes, festivals) and transnational popular culture (Adele, Louis Vuitton). Continuing a focus on successful directors from Quebec, Lee Carruthers surveys the film corpus of Denis Villeneuve. Hailed by Hollywood critics as the "filmmaker of the decade," Villeneuve's leap from Canadian independent filmmaking to big-budget Hollywood productions invites comprehensive assessment. Carruthers argues that despite Villeneuve's commercial success and critical acclaim, his creative signature remains elusive: submitting the films to rigorous analysis while revising traditional notions of the auteur, Carruthers asks whether the forms of Villeneuve's cinema can be tapped for meaning.

The next two chapters consider women filmmakers who have gained new prominence since 2000. Tanya Horeck discloses subtle forms of female subjectivity in two films by Sarah Polley, reading Polley's early short, *I Shout Love* (2001), and her subsequent feature, *Take This Waltz* (2011). Horeck's discussion develops a persuasive frame for situating Polley's work as a new feminist cinema, foregrounding complex modes of affect and experience. Next, Karine Bertrand provides an entry point to the film and media practice of Indigenous women in her conversation with Mohawk filmmaker Sonia Bonspille Boileau. Bertrand traces the generational shift that has occurred within this group, aligning filmmakers like Alanis Obomsawin to emerging directors. For Boileau, filmmaking provides an opportunity to explore the multidimensional relationships between Quebec and Indigenous culture, as well as the role of women as knowledge-keepers and storytellers within those groups.

The remaining four essays in this section focus on Canadian directors working in different ways within low-budget and microcinema modes of production. Jean-Pierre Sirois-Trahan sketches Denis Côté's rise from film critic to festival darling, detailing the low-budget film movement that Côté ushered in – the *renouveau* of Quebec cinema. Though often acclaimed by critics, Côté has received less mainstream attention than figures like Dolan and Villeneuve; for Sirois-Trahan, this lapse relates to the way Côté's work resists easy interpretation, opening out a new terrain of film aesthetics. English-language cinema

Introduction: Towards a Renewed Critical Optics

in Canada has also seen something of a rebirth in recent years through Telefilm Canada's microbudget funding category for first-time directors. Jennifer VanderBurgh examines two coming-of-age films from this grouping, *Wet Bum* (MacKay, 2014) and *Sleeping Giant* (Cividino, 2015). Examining correspondences between narrative space, geography, and the thematic uses of water in these titles, VanderBurgh deploys close textual analysis to complicate notions of "the national" in relation to cinema in Canada since 2000. Next, David Davidson considers the phenomenon of "Toronto DIY" cinema, discussing the young filmmakers who emerged from film school in the late aughts at a time when there were few opportunities or viable role models available to young directors. Specifically, Davidson traces the early careers of Kazik Radwanski and Matt Johnson, who spearheaded the super low-budget DIY trend in Toronto and carved out new ground for small-scale film production in Canada. Finally, turning from individual filmmakers to broader categories of production, Murray Leeder's overview of Canada's horror cinema since 2000 shows how prominent the genre has become within Canadian film production. Standing as a kind of counterpoint to the small-budget art cinema, horror filmmaking serves as a venue for Canadian filmmakers to break into the industry without having to compete directly with Hollywood's ample budgets. Leeder argues that the heterogeneity of the horror film category challenges some of our most familiar frameworks for thinking about Canadian cinema.

The second section of the volume examines documentary and experimental films produced in Canada over the past two decades. It begins with Michael Meneghetti's assessment of the altered legacy of direct cinema in our contemporary context. Meneghetti uses Jay Cheel's *Beauty Day* (2011) as a case study to interrogate the way stylistic shifts in documentary film practice resonate with crises of creative labour and autonomous self-actualization under neoliberal late capitalism. Through a nuanced analysis of the film, Meneghetti shows how the direct cinema style has been evacuated of the meanings it embodied when it arose in the 1960s.

From short experimental works to stylized features, Guy Maddin's films have been among the most recognized (and recognizable) Canadian productions released since 2000. In Miriam Siegel and Charlie Keil's chapter, the authors examine the "docu-fantasia," an alternative mode of documentary featured in Maddin's recent work. Focusing on *My Winnipeg* (2007), Siegal and Keil read the film as incorporating strategies of personal recollection, re-enactment, and archival documentation to generate new mythologies of place.

The next pair of essays details the ways the National Film Board of Canada has adapted in recent decades. Gillian Roberts discusses the NFB's archive of images of Indigenous people and how they have been recombined and given new meaning by recent Indigenous filmmakers. The *Souvenir* series (2015) comprises short works by Indigenous filmmakers – Jeff Barnaby, Caroline Monnet, and Kent Monkman – each a distinctive project that draws on the NFB as an archive.[26] Roberts explores the way in which this reinterpretation of the NFB archive marks an intervention and repatriation of images of Indigenous peoples. Seth Feldman's contribution also focuses on changes within the NFB, explaining how recent technologies have transformed the field of documentary film. By analyzing interactive documentary (i-doc) productions such as *Bear 71* (Allison and Mendes, 2012) and *Highrise* (Cizek, 2010–15), Feldman reveals the Janus-faced nature of this mode of media production: on one hand, the films look backward to the history of NFB film styles, and often make use of the extensive (and now digitized) NFB archive; on the other, they seek to reimagine media documentary through new multi-platform and interactive modes.

Much as documentary in Canada has explored new forms and categories, experimental works have developed in ways that challenge traditions of Canadian filmmaking as well. Dan Browne examines recent examples of Canadian poetic filmmaking, addressing works preoccupied with diasporic images and narratives. In particular, Browne surveys films by Gariné Torossian, Izabella Pruska-Oldenhof, Solomon Nagler, Francisca Duran, and Cecilia Araneda, describing the manner in which these works engage issues of geographical displacement as well as historical and personal trauma. The past two decades have also seen some intriguing developments in film-based artmaking and exhibition practices. To this point, Melanie Wilmink looks at the film installations of Montreal artist dominique t. skoltz and considers how these projects provoke new encounters with the materiality of the moving image. In particular, Wilmink suggests that skoltz's *y2o* (2013) installations actuate a dialogue between film and gallery space, foregrounding the formal and social conventions of both. Through this intriguing case study, Wilmink suggests that contemporary visual art practice in Canada can reposition cinema and spectator in challenging ways.

The final section of the book contemplates some of the contexts and institutions that shape film production and circulation in Canada. These studies serve as a complement to the previous sections, pulling back from particular films and filmmakers to provide a more encompassing view of political and economic factors that condition the ways

Canadian films are made and consumed. To this end, Charles Acland raises a provocative paradox for Canadian film studies: how should we talk about the robust film industry devoted to service production in the context of Canadian cinema? While in recent years Canada's industry has become extremely successful at supporting the production of popular films – including nominally Canadian titles like *Resident Evil: Afterlife* (Anderson, 2010) and American-financed films like *The Shape of Water* (del Toro, 2017) – such productions are not typically read as expressions of "Canadian" culture. Acland charts the effect of various tax credit regimes that have stimulated film production in Canada and evaluates the implications of these policy decisions on both culture and labour. This question of the labour entailed in Canadian cinema and its determining impact on Canadian media production lies at the centre of Amanda Coles's chapter. While Canadian film studies has largely been silent on the labour practices of film production, Coles's discussion makes an important intervention, tracing the role that unions play in Canada's film and television industry. Her assessment not only sheds light on aspects of the industry that are typically overlooked by film scholars, such as the conditions of film production, but also highlights the ways that unions influence cultural policy decisions and therefore the kinds of films that are made and seen. Peter Lester's chapter on international co-productions surveys another facet of Canadian film production that has grown in scale and prominence in the past two decades. Using Lenny Abrahamson's *Room* (2015) as a case study, Lester probes the both the policy and discourse of co-productions, finding fertile ground for a reconsideration of the "national" as it is understood in cultural terms. Is it necessary for Canadian films to tell Canadian stories, or to be "visibly Canadian"? In an incisive corollary to Acland's analysis, Lester's investigation sheds additional light on the ways that Canada's tax credit policy serves as a cultural and economic stimulant.

Moving from film production to exhibition, the final two chapters present new research on film festivals in Canada. First, Aimée Mitchell details the ambitious energies of the Toronto Queer Film Festival. Launched in 2016 as an alternative to the Inside Out LGBT festival, TQFF focuses on the small-scale film cultures that provide spaces for experimentation and transgression. Mitchell compares TQFF to Inside Out's history from the latter's radical, grassroots origins to its rise as a major event with corporate sponsors, tackling the thorny question of what is lost when a community-oriented festival goes mainstream. Next, Diane Burgess's essay considers the film festival circuit in Canada at a national scale, critically examining the prominent role that the Toronto International Film Festival now plays on the Canadian scene. Beyond its annual festival, the opening of the TIFF Bell Lightbox in 2010 supplies a year-round home for the organization, securing TIFF's status as perennial programmer and tastemaker for Canadian cinema.

* * *

In late 2020, members of the Directors Guild of Canada released a document they called the "Directors Manifesto," urging Telefilm Canada to reformulate their funding adjudication process to fully engage the needs of emerging filmmakers and the creative merits of individual film projects. The committee also called on the organization to prioritize inclusiveness for all historically underrepresented groups, initiating targets for gender, race, and region, and to embrace a more collaborative model of support for filmmakers to facilitate career growth at home and abroad.[27] These developments are notable in a general sense, and also cohere with the interests and objectives of this book in important ways: the DGC document asks us to recognize the tenuous balance between commercial and creative agendas, the value and richness of individual works, and the evolving and diverse profile of Canada's artists and their creative practices. These are not just rhetorical signposts, but substantial considerations that impact the livelihood and enduring legacy of Canadian filmmakers and the industry as a whole. We present this volume as an effort to catalyze a related kind of dialogue, responding to Canadian cinema both conceptually and at the ground level, in hopes of cultivating a comparably flexible framework of assessment.

This book invites readers to discover new things in Canadian cinema, and to see familiar elements in unfamiliar ways. This entails a rearticulation of the way film in Canada is produced by and speaks across multiple cultures, forging new affinities among anglophone, francophone, and Indigenous-language examples, set alongside diasporic, multiple, and hybrid works. The productions analyzed here are interesting and multifarious, spanning feature films, television, digital and media art, short form projects, archives, and interactive works, reflecting the ways that the media object itself has been transformed over the past two decades and assumes new forms. Taken as a whole, this collection offers what we might call "polite provocations" to received frames of reference, unsettling any outmoded picture of Canada's cinema by enumerating the diverse individuals who are actually making films, the varied aesthetic strategies the films employ, and the reconfigured conditions from which Canadian film practice springs.

This is not to replace old frameworks with another limiting schema, but to decisively launch a renewal of critical activity. As this book's case studies ably demonstrate, we need to keep noticing and talking about Canada's film practice because it deserves our sustained attention; these films and contexts ask to be assessed on their own terms, as distinctive and heterogeneous phenomena, even if we are not yet able to say how they add up, or what they will ultimately tell us about our current situation. Bringing a selection of recent works into scholarly focus and speaking to Canadian cinema of the last twenty years is a way of answering this challenge concretely.

Notes

1 Charles Tepperman, "Bureaucrats and Movie Czars: Canada's Feature Film Policy since 2000," *Media Industries Journal* 4, no. 2 (fall 2017).

2 See Burgess essay in this volume; see also Liz Czach, "Film Festivals, Programming, and the Building of a National Cinema," *The Moving Image* 4, no. 1 (spring 2004).

3 Guy Maddin, whose career began in the 1980s, is the main exception to this trend.

4 Jim Leach, *Film in Canada* (Toronto: Oxford University Press, 2006); a second edition was published in 2010.

5 Jerry White, ed., *The Cinema of Canada* (London: Wallflower Press, 2006).

6 William Beard and Jerry White, eds., *North of Everything: English-Canadian Cinema since 1980* (Edmonton: University of Alberta Press, 2002).

7 André Loiselle and Tom McSorley, eds., *Self Portraits: The Cinemas of Canada since Telefilm* (Ottawa: Canadian Film Institute, 2006).

8 David L. Pike, *Canadian Cinema since the 1980s: At the Heart of the World* (Toronto: University of Toronto Press, 2012).

9 See, in addition, Chris Gittings, *Canadian National Cinema: Ideology, Difference and Representation* (New York: Routledge, 2001); George Melnyk, ed., *Great Canadian Film Directors* (Edmonton: University of Alberta Press, 2007) as well as his *Film and the City: The Urban Imaginary in Canadian Cinema* (Edmonton: Athabasca University Press, 2012) and *One Hundred Years of Canadian Cinema* (Toronto: University of Toronto, 2004); Peter Urquhart and Ira Wagman, eds., *Cultural Industries.ca* (Toronto: Lorimer, 2012); Elaine Chang, ed., *Reel Asian: Asian Canada on Screen* (Toronto: Toronto Reel Asian Film Festival, 2007); Tom Waugh, *The Romance of Transgression in Canada: Queering Sexualities, Nations, Cinemas* (Montreal: McGill-Queen's University Press, 2006); Janine Marchessault and Susan Lord, Fluid Screens, eds., *Expanded Cinema* (Toronto: University of Toronto

Press, 2007); Malek Khouri and Darrell Varga, eds., *Working on Screen: Representations of the Working Class in Canadian Cinema* (Toronto: University of Toronto Press, 2006); Faiza Hirji, *Dreaming in Canadian: South Asian Youth, Bollywood and Belonging* (University of British Columbia Press, 2010); and Baldur Hafsteinsson, *Indigenous Screen Cultures in Canada* (University of Manitoba Press, 2010).

10 With a somewhat narrower focus, Liz Czach and André Loiselle's recent collection, *Cinema of Pain: On Québec's Nostalgic Screen* (Waterloo: Wilfrid Laurier University Press, 2020), provides a valuable examination of recent filmmaking in Quebec.

11 Janine Marchessault and Will Straw, eds., *The Oxford Handbook of Canadian Cinema* (New York: Oxford University Press, 2019), xiv.

12 André Dudemaine, Gabrielle Marcoux, and Isabelle St-Amand, eds., *Canadian Journal of Film Studies* 29, no. 1 (spring 2020), special issue on "Indigenous Cinema and Media in the Americas: Storytelling, Communities, and Sovereignties."

13 For a recent overview of these issues see Chrisopher Gittings, "Canadian Cinema(s)," in *The Routledge Companion to World Cinema*, edited by Rob Stone et al. (New York: Routledge, 2017).

14 Toby Miller et al., *Global Hollywood 2* (London: BFI, 2005).

15 On the transnational turn, see Nataša Ďurovičová and Kathleen E. Newman's co-edited volume *World Cinemas, Transnational Perspectives* (Routledge, 2010) and Will Higbee and Song Hwee Lim's essay "Concepts of Transnational Cinema: Towards a Critical Transnationalism in Film Studies" in *Transnational Cinemas* 1, no. 1 (2010). For related critiques of national cinema see, in particular, Ian Christie, "Where Is National Cinema Today (and Do We Still Need It)?," *Film History* 25, no. 1–2 (2013): 19–30. See also Miller et al., *Global Hollywood 2*, and Dudemaine, Marcoux, and St-Amand, "Indigenous Cinema and Media in the Americas."

16 Figures from *Profile 2020* (Ottawa: Canadian Media Producers Association, 2020), completed March 2020, just before the pandemic effect was really felt.

17 Andy Fry, Jordan Maxwell, Marc Glassman, and Sada Ahsan, "Acts of Service: Balancing the Two Sides of Canada's Booming Production Sector," *Playback Online*, 20 December 2021, https://playbackonline.ca/2021/12/20/acts-of-service-balancing-the-two-sides-of-canadas-booming-production-sector/#ixzz7HgMGCQS1.

18 Christopher Gittings estimates that between 2008 and 2012 Indigenous films accounted for only 1.6 per cent of Canadian feature film production; see C.E. Gittings, "Indigenous Canadian Cinemas: Negotiating the Precarious," in *The Precarious in the Cinemas of the Americas: Global Cinema*, ed. C. Burucúa and C. Sitnisky (London: Palgrave Macmillan, 2018).

19 Fry et al., "Acts of Service."
20 This figure is subject to significant fluctuations, with a decade low of 8.7 per cent in 2016 and high of 18.5 per cent the following year. See *Profile 2020*, 86.
21 C-18.1 *Loi sur le cinema* (Quebec: Publications Québec, 31 October 2021), http://www.legisquebec.gouv.qc.ca/fr/document/lc/C-18.1/.
22 Described by Wente as a New Wave in Dudemaine, Marcoux, and St-Amand's special issue of *Canadian Journal of Film Studies*.
23 Jesse Wente, "Doing All Things Differently," *Film Quarterly* 72, no. 3 (2019): 42–3, https://filmquarterly.org/2019/02/27/manifesto-eleven-calls-to-action/#doingallthings.
24 Ibid.
25 In key respects, this approach coheres with the practice of "surface reading" that has emerged in recent literary criticism, focusing on "what is evident, perceptible, apprehensible in texts; what is neither hidden nor hiding." Stephen Best and Sharon Marcus, "Surface Reading: An Introduction," *Representations* 108, no. 1 (2009): 9.
26 A fourth film in the series was directed by Michelle Latimer. In December 2020, Michelle Latimer acknowledged that her claim to Indigenous identity was based on ancestral ties that have been called into question by Indigenous communities and elders. Barry Hertz, "'I Made a Mistake': Canadian Filmmaker Michelle Latimer Addresses Indigenous Ancestry Questions," *Globe and Mail*, 17 December 2020 (online version), https://www.theglobeandmail.com/arts/film/article-i-made-a-mistake-canadian-filmmaker-michelle-latimer-addresses/.
27 See the Director's Guild of Canada, Directors Manifesto; Telefilm Canada Consultations Fall 2020, Independent Filmmakers Committee, 18 November 2020, https://www.dgc.ca/assets/PDF/Telefilm-Consultations-DGC-Manifesto-Nov-18-2020.pdf.

PART ONE
Feature Films and Filmmakers

1

Speaking across Borders
Xavier Dolan and the Transnationalism of Contemporary Auteur Cinema in Quebec

Ian Robinson

This chapter considers the strategic use of national and transnational frames in both the production and reception of Xavier Dolan's films. Dolan's distinction among Quebec filmmakers lies in the ways his films speak to audiences and circulate across borders. For Dolan, the fluid movement between national and transnational scales is associated with both his critical and commercial achievements, as well as the substantial amount of critical attention – both positive and negative – directed at his films.

I begin by framing Dolan's work within contemporary Quebec cinema and its transnational contexts before turning to a discussion of Dolan as an auteur-star. Dolan's brand of stardom has been constructed around his international success at festivals and his outspoken confidence as a filmmaker. Critics have focused again and again on Dolan's relatively young age and the pace of his rapidly expanding filmography. His films frequently utilize a pastiche of images and styles from popular culture and art cinema alike; for critics, Dolan's cinema is often found to be either extraordinary and precocious, or naive and even narcissistic. The second section of the chapter traces the construction of Dolan's image – a rarity in Canadian and Quebec cinema for his international stardom – across media and interviews. Dolan's cinema is situated in a transnational context given Dolan's international acclaim, revealing tensions between national identity and Dolan's globalist approach. The importance of the international film festival circuit, and Cannes in particular, is a theme that reoccurs throughout this chapter. The third section discusses the critical role of transnational festivals in the development and circulation of Dolan's films. In the final section, I address how Dolan's films problematize the dominant national allegory of national film criticism in Quebec, asking in what ways Dolan's films enter into dialogue with *place* at the national and transnational scales, particularly in their use of music and language. Upon analysis of Dolan's films, place is neither immutable nor a clearly demarcated geographical or cultural concept. Rather, the transnational circulation of Dolan's films across borders, and their appeal to global audiences through the vernacular languages of popular music and stardom, complicates a national frame of interpretation.

I

Dolan's filmmaking career took flight at a time when Quebec film was undergoing a significant renaissance. The contested terms and grounds of the Quebec "*renouveau*," or "New Wave," in the new millennium are difficult to pin down, with many critics identifying the *renouveau* with the work of directors such as Denis Côté, Stéphane Lafleur, Simon Lavoie, Anne Émond, and Sophie Deraspe, among others.[1] Films referred to in the context of the *renouveau* vary widely in terms of form and aesthetics, but often share an emphasis on character-driven drama and a realist orientation towards Quebec's suburban and rural settings. The movement is often further characterized by themes of present-day ennui, the search for meaningful relationships, and a move away from the overt nostalgia of some popular cinema and the aesthetics and speed associated with digital culture.[2] This new strand of Quebec art house cinema has found success at international festivals such as Rotterdam, Sundance, Locarno, Quebec's Festival du nouveau cinéma, and Berlin, where Denis Côté took the Alfred Bauer Prize in 2013 for *Vic + Flo ont vu un ours/Vic + Flo Saw a Bear*. With some success in Quebec markets, many of these films received little international distribution, especially in the lucrative American market. And while critically successful in Quebec, they have mostly achieved modest levels of commercial success. Even *Vic + Flo ont vu un ours*, which has played at forty-five festivals since its premiere in Berlin, brought in a total of less than $60,000 at the Quebec box office, ranking it the fifteenth most commercially successful Quebec film in its home province.[3]

Outside of Canada, discussions of Quebec's renewed film culture and its place on the international scene are more likely to point to an altogether different set of films produced in Quebec since the late 2000s. The international success of Denis Villeneuve, Jean-Marc Vallée,

Philippe Falardeau, and Kim Nguyen has drawn curiosity and attention both inside and outside of Canada. These directors have advanced their careers by crossing over from popular and art house French-language Quebec cinema to English-language American indie and Hollywood filmmaking. Although the styles of these filmmakers are again quite different from one another, their careers have all followed a similar trajectory in which a broadly critical and commercial success in Canadian and international markets paved the way for entry into American markets. For Jean-Marc Vallée, the success of his Quiet Revolution coming-of-age drama C.R.A.Z.Y. (2005) in virtually every market except the United States (where it was never distributed) brought Vallée to the attention of international producers Martin Scorsese and Graham King, who were seeking to bring *The Young Victoria* (2009) into production. King described hiring Vallée thus: "I very much wanted to find a director who would steer us away from the traditional BBC-type costume drama. I knew that I wanted to make a period movie for an MTV audience and suddenly C.R.A.Z.Y. showed up on my desk."[4] For Denis Villeneuve, the success of *Incendies* (2010) both in terms of awards on the international festival circuit and its Academy Award nomination led to the director's first Hollywood studio film, *Prisoners* (2013). Philippe Falardeau similarly caught the eye of Hollywood with *Monsieur Lazhar* (2011) before his first English-language film with Hollywood, *The Good Lie*, in 2013.

The recent re-emergence of Quebec cinema on the international scene points to different models of articulation of the national and the transnational in film culture. In both instances there is a movement away from overt national themes – even though directors such as Vallée, Villeneuve, and Falardeau made their names in cinema by exploring some of the problematic social, historical, and political themes of Quebec in C.R.A.Z.Y., *Monsieur Lazhar*, and *Polytechnique* (2009). While these filmmakers have largely adapted to the conventions of Hollywood, the directors most often associated in Quebec with *renouveau*, including Denis Côté and Stéphane Lafleur, have largely turned away from overt treatments of national issues in favour of local settings and stories that speak to broader concerns, such as the loneliness and anxiety of those left behind by globalization and the speed of digital culture. The Hollywood films of Villeneuve, Vallée, and Falardeau might exemplify one trend in transnational cinema: a strategic form, or what Mette Hjort has labelled "opportunistic transnationalism," and a cinema that is relatively unmarked in its transnational connections.[5] The cinema of these directors signals an emerging regime of transnational mobility among directors, and occasionally other crew, between Hollywood and French-language Quebec national cinema. Their films are situated locally and nationally through a rather latent form of national "aboutness," achieved through background references to place and setting in a cinema that otherwise appeals to the sober and minimalist aesthetics of international art house festivals.[6] Adapting Hjort's scalar measure of national and transnational affinities, we can say that both trends, or cinematic groupings – the art cinema of the *renouveau* and the Hollywood cinema led by Quebec auteurs – are characterized by relatively weak levels of transnationalism, associated primarily with their modes of circulation at international festivals and their reception across linguistic borders.[7]

The cinema of Xavier Dolan fits imperfectly into either category of contemporary Quebec film culture. On the one hand, Dolan's films would seem to fit within the discursive frame of the *renouveau*, although Dolan himself has refuted that he is part of any movement or renewal of Quebec cinema. Two further points distinguish Dolan's films from the emergent Quebec art house tradition. First, Dolan's films adopt a particular sensibility to the freedom of blending popular culture with artistic expression. Dolan's films frequently break with the austere minimalism of his contemporaries in favour of hyper-aestheticized mise-en-scène. Departing from the dominant tendency of realism in art house cinema, Dolan's films often include brief moments in which the mise-en-scène erupts in either an expressionist or dialogic relationship to the characters' state of mind. In a famous scene in *Laurence Anyways*, a waterfall suddenly crashes down on Fred (Suzanne Clément) as she sits dejected in her living room. *Mommy* received rare mid-screening applause from festival audiences in Cannes in a scene in which Steve (Antoine Olivier Pilon) reaches out of the diegesis to stretch apart the frame's aspect ratio. In these moments and others, Dolan has displayed a willingness to play with the conventions of mise-en-scène at the limits of diegetic realism. However, rather than drawing sole inspiration from the canon of new wave cinemas, Dolan's post-classical aesthetic derives as much from the flexible mode of narration associated with music and video culture, a point that I will discuss further in the final section of this chapter. Second, over the course of his career, Dolan has managed to achieve both critical and commercial success. He has capitalized on his status as an award-winning auteur to succeed in commercial markets. Furthermore, he has leveraged the transnational possibilities of co-productions, festivals, international distribution, and critical attention in order to translate symbolic forms of capital into considerable commercial success. Without yet leaping to Hollywood,

Figure 1.1 The scene is flooded with excessive emotion as a waterfall suddenly descends upon Fred's living room in *Laurence Anyways* (2012).

Dolan has forged a distinct transnational path for Quebec and Canadian cinema. His cinema exemplifies a transnational approach to production, distribution, and exhibition, while also participating in a transnational network of auteur aesthetics and audience viewing practices.[8]

2

Critical commentary on Dolan has contributed to a normative set of discursive frames which mark him as an auteur and star. While star theory typically refers to the discourses by which the images and identities of movie celebrities are developed intertextually, Dolan exemplifies a trend in which stardom is negotiated within the "commerce of auteurism." As Corrigan has written, film "auteurs have become increasingly situated along an extratextual path in which their commercial status as auteurs is their chief function as auteurs."[9] Of interest here is the way that Dolan has "strategically embrace[d] the more promising possibilities of the auteur as a commercial presence" at both textual and extra-textual levels.[10] This phenomenon of the auteur-star is of course not new in international film culture. However, the extent to which Dolan has strategically crafted and embraced his status as an auteur-star, in both his acting and directing roles, distinguishes him in the contemporary film culture of Quebec. Moreover, Dolan's auteur stardom has been developed at a transnational scale rather than the national playing field of Quebec cinema, which is dominated by names that seldom cross national borders.[11]

The trajectory of Xavier Dolan's filmmaking career to the present has been widely remarked upon in film criticism and the news media. Critical reception of his films has frequently focused on Dolan's biography and his burgeoning career alongside discussions of his films. This is most obviously due to the fact that Dolan's first feature, *J'ai tué ma mère/I Killed My Mother* (2009), was inspired by the writer-director's own turbulent adolescent years. However, the extensive media attention that grew out of *J'ai tué ma mère* has cultivated a particular auteur mythology that is unique, even unprecedented, among Canadian and Quebec directors. For the uninitiated, the oft-repeated Dolan story in brief: Dolan began writing the first draft of the script of *J'ai tué ma mère* at age sixteen after dropping out of school, partly as a way to write himself an acting role. A child actor from the age of four, Dolan's acting career had stalled during his teenage years. He continued to work in the film industry as a French-language voice actor for dubbed Hollywood films released in Quebec, recording the role of Ron Weasley in all eight *Harry Potter* movies and most recently the role of Jake in Richard Linklater's *Everybody Wants Some* (2016). More importantly, the origin myth of Xavier Dolan highlights his initial rejection by both Telefilm and SODEC for production funding, his ambitions for a Cannes premiere, and his ultimate triumph with an eight-minute standing ovation at the film's opening in the Director's Fortnight. Here he received three awards including the prix Regards jeunes, a prize he again claimed the following year for *Les amours imaginaires/Heartbeats* (2010). Dolan released his first six feature films in the seven years between 2009 and 2016, five of which premiered and won awards at the Cannes Film Festival. In 2014 his most widely acclaimed film, *Mommy*, shared the Jury Prize at Cannes alongside Jean-Luc Godard's *Adieu au langage/Goodbye to Language* (2014); *Juste la fin du monde/It's Only the End of the World* won the Grand Prix in 2016.[12] Dolan's long-awaited seventh feature, his English-language debut and first Canada-UK co-production *The Life and Death of John F. Donovan*, opened at the Toronto International Film Festival in 2018, with a limited release the following year. The film starring Kit Harrington, Natalie Portman, and Susan Sarandon was met with mild to harsh disapproval from critics. Critical reviews of the film often focused on Dolan's biography, evaluating the film as the director's personal statement about stardom and celebrity.[13] Dolan's eighth feature returned to more familiar ground, with Dolan himself taking a lead role in the French-language *Matthias & Maxime*. The film opened at Cannes in 2019.

Perhaps more than any other Canadian director, Dolan has carved out an auteur-star image which traverses the transnational arenas of art cinema and popular culture. In his still-young career, he has garnered a reputation as outspoken and defensive against criticism of his films. Quebec critics have had difficulty squaring him with received categories of national cinema, and Dolan has often rejected a national perspective on his work in favour of a globalist and generational attitude. It is the latter discourse, an emphasis on his age, which has been the most significant in framing Dolan's stardom. Arguably, Dolan's youthful success as a filmmaker has been the defining discourse of his image as an auteur-star. Dolan has embraced this image as well, positioning himself as an ambassador for transnational millennial popular culture and its intersections with the global art cinema.

Labels such as "enfant terrible," "wunderkind," "génie," "precocious," and "rock star" continue to precede Dolan's name in critical and media accounts. Much more than any of his contemporaries on the Quebec film scene, Dolan has become an important subject of criticism, beyond any discussion of his films. As one critic writes, "Xavier Dolan 'the phenomenon,' since *J'ai tué ma mère*, has been the subject of immeasurable attention whose scope clearly exceeds that of his cinema."[14] For such critics, far from embodying an authentic Quebec film culture, Dolan's films betray the narcissistic sensibility of the director. This notion of youthful narcissism has been the theme of some of the most biting criticism of Dolan, including a review of *Tom à la ferme* in the *Hollywood Reporter* accusing the film of an obsession with close-ups of the actor-director's face. While such personal criticism hardly seems warranted, Dolan's penchant for outspoken rhetoric – such as lashing out at SODEC and Telefilm as outmoded institutions, complaining about *Laurence Anyways* not being included in the main competition at Cannes, and reproaching the Cannes press for their disapproving reviews of *Juste la fin du monde* – has brought him a great deal of attention. Outside of his films, the Dolan brand consists of his own image, including his hairstyle, tattoos, and fashion sense. As the face of Louis Vuitton, Dolan has not only embraced commercial culture but has taken a position within the image-making culture industry of stars and models. His crossover to mainstream popular culture was most clearly evident in his direction of Adele's 2015 record-breaking music video for "Hello," parts of which were shot on IMAX film. The "Hello" video not only granted Xavier Dolan new star status in anglophone markets and cultural spheres far from the art house cinema of *J'ai tué ma mère*, but redefined his brand as a transnational icon of popular culture.

3

International film festivals have been instrumental to Dolan's success. Film festivals function as transnational cultural nodes in several ways. As Dina Iordanova argues, "the film festival has always been the site where the inherently transnational character of cinematic art reveals itself most glaringly. If it were not for the festival recognition and awards that bring important and nascent filmmakers to the attention of international audiences – filmmakers often under-appreciated in their own countries – how would we know and cherish the oeuvre of some of the greatest Japanese or Iranian directors today?"[15] Despite the rather simplistic description of festivals' role in programming new and under-appreciated filmmakers and genres, Iordanova's point raises some other pertinent questions regarding the way that festivals articulate a transnational and cosmopolitan view of the world, translating national cultures to global audiences. As Marijke de Valck observes, festivals such as Cannes are in the "business of cultural prestige."[16] This economy of prestige, in which films compete for awards and recognition, offers a form of symbolic capital to filmmakers and often opens up new distribution channels and access to audiences across international borders. Symbolic capital in the form of recognition by the prestigious festival jury can therefore facilitate an economic return, albeit usually a modest one compared to studio-produced Hollywood cinema.[17] Film festivals such as Cannes have considerable power in terms of what de Valck refers to as gatekeeping and tastemaking functions.[18] As gatekeepers, festivals create thresholds of entry, such that even participation in the Cannes Film Festival is a mark of prestige. As tastemakers, festivals are influential in legitimizing certain forms of cinema. Furthermore, the influence of a festival like Cannes can be seen not only in the international sales of films that have screened at Cannes, but in the critical and commercial success of the films in reviews and criticism and at the box office.

While he is not alone among contemporary Quebec filmmakers to be invited to the Cannes Film Festival – Denis Villeneuve's first film *Un 32 août sur Terre* opened in Cannes in 1998, as did *Polytechnique* (2009) and *Sicario* (2015), while Stephane Lafleur's *Tu dors Nicole* screened in the Director's Fortnight in 2014 – Dolan's films most closely and consistently identify with Cannes's transnational prestige and unique capacity to generate star power outside of Hollywood. For Dolan, bringing *J'ai tué ma mère* to Cannes certainly opened doors for future success, both at the festival and in the French market. With a reputation as a "Cannes filmmaker," Dolan was catapulted into a pantheon of elite international directors including the likes of Wong Kar-Wai and Pedro Almodovar, both influences on the pop-infused style of Dolan's films. The unusual success of a Quebec filmmaker in French theatres has been noted by critics, with Dolan's *Mommy* and *Juste la fin du monde* reaching levels of ticket sales not seen for a Quebec filmmaker since Denys Arcand's hits, *Les invasions barbares* (2003) and *Le déclin de l'empire américain* (1986).[19] After *Mommy*'s 2015 César Award for Best Foreign Film, *Le Figaro* took note of Quebec cinema's transnational momentum towards Europe, especially France: "Celine Dion isn't the only cultural ambassador for Quebec around the world. Gradually the cinema of our cousins is finding its place in Europe and especially in France."[20] The new cachet of Quebec cinema is often read as directly linked to Dolan's successes in Europe, as comments by Odile Tremblay, journalist for *Le Devoir*, suggest: "[Dolan] has changed the way the French look on our cinema, because they associate the film and the director with youth, modernity, and the future, too. Previously, they could admire filmmakers [from Quebec] but did not see them as visionaries."[21]

Following his second film, *Les Amours imaginaires* (2010), Dolan has increasingly turned to the co-production market to get his films produced. *Laurence Anyways* (2012), *Tom à la ferme* (2013), and *Juste la fin du monde* (2016) are all official Canada-France co-productions, benefitting from tax incentives and state investments in both countries. With the exception of *Mommy*, his films have increasingly starred French actors including Melvil Poupaud, Nathalie Baye, Marion Cotillard, Léa Seydoux, and Vincent Cassel, and the prestige that this confers has largely functioned as the gatekeeper in Dolan's transnational passage from Quebec to France. It has also gone some way to legitimize Dolan and Quebec cinema on the world stage, thus fulfilling a cultural taste-making function as well. The three co-productions with MK2 (*Laurence Anyways*, *Tom à la ferme*, and *Juste la fin du monde*) all benefit from the higher budgets that accompany projects with multiple production partners. However, MK2 also offers a vertically integrated production, sales, and distribution agency with ownership of a network of cinemas in France and Spain. Dolan's partnerships with MK2 have guaranteed his work a strong presence in France and, in the cases where MK2 has handled international sales, a strong presence in theatres across Europe. Finally, MK2 also sells a particular brand of international films by auteurs such as Jia Zhangke, Pawel Pawlikowski, and Abbas Kiarostami, and its brand is created in close connection with major European film festivals including Cannes. In working with one of the leading auteur film producers and distributors in Europe, Dolan's films have become associated with a transnational body of auteur cinema that circulates above and beyond its national origins. And like Cannes, which stands at the epicentre of transnational art cinema, the ethos of this brand is the discovery of the new and the canonization of international auteurs.

4

In his analysis of the Toronto International Film Festival and the success of New Iranian Cinema, Bill Nichols raises the question of what kind of knowledge of place is offered by transnational cinema, and in what ways cinema translates and transposes knowledge of national and transnational cultures.[22] The transnational production and circulation of Dolan's films prompts consideration of where his films take place and how they speak to themes of nationhood or of the transnational. This recalls one of the perennial questions haunting Canadian and Quebec film studies. What is it that defines a film's place in the country's national cinema? In what ways does the cinema allegorize a condition of national belonging?[23] Dolan's films are problematic for a notion of national cinema in which film allegorizes the province's social and cultural aspirations for nationhood and its historical struggles against the legacies of colonialism. In Dolan's films, the recurring instabilities and contradictions of intimate and familial relationships resist simple allegorizing as a condition of participation in the Quebec nation.[24] As I argue below, Dolan's fluid deployment of accents, music, settings, and references to popular culture preclude a straightforward metaphoric reading of nationhood in his films. A more satisfactory approach to questions of nationhood in Dolan's films then considers how the national and the transnational are marked thematically, in both overt and latent forms. In other words, in what ways do Xavier Dolan's films enter into dialogue with *place*, at either the national or transnational scales?

Accents, setting, and popular music in Dolan's films provide the most important markers of national and transnational place. With the exception of *The Life and Death of John F. Donovan*, which is set predominantly in the UK, Dolan's films all take place in Quebec, in or around Montreal. For the most part, the settings provide the kind of "banal aboutness" that can be identified in cinema produced for transnational audiences. Audiences are presented views of the Montreal suburbs (*Mommy*, *J'ai tué ma mère*), the hip backdrop of Montreal's Mile End (*Les Amours imaginaires*, *Laurence Anyways*), and the Quebec countryside of farms and small towns (*Juste la fin du monde*, *Tom à la ferme*). When action does move to the countryside as in *Tom à la ferme*, the rural countryside is reduced to a trope: city-dweller protagonist is seduced and held captive through his own disorientation away from home in Montreal. *Juste la fin du monde*, a film in which place is virtually unmarked, similarly revolves around an outsider (a successful playwright) returning home to visit his small-town family with whom he has never been able to communicate properly. In this case, the protagonist's complex relationship with the periphery, a relationship marked by both nostalgia and apprehensiveness, contrast with his professional life and the energy of the cultural centre of Paris. *Tom à la ferme* and *Juste la fin du monde* thus confirm André Loiselle's observations about the transformation of the rural in the Quebec imaginary, from its connotations of national heritage and values to its association with regressive forms of conservatism. In the rural, Loiselle finds the site of the contemporary horror film, set away from the imagined cosmopolitanism of the city in Quebec culture.[25] While the city functions as a cosmopolitan and anxiety-ridden space in *Les amours imaginaires* and *Laurence Anyways*, Dolan's rural settings evoke a disquieting sense of a past homeliness that cannot be returned to. In this way, the rural conjures the nostalgia of a former Quebec culture no longer accessible by Dolan's urban characters. Adding a transnational dimension to the urban-rural dialectic, *Juste la fin du monde* relocates the cosmopolitan centre from Montreal to Paris, a place only alluded to in dialogue and in the opening sequence.

Of any type of space, it is the suburban zones of *Mommy* and *J'ai tué ma mère* that are most closely identified with Quebec nationhood. These domestic zones of life, where the adolescents Hubert and Steve struggle against their familial environments, are also the sites where participation in a national community, however dysfunctional, is most fully articulated. This relationship between suburb, family, and the state is most apparent in *Mommy*. The narrative opens and closes with reference to its fictional premise, a national policy that allows disadvantaged families to surrender their problem children to be incarcerated by the Canadian state. The state's regressive family policy appears in direct opposition to the promise of the suburban domestic sphere. In its pessimistic conclusion – Diane, Steve's overburdened mother, takes the unwitting Steve to the federal detention centre – *Mommy* points to the breakdown of the suburban family as a space for the reproduction of Quebec nationhood. In addition, the suburban worlds of *Mommy* and *J'ai tué ma mère* are coded as working-class and family-oriented spaces. Whereas the young and childless creatives in *Les amours imaginaires* appear to have an excess of time for tea dates and strolling the clothing boutiques in Mile End, for Diane in *Mommy*, time is fully commodified. The impossible reconciliation of work-time with the time required to manage her troubled son leads her to lose her job, and ultimately, to the horror of Steve's final incarceration.

Accents in Dolan's films range between Québécois and international French, reflecting the transnational character of the productions and the nationality of the actors. While films such as *J'ai tué ma mère* and *Mommy* rely fully on Quebec accents and exploit local idiomatic language to evoke a measure of nation-specific linguistic culture, by *Juste la fin du Monde* Dolan has moved towards an all-French cast including international art house and Hollywood stars Marion Cotillard, Léa Seydoux, and Vincent Cassel. It is *Laurence Anyways* that provides an interesting example of a film that combines different French-language accents in the same cast. In this case, the French actor Melvil Poupaud stars alongside Suzanne Clément, a Quebec actress and recurring Dolan collaborator. According to scholar Valérie Mandia, the linguistic hybridity formed not only varying accents but by diction, idioms, and the inclusion of English phrases and expressions in Dolan's films functions as a means of reconciling both Quebec and European francophone audiences and of bridging the normally large gulf between French-language Quebec and English-speaking North American popular cultures.[26]

Music is the most significant marker of national and transnational culture in Dolan's films, and the expressive character of his cinema is profoundly shaped by its diegetic and extra-diegetic soundtracks. The films are often punctuated by a mix of both national (Quebec) and international popular music, recognizable and specific to Quebec audiences while also made accessible to a transnational film culture. Again, the balance achieved in Dolan's films is an orientation towards both Quebec and international Francophone cultures, marked by the inclusion of mainstream anglophone pop cultural references. The eclectic soundtrack for *Laurence Anyways*, for instance, conveys the transnational sensibility of the film, composed of songs from internationally popular anglophone bands such as Duran Duran, Depeche Mode, and the Cure, pieces by classical composers including Erik Satie, Sergei Prokofiev, and Antonio Vivaldi, and French-language Quebec pop musicians Jean Leloup and Julie Masse. In a further nod to Quebec culture and nationhood, the film includes a famous sovereigntist anthem, "Gens du pays" by the Quebec national folk legend Gilles Vigneault.

In *Mommy*, the most widely acclaimed of Dolan's films and arguably one of his most locally oriented films in terms of language and theme, one of the functions of the soundtrack's popular music is to communicate the contradictory feelings and situations evoked by the film's narrative. Operating as a global vernacular, hit songs by Counting Crows, Oasis, Lana Del Rey, and Céline Dion translate the film's problematic for transnational audiences at the level of affect. As is typical of many aspects of Dolan's films, music is often oriented towards both a national identity and a transnational audience. A memorable scene in *Mommy* finds Steve, Diane, and Kyla singing along to Céline Dion's 1990s hit, "On ne change pas." Encouraging the others to dance, Steve announces, "C'est un trésor national!" Dion's hit was of course a major national success in Quebec and Canada, but the choice of Dion as a signifier of Quebec national culture is also more complex, since Dion's career has been marked by her movement between the linguistic spheres of anglophone and francophone culture. In fact, Dion, as one of the most successful pop singers in either language, is fairly unique among pop singers for her ability to cross national and linguistic borders so fluidly. The 1998 album on which "On ne change pas" was released, *S'il suffisait d'aimer*, remains the world's second-bestselling French-language album of all time.

If the soundtracks of films such as *Laurence Anyways* and *Mommy* bring a transnational appeal to Dolan's cinema, and in effect soften or translate the locally specific themes and language for global audiences, they also make use of the vernacular of popular music video at the level of form. Several sequences draw on the aesthetic qualities of popular music video. Typical examples can be found in *Mommy*, including the aforementioned scene in which the skateboarding Steve reaches up and pulls apart the frame of the screen, in the process expanding the aspect ratio from its distinct square format to widescreen. The accompanying song, "Wonderwall" by Oasis, sets the scene apart as a discrete unit in the film with its own textuality. As a music video, it is set apart by a highly performative and reflexive mode of address. In another such self-contained sequence, Diane envisions an alternate outcome for Steve in which he attends college and enjoys a successful life. This dreamlike sequence, unmarked as such except for a newly widened aspect ratio, is set to "Experience" by Ludovico Einaudi. According to Dolan, this was the first scene to be conceived; the entire film was written around this alternate ending. A third self-contained music video, set to "Colorblind" by Counting Crows, follows Steve as he skateboards to an empty parking lot, spins around with a shopping cart, and catches up with some other teenagers outside of a strip mall. As in the other examples, this sequence presents itself as a discrete textual unit, independent from the rest of the film. As "Colorblind" plays in its entirety, Steve listens and dances to different music through his headphones. The interplay between the two sources of music – the non-diegetic "Colorblind" and the inaudible headphone music that Steve hears, functions to again unsettle the viewer from their identification with Steve. Carol Vernallis has described the intertextual and intermedial connections between cinema, music videos, and commercials in terms of a process of "youtube-ification" in which "all media – from post-classical cinema to music videos and commercials – start to resemble or refer to YouTube."[27] This is a transnational screen culture in which Dolan knowingly participates by constructing art films largely composed of discrete, memorable units that refer as much to other online videos – on YouTube – as they do to the singular films in which they appear. Borrowing from the culture of online music videos, sequences from Dolan's films, such as the ones mentioned above from *Mommy*, utilize a more flexible textual structure in which music can fluidly move between the diegetic and the non-diegetic.

Over the course of his first six films, Xavier Dolan has pursued cinema with a dual orientation towards the national spaces of Quebec cinema and to the transnational flows of global film culture. His films circulate within a cultural field – from financing structures to director's interviews, to awards galas and criticism – that operates within and across national scales. In his balance of national and transnational acceptance, Dolan has largely rejected the national allegory as a mode of representation and storytelling. Instead, his generational cinema speaks to the flexible allegiances to city, nation, language, and transnational community that are common to millennial digital culture. Dolan's rise as a transnational auteur-star has been facilitated by his pursuit of a strategic form of transnationalism; his frequent co-production financing; his appeal to the vernaculars of Anglo popular culture through retro pop music; his acclaim at international festivals; and his collaboration with Québécois, French, English, and American film stars. For Dolan's films, Cannes and the international festival circuit, with all the prestige that it confers, has been a crucial source of symbolic capital. It is the guarantee of entry to an exclusive milieu of recognized auteurs. If

Figure 1.2 Steve rides his skateboard in a sequence set to Counting Crows' "Colorblind" in *Mommy* (2014).

Dolan has one foot in the canonized house of cinema auteurs, his other belongs in the popular culture of Céline Dion, Adele, and the aesthetics of online music videos. Both of these cultural fields – the exclusive enclave of Cannes and the mass industry of pop – are transnational spaces. Furthermore, in his articulation of local places, including Montreal and its environs, and in his globally appealing stories about queer coming of age and the insecurity of personal relationships, Dolan's films have capitalized on the enduring appeal of the small nation as a source of international art house acclaim. His strategic transnationalism reflects a negotiated positionality with respect to an identification with a national film culture and the prestigious and capital-intensive currents of global art cinema. From a small nation with a cinema that rarely ventures beyond its borders, Dolan's youthful cinema has provided a new model for the crossing of cultural, linguistic, and national borders.

Notes

1 Simon Galiero, "Du cinéma d'auteur et du 'renouveau' dans le cinéma québécois," *Liberté* 299: 27–9; Bruno Dequen, "Table ronde sur le renouveau du cinema Québecois," *Nouvelles Vues*, 12 (spring–summer 2011).
2 Patricia Bailey, "A New Generation of Quebec Filmmakers Captures a Culture Adrift," THIS, May–June 2010: https://this.org/2010/07/06/quebec-film/.
3 Observatoire de la culture et de communications du Québec, *Statistiques sur l'industrie du film et de la production télévisuelle indépendante: Édition 2014* (Quebec: Institut de la statistique du Québec, 2014), 56.
4 Chloe Fox, "The Young Victoria: We Were Amused," *The Daily Telegraph* (31 January 2009).
5 Mette Hjort, "On the Plurality of Cinematic Transnationalism," in *World Cinemas, Transnational Perspectives*, ed. Natasa Ďurovičová and Kathleen Newman (New York: Routledge, 2010), 19.
6 See Mette Hjort, "Themes of Nation," in *Cinema and Nation*, ed. Mette Hjort and Scott MacKenzie (London: Routledge, 2000), and Bailey, "A New Generation."
7 Hjort, "Themes of a Nation"; Hjort, "On the Plurality of Cinematic Transnationalism," 13.
8 Shaw identifies fifteen analytical categories of transnationalism in film culture: transnational modes of production, distribution and exhibition; transnational modes of narration; cinema of globalization; films with multiple locations; exilic and diasporic filmmaking; film and cultural exchange; transnational influences; transnational critical approaches; transnational viewing practices; transregional/transcommunity films; transnational stars; transnational directors; the ethics of transnationalism; transnational collaborative networks; national films. Deborah Shaw, "Deconstructing and Reconstructing 'Transnational Cinema,'" in *Contemporary Hispanic Cinema: Interrogating Transnationalism in Spanish and Latin American Film*, ed. Stephanie Dennison (Woodbridge: Tamesis, 2013).
9 Timothy Corrigan, *A Cinema without Walls: Movies and Culture after Vietnam* (New Brunswick, NJ: Rutgers University Press, 1991), 105.
10 Ibid.
11 On the star system in Quebec national cinema, see Bill Marshall, *Quebec National Cinema* (Montreal: McGill-Queen's Press, 2000), chapter 7.
12 The Grand Prix is the second most prestigious prize at the Cannes Film Festival after the Palme d'Or, while the Jury Prize is akin to a third-place award.
13 The review in *Variety* was particularly harsh: Peter Debruge, "Toronto Film Review: 'The Death and Life of John F. Donovan,'" *Variety*, 13 September

2018, https://variety.com/2018/film/reviews/the-death-and-life-of-john-f-donovan-review-1202939893/.
14 Author's translation. Alexandre Fontaine Rousseau, "Culte de la personalité: Le cinema de Xavier Dolan," *24 images*, no. 173 (2015): 11.
15 Dina Iordanova, "Foreword," in *Film Festivals: History, Theory, Method, Practice*, ed. Marijke de Valck, Brendan Kredell, and Skadi Loist (London: Routledge, 2016), xiii–xiv.
16 Marijke de Valck, *Film Festivals: From European Geopolitics to Global Cinephilia* (Amsterdam: Amsterdam University Press, 2007), 106.
17 Marijke de Valck, "Fostering Art, Adding Value, Cultivating Taste: Film Festivals as Sites of Cultural Legitimacy," in *Film Festivals: History, Theory, Method, Practice*, 104–8.
18 Ibid., 109.
19 Marc-André Lussier, "Films québécois en France: un public à séduire," La Presse.ca (8 March 2017), http://www.lapresse.ca/cinema/cinema-quebecois/201703/17/01-5079717-films-quebecois-en-france-un-public-a-seduire.php.
20 Author's translation. Nathalie Simon, "Québec: la Belle Province du cinéma," *Le Figaro*, 18 March 2015: A28.
21 Author's translation. Quoted in ibid.
22 Bill Nichols, "Global Image Consumption in the Age of Late Capitalism," *East-West Film Journal* 8, no. 1 (1994): 68–85.
23 The question of national allegories in cinema has been a recurring theme in Canadian and Quebec film studies following Frederic Jameson's groundbreaking essay "Third-World Literature in the Era of Multinational Capitalism," *Social Text* 15 (fall 1986): 65–88.
24 For an alternative and allegorical reading of postnational Quebec society in contemporary cinema, see Mercédès Baillargeon, "Romantic Disillusionment, (Dis)Identification, and the Sublimation of National Identity in Québec's 'New Wave': *Heartbeats* by Xavier Dolan and *Night #1* by Anne Émond," *Québec Studies*, no. 57 (2014): 171–91.
25 André Loiselle, "Popular Genres in Quebec Cinema: The Strange Case of Horror in Film and Television," in *How Canadians Communicate III: Contexts of Canadian Popular Culture*, ed. Bart Beaty et al. (Edmonton: Athabasca University Press, 2010).
26 Valérie Mandia, "Le septième art hors des frontières nationales: le pouvoir de la langue et de l'imaginaire culturel dans les films du cinéaste québécois Xavier Dolan," *Francophonies d'Amérique*, no. 37 (spring 2014).
27 Carol Vernallis, *Unruly Media: YouTube, Music Video, and the New Digital Cinema* (Oxford: Oxford University Press, 2013), 14.

2

An Equivocal Auteur

Gauging Style and Substance in the Films of Denis Villeneuve

Lee Carruthers

> It's not exactly a masterpiece of cinema, but it might keep you amused for an hour and a half.
>
> José Saramago, *The Double* (7)

For the purposes of a volume on contemporary Canadian cinema, writing about Denis Villeneuve should be easy. The most commercially successful director to emerge from Quebec in recent years, and heralded as "filmmaker of the decade" by the Hollywood Critics Association in 2019, Villeneuve's thirty-year trajectory from NFB shorts and modest SODEC-funded features to internationally acclaimed blockbuster filmmaking seems a straightforward phenomenon to characterize, a kind of success that is both impressive and readily legible.[1] Yet a comprehensive examination of Villeneuve's cinema to date, spanning the mid-nineties to the present, shows this task to be a little unwieldy: on reflection, it's harder than one might expect to situate Villeneuve resolutely as a "Canadian auteur."

One aspect of this dilemma concerns the predictable problem of reconciling a filmmaker based in Hollywood, whose work often observes generic formulae, with established models of Canadian national cinema: David Cronenberg has long been the best-known demonstration of this problem, and his films still resist critical appropriation in important ways. But this chapter actually focuses on the other side of the issue, casting the question of how we should conceptualize Denis Villeneuve as an auteur – Canadian or otherwise. In reviews, interviews, and other press coverage, Villeneuve routinely receives this designation, based on the high style and perceived intelligence of his work. Yet I will confess to finding this connection surprisingly unpersuasive. While Villeneuve's iconic status as a filmmaker is indisputable, it's not clear that this constitutes authorship in the usual sense: critics have not laid bare the distinctive contours of a stylistic signature in his work, or conclusively explained what such a signature might mean. The status of auteur carries with it the expectation of a thoughtfully cultivated aesthetic that leads us to the filmmaker's ideas. With assessments of Villeneuve, however, what stands in for these criteria are more or less approximations: his work is enormously stylish, and sometimes gives the appearance of conceptual depth.

This chapter will clarify the constitutive elements of Villeneuve's oeuvre, first as a matter of style, and then, in pursuit of meaning, driven by a close analysis of nine feature films. Grounding this assessment is the idea that an auteurist critical practice retains some scholarly purchase, though necessarily in a modified, contemporary form. Historically, auteurist frameworks have tended to prioritize the creative achievements of white, male artists above all others, while claiming only to be casting objective hierarchies between "greater" and "lesser" works. To some degree, it remains an organizing premise for film festivals, retrospectives, and academic publishing, aligning critical and scholarly work with the formation of publics, and with pleasurable practices of film viewing.[2] Recently scholars have emphasized the extent to which this lens necessarily suppresses the range and diversity of cinema, especially for cinema made by marginalized people. In other words, auteurism too easily functions as criteria of exclusion rather than as a starting point for programs of film research or cinephilic discovery.[3] Although my discussion does not specifically interrogate this issue, it does underscore the ease with which a decidedly uneven film corpus has earned Villeneuve the prestige status of auteur, while other filmmakers remain comparatively undervalued. This discussion also recognizes that Villeneuve's cinema is strongly collaborative, often featuring the same technical personnel across multiple productions: sustained creative partnerships that have shaped the work include cinematographer Roger Deakins (*Prisoners, Sicario, Blade Runner 2049*); composer Jóhann Jóhannsson (*Prisoners, Sicario, Arrival, Blade Runner 2049*); sound designer and editor Sylvain Bellemare (*Incendies, Arrival*), storyboard artist Sam Hudecki (*Enemy, Prisoners, Sicario, Arrival, Blade Runner 2049*), and production designer Patrice Vermette (*Enemy, Prisoners, Sicario, Arrival*). My aim, therefore, is not to submit Villeneuve's cinema to an outworn critical category, but to retrieve some of its productive specifications, reading the aesthetic of his work as something both protean and persistent that is shaped by contextual and collaborative factors. As the pages to follow will indicate, these terms can help us to understand Villeneuve's filmmaking better, sharpening our sense of his contribution to Canadian and Hollywood cinemas.

The Auteurist Background

While the notion of the film director as "auteur" is a familiar formulation, I want to offer a brief review of its underlying assumptions so as to situate the subject of this chapter more concretely. A version of this idea first circulated within French critical culture of the 1920s, appearing in the writings of Louis Delluc and Léon Moussinac, before acquiring additional shadings in the pages of *Cahiers du Cinéma*, where thinking about the filmmaker as auteur was pursued as a lively practice and loose editorial policy (or "politique") across the 1950s. For these critics, understanding the auteur involved reading a film's mise-en-scène, a variable term that on one hand refers to the dynamic organization and content of filmic space, and on the other, to a more elusive relation between the filmmaker and material that the film's visual arrangement is said to convey.[4] The auteur "theory" is a further variation imported into Anglo-American film criticism by Andrew Sarris, beginning with his influential *Film Culture* essay, "Notes on the Auteur Theory in 1962."[5] Sarris's appropriation of the French discussion is transformative, distilling its terms into a theoretical stance (though never quite a theory) and explicit critical method that drives the arguments and evaluative hierarchies outlined in *The American Cinema* (1968).[6] Sarris's clarity of purpose is surely one of the reasons auteurism's legacy has proved so generative: a galvanizing force for 1960s film culture and beyond, it is a concept intended to spark critical activity, inspiring extensive film viewing and comparative assessment, spanning both art cinema and the commercial products of Hollywood.

Before proceeding to Villeneuve, it's worth pausing to review Sarris's arguments briefly, which in revised form help to frame my discussion below. Sarris's conceptualization of the auteur rests upon three overlapping premises. The first is simply a baseline expectation of technical proficiency: the director must possess an "elementary flair for the cinema," as one might expect in the adjudication of any art. The second principle concerns the "distinguishable personality of the director," as reflected in the films' aesthetic arrangements: thus, a survey of an auteur's output will exhibit discernible and recurrent stylistic features for the perspicacious critic, which appear as a creative signature across the work. In other words, an auteur's work is not just bound by common narrative or thematic elements, but by its formal orchestration: as Sarris expresses it, the way a film "looks and moves should have some relationship to the way a director thinks and feels."[7] The third premise is closely tied to the second, but is more difficult to articulate, perhaps because what it describes so often registers as textual opacity. At the heart of the auteur's project lies what Sarris calls "interior meaning" – a way of naming the governing idea that can be glimpsed in the auteur's films and is continually worked out by them cinematically.

What is at issue for Sarris is a kind of distinctive energy that infuses the films and continually generates their meaning: this dimension of the work lends depth to its stylistic patterning and also to the ways its aesthetic contours are in some sense "personal." More than the form alone, and more than the expression of personality, the work produces a dynamic picture of the world that is also, tacitly, a kind of argument about it, catalyzed by the auteur's persistent, creative risk. I expect that it's something along these lines that encourages scholars to suggest (for instance, in relation to Terrence Malick's films) that the medium at its best carries out a kind of thinking: it is the auteur's stake in the world that matters here, and which cinema raises to visibility. "Interior meaning" does not entail undue seriousness or even self-consciousness, however: it is a kind of alchemizing force that is equally playful, and continually relates style to substance.[8]

Directed to the cinema of Denis Villeneuve, Sarris's formulations motivate two kinds of knowledge-seeking: first, they invite us to specify the terms of Villeneuve's film aesthetic, which, on the basis of received commentaries, remains unfocused; second, and more substantially, they ask us to think seriously about the creative strengths and limitations of Villeneuve's corpus, reckoning with the expectation of a style that yields meaning. For my purposes, the auteur designation allows us to group a wide-ranging body of films cohesively, uncovering their textual logics by comparative means. That this practice centres upon a single director is a productive rhetorical device, but never a refusal of contextualization: as we will see, the chapter also foregrounds the mediated nature of Villeneuve's work, set in relation to other traditions and texts, creative collaboration, and social realities.

Identifying Villeneuve's Style

The sections below present the stylistic trends of Villeneuve's cinema in two ways: first, as a condensed chart of formal strategies that clearly maps the continuities and differences across his filmography (table 2.1); and second, through a more detailed discussion of representative examples.

My analysis is based on repeat viewings of each title, proceeding at first freely and then chronologically through the corpus. The stylistic categories outlined here therefore derive from a patient process of elimination, forming initial hypotheses about a wide spectrum of trends that are then winnowed down to those that can be confirmed, and eventually consolidating a picture of the stylistic elements that most strongly shape the work as a whole. To qualify as a formal trend, the strategy in question must be salient (noticeable, marked, prominent) and consistent (forming a continuity across all, or most, of the films). On the chart itself, its presence in each film is indicated as "Y" (yes) or "N" (no).

Though harmonized with classical procedures, these elements register the sort of formal self-consciousness once associated with the international art cinemas, and now fairly pervasive across mainstream film practice: their peculiar appearance and interaction within Villeneuve's cinema, however, suggests a distinct aesthetic. After completing this assessment, an additional trend was charted retrospectively to address the ways each film announces a conceptual frame to shape its interpretation: on this point, see the more detailed discussion below. What emerges from this process is an overview of six strategies, five exclusively formal, and the last formal-conceptual: of the formal categories, two concern editing, and three relate to compositions within the frame. Although summarized as discrete procedures in the interest of clarity, the techniques evaluated here work synergistically, heightening their effects.

1. EDITING INFLECTIONS: TIME STRUCTURES. This category proves to be a key descriptor for many of Villeneuve's feature films, charting editing manipulations that call attention to the temporal organization of the work. Arguably, the prominence of time as a formal effect and theme in Villeneuve's cinema is forecast by his early NFB project, REW-FFWD (1994): this reflexive documentary short uses a puzzle structure to frame its playful exploration of medium and memory. At the core of this formal category are occasions of ambiguity, where the ordering of shots and sequences departs from classical procedures. Scanning Villeneuve's first four features, these manipulations occur as marked temporal ellipses, suspending narrative action and motivation in conspicuous ways, and through repetitions, replaying narrative events from multiple perspectives. In *Arrival*, temporal play affects narrative sequencing on a larger scale, and coheres with the film's overarching concern with lived temporality. While *Blade Runner 2049* is cast into the future, and invested

in questions of memory, the film's temporal organization is surprisingly conventional, generating reliable narrative cues for its spatiotemporal coordinates. A plausible rationale for this difference is that with this production, mise-en-scène and atmosphere are of supreme importance, and are delivered with greater force within a narrative design that is free from distracting temporal ruptures. Something similar likely applies to *Sicario*, which develops a straightforward timeline to support its extended action sequences, and to Villeneuve's most conventional film, *Prisoners*, which also pursues a linear temporal trajectory.

II. EDITING INFLECTIONS: CLOSE VIEWS AND MANNERED MONTAGE. The second category focuses on editing techniques as they work to articulate space. To this end, an observable operation of Villeneuve's cinema entails a limited play of shot scale that resists a conventional establishing shot: instead of commencing with a wide, legible view of the space to situate narrative activity, the film proceeds with close views of an object, or a character, rendering these as a series of slightly disordered, representative pieces. These decontextualized views generate tension because they analyze the space before it has attained full legibility. This kind of stylization aligns with recognized practices of contemporary cinema, such as the pervasive use of close-ups that David Bordwell has termed an "intensified continuity," but here operates in ways that are distinctive. The car crash that opens *Un 32 août sur terre* is conveyed through suffocating shot alternations, first framing the car's headlight so closely as to seem nearly abstract, and then producing successive views of the protagonist's face, her muddied driver's licence, and her flailing hand as she struggles for the door, shifting between interior and exterior views before opening out to a wider perspective. Looking to films as different as *Incendies* and *Sicario*, these titles likewise exhibit a similar reverse-establishing pattern, moving from an isolated detail to the broader environment in patient gradations. In a handful of titles, these editing mannerisms are accompanied by more legible structures, or replaced by them entirely (*Prisoners*, *Enemy*); in *Blade Runner 2049*, for example, close, not-yet-contextualized perspectives are folded into establishing shots with greater efficiency.

Another self-conscious editing mode that characterizes the early work, in particular, involves digressive episodes of montage. A quiet passage from *Polytechnique*, for example, is a purely descriptive and silent observation of snow falling in a park. The episode unfolds as a succession of five lingering images, comprising about twenty seconds in total, fragmenting the wintry space into discrete components: first,

Table 2.1 Formal and conceptual trends in the films of Denis Villeneuve

Production information	Time structures	Close views and mannered montage	Aerial perspectives	Lateral compositions	Colour design	Conceptual framings
Un 32 août sur terre (CANADA, 1998)	Y	Y	Y	Y Wide landscape	Y	Y Title signals the film's concern with "impossible time"
Maelström (CANADA, 2000)	Y	Y	N Not aerial, but an extravagant camera rotation	Y	Y	Y Existential commentary on human finitude: "All human action is a manifestation against death."
Polytechnique (CANADA, 2009)	Y	Y	Y	Y	Y	Y Lecture on entropy
Incendies (CANADA-FRANCE, 2010)	Y But initially restricted: red titles indicating location shore up narrative legibility	Y But retaining legibility	Y	Y Wide landscape	N Striking visuals, but colour is not a dominant technique.	Y From Wajdi Mouawad's play: "Childhood is a knife stuck in your throat. It can't be easily removed." A lecture on pure mathematics
Prisoners (USA, 2013)	N Conventional	N Conventional, not distinctive	N	Y Natural and suburban spaces extend across wide frame	Y Warm/cool contrasts Amber interiors, explosive colour at the film's conclusion: rain and fire	Y But simple: the Lord's prayer

Production information	Time structures	Close views and mannered montage	Aerial perspectives	Lateral compositions	Colour design	Conceptual framings
Enemy (CANADA-SPAIN, 2013)	Y	N	Y Rooftop scene highlights perceptual instability	Y Urban spaces, skyline, segmented interiors	Y Amber, sickly tone	Y A line from Saramago's novel: "Chaos is order yet undeciphered." A history lesson on power
Sicario (USA, 2015)	N Straight-ahead plotline	Y	Y Helicopter	Y Wide terrain (land, sky, city); horizon at sunset	Y Warm/cool contrasts Amber interiors, explosive colour at the film's conclusion: rain and fire	Y Definition of "sicario"; the idea that violence is universal
Arrival (USA, 2016)	Y	Y	Y Helicopter	Y Wide terrain (land, sky, city) and modular spaces	Y Warm/cool contrasts	Y Time and memory: in voice-over, "We are so bound by time …" Professor's lecture on linguistics
Blade Runner 2049 (USA, 2017)	N	Y But limited	Y From the film's opening shots, drone	Y Wide terrain (land, sky, city) and modular spaces	Y Warm tones vs cool: striking amber filter in casino sequence	Y Opens with the film's backstory; later, referencing Vladimir Nabokov's *Pale Fire*

a wide view of the skyline from a snowy balcony; then, a slightly closer view, tipped upward, of a statue; next is another broad perspective, framing a pair of lion statues at frame right; then, a close shot of the lion's face, from a reversed angle; and finally, one last wide framing of the park, looking up at the snow-edged trees, their branches stretched toward the left side of the frame. What motivates this episode aesthetically is surely the tonal contrast it effects with the eruptions of violence that will follow: here is the calm before the storm. But notably, it also elaborates this contrast by a method that seems nearly Eisensteinian, asking us to notice small shifts in scale, camera angle, and figure direction from shot to shot – and thus the way our view of things can be altered in an instant. We might describe the editing style here as a constrained, or conventionalized, "cubism" – that is, as a perceptual fragmentation that is visually arresting, yet remains in the service of storytelling. Though dynamic and sometimes disorienting, the fragmented optics of Villeneuve's cinema nonetheless advance narrative unity. Interestingly, the two transitional titles marking Villeneuve's first forays into Hollywood, *Prisoners* and *Enemy*, largely dispense with these embellishments, instead relying on unadorned storytelling logics.

III. COMPOSITIONAL STRATEGIES: AERIAL PERSPECTIVES. Perhaps the most distinctive aesthetic trend of Villeneuve's cinema, and certainly the most impressive, is the preponderance of dramatic aerial views that appear across the work. One of the benefits of aerial cinematography is its visceral articulations of scale: to this end, the richest moments aesthetically in *Un 32 août sur terre* and *Incendies* involve this play of relative size, contrasting the progress of a vehicle, which registers as a tiny object in the frame, with the wide, white expanse of desert. In a spectacular variation, the inverted aerial shot featured late in *Polytechnique* initially observes the path of a car on the roadway below, but then changes course, sweeping upward steeply to trace the frozen shoreline of the St Lawrence River. This view of jagged ice floes suspended in dark water possesses a nearly abstract quality, strongly (and deliberately) recalling the flattened cubist forms of Picasso's *Guernica*, featured earlier in the diegesis.[9] On the basis of *Sicario*, and *Blade Runner 2049*, one might assume that such visual effects were the byproduct of Villeneuve's collaboration with celebrated cinematographer Roger Deakins; it's worth noting, however, that these stylized views long predate this partnership, and are in fact excluded from the first Villeneuve/Deakins collaboration, *Prisoners*. The other exception to the trend is *Maelström*, which does, however, generate something similar, replacing the trademark shot with a dynamic camera rotation that seems to lift off from the ground below. In more recent films, aerial views are justified narratively as extended helicopter excursions, complete with blaring engine noise. In *Sicario*, the camera is so distant as to produce map-like perspectives, capturing the remote patterns of intersecting roadways below; conversely, *Arrival* reimagines these perspectives over a verdant terrain, positioned amid low clouds over a green landscape. While these perspectives are not always steeped in meaning, they are often glorious, and in this sense serve as their own reward: paired with the compositional strategies outlined below, Villeneuve's cinema insists that seeing things in a fresh, unprecedented way is one of the central pleasures of cinema.

IV. COMPOSITIONAL STRATEGIES: THE LATERAL FRAME. A consistent aesthetic feature of Villeneuve's cinema, and a firm basis for his reputation as a stylist, concerns the way his films exploit the compositional options of the widescreen frame. Whether to picture a vast terrain or an ebbing sunset, as in *Un 32 août sur terre*, *Incendies*, and *Sicario*; to present a stretch of skyline or urban sprawl, as in *Enemy* and *Prisoners*; or to emphasize discrete, modular zones like those of *Blade Runner 2049*, Villeneuve's images cultivate a strong sense of design, and sometimes emulate a modernist aesthetic. For example, *Arrival*'s complex linear compositions divide the frame into broad sections, highlighting their horizontality, often forming frames within the frame. Thus, the wide, illuminated space in which the aliens appear resembles nothing so much as a movie screen, in acknowledgment of the film's own compositional materials. This lateral emphasis also prepares a memorable graphic contrast, juxtaposing the width of the frame with the towering, tapered forms of the heptapods, and the fluid logograms that constitute their language. But the more important connection here is with the work of American light artist James Turrell, whom Villeneuve cites as an influence. Turrell's large-scale, immersive installations are internationally acclaimed; his astonishing projection piece *Breathing Light* (2013) serves as a model for *Arrival*'s alien interview room, and is very similar in appearance. Restaging the optics of a Ganzfeld experiment, *Breathing Light* facilitates an intense form of perceptual play that strongly alters the experience of spatial depth. When photographed, the installation space appears flattened out as a wide, luminous rectangle, or an illuminated screen: against this bright backdrop, viewers stand as diminutive figures in a countourless space. It's easy to see the way Turrell's aesthetic informs aspects of *Arrival*'s production design, though the diegetic zone it yields

Figure 2.1   *Breathing Light* (2013) serves as a model for the alien interview room in *Arrival* (2016).

within the film is more rational than hallucinatory. Villeneuve's vision for these details emerged in collaboration with production designer Patrice Vermette, another admirer of Turrell's work: Vermette has shaped the aesthetic of four of Villeneuve's films, working on *Prisoners*, *Enemy*, *Sicario*, and *Arrival*. For comparative purposes, images of *Breathing Light* and Turrell's other Ganzfeld pieces can be viewed online.[10]

V. COMPOSITIONAL STRATEGIES: COLOUR DESIGN. While his three films with Roger Deakins share a particular colour aesthetic – elaborating warm and cool zones within the frame, exaggerated and diminished saturation, and vivid splashes of orange and scarlet – Villeneuve has always been something of a colourist. The early feature, *Un 32 août sur terre*, already signals this tendency with its blue-lit interiors and repeated contrasts of sand and sky. Perhaps the most self-conscious colour design appears in *Maelström*: the film's blue-red palette is strongly emphasized from scene to scene, and localized in horizontal segments of the frame. A particularly striking image pictures the film's protagonist waiting at a subway platform: she sits on a low bench at frame left, joining a man who sits some distance away, frame right (figure 2.2). This studied composition invites the viewer to remark its careful symmetries: the vivid blue backdrop set against the long line of the red bench recalls the restricted primary palette of a Mondrian painting, or the color field work of Rothko, suggesting an evident calculation about its arrangement. While these elements furnish intense graphic appeal and contribute an encompassing sense of design to Villeneuve's cinema, they do not constitute a signifying system (as one might find, for instance,

Style and Substance in the Films of Denis Villeneuve 53

Figure 2.2 Symmetrical composition in *Maelström* (2000).

in Godard's use of colour) but rather a spectacular one, aimed at visual interest and visceral effects. The hot and cold hues that organize the environments of *Blade Runner 2049* – as when red lights on K's drone pierce the leaden sky, or a yellow flower miraculously grows beneath a greyed tree – carry significance insofar as they reflect the narrative's continual parsing of human/replicant energies. The film's most assertive use of colour, the long, amber-saturated casino sequence, clearly bears the signature of cinematographer Deakins, and also references, without special innovation, the chromatic atmosphere of Tarkovsky's *Stalker* (USSR, 1979).

VI. CONCEPTUAL FRAMINGS: TELEGRAPHING THE BIG IDEA. Compiled retrospectively, this category departs from matters of film style to consider conceptual frameworks: specifically, it marks an observable routine across the corpus by which the films telegraph a sophisticated idea or theme to condition their interpretation. In each case, a title, quotation, or piece of dialogue is supplied at the front end of the film, proposing a leading concept. The very title of *Un 32 août sur terre*, for example, frames the narrative as a problem of illogical or impossible time; in *Maelström*, a philosopher's existential commentary is referenced, discoursing on human finitude ("All human action is a manifestation against death"); in *Enemy*, an opening title provides a pithy line from José Saramago's novel ("Chaos is order yet undeciphered"). Across four other films, professors lecture on entropy (*Polytechnique*), pure mathematics (*Incendies*), Hegel's conception of history via Marx (*Enemy*), and linguistics (*Arrival*). In *Blade Runner 2049*, Nabokov's literary experiment *Pale Fire* is repeatedly highlighted, first as lines recited, and then as a book held up to the camera's gaze. The two films most resistant to this schema still deploy related framing devices: there is the historically inflected definition that opens *Sicario* ("The word *Sicario* comes from the zealots of Jerusalem. Killers who hunted the Romans who invaded their homeland. In Mexico, *Sicario* means *hitman*"), which aligns the narrative, albeit in a plainspoken way, with universal themes; likewise, *Prisoners* initiates its exploration of righteous violence, not subtly, with a recitation of the Lord's Prayer over its opening images.

By these weighty additions the films seek to establish a certain tone, if not of seriousness than of intellectual investment, that is meant to shade the work as a whole. They are consistent with Villeneuve's effort to incorporate aesthetic elements from the international art scene within his films: we might think of the sustained stare at Picasso's *Guernica* that occurs in *Polytechnique* and inspires the film's monochrome aesthetic; the giant spider that concludes *Enemy*, modelled on Louise Bourgeois's large-scale sculpture *Maman*; or the way the work of James Turrell is a clear reference for *Arrival*'s minimalist set design. Such details are part of the reason that critics routinely characterize Villeneuve's cinema as smarter and more thoughtful than standard fare. Operating in concert with the aesthetic strategies outlined above, such references contribute additional layers of self-consciousness to Villeneuve's project, aiming to align his work with certain kinds of cultural capital, with an appreciation (or at least awareness) of cinema's upscale affinities. In other words, these references successfully situate Villeneuve's work at the interface of Hollywood filmmaking and global art cinema practice, forming what critics have termed "blockbuster[s] with brains."[11] The question that I want to raise with respect to this canny positioning concerns what, if anything, lies beneath the films' sophisticated surfaces.

Critical Reception and the Problem of Style

While Villeneuve's work is acclaimed by critics, receiving wide recognition and numerous awards, a longer view of its reception proves less uniformly positive, and illuminates a common line of complaint related to matters of style. The most emphatic assessments emerge from critics and scholars in Quebec, directed at the early Canadian features. Given *Polytechnique*'s status as the first feature-length dramatization of the 1989 École Polytechnique massacre, and the media furor surrounding its release, this intense response is unsurprising. But it's a mistake to understand such critiques as "local" readings of the work, or purely as responses to a controversy; instead, what distinguishes these commentaries is the way they submit Villeneuve's films to a robust level of scrutiny. The assessments offered by André Habib and Jean-Pierre Sirois-Trahan, in particular, hold the work to a high standard, enumerating its strengths and weaknesses in a Bazinian language that is part of a larger effort to envision a renewed Québécois cinema. This effort entails a certain kind of film poetics, grounded in the expectation that form and content serve each other reciprocally, and are fused in significance; in this respect, their criteria should remind us in important ways of Sarris's concept of "interior meaning."

Though recognizing the technical mastery of Villeneuve's films, received critiques have levelled two intertwined charges at them: the first suggests that the work indulges in an empty formalism, while the second is troubled by its aestheticization of violence and other sensitive content. In a scathing review of *Polytechnique*, André Habib suggests that the film has indifferently transposed the reality of the massacre into aesthetic material for the cinema: by its generic applications of style, the film flattens out what is horrifying and historically charged, and for this reason lacks a "moral vector."[12] The film's calculated monochrome aesthetic similarly disturbs Montreal-based critic Brendan Kelly, who also finds it lacking in insight: in an especially damning assessment, he remarks that "there's something wrong when the visuals are the most arresting thing in a film about the Polytechnique murders."[13] Then there is the issue of the film's structuring viewpoint: Mélissa Blais's trenchant analysis suggests that the film's narrative design gives equal importance to the male perspective, and in so doing, facilitates a reading of the massacre via masculinist discourse that radically diminishes its political impact.[14] It is notable that the film was shot in dual-language versions, seeking to broaden its appeal in another way, capturing both French- and English-speaking audiences.

Although *Polytechnique* is evidently a flashpoint for critics, these objections extend to other titles and to wider critical contexts. In a lively discussion from 2011, Sirois-Trahan characterizes Villeneuve's filmmaking more broadly as a surface-driven "cinema of the image" that merely elaborates in filmic form the commercial aesthetic of music videos and advertising – two professional domains with which Villeneuve is quite familiar. In contrast to the sustained ambiguities of Denis Côté's cinema, the films perform a kind of empty embellishment, mobilized by a camera that "transforms tragic events into a show, without developing a real view of the world."[15] Writing for *New York Magazine*, David Edelstein wonders if *Prisoners*, in the vein of *Incendies*, doesn't use the peril of children to generate "easy shocks."[16] Likewise, *Cinemascope*'s critic Richard Porton suggests that the favorable reviews of *Sicario* that emerged after its Cannes premiere effectively endorsed a vapid formalism while failing to interrogate "the shallow and exploitative nature of the material." Like the dual-language versions of *Polytechnique*, *Sicario* "hedges its bets in order to remain shamelessly crowd-pleasing."[17] On the same film, A.O. Scott of the *New York Times* wonders if *Sicario*'s powerful sounds and images aren't just expressions of technique: their interplay is "at once numbing and sensational ... instead of a movie about violence we're watching another violent movie, after all."[18]

For my purposes, the most emblematic titles for this problem of style are the very different features *Maelström* and *Enemy*: separated by more than a decade, the first was produced in Canada, and the other in Hollywood with mainstream star Jake Gyllenhaal. While *Maelström* received a number of Canadian film prizes, a mixed review in *Variety* sounds a familiar theme: "Whether there's much substance beneath all the surface eccentricity may be the largest among many puzzles here ... viewers may sometimes wonder whether there's any guiding principal [sic] here beyond quirkiness for its own sake."[19] But the quirkiness of the narrative is not quite the issue: it's the way each scene unfolds as an occasion for aggressive stylization, rendering the protagonist's abortion, car accident, and ride on the Métro as dramatic equivalences wrought in the same vivid colour scheme. While *Maelström*'s investment in a pop surrealism is obvious – the film is narrated by a fish, after all – this association does not bind the film's choices in a meaningful way; rather, it supplies a soft justification for eclectic and incongruous narrative effects.[20]

Turning to *Enemy*, we encounter something similar: the film's treatment of José Saramago's *The Double* retains only the sparest thread of its source material, harnessing certain of the novel's story elements to the machinations of a conventional thriller, set within the drabbest urban milieu. In its looseness of adaptation, Villeneuve's film sets aside the funny, dark, existential voice of the literary work and its complex picture of history: what it offers instead is an enigmatic ending that would have surprised Saramago, manifesting the narrative's subterranean energies as a giant spider poised above Toronto's skyline. Publicity for the film suggests that Villeneuve asked his cast not to reveal the spider's significance during media events, and it's little wonder: the film's conclusion makes better sense as a quasi-Cronenbergian gesture than as a consequential outgrowth of the film's style and themes.[21]

This uneasy fit of style and substance in Villeneuve's cinema certainly makes it harder to call him an *auteur*, in the established sense: one feels too often that the aesthetic contours of the work exist only to please themselves, and not as catalysts for meaning. There is also a way in which Villeneuve's films can seem more accommodating than personal, as though designed to reach every available audience; as we have seen, this effort to maximize the films' commercial reach can register as tone-deaf, or at worst, exploitative. Yet in the final sections of this discussion, I will look at the workings of a single title to see if Villeneuve's recent work might enframe richer possibilities.

The Interpretive Tasks of *Arrival*

Arrival is based on Ted Chiang's novella "Story of Your Life," which first appeared in the science fiction anthology *Starlight* in 1998 and garnered several major science fiction prizes. Adapted for the screen by Eric Heisserer, it relates the story of a linguist who reflects on the loss of her daughter while working to decipher an alien language and writing system. The source material supplies Villeneuve's film with its imbricated temporal structure and with the related premise, traced via principles of linguistics and classical physics, that time operates as a simultaneous mode of awareness rather than sequentially. At the narrative level, this idea takes shape in the protagonist's ability to engage multiple temporalities: most poignantly, she knows in advance that her daughter will die prematurely, and yet chooses to endure this heartbreak rather than alter its course. Thus, story and film make a claim that is both epistemological and existential in nature, proposing that the outcome of things must be known in order to begin.

The story's complex temporal configurations register on the page through a finely calibrated syntax, cultivating a play of tenses even within a single sentence to acutely convey overlaid processes of anticipation and recollection. In one of many addresses to her daughter, the narrator recalls, "When it comes to language-learning anecdotes, my favorite source is child language acquisition. I remember one afternoon when you are five years old, after you have come home from kindergarten. You'll be coloring with your crayons while I grade papers" (9). The linkage of "I remember" with "you are," and also "you have" and "you'll be," is nearly confounding: though the sense of the passage is clear enough, it conjures a murkiness that entwines past, present, and future. In this respect, Chiang's story seems an ideal object to be adapted into film, as it appears to share the medium's affinity for temporal mediation. But as a work of short fiction, its temporal folds are packed more densely, continually augmenting each other: within the narrator's recollections, her thoughts frequently attach themselves to disparate events, occurring at other moments, and draw them into focus so that every recalled episode is intercut and qualified by competing temporal contexts. Like these temporal fractures, the story's narrative content – its "heptapods" and "logograms" – seem designed for cinematic expansion, particularly to emphasize their vast scale and intricate graphic elements. Chiang's prose often invites the detailed gaze of cinema, as when a logogram is said to resemble an "Escheresque lattice" (16), or a series of semagrams are observed "sprouting like frost on a windowpane" (26).

There are important differences between these texts as well. Key narrative details are elided or changed outright in the film adaptation: most noticeably, the global panic that ensues related to the aliens' arrival, with its military intrigue and spectacular explosions, are heightened additions to the story, projected by Villeneuve's film as extended visual set pieces. Yet despite these amendments, the film remains more like the story than not in its central preoccupations: indeed, the shared terrain between the texts is an essential interface, and marks a deepening of significance in Villeneuve's work. Unlike the trivial adaptation of Saramago's fiction for *Enemy*, *Arrival* stands as a rich amalgamation of form and content, deploying cinematic technique in a considered way to extrapolate the narrative's core arguments. While the film in some respects transforms its source material into hyperbolic Hollywood action, an examination of its careful orchestration of images shows us that the novel's ideas endure in cinematic form and are sometimes powerfully concentrated by the unique capacities of the medium.

Looking to the film's opening moments, one is struck by the delicate tension initiated beneath the scene's sentimental content. The first images picture the film's protagonist, Louise Banks, playing with her child on a lakeside lawn: in close, accessible framings, the camera does more than observe their movement, instead relaying it sympathetically, as though swept up in the rhythms of their game. The visual field is carefully delimited, using the wide frame to create an airy, expansive space that is repeatedly split by figure movement and the dissective action of the camera. Much is achieved here with ease and efficiency, foregrounding the nearness of things in experience, dynamic and tactile, and also the way such proximate textures are pulled away from us in time. Admirers of contemporary American art cinema will remark that the idyllic scene, surging camera movement, and classical score recall the cinematography of Emmanuel Lubezki, particularly in the arrangements that animate Terrence Malick's *Tree of Life* (2011). But the aesthetic strategies at work here, via Bradford Young's camera, are not derivative: instead, they begin to formulate an encompassing formal system that asks for a special attentiveness from the viewer.

Perhaps the simplest way to explain *Arrival*'s aesthetic method is to point to a subtle visual game that it develops across the film as a whole. Here is the gist of it: a shot begins in darkness, and is filled with music; then, the camera tilts down from its initial positioning to locate the screen-like contours of a lit space, wedged between areas of darkness above and below. What the camera pictures is not necessarily unusual: it has simply found an area of focus and narrative activity, set between floor and ceiling, or lake and sky. The film's opening performs this action, and it recurs in the presentation of other spaces, such as Louise's home and the desolate zones of the university. Quite apart from narrative content, this way of introducing things involves the viewer in an unhurried routine of revelation: narrative information is delivered in a way that is a little drawn out, attaining legibility incrementally, over time. We might think of these moments as minor instances of defamiliarization, or as repeated delays that contribute a slight roughening of the film's narrative language. But more pertinently, it's valuable to see them as a form of conditioning for the viewer, engaging us in an expectant mode of looking. Such small postponements invite us to notice resemblances across the film's images, and to wait for confirmation: in other words, the film asks us to receive its images by actively interpreting them, so as to receive their communication.

This priority is made clearer through another interpretive task set before the viewer. Less than an hour into the film, there is a scene in which Louise recollects a moment shared with her daughter: they stand together in a dimly lit space, perhaps a horse's stable, gazing upward at the large animal. The shot is out of focus, so the horse's body is blurred and indistinct, appearing as an exaggerated line stretching upward, like a glyph rather than a familiar figure. On an initial viewing, the scene reads as a flashback, summoning a moment from Louise's past; with a fuller knowledge of the film's story, we will understand its temporal placement differently. But crucially, the uncertain push-pull of time is encoded in the image already, if we know how to read it: it registers in the instability of the animal's form, testing the limits of what we can recognize and name based on what we have seen before. Notably, the image also serves as a visual rhyme, reiterating certain graphic elements from the previous scene and thus blurring their separation in time.[22] Such "memory" episodes gather around common shapes and gestures in Villeneuve's film, compelling viewers to notice quiet details and visual alignments as a way of making meaning: by this, the film engages us in a version of Louise's work – attending to patterns and decoding them, reading the film's materials like a language. The mirrored activity of film and viewer is intimated in the scenes that present Louise's learning sessions with the aliens: to understand their discourse requires a patient doubling of movements, her hand raised to the illuminated screen. It's profoundly suitable that Villeneuve's cinema should finally cultivate a bold synthesis of form and content with *Arrival*, given that the grounding claim of Chiang's story addresses the complex ways that images constitute significance, bending their fluid configurations to the work of a visual syntax. Unlike the riffing stylization of Villeneuve's other films, *Arrival*'s style encourages continual interpretation, making the process of discovery and the meaning-bearing nature of images a shared project of film and viewer. In this sense, *Arrival* both animates and resolves the problem of empty style that we have traced across Villeneuve's corpus: the film's aesthetic is meticulous and rhetorical, generating a spectacle that is also keenly aware of its own representational forms.

This is not to say that Villeneuve's films are devoid of meaning otherwise, or that every production should aspire to *Arrival*'s meditative aesthetic. One look at the elegant interplay of scale and movement across the white desert of *Un 32 août sur terre*, or at the roaring Juarez sequence in *Sicario* – a perfect quarter-hour of bristling tension – confirms the mindfulness of medium that is shared by Villeneuve and his collaborators, exploiting the most cinematic of possibilities. The difference of this film is that the ideas are actively generated by the form, and not incidental to it; through its images and sounds, *Arrival*'s style tells us that time is often difficult to parse, and moves like a language. What we encounter in the film are the familiar design elements that characterize the whole of Villeneuve's work, but here they have acquired new force. By this, *Arrival* draws nearer to what Andrew Sarris called "interior meaning," because in the creative shaping of its sounds and images, Villeneuve's film gives rise to an idea rather than merely gesturing toward it. The distance between a work that thematizes and one that brings something new into being is captured in an incisive observation from James Turrell, whose forms *Arrival* knowingly appropriates: asked to say what his installations represent, or to what they allude, Turrell makes a sharp distinction: "It's not about light – it *is* light."[23] This point might also be extended to my assessment of Villeneuve's cinema in an overarching way, emphasizing the artist's responsibility to forge rather than borrow meanings.

Toward a Conclusion

At about the time Villeneuve's *Maelström* was released, Piers Handling contributed a short essay to a published *festschrift* for Andrew Sarris, called "Auteurism in Canada." In those pages, he described the transformative power of the auteur concept, particularly in its application to Hollywood filmmaking, extolling its way of inspiring both enthusiasm and intellectual rigor for the cinema. Turning to the Canadian context, however, he writes, "Despite the auteurs who have worked in the margins ... Canadian cinema attains depth when looked at as a national cinema, not as a group of heroic individuals struggling to make their films. David Cronenberg, Atom Egoyan, Denys Arcand are true auteurs, but even their films are rewarded when placed next to one another, their work seen as part of a cultural continuum."[24] Handling's refusal of auteurism in this context isn't very pliable, and equates the term, more or less, with a scrappy individualism: thus, the Canadian industry is simply too small, and too collaborative by nature, to sustain or require the auteur's creative resistance. Second, he also suggests that the output of Canada's auteurs, though impressive, needs the cohesion and conceptual ballast of a national framework to attain full legibility. Looking back on this assessment, one recognizes familiar terrain, debating the relative "Canadian-ness" of our film directors, while also wishing to account for the films made across global production contexts. More recently, formulations of transnational cinema have proved better equipped to describe the complex exchanges of the contemporary situation; the breadth of these frameworks, however, does not always lend itself to a specific understanding of the films themselves. To some degree, this discussion has sought to intervene in these arguments, though focused on a filmmaker who had not yet broken through to the festival circuit at the time Handling was writing. This has involved laying bare the aesthetic strategies that characterize Villeneuve's work, so we might think about his cinema with greater precision, and as an evolving film practice spanning three decades rather than one splintered into antagonistic phases of Canadian and Hollywood production.

But another part of this effort has been to clarify what the value of the auteur concept has been for film critical culture, for taking substantial and sometimes resolutely commercial work seriously, gauged on its merits. I admire Patricia White's recent formulation of authorship, apropos of Greta Gerwig's cinema, as "what critics call it when the director's vision shines through the commodity form of cinema."[25] In this chapter, I have interpreted this vision not as "personality," nor just as a discernible style, but as a phenomenon that permeates the work in a meaningful way, potentially raising something new to visibility. Perhaps such expectations are too high, or too particular, for Villeneuve's cinema – but even the discrepancies we have observed between these standards and the work itself are instructive as they shed light upon both creative and critical tasks.

So where does this leave us, with Villeneuve as auteur? It may be best to situate him as a hybrid filmmaker whose most consistent effort has been to straddle disparate classifications, speaking to both French and English markets, festival juries and mainstream audiences, occupying the lucrative terrain that spans high art and high concept. This positioning, though equivocal, may be more helpful than it first appears: it provides a picture of Canadian cinema that has not often been acknowledged in scholarly work, because it frustrates some of our favoured critical categories. It remains to be seen whether Villeneuve's films will continue along the promising path held out by *Arrival*. The more recent *Blade Runner 2049* is hard to scrutinize in this way, as it seems simultaneously buoyed up and obscured by the powerful aura of Ridley Scott's original and by its own intertextual references. Likewise, the critical reception of Villeneuve's *Dune*, an ambitious adaptation of Frank Herbert's iconic sci-fi novel, appears strongly conditioned by the film's pandemic context: reviewers demand little of the project beyond its spectacular scale and effects, instead echoing the director's own statements about the production as designed to deliver "a unique big screen experience."[26] Yet we might recall one last aspect of *Cahiers*' auteur policy here – though qualified by Bazin – which suggests that a director's later works are more valuable to us because they are more personal, born of longer creative experience.[27] While the argument is disputable, there may be something to take away from it: in line with this discussion's metacritical approach, we should seize the idea that our scholarly categories need to accommodate the films and filmmakers we have, and not the reverse. With this in view, Villeneuve may prove to be a Canadian auteur eventually, even as the concept undergoes continued reassessment: only his future work, and our own critical transformations, will tell.

Notes

1 Denis Villeneuve was born in 1967 in Gentilly, Quebec, near Trois-Rivières. His studies began in the sciences at a CEGEP – by his account, very unhappily – before he transferred to the communications program at the Université du Québec à Montréal, with a concentration in film. Villeneuve participated in Radio-Canada's Europe-Asia Competition (later called La Course Destination Monde), travelling around the world for six months, producing short creative documentaries to a total of twenty-five films. He ultimately won first prize in the 1990–91 season, and secured a one-year internship at the National Film Board. A collaboration between the NFB and the Canadian International Development Agency on the topic of multiculturalism facilitated a semi-documentary project, which Villeneuve wrote and directed, *REW-FFWD* (1994). At this time, Villeneuve also began making music videos for various Québécois artists, receiving awards for several of these projects. A look at these early efforts discloses something of Villeneuve's burgeoning aesthetic in their playful visuals and formal experimentation. A video for musician Kevin Parent (*La jasette*, 1995) perhaps anticipates Villeneuve's style most clearly: shot largely in monochrome with occasional flashes of colour, aggressively structured by montage while generating Buñuelian image combinations, it's not difficult to relate the video's visual flourishes to Villeneuve's subsequent image-making. These projects introduced Villeneuve to André Turpin, who would serve as director of photography for Villeneuve's first three features. Both men contributed to Roger Frappier's anthology film *Cosmos* (1996) alongside emerging filmmakers Jennifer Alleyn, Manon Briand, Marie-Julie Dallaire, and Arto Paragamian. Villeneuve's segment, "Le Technétium," focuses, with characteristic self-consciousness, on a nervous filmmaker's preparations for a television interview. *Cosmos* won the Prix International des Cinémas d'Art et d'Essai at the Cannes Film Festival and was Canada's official submission for Best Foreign Language Film.

2 Richard Brody speaks to the conflicted status of the auteur in the contemporary moment – both as a figure that has "never been celebrated more liberally than now," and as the subject of unprecedented backlash. See "An Auteur Is Not a Brand," *The New Yorker* 10 July 2014, https://www.newyorker.com/culture/richard-brody/an-auteur-is-not-a-brand.

3 See, for example, Girish Shambu's interview with Niki Little, artistic director of the imagineNATIVE festival ("ImagineNATIVE Cinema: A Conversation with Niki Little," Criterion Collection, 19 May 2021, https://www.criterion.com/current/posts/7393-imaginenative-cinema-a-conversation-with-niki-little). Shambu's accompanying essay, "Indigenous Cinema and the Limits of

Auteurism," is also valuable (Criterion Collection, 19 May 2021, https://www.criterion.com/current/posts/7388-indigenous-cinema-and-the-limits-of-auteurism).

4 An important figure in the context of *Cahiers* is André Bazin, the intellectual centre of the journal in this period. Bazin strongly shaped the director-focused approach developed by François Truffaut, Jean-Luc Godard, Eric Rohmer, Jacques Rivette, and others, but also sought to temper its critical excesses, calling for greater attention to the contextual factors that condition filmic texts. See, for example, Godard's review of Hitchcock, "The Supremacy of the Subject" (*Cahiers*, March 1952, no. 10); Jacques Rivette's review of Preminger, "The Essential," translated in Jim Hillier ed., *Cahiers du Cinema: The 1950s* (London: Routledge and Kegan Paul, 1985), 135; and Alexandre Astruc's "What Is *Mise en Scène*?," translated in *Film Culture*, nos. 22/3 (1961): 65.

5 Andrew Sarris, "Notes on the Auteur Theory in 1962," *Film Culture*, no. 27 (winter 1962–63), reprinted in *Auteurs and Authorship: A Film Reader*, ed. Barry Keith Grant (Malden: Wiley Blackwell, 2008), 35–45.

6 Andrew Sarris, *The American Cinema* (New York: Dutton, 1968).

7 Sarris, "Notes on the Auteur Theory," 43.

8 As signalled by the essay's epigraph, Sarris's formulation takes inspiration from Søren Kierkegaard's discussion of shadowgraphs in *Either/Or*, which concerns the way an understanding of what is most valuable can be achieved indirectly, looking past external elements to glimpse an "inner picture." See Kierkegaard's *Either/Or*, vo. 1, trans. David F. Swenson and Lillian M. Swenson (Princeton: Princeton University Press, 1944), 142.

9 Brenda Longfellow's analysis of *Polytechnique* speaks to these moments very acutely: see "The Practice of Memory and the Politics of Memorialization: Denis Villeneuve," *Canadian Journal of Film Studies* 22, no. 1 (spring 2013).

10 *Breathing Light* is featured on LACMA's website for its 2014 Turrell retrospective here: https://www.lacma.org/art/exhibition/james-turrell-retrospective. His work can be viewed more comprehensively at https://jamesturrell.com. Interestingly, *Arrival* was not the only pop cultural artifact to reference Turrell's work in 2016: perhaps the better-known tribute is the music video for "Hotline Bling" (2016), in which Canadian rapper Drake deploys a series of Turrell-style spaces as a dynamic backdrop, launching many memes.

11 Ben Child, "Has *Blade Runner 2049*'s Failure Killed Off the Smart Sci-fi Blockbuster?," *The Guardian*, 14 November 2017, https://www.theguardian.com/film/2017/nov/14/blade-runner-2049-killed-the-smart-sci-fi-blockbuster-denis-villeneuve.

12 See André Habib, "Mortes tous les après-midis," *Hors Champ* (2009), http://www.horschamp.qc.ca/spip.php?article364.

13 See Kelly's article "Murderous Rampage Recreated, but with No Particular Insight," *The Gazette*, 6 February 2009, D1. It should be noted that critics

also supported Villeneuve's project, calling it a necessary reckoning: see for example Nathalie Petrowski's review in *La Presse*, "*Polytechnique*, Un Film à Voir" (28 Janvier 2009: Arts Spectacles, 1).

14 Melissa Blais, "Negotiating the Representation of the December 6 Massacre, or When Feminism and Anti-Feminism Coexist in the Same Film," in *'I Hate Feminists': December 6 1989 and Its Aftermath* (Halifax: Fernwood Publishing, 2014), 79–97. Blais's essay also appears in a special issue of the *Canadian Journal of Film Studies* 22, no. 1 (spring 2013), which is a superb resource on this topic: of particular relevance here is Scott MacKenzie's account of Villeneuve's film as generating a "universalist discourse" that "relativizes the experiences of men and women ... giving the male characters equal claim to the trauma that flows from the massacre." See "It's Not Always That Black and White: Universalism, Feminism, and the Monochromatic Worldview of *Polytechnique*," 69. In the language of recent media discourse, the film's parallel structure might be described as a species of bothsidesism.

15 "Table ronde sur le renouveau du cinéma québécois," *Nouvelles Vues: Revue sur les Pratiques et les Théories du Cinéma au Québec*, no. 12 (spring–summer 2011), 5–6. In the same issue, see also Sirois-Trahan's introduction, "Du renouveau en terrains connus." For more about Côté's films see Sirois-Trahan's chapter in this volume.

16 David Edelstein, "Torturous," *New York Magazine*, 12 September 2013.

17 Richard Porton in *CinemaScope Online*, TIFF 2015, https://cinema-scope.com/cinema-scope-online/tiff-2015-sicario-denis-villeneuve-us-special-presentations/.

18 A.O. Scott, "*Sicario* Digs into the Depths of Drug Cartel Violence," *New York Times*, 17 September 2015.

19 Dennis Harvey, "*Maelstrom*," *Variety*, 18 September 2000.

20 Opinions differ, of course: the notes that accompany TIFF Cinematheque's 2017 Villeneuve retrospective describe this aspect of Villeneuve's work as an "entertaining dose of pop metaphysics." See Adam Nayman's "High Concept: The Films of Denis Villeneuve," TIFF, 22 September 2017, https://www.tiff.net/the-review/denis-villeneuves-high-concept-cinema.

21 Villeneuve has suggested in interviews that the spider is intended to convey some of *The Double*'s ideas, though the connection seems tenuous. See David Gregory Lawson's interview with Villeneuve in *Film Comment*, 26 February 2014, https://www.filmcomment.com/blog/interview-denis-villeneuve/.

22 Although Villeneuve has indicated that this shot is essential to the film's meanings, he has not clarified the connection. See Ariston Anderson's interview in *The Hollywood Reporter*, 6 September 2016, https://www.hollywoodreporter.com/news/venice-arrival-director-denis-villeneuve-925854.

23 Italics added for emphasis. See Patricia Failing's piece in ARTnews, 4 September 2013, https://www.artnews.com/art-news/artists/assessing-james-turrell-2284/.

24 Piers Handling, "Auteurism in Canada," in *Citizen Sarris, American Film Critic: Essays in Honor of Andrew Sarris*, ed. Emanuel Levy (Lanham: Scarecrow Press, 2000), 277–80.

25 Patricia White, "Ambidextrous Authorship: Greta Gerwig and the Politics of Women's Genres," *Los Angeles Review of Books*, 7 February 2020, https://lareviewofbooks.org/article/ambidextrous-authorship-greta-gerwig-and-the-politics-of-womens-genres/.

26 See Villeneuve's statement about Warner Bros' decision to release the film simultaneously via HBO Max and in theaters: Denis Villeneuve, "'Dune' Director Denis Villeneuve Blasts HBO Max Deal," *Variety*, 10 December 2020, https://variety.com/2020/film/news/dune-denis-villeneuve-blasts-warner-bros-1234851270/. Concerning the film's critical reception, *Rolling Stone*'s generous review is representative: K. Austin Collins, "'Dune' Wages an All-Out Attack on the Senses – and Wins," *Rolling Stone*, 20 October 2021, https://www.rollingstone.com/movies/movie-reviews/dune-review-denis-villeneuve-1243908/.

27 André Bazin, "On the *politiques des auteurs*," *Cahiers du Cinéma*, no. 70 (April 1957), reprinted in *Cahiers du Cinéma: The 1950s: Neo-Realism, Hollywood, New Wave*, ed. Jim Hillier (Cambridge, MA: Harvard University Press, 1985), 248–59.

3

A "Momentary Melancholy"

Female Desire and the Promise of Happiness in the Cinema of Sarah Polley

Tanya Horeck

> I hope that the ways in which women are degraded, both obvious and subtle, begin to seem like a thing of the past ... For that to happen, I think we need to look at what scares us the most. We need to look at ourselves. What have we been willing to accept, out of fear, helplessness, a sense that things can't be changed? What else are we turning a blind eye to, in all aspects of our lives? What else have we accepted that, somewhere within us, we know is deeply unacceptable? And what, now, will we do about it?
>
> Sarah Polley, "The Men You Meet Making Movies"

Actor-turned-director Sarah Polley is one of Canada's most high-profile female directors and is therefore an essential part of any story to be told about Canadian cinema post-2000. Polley has a small but significant oeuvre which, to date, consists of four short films, two feature fiction films (*Away from Her* [2006], *Take This Waltz* [2011]), one documentary (*Stories We Tell* [2012]), and two TV series (*Alias Grace* [2017] and *Hey Lady!* [2020–]).[1] Polley's directorial career, which began at the turn of the millennium, is filled with accolades and critical plaudits: she is the first woman in Canadian history to receive a Genie Award for Best Director for her 2006 film *Away from Her* (which also earned her an Oscar nomination for Best Adapted Screenplay); she is listed as the "top Canadian female director" on a ranking by imdb.com; and her 2012 documentary *Stories We Tell* has been named as one of the best Canadian films of all time by TIFF in a 2015 poll.[2] In 2017, she received international acclaim as the showrunner of a six-part adaptation of Canadian literary giant Margaret Atwood's 1996 novel *Alias Grace* for CBC and Netflix.[3]

As a filmmaker Sarah Polley is often spoken of and celebrated as "exceptional," whether it be for her determined Canadian-ness, her youth (she began filmmaking in her early twenties), her keen intelligence, or her adept shift from actor to auteur.[4] But while Polley is seen to epitomize a certain conventional notion of the auteur as individual creative genius, her cinema is, in fact, a study in the work of feminist adaptation and collaboration. In addition to writing her own original screenplays, Polley regularly adapts Canadian literary works, especially those of Canadian women authors, including Alice Munro's "The Bear Came over the Mountain" (*Away from Her*) and Atwood's *Alias Grace*. At the end of 2020, it was announced that Polley is directing (and writing the screenplay for) the film adaptation of Canadian author Miriam Toews's acclaimed 2018 novel, *Women Talking*, about a group of Mennonite women who have been sexually assaulted by some of the men in their religious colony and meet to decide how to protect themselves and their daughters.[5] While all film is, of course, collaborative, one can argue that Polley's films – especially *Stories We Tell* but also her fiction films – are self-reflexive examinations of the conditions of authorship and the politics of truth and narrative, and that this critical preoccupation is closely bound up with her attempt to engage with what Shelley Cobb calls "the cultural politics of female agency."[6]

Although Polley's life-long political activism is always included in media profiles of her work, until recently her politics and her films have tended to be kept separate, even by the director herself. As Polley has noted: "I feel like I've always had two selves – the part of me that makes films and the part of me that's political, and they haven't really connected that much."[7] However, with *Alias Grace*, and with the forthcoming *Women Talking* (expected to be released in 2022), this separation has lessened. The politicized and historical exploration of patriarchal violence against women in these films relates to Polley's political statements on the contemporary #MeToo movement, including the epigraph to this chapter. Not long after the release of *Alias Grace*, and in the wake of the fallout over the Harvey Weinstein exposé, Polley penned an important and highly publicized *New York Times* op-ed, "The Men You Meet Making Movies," which details her own disturbing encounter with Weinstein as a young actress in the 1990s and provides a salient account of the exclusionary gendered cultures at work in the film industry. With this piece, Polley offers a powerful new origin story of her turn to directing: as a form of cultural resistance against the objectification and denigration of female actors. Not long after her meeting with Weinstein, Polley states, "I started writing and directing short films.

I had no idea, until then, how little respect I had been shown as an actor. Now there were no assistant directors trying to cajole me into sitting on their laps, no groups of men standing around to assess how I looked in a particular piece of clothing. I could decide what I felt was important to say, how to film a woman, without her sexuality being a central focus without context."[8] This is an important feminist statement for the new millennium, one which connects the sexual objectification and sexual harassment of women – both on and off the screen – to the determined intent to overturn prevailing gendered power dynamics by seizing control of what Laura Mulvey famously called the "camera's look."[9] In the chapter that follows, I explore Polley's strategies for filming women, and for evoking an embodied female subjectivity, with a special focus on the fiction films that bookend her work in the first decade of the twenty-first century: the short film *I Shout Love* (2001) and her feature-length film *Take This Waltz* (2011) (both shot by cinematographer Luc Montpellier). Both films have been labelled by critics as "romantic comedies," even though, as I will demonstrate, they actively work to deconstruct the genre, deploying and unsettling its key tropes and devices, from the "meet cute" to the "happy ending."

While Polley has hinted that the time has come for her work to take a more overtly political turn,[10] I suggest that her existing corpus, whether openly feminist or not, is already thoroughly imbued with the socio-political through her films' complicated, ambivalent, and highly nuanced explorations of what Lucy Bolton calls "female consciousness."[11] Writing on the films of Jane Campion, Sofia Coppola, and Lynne Ramsay, Bolton draws on the work of feminist theorist Luce Irigaray to account for how these film directors "create space for the female characters to explore themselves and others, using language, the body, and consciousness, offering a vision of a possible alternative way of being for women in cinema."[12] Resisting any essentialist or categorical notion of what "woman" is, Bolton suggests that what interests her about the work of these female directors is their "introspective contemplation" of the "inner lives" and "self-expression" of their female protagonists.[13]

The significance of Polley's work for feminist film criticism, and for wider debates surrounding female filmmaking in twenty-first-century Canadian cinema and beyond, is found in her sustained focus on male-female relations and the themes of adultery, love, and marriage, as well as in the less remarked-upon tactility and emotional/affective textures of her work. Polley's "insistently contemplative" films, with their focus on female embodiment and identity, invite comparison to the work of other twenty-first-century transnational anglophone female filmmakers including Andrea Arnold, Lynne Ramsay, and Jane Campion.[14] In their emphasis on what Liza Johnson terms "negative affect," including anger, anxiety, shame, and disgust, these female filmmakers are offering new ways of screening female subjectivity and perspectives through a phenomenological approach that "show[s] bad feeling as producing its own unexpected desires."[15] I reveal how Polley's examination of the melancholia of her white female protagonists – which plays out at the level of narrative but also, significantly, at the level of the films' visual grammar and affective atmospherics – is central to the political purchase of her critical reframing of the filmic female body. Refusing any easy generic classification, these films detail scenarios of failed romantic love and mine bad feelings in ways that upend scripts of what Lauren Berlant terms the "good life fantasy."[16] According to Berlant, "cruel optimism" is a "relation of attachment to compromised conditions of possibility whose realization is discovered to be *im*possible, sheer fantasy, or *too* possible, and toxic."[17] Berlant's description of desire as a "cluster of promises" is resonant for an understanding of Polley's female protagonists, and their attempt to strike "affective bargains" that keep them "in proximity to the scene of desire/attrition."[18] Most significantly, by focusing attention on the romantic and sexual unhappiness of her female protagonists at a moment of apparent impasse in their lives, Polley's films can be seen to expose the psychic and emotional costs of what Sara Ahmed has referred to as the "sentimentalization of heterosexuality as 'domestic bliss.'"[19] It is in her strong evocation – and critique – of intimate domestic bonds, which are shown to be simultaneously light and cloying – life-affirming *and* soul-destroying – that Polley situates her filmic examination of sexual politics and the ambivalent lure of what Ahmed calls the "promise of happiness."[20]

I Shout Love

Polley's 2001 short film *I Shout Love*, which won a Genie Award for Best Live Action Short Drama in 2003, opens with close-up images of a woman sobbing hysterically.[21] In her director's commentary, Polley, who wrote and directed *I Shout Love* when she was twenty-two years old, says that it began as an experiment: "could you start a film on somebody's face who was totally hysterical without knowing why and throughout the course of the film develop an empathy for why they were so hysterical?"[22] With this opening image, and its demand that the viewer become immediately involved in the embodied experience of her female protagonist, Polley sets the scene for the films that follow in her career, all of which, in one way or another, invite us to empathize with, rather than judge or condemn, her desiring female characters as they engage in transgressive, sometimes inexplicable/self-destructive and/or socially unconventional behaviours that gently kick out against patriarchal norms and strictures, particularly regarding heterosexual relationships and the institution of marriage.

The plot of *I Shout Love* is this: Tessa, the histrionically sobbing woman of the opening images (played by Kristen Thomson – a favourite Canadian actor of Polley's who also appears in *Away from Her*), pleads with her soon-to-be-ex-live-in-boyfriend, Bobby (Matthew Ferguson), to stay with her for one more day and night as they re-enact their relationship rituals for her video camera. Before we even see a face onscreen, or know what is happening, we hear Tessa's loud heaving sobs and screams as a man's voice asks her to "put down the camera please." What follows next is a series of jump cuts of Tessa's face in extreme close-up looking into the camera as she ugly-cries in a highly performative display of grief over her boyfriend leaving her for another woman; this opening sequence ends as the camera pulls back to reveal Bobby standing by a taxi with his suitcases: "Please Tessa, you're making it worse." Tessa's defiant response – "So what if I'm making it motherfucking worse, cock-sucking asshole?" – complicates any easy read of her as a victim in the scenario. In the semi-comical exchange between the two that follows, Tessa finally tells Bobby to leave – only after the taxi pulls away with Tessa's body still draped over it. Bobby tells her he now can't, picking her up and carrying her over his shoulder and back into their apartment in a parody of the old-fashioned patriarchal ritual of the husband carrying the wife across the threshold.

It is significant that the video camera is the important third character throughout *I Shout Love*, its insistent buzzing noise a constant audio reminder of its presence. The device of a film-within-a-film is central to Polley's fascination with how events get framed – and re-framed – by individuals in ways that give the lie to any idea of an "objective" truth.[23] The camera crashes to the ground during Tessa and Bobby's opening emotional exchange, and Bobby retrieves it when he returns outside to get his suitcases, but back in the apartment Tessa soon resumes her control of filming in a rotating circular shot of Bobby sitting on the couch, as she roller-blades around him – as insistent as he is skeptical about the need to film the events between them as they unfold.

In this image of Tessa as female director, we see an early example of Polley's interest in the figure of the female author, and beyond that, in questions of control, storytelling, memory, and the politics of

Figure 3.1   Tessa as filmmaker in *I Shout Love* (2001).

re-enactment. Tessa is shown to be firm – at times almost cruel – in her insistence on filming a kind of "top ten" list of what she describes as the "stuff about us I want to keep," which Bobby reluctantly goes along with. The focus on re-enactment, and on the diegetic inclusion of the figure of the female filmmaker calling the shots behind the camera, presages Polley's acclaimed documentary *Stories We Tell*, which includes a controversial mixture of actual home video footage and reconstructed "pretend" Super 8 home movie footage in which actors play her family members, including her deceased mother. Initially, the difference between the actual and re-enacted home movie footage in *Stories We Tell* is not apparent; it is not until the last part of the film that viewers see an image of Polley behind the camera directing the actors who play her family members, letting viewers in on the fact that some of the home movie footage is "fake." While *I Shout Love* is not a documentary, and therefore does not trade in the same distinctions regarding "real" and "fake," I suggest that the self-conscious role of re-enactment in this early short film is used to raise a similar set of questions about the processes of memory, the vicissitudes of desire, and the affective remediation of the past. Most significantly, as with *Stories We Tell*, re-enactment in *I Shout Love* is the means through which the female author/director attempts to create a new space of agency for herself. In Tessa's annoyed response to Bobby's question about whether they are supposed to "act" in the re-enactments – "no, not all phoney like that!" – there is an echo of Polley's justification for including the hybrid of actual and reconstructed home movie footage in *Stories We*

Tell, not as mere trickery or phoniness but as an attempt to find a kind of emotional "truth" in competing versions of the past.[24]

The point of the re-enactments for Tessa is not chiefly to recapture the moments of her relationship with Bobby, nor is it exactly about "working through" the trauma of her loss, though it is both of these things to a degree; rather, as Agnieszka Piotrowska has suggested of *Stories We Tell*, there is a "'reviewing' of the self" that occurs in order to find new forms of subjectivity and ways of being in the world.[25] To a certain extent, Tessa is an example of what Piotrowska calls the "nasty" female filmmaker: "nasty," that is, in terms of the patriarchal conventions she is seen to subvert.[26] She refuses to be "nice" and compliant about the break-up, and she yells and swears and carries on before assuming a calm, if domineering, control of the proceedings. While the initial image of the hysterical woman could be seen to conform to certain patriarchal notions of the woman as "shrew," Tessa resists such a categorization through her humour, her wisdom, and her creative deployment of technology to recast the terms of her separation from her boyfriend.

The re-enactment of the things Tessa wants to remember about their relationship, from the recreation of a paint fight they once had, to watching Bobby sleep, to her masturbating and orgasming under the tap in the bathtub while she lies in his arms, conjures up the "lost object" of their relationship.[27] To borrow a quotation from documentary theorist Bill Nichols, the re-enactments in *I Shout Love* can be understood as moments "in which the participants attempt to will themselves back to the past and yet know very well that the effort must fail."[28] Re-enactments, as Nichols writes, are affective formations that "take past time and make it present" and that "take present time and fold it over onto what has already come to pass. They resurrect a sense of a previous moment that is now seen through a fold that incorporates the embodied perspective of the filmmaker and the emotional investment of the viewer."[29] While the imbrication of a co-existing past and present may represent what Nichols refers to as the "impossible space of a fantasmatic," it is within this liminal, "impossible" space that Polley works to bring the embodied desire of her female protagonists "into being."[30]

Over the course of the film, Bobby becomes increasingly emotionally engaged in the enterprise of reviewing their relationship, and by the film's end Tessa is the one to gently but firmly tell him it is now time for him to leave. The film concludes with a composed Tessa on her own in the apartment, re-playing the close-up video images of herself sobbing, seen at the start of the film, on her television screen; the audio on the video images is muted and overlaid with news commentary on the protests at the Summit of the Americas in Quebec in 2001 and blow-by-blow commentary of a Toronto Maple Leafs hockey game. Polley has described the anti-globalization protests in Quebec and the situation of being a fan of the ever-losing Leafs team (both of which feature as social texture and backdrop in the film) as metaphors for the thematic emphasis on the importance of fighting "losing battles." However clunky these metaphors may be, they are used to underscore the film's wider attempt to puncture dominant narratives that would insist on a linear narrative of happiness with clear markers of success and attainment. As film theorist Anna Backman Rogers suggests of the potential that might come from "welcoming unhappiness": "In not subscribing to a set of clichés that designate what a good and successful life is, new pathways are opened up."[31]

In the final images of the film, Tessa circles around the television set on her roller blades, before the film comes to rest on a freeze frame image of the video footage of her sobbing face from the start of the film – now re-framed through the TV screen – in extreme close-up. This video image of a woman's face in a film-within-a-film runs across much of Polley's cinema.[32] In *Away from Her* the film begins and ends with an image of a young Fiona (Julie Christie) before she was afflicted with Alzheimer's (she had the "spark of life about her"), and in *Stories We Tell* video footage of Polley's dead mother, Diane, when she was alive and vibrant, plays a critical framing role for the film's narrative.

Retrieving images from the past and coming to terms with loss is a central preoccupation of Polley's filmmaking and its foregrounding of the critical possibilities of melancholia. As Ahmed has noted in her discussion of Freud's distinction between mourning and melancholia: "For Freud, mourning is a healthy response to loss, as it is about 'letting go' of the lost object, which may include a loved person or an abstraction which has taken the place of one."[33] Melancholia, on the other hand, is seen to be "pathological: the ego refuses to let go of the object, and preserves the object 'inside itself.'" Ahmed, however, challenges the notion that it is "good or healthy to 'let go' of the lost object."[34] Instead, she argues that the "desire to maintain attachments with the lost other is enabling, rather than blocking new forms of attachment"; indeed, she further asserts that "keeping the past alive, even as that which has been lost, is ethical: the object is not severed from history, or encrypted, but can acquire new meanings and possibilities in the present."[35] This critical re-reading of melancholia holds importance for an examination of how Polley depicts the ennui of her female protagonists as productive of certain new desires. When the film's credits play out over images of Tessa's face as her mouth opens up wide into a cheeky, slightly naughty grin, I read this not as a simple assertion of success and closure (all's well that ends well), but, rather, as an acknowledgment of a different set of possibilities for self-fashioning and determination that come from her affective, technological re-purposing of past attachments.

Take This Waltz

Take This Waltz is another film about the dissolution of a heterosexual relationship between twenty-somethings in Toronto, which extends and expands upon *I Shout Love*'s examination of female melancholy. Released after the mainstream success of *Away from Her*, a film that explores infidelity through the relationship of an older couple coming to terms with the wife's Alzheimer's diagnosis, Polley has described her second feature-length film, based on her own original screenplay, as another "love story" – albeit one that is "about people at the beginning of something."[36] In the character of Margot, played by Hollywood actress Michelle Williams, Polley offers her most sustained – and I argue her most critically significant – illustration of the double binds of love, domesticity, infidelity, and desire.

Take This Waltz begins and ends with the same image: its central female character, Margot, is baking blueberry muffins in a kitchen. The scene is bathed in warm colours, and gives off the impression of heat; the camera stays close to Margot's body as she languidly brushes her hair away from her face, and sits on the floor, leaning her head against the door of the stove. A shadowy male figure (blurry and out of focus) passes by the melancholy Margot to look out of the window: it could be her husband or her lover, and ultimately it does not matter which, because over the course of the film the two figures become interchangeable as the woman finds herself locked into the very same scenario of a cosy – and suffocating – heterosexual domesticity.

This scene, and indeed the film as a whole, can be seen to grapple with the following question, posed by Ahmed in *The Promise of Happiness*: "What happens when domestic bliss does not create bliss?"[37] Ahmed asks this question as part of her analysis of the film *The Hours*, based on Virginia Woolf's *Mrs Dalloway*, in particular a scene in which the character Laura (Julianne Moore) bakes a cake, "which ought to be a happy endeavor, a labor of love."[38] And yet, as Ahmed writes, "a sense of oppression lingers in the very act of breaking the eggs" to make the cake. Ahmed argues:

> If … happiness creates its own horizon, as a horizon of likes, then it is possible to be surrounded by likes that are not your own, and by promises that haunt you in their emptiness. Not only do such objects not cause your happiness but they may remind you of your failure to be made happy; they embody a feeling of disappointment. The bowl in which you crack the eggs waits for you. You can feel the pressure of its wait. The empty bowl feels like an accusation. Feminist archives are full of scenes of domesticity in which domestic objects, happy objects, become alien, even menacing.[39]

This idea of the menace of domesticity or domesticity-as-menace is very apt for *Take This Waltz*, a film that dissects the ways in which the curious intimacies of marriage can deaden one's sense of self and squelch desire. Margot, a freelance copywriter who aspires to greater things, is married to the kind-hearted Lou (Seth Rogen), who spends almost all of his time in the kitchen, as he is writing a cookbook on the various ways to cook chicken. If the constant smell of chicken wafting through the house isn't exactly menacing, it is not conducive to thrilling sexual encounters either. The two are comfortable enough in their well-worn domestic routines, even if their baby talk ("I wuv you," Margot tells him, in deliberately cringe-inducing moments), constant play-fighting, and jokey habit of saying the violent things they would like to do to one another as a sign of their love ("I love you so much I'm gonna mash your head in with a potato masher") are revealed as the desexualized mechanics of a relationship that has become somewhat oppressive and stale. When Margot meets handsome artist/rickshaw driver Daniel (Luke Kirby) in a meet cute to match all meet cutes, her desire for desire takes hold, and the rest of the film examines Margot's dilemma over whether she should stay or she should go.

To write out the plot of *Take This Waltz* is to feel as though one is writing out the plot to a Harlequin romance, and yet the film is anything but clichéd. It has been described, variously, as an "indie quirkfest,"[40] an "arthouse version of romantic escapism,"[41] and "a slice-of-life style of romantic comedy with dramatic elements."[42] For some critics, the film is "torn between naturalism and lyricism" and its generic uncertainty is viewed as a problem.[43] In the words of David Rooney of *The Hollywood Reporter*: it has a "hard time deciding if it wants to be a happy-sad, flaky comedy or a dreamy mood piece."[44] However, in contrast to these critics, I contend that the affective tone of the film, and its poetic realism, is not a matter of indecision at all – or rather, that that indecision is somehow the point: it is in the interstices of happy/sad and reality/fantasy that the critical force of Polley's investigation of female desire lies. As Ahmed writes, "Desire is both what promises us something, what gives us energy, and also what is lacking, even in the very moment of its apparent realization. There can be nothing more terrifying than getting what you want, because it is at this moment that you face what you want."[45] *Take This Waltz* offers an account of this central paradox of desire – its simultaneous energy and its inherent lack – through its treatment of the profound ambivalence that attends the psychic need to preserve the "fantasy that getting what you want would make you happy."[46] It does not judge its characters: everyone, including Margot, behaves pretty decently, and the film is not delivering a docu-style socio-political exposé of marriage as an institutional trap. Instead, *Take This Waltz* is most interesting for how it plays out at an affective, corporeal level, in which viewers are invited to spend time with Margot's melancholia and the "in-between" stasis of her ambivalent longing.[47]

Critic Stella Papamichael has asserted that "it's rare to see a woman on screen who is this difficult to pin down," and it is certainly the case that many reviews express an unease over how to respond to the character of Margot.[48] While Williams's performance is much-praised, the character of Margot is judged rather harshly, in ways that she never is by Polley's film itself. Margot has been described in reviews as "fitful and possibly manic depressive"; "immature"; "solipsistic"; "deeply flawed"; "selfish"; and "self-pitying."[49] Even the normally measured Roger Ebert had unusually strong judgment to pass: in his review of the film he suggests that Williams is perhaps too "lovable" an actress to play Margot and concludes by imagining what would happen if acerbic comedian Sarah Silverman (who plays Margot's sister-in-law in the film) were to have played the role: "That would never work. Michelle Williams enlists our sympathy. With Silverman playing that character, we'd see Margot as the shameful woman she is."[50] Such moralistic judgments of Margot appear to bear out Polley's observation that "people try to pin down and categorize women more than they do men" and that "restlessness" in a woman is something "we can't quite handle."[51]

As reviewer Katherine Monk writes, "As far as Polley sees it, we live in a world that loves to show us the giddy beginning and the pathos-laden end of the affair, but never the middle."[52] In showing us the long middle, Polley could be said to be performing the work of Ahmed's feminist killjoy: to "disturb the very fantasy that happiness can be found in certain places," namely in conventional romantic love.[53] Polley has said that *Take This Waltz* is a film about the "concept of emptiness";[54] I suggest that it is also a film about the burden of "the promise of happiness." In Margot, we have the figure of the melancholic who cannot shake off the feeling of loss, who holds onto it and does not let go.[55]

The quotation that forms part of the title to this chapter, "A Momentary Melancholy," is taken from a scene in which Margot is trying to account for what her lover-to-be Daniel has described as her permanent "restlessness." Margot explains to Daniel that, like a young child who cannot be consoled, she is sometimes overcome by a "momentary melancholy" in which she is suddenly flooded by an unspeakable sadness. Margot's speech to Daniel about melancholia and the difficulty of dispelling it is one of the stagier moments of dialogue in the film, and some critics have called it out for its "phoniness." Although the force of Margot's melancholy is more compellingly depicted through the film's visceral moments, which I will soon discuss, this scene, which holds the camera on Margot's face in mid-shot, heralds the film's commitment to spend time with the ambivalence and "bad feelings" of its female characters.

It needs to be noted that Polley's films are certainly not "feel-bad films" in the sense outlined by Nikolaj Lübecker: of being directly confrontational for the spectator, refusing any and all forms of catharsis, and creating such a degree of exhausting intensity that "spectators begin to worry where things are going."[56] Indeed, the tone of her films is often light and comedic, with emotive musical soundtracks, even as the narratives explore broken relationships and injured feelings.[57] However, both *I Shout Love* and *Take This Waltz* do stay with the bad – or at least the thoroughly ambivalent – feelings of their female protagonists over the course of their duration (respectively, 38 minutes and 116 minutes), and frustrate many of the genre-directed expectations of the romantic comedy genre: there are no conventional endings with happy heterosexual couplings and resolutions found here. Moreover, the films manage to keep uncertainty alive about "where things are going" with the characters and plot, which is a testament to how closely they stay with the embodied experiences of their female protagonists. In a very perceptive review of *Take This Waltz*, which acknowledges that ambivalence is the film's "principal subject and dominant mood," A.O. Scott of *The New York Times* writes: "Nobody in this film is just one way ... Polley, as a writer, a director of actors and a constructor of images, excels at managing the idiosyncrasies and contradictions of her characters so that our knowledge of them is both intimate and mined with potential surprise. Margot and Daniel don't know what they are going to do, and Lou does not know what is happening, and for most of the movie we dwell in a similar state of suspense and partial knowledge."[58] We wait with Margot in the "in-between," uncertain of how she will respond: in those scenes when Daniel is not present, we share in her yearning for him to return not necessarily because of the force of his individual character, but because of the film's ability to involve us in the mise-en-scène of Margot's desire.[59]

In light of Polley's expressed concern over how to film the female body in a non–sexually objectifying way, it is notable that there is very little overt sex in the film and that when Margot does appear naked it is generally not in the context of sex at all. In addition to a domestic scene, in which Margot takes her clothes off to get into the shower, there is an earlier sequence in the showers at the public swimming pool, with Margot and her friends, Karen (Jennifer Podemski) and Geraldine (Sarah Silverman), shown in full-frontal nudity. The women shower together, and discuss the banalities and comforts of marriage, with Geraldine directing some pointed commentary at her sister-in-law about the risks of falling in thrall to the allures of the "new." Also present in the shower are a group of much older women, with bodies of all shapes and sizes. The camera films all of the women neutrally as they clean their bodies and discuss marriage, sexuality, and aging.

The film's most powerful depiction of Margot's ambivalence and melancholia, along with the scope of her desire, comes not from any sexual encounter (and its potential objectifications) but from a striking dialogue-less scene, which produces affect through physical movement and bodily expression. Spending an illicit day together, Margot invites Daniel to go on a ride on Toronto's Centre Island called "The Scrambler." She pitches it to Daniel as a space that is dark with lots of loud music, where "it's way too fast to do anything stupid." Set to the Buggles' 1979 hit "Video Killed the Radio Star," the sequence pictures Daniel and Margot as they ride the Scrambler, their bodies swaying back and forth against each other in the darkness, with strobes and flashes of light passing over their faces. The choreography of the scene, set to the beats of the song and the movement of the ride, is significant in its visceral capture of the thrill and abandon of their youthful desire but also the sadness and impossibility of it – not only in terms of the obstacle of Margot's husband, but in wider terms of the fleeting nature of life's passions. A range of palpable emotions pass across Margot's face, from joy to sadness and back again, as the viewer follows the pleasurable motions of her body, which sways with the rise and fall of the music. The scene ends abruptly, joltingly, as the ride comes to an end: the music stops, harsh fluorescent lights flick on, and the ride operator

Figure 3.2 Margot and Daniel on the Scrambler in *Take This Waltz* (2011).

opens the doors of their aluminum seat. Jolted out of their reverie, the couple look brutally exposed, their bodies now noticeably apart from one another as they awkwardly exit the ride and the frame of the shot.

What I admire most about *Take This Waltz*, and even find radical at times, is how it stays with this vision of happiness-as-loss. To quote again from Ahmed: "Feminism involves challenging the very 'pressure' of happiness, the way it restricts the possibilities for finding excitement, of being excited."[60] At its most challenging, *Take This Waltz* raises consciousness "of what women are asked to give up for happiness" as it explores Margot's refusal "to give up desire, imagination and curiosity for happiness."[61] Margot knows very well how to perform the role that is expected of her – as wife, aunt, daughter-in-law, and sister-in-law (as demonstrated in the scenes with Lou's big, boisterous family) – and she even derives a certain enjoyment from it, but the sadness resides "in the realization of what one has given up" for such domestic bliss.[62] The film's critique of the promise of happiness is all the more powerful for the fact that Lou is a kind, understanding man: Margot is not fleeing from a scene of violence or persecution, in other words.

At the end of *Take This Waltz*, Polley provides the sex scene that has been withheld throughout the film. The critical response to the scene suggests that it did not give (some) viewers what they wanted. Peter Bradshaw of *The Guardian*, for example, calls it "one of the most odd and unsexy sex scenes in cinema history."[63] Set to Leonard Cohen's song "Take This Waltz," from which the film takes its name, the highly stylized scene, which is almost five minutes long, takes place in an empty loft apartment that gradually fills up with belongings and furniture, as it shows the passage of time in Daniel and Margot's relationship, after she finally leaves Lou for him. In a 360-degree shot, the camera circles around the couple as they first kiss and embrace, and then have sexual intercourse on a bed; the circular shot continues as it shows the progression through the different seasons of their sexual relationship with various other participants joining in (there is a ménage à trois with another woman, and one with another man). The circular tracking shot moves from wild sex to domestic scenarios, and finally ends with Daniel and Margot sitting companionably on the couch watching television, as Margot's baby talk of "I wuv you" from the Lou days resumes. Margot's return to the baby talk is pointed, and suggests the ways in which the binds of marriage work to infantilize the woman and her desires.

While some critics have queried the "realism" of the stylized sex scene, and whether it makes narrative sense, I argue that it functions in more symbolic terms. As a set piece, the scene is examining – on an intellectual and cinematic level – what happens when your wildest fantasies of desire are realized. What happens, in other words, when all obstacles are finally removed? And more than that, what does it mean to recognize that "something you desire is actually an obstacle to your flourishing?"[64] The answer, for Polley, lies in the next shot of the couple brushing and flossing their teeth together; in a replay of earlier scenes, Margot sits on the toilet and pees, and the dull, deadening routines of domesticity take hold once again.

In her review of the film, Catherine Wheatley suggests that Margot emerges as the "film's victim": "For all the sense of possibility and potential, of doubt and regret, the wheel of fate turns and Margot lands in the same place every time."[65] I agree with Wheatley that the film is interested in the notion of return and repetition, but I am not as willing to concede to the final view of Margot-as-victim. As with the re-enactments in *I Shout Love*, Polley replays certain scenes and images at the film's conclusion as part of her sustained examination of what Berlant would term the "affective structure" of optimistic longing and desire in the context of domesticity and romantic love.[66] What's so cruel about optimism, Berlant argues, is how the "affective structure of an optimistic attachment involves a sustaining inclination to return to the scene of fantasy that enables you to expect that *this* time, nearness to this thing will help you or a world to become different in just the right way."[67] *Take This Waltz* is a study of how the female subject becomes bound and attached to the terms of a "good life" fantasy of love and domesticity, and if it does not suggest a clear way out of this scenario, it does, at least, force a recognition of its power to both enthrall and entrap.

At the film's end, there is a replay of Margot in the kitchen baking muffins; a man now clearly identifiable as Daniel walks by to look out the window and Margot goes over to him, closes her eyes, and hugs him from behind (a familiar gesture from her relationship with Lou). But this time, during the replay of the scene, "Video Killed the Radio Star" begins playing and the next and final image of the film is of Margot on the amusement park ride, the Scrambler, on her own. The motion of the ride takes over, as Margot moves in time to the music, her body swaying back and forth, the light playing over her face, which expresses a range of happy-sad emotions, never settling on just one feeling or one way of being. Viewers are invited to engage with Margot on a visceral level and it is significant that the film ends in this moment of pleasurable motion, as it were: Margot's body continues to move in space, alive to possibility; it is the film that stops as the screen goes to black.

In this chapter, I have suggested that the feminist politics of Polley's cinema lies in her nuanced exploration of female desire, melancholy, and the "promise of happiness." With its focus on conflicted psychic states, "bad feelings," and the embodied experiences of its female characters, Polley's work demands to be situated in relation to what So Mayer calls a twenty-first-century "new feminist cinema," which is characterized by its political awareness and its commitment to the production of "resistant subjects."[68] In what is a signature moment across Polley's oeuvre, both *I Shout Love* and *Take This Waltz* conclude with strikingly tactile images of their female protagonists: the camera captures their bodies in movement. Notably, both films insist upon an intimate engagement with the terms of Tessa's and Margot's ambivalence right up to the very ending and beyond. It is within this cinematic space of the "in between" that Polley locates the struggle of her desiring female protagonists, and where I argue that the wider significance of her work as a filmmaker lies.

Notes

1 Polley also directed an episode of the TV mini-series *The Shields Stories*, which dramatizes the short stories of Canadian writer Carol Shields, called "The Harp" (2004).
2 Polley completed the Directors' Lab program at the Canadian Film Centre in 2001. For IMDB ranking see https://www.imdb.com/list/ls069341857/.

3 Polley wrote and executive produced the series, while fellow Canadian Mary Harron directed.
4 On the discourse of exceptionalism that surrounds women filmmakers see Shelley Cobb, *Adaptation, Authorship and Contemporary Women Filmmakers* (Houndsmill, Basingstoke: Palgrave Macmillan, 2015), 5.
5 See Dave McNary, "Frances McDormand to Star in 'Women Talking' from Director Sarah Polley," *Variety*, 17 December 2020, https://variety.com/2020/film/news/frances-mcdormand-women-talking-sarah-polley-1234865603/.
6 Cobb, *Adaptation, Authorship*, 16.
7 Quoted in Katie Underwood, "Sarah Polley on *Alias Grace* and Canadian TV's 'Embarrassing' Diversity Problem," *Chatelaine*, 21 September 2017, https://www.chatelaine.com/living/entertainment/sarah-polley-alias-grace/.
8 Sarah Polley, "The Men You Meet Making Movies," *New York Times*, 14 October 2017, https://www.nytimes.com/2017/10/14/opinion/sunday/harvey-weinstein-sarah-polley.html. As this book goes to press, Polley has published a collection of personal essays, *Run towards the Danger: Confrontations with a Body of Memory* (London: September Publishing, 2022). In one of the essays, "The Woman Who Stayed Silent," Polley speaks out about her sexual assault by Canadian broadcaster Jian Ghomeshi when she was sixteen. The essay situates her traumatic experience in the context of #MeToo.
9 Laura Mulvey, "Visual Pleasure and Narrative Cinema," *Screen* 16, no. 3 (1975): 18.
10 On Polley's political turn, see Underwood, "Sarah Polley on *Alias Grace*," and Anna Silman, "What Would Sarah Polley Do? The Unorthodox Film Heroine's 20-Year Journey to *Alias Grace*," *The Cut*, 26 October 2017, https://www.thecut.com/2017/10/sarah-polleys-20-year-journey-to-adapt-atwoods-alias-grace.html.
11 Lucy Bolton, *Film and Female Consciousness: Irigaray, Cinema and Thinking Women* (Houndsmill, Basingstoke: Palgrave Macmillan, 2015), 3.
12 Ibid., 3–4.
13 Ibid., 3.
14 Amelie Hastie, "The Vulnerable Spectator: Vagaries of Memory, Verities of Form," *Film Quarterly* 67, no. 2 (2013): 61.
15 Liza Johnson, "Perverse Angle: Feminist Film, Queer Film, Shame," *Signs* 30, no. 1 (2004): 1362.
16 Lauren Berlant, *Cruel Optimism* (Durham/London: Duke University Press, 2011), 3.
17 Ibid., 24.
18 Ibid., 25.
19 Sara Ahmed, *The Promise of Happiness* (Durham/London: Duke University Press, 2010), 2.

20 *The Promise of Happiness* is the title to Sara Ahmed's book (Durham/London: Duke University Press, 2010), which interrogates the concept of "happiness" and in particular the insistent "demand for happiness," which, she argues, is in fact a "demand to return to social ideals" (31) and normative identities and behaviours.
21 The title *I Shout Love* comes from the 1958 poem by Canadian poet Milton Acorn. Polley includes the poem in full at the end of her short and it can also be found here: https://canpoetry.library.utoronto.ca/acorn/poem2.htm.
22 This quotation is from Polley's voice-over director's commentary on *I Shout Love*, which is included on a two-disc special edition of *Away from Her* by Mongrel Media.
23 Polley attributes her awareness of the complexity of notions of truth and "objectivity" to her Canadianness: "I think the uncertainty of a basic objective truth is in my films, and that's part of me as a Canadian. That's a cultural thing that has been handed down to me ... That there's not one truth that everyone must obey, but that there are different realities for everyone"; quoted in Soraya Roberts, "The Evolution of Sarah Polley," *Hazlitt*, 3 November 2017, https://hazlitt.net/longreads/evolution-sarah-polley.
24 Polley discusses the role of the re-enactments in *Stories We Tell* as honouring "the truth that exists in between all the different versions that people have of the same story"; quoted in Jose Solis, "Further Illuminating the 'Stories We Tell': An Interview with Sarah Polley," *Pop Matters*, 15 May 2013, https://www.popmatters.com/171347-further-illuminating-the-stories-we-tell-2495758091.html.
25 Agnieszka Piotrowska, *The Nasty Woman and the Neo Femme Fatale in Contemporary Cinema* (London/NY: Routledge, 2019), 79–80.
26 Ibid., 65–8.
27 Bill Nichols, "Documentary Reenactment and the Fantasmatic Subject," *Critical Inquiry* 35 (autumn 2008): 74.
28 Ibid., 75; the author is discussing Andrew Jarecki's 2003 documentary, *Capturing the Friedmans*, here.
29 Ibid., 88.
30 Ibid.
31 Anna Backman-Rogers, "Lena Dunham's Girls: Can-Do Girls, Feminist Killjoys, and Women Who Make Bad Choices," in *Feminisms: Diversity, Difference, and Multiplicity in Contemporary Film Cultures*, ed. Laura Mulvey and Anna Backman-Rogers (Amsterdam: Amsterdam University Press, 2015), 52.
32 Polley's use of video might be viewed, in part, as a homage to fellow Canadian director and mentor Atom Egoyan, who also has a thematic interest in video recordings in his films. Egoyan directed Polley in *Exotica* (1994) and *The Sweet Hereafter* (1997) and was also an executive producer on her first feature-length film, *Away from Her*.

33 Sara Ahmed, *The Cultural Politics of Emotion* (Edinburgh: Edinburgh University Press, 2004), 159.
34 Ibid.
35 Ibid.
36 Quoted in Michael Koresky, "Sarah Polley," *Reverse Shot*, 1 May 2007, http://www.reverseshot.org/interviews/entry/1291/sarah-polley.
37 Ahmed, *The Promise of Happiness*, 76.
38 Ibid.
39 Ibid.
40 Tasha Robinson, "Take This Waltz," *The A.V. Club*, 28 June 2012, https://film.avclub.com/take-this-waltz-1798173309.
41 Roger Ebert, "*Take This Waltz*," RogerEbert.com, 11 July 2012, https://www.rogerebert.com/reviews/take-this-waltz-2012.
42 Katherine Monk, "Sarah Polley on *Take This Waltz* and Her Fascination with Desire," *National Post*, 8 September 2011, https://nationalpost.com/entertainment/sarah-polley-on-take-this-waltz-and-her-fascination-with-desire.
43 Adam Nayman, "Split Decision: Sarah Polley's *Take This Waltz*," *Cinema Scope* (2011), http://cinema-scope.com/currency/split-decision-sarah-polleys-take-this-waltz/.
44 David Rooney, "*Take This Waltz*: Toronto Review," *The Hollywood Reporter*, 9 November 2011, https://www.hollywoodreporter.com/review/take-waltz-toronto-review-233892.
45 Ahmed, *The Promise of Happiness*, 31.
46 Ibid., 32.
47 Early on in the film, in a strong signposting of the film's thematics, Margot tells Daniel she does not like "being 'in between' things."
48 Stella Papamichael, "'Take This Waltz' Review: Michelle Williams Strays from Seth Rogen: Michelle Williams Considers Cheating on Seth Rogen in This Daring Love Story," *Digital Spy*, 12 August 2012, http://www.digitalspy.com/movies/review/a397838/take-this-waltz-review-michelle-williams-strays-from-seth-rogen/.
49 Ryan Gilbey, "*Take This Waltz*: Review," *The New Statesman*, 15 August 2012, https://www.newstatesman.com/culture/culture/2012/08/take-waltz-review; Linda Barnard, "*Take This Waltz*: Last Dance for Romance," *The Star*, 28 June 2012, https://www.thestar.com/entertainment/movies/2012/06/28/take_this_waltz_review_last_dance_for_romance.html; Catherine Wheatley, "Film Review: *Take This Waltz*," *Sight and Sound* (2011); James Rocchi, "Tribeca Review: Sarah Polley's 'Take This Waltz' Has Insights and Edges Sharp Enough to Stab," *IndieWire*, 23 April 2012, https://www.indiewire.com/2012/04/tribeca-review-sarah-polleys-take-this-waltz-has-insights-and-edges-sharp-enough-to-stab-252457/; A.O. Scott, "Sometimes Attraction Becomes a Slow Dance around a Subject: 'Take This Waltz,' Directed by Sarah

Polley," *New York Times*, 28 June 2012, https://www.nytimes.com/2012/06/29/movies/take-this-waltz-directed-by-sarah-polley.html; Louisa Mellor, "*Take This Waltz* Review," *Den of Geek*, 12 August 2012, http://www.denofgeek.com/movies/take-this-waltz/22300/take-this-waltz-review.

50 Ebert, "*Take This Waltz*."
51 Quoted in Silman, "What Would Sarah Polley Do?"
52 Monk, "Sarah Polley on *Take This Waltz* and Her Fascination with Desire."
53 Ahmed, *The Promise of Happiness*, 32.
54 Quoted in Peter Knegt, "Sarah Polley Talks 'Take This Waltz': 'I Wanted to Make a Film about the Concept of Emptiness,'" *Indiewire*, 29 June 2012, https://www.indiewire.com/2012/06/sarah-polley-talks-take-this-waltz-i-wanted-to-make-a-film-about-the-concept-of-emptiness-46268/.
55 Ahmed, *The Promise of Happiness*, 139.
56 Nikolaj Lubecker, *The Feel-Bad Film* (Edinburgh: Edinburgh University Press, 2015), 3.
57 Polley has spoken of the importance of music to her films' narratives. Indeed, a less-remarked-upon feature of her collaborative work is her deployment of the music of mainly Canadian singers in her films such as Gord Downie, Joni Mitchell, Leonard Cohen, and k.d. lang.
58 Scott, "Sometimes Attraction Becomes."
59 Catherine Wheatley has called Daniel a "balletic cipher" and it is true that he exists mainly as a blank slate for the projection of Margot's desires; Wheatley, "Film Review: *Take This Waltz*."
60 Ahmed, *The Cultural Politics of Emotion*, 69.
61 Ibid., 70.
62 Ibid.
63 Peter Bradshaw, "Take This Waltz – Review," *The Guardian*, 16 August 2012, https://www.theguardian.com/film/2012/aug/16/take-this-waltz-review.
64 Berlant, *Cruel Optimism*, 1.
65 Wheatley, "Film Review: *Take This Waltz*."
66 Berlant, *Cruel Optimism*, 2.
67 Ibid.
68 So Mayer, *Political Animals: The New Feminist Cinema* (London: Bloomsbury, 2016), 9.

4

Indigenous Women's Cinema in Quebec
The Works and Words of Mohawk Filmmaker Sonia Bonspille Boileau

Karine Bertrand

In the last twenty years, there has been an array of books (most of them in English) written by Indigenous women of Turtle Island, who represent both older and newer generations of healers, warriors, dreamers, and artists reclaiming sacred spaces (land, water, community, family, inner spaces) and educating Indigenous and non-Indigenous populations by telling their personal stories as well as the stories of their people. Thus, inspiring readings such as Lee Maracle's *I Am Woman* in which the Sto:lo author reveals her intent to "remove three mountains (racism, sexism and nationalist oppression) from the path to liberation," or Nishnaabeg author Leanne Simpson's *Islands of Decolonial Love*, which shows us the magnitude of the Indigenous revival through *survivance* stories, are there to reaffirm Indigenous women's positions as leaders and change makers.[1] In a similar way, the more recent writings of First Nation poets from Quebec (Innu authors Joséphine Bacon, Nathasha Kanapé Fontaine, Manon Nolin)[2] present themselves as flourishing, healing landscapes that bring the beauty and power back in the meaning of the word "Woman," a word intrinsically connected to their identity through their relationship to the land:

Among the dying trunks of the Land
I will offer my heart to Assi

She will be my mother
my wealth
my reason to live

my dirty drug
my undrinkable liquor
my restorative tea[3]

Alongside these writers, three generations of Indigenous women filmmakers, from Alanis Obomsawin to Amanda Strong, take us on a circular path where the definition of Indigenous womanhood continues to engage with the words "educators," "knowledge transmitters," "activists," and "creators." Emerging artists such as Elle-Máijá Tailfeathers, Lisa Jackson, Amanda Strong, and Zoe Hopkins are now moving beyond the documentary realm to offer fresh perspectives and new stories, incorporating in their animated and experimental films bouts of tradition and modernity. Their work advocates what M. Raheja calls *visual sovereignty*: "engaging and deconstructing white-generated representations [and] intervening in larger discussions of Native American sovereignty."[4] In Quebec, the ongoing work of the Wapikoni Mobile, a nomad film and music studio that travels to Indigenous communities and provides the younger generation tools and training to create short films and music videos, has travelled in recent years well beyond the borders of Quebec, touring the festival circuits and organizing workshops in Polynesia and South America. Emerging from that initiative, artists such as famous rap singer Samian, Idle No More Québec representative Mélissa Mollen Dupuis, and multi-disciplinary artist Jemmy Echaquan Dubé (also spokesperson for the Réseau Jeunesse des Premières Nations du Québec) are all contributing to this new generation's survivance movement, that is, moving well beyond survival to construct new discourses of change. Alongside these artists, filmmakers Caroline Monnet (Algonquin), Kim O'Bomsawin (Abénaki), and Sonia Bonspille Boileau (Mohawk) are also presenting original, creative works that engage with the challenges of being an Indigenous woman today, dealing with issues such as identity (Caroline Monnet's *Portrait of an Indigenous Woman*, 2014), cultural reappropriation (Sonia Bonspille Boileau's *Princesses*, 2016), and missing and murdered Indigenous women (Kim O'Bomsawin's *Quiet Killing*, 2017 and Sonia Bonspille Boileau's *Rustic Oracle*, 2019).

Because of her abundant work on documentaries (*Last Call Indien*, 2010; *The Oka Legacy*, 2015) and fiction films (*Le Dep*, 2014; *Rustic Oracle*, 2019), as well as working on multiple shows for APTN (*Princesses, Skindigenous*), and because she was the first female Indigenous filmmaker in Canada to release a feature-length film, *Le Dep* (2014), I have chosen to focus on Sonia Bonspille Boileau's award-winning work, first by describing and analyzing some of her films/television shows, and second through an interview which allowed me to dig deeper into

Figure 4.1 Sonia Bonspille Boileau (right) with Eve Ringuette and Charles Buckell-Robertson on the set of *Le Dep* (2014).

subjects such as the role of Indigenous women in cinema, the disparities between Quebec and Canada in regards to First Nations and non-Indigenous relationships, and this generation's creative goals and dreams. I tried as much as possible to transcribe Sonia's words and intents without any modifications, so as to communicate with precision her words and stories. Moreover, because Sonia B. Boileau admits to having been inspired by Abénaki filmmaker Alanis Obomsawin's work, I was able, when it fit accordingly, to put her work in conversation with Obomsawin's films.

Quebec and Its Relationship with Indigenous Peoples

It is to be said that on the northeastern side of Turtle Island – also known as Quebec – the more recent emergence of First Nations writers and filmmakers can be partially explained by the complex relationship and history the province has with Indigenous populations. Indeed, it is a history that starts with some forms of collaborations and mixed marriages at the time of colonization, and at the same time the invasion of Indigenous lands and the desire to convert Indigenous peoples to Christianity. The troubled relationships between First Nations in Quebec are further complexified by French Canadians' own struggles with the English invader/oppressor (in the eighteenth century) and their fight for independence (1960s). This was a time when the *Indigenous Other* was excluded from the Québécois social and political landscape, with French Canadians thinking they were colonized just like First Nations were, thus choosing for a long time to ignore their own role as colonizers. The Oka Crisis (1990), a seventy-eight-day stand-off between the Mohawks of Kanehsatake, the Quebec police force, and the Canadian military over a land dispute, was certainly a turning point in this complicated relationship; the "Invisible people," as filmmaker and activist Richard Desjardins named them, became a *visible nuisance* in the colonizer's eyes. Indeed, the Oka Crisis marked the moment in Canada's history when it was no longer possible to completely ignore First Nations presence. The incredible amount of media coverage and the release of the Alanis Obomsawin film *Kanehsatake: 270 Years of Resistance* (1993) both contributed to the construction of a narrative in which stereotypes (on the media end of things) were confronted with actual facts and history (the Native point of view, as seen in Obomsawin's documentary). The three decades succeeding these events saw the release of the reports of the Royal Commission on Aboriginal Peoples (1996) and the Truth and Reconciliation Commission (2015). Both of these shed light on the reality of colonization and its consequences, including residential school syndrome, the treatment of Indigenous women (who are three times more likely to experience violence than non-Indigenous women), the validity of the land claims, and the need for Canadians to "reconcile" (but was there ever conciliation?) or at least build better relationships with First Nations.

On the cultural front, the failed referendum of 1995, the considerable increase in immigration, the changing multicultural landscape, and Quebec's everlasting nostalgia for the past and ongoing identity quest have all contributed to a recent movement where seeking Québécois identity resonates with a *retour à la terre* (i.e., connection to the territory) which can be epitomized by Indigenous cultures and what they symbolize in regards to Québécois connection to the land. Thus, in documentaries such as *L'empreinte* (C. Poliquin, 2014) and *Québékoisie* (O. Huggins and M. Carrier, 2013), the filmmakers put forward the thesis of mixed-blood ancestry, with well-known anthropologist Serge Bouchard stating that the influence and impact that Indigenous cultures have had on Québécois culture is far greater than what we realize. In the same way, Bill Marshall, in his chapter on *The Indigenous Other*, quotes a report stating that "Quebec contained the lowest social distance of any province between the aboriginal and non-aboriginal population."[5] Although these arguments have been debated, it is still interesting to see that many Indigenous artists, who identify themselves as Indigenous – for example, Innue poet Josephine Bacon and Attikamek visual artist Eruoma Awashish – also admit the presence of mixed-blood ancestry in Quebec and within their own nation, acknowledging the relative impact that having French-Canadian ancestry (and, we should add, the impacts of centuries of assimilation) have had on their work. It is, in a way, the same case for Sonia Bonspille Boileau, born out of the union between a French-Canadian father and Mohawk mother.

Last Call Indien: Sonia Bonspille Boileau's Work and Art: Seeking Mohawk Culture and Identity

At the very beginning of her documentary film *The Oka Legacy* (2015), Mohawk filmmaker Sonia Bonspille Boileau speaks of the impact of the Oka Crisis on Indigenous identity, and more specifically of the impact the crisis had on her, an eleven-year-old girl who, at the time, didn't know that much about her maternal culture or what it meant exactly to be Mohawk. Five years before her documentary came out, Sonia B. Boileau had done *Last Call Indien,* a medium-length film in which she tries to hold on to her Indigenous roots and identity, after finding out her grandfather had been taken away to residential school and assimilated into a non-Indigenous world and culture. The project was also the occasion for her to reconnect with her mother and bond over her family history.

Coming back to *The Oka Legacy*, the famous conflict had her find out that during those seventy-eight days, it was better for her and her family to hide behind her dad's French-Canadian name, Boileau, than to be Indigenous and the victim of racism and prejudice. The forty-four-minute narrative is carefully built using testimonies from people who lived the Oka Crisis and its aftermath, either from up close or from afar. We get to hear, for example, the story of Waneek Horn-Miller, an Olympic water polo champion, who, before getting into the sport, was caught in the middle of a riot that left her with a knife wound and the will to fight back through Olympic competition. Watching from a distance, we learn that Innue activist Melissa Mollen Dupuis was inspired to become involved in the *Idle No More* movement by individuals such as Ellen Gabriel and Kahentiiosta, two Mohawk women who stood up to the police and military to protect their land for the future generations. The role these women played in the crisis is mainly put forward in Obomsawin's film *Kanehsatake: 270 Years of Resistance*, where the two protagonists are depicted as the voices of reason and justice.

Years later, in her first feature-length film *Le Dep*, Sonia would mould her main protagonist, played by Innue actress Eve Ringuette, directly on the female role models she had met, and also on Eve herself, placing a female character once again at the heart of the narrative and having her survive and thrive through a horrific ordeal – not unlike the protagonists of Obomsawin's *Kanehsatake*. It was when receiving the filmmaker's permission to use footage from *Kanehsatake* that Sonia B. Boileau decided to incorporate interviews and images to illustrate the impact that Mohawk women's voices had at the time of the conflict and well after. Therefore, at the heart of this *Oka Legacy*, as well as at the heart of Indigenous communities, Indigenous women hold a place that the filmmaker is eager to put forward – even in the testimonies of men such as Oka warrior[6] Clifton Nicholas, who declares that the women give direction to the men, they are the ones who decided that they need to protect the land instead of go to war.

Another significant testimony present in the film is Francine Lemay's narrative. It tells the story of a woman whose policeman brother was killed in the crossfire during the Oka events and who surmounted her grief and ignorance of Mohawk culture by reading and eventually translating a book written by Mohawk women about the numerous challenges their people had to overcome, which were mostly brought on by colonization. In this way, we are shown that the Oka legacy, beyond the Aboriginal Royal Commission and the Truth and Reconciliation report, beyond exacerbating tensions and creating new relationships between Indigenous and non-Indigenous communities and peoples, is about assuming and embracing an identity that is surrounded by a heavy history of power relations and injustices. By putting women and their families at the heart of the conflict, acting as fair and determined warriors and peacemakers, just as Alanis Obomsawin had done in her documentary, Sonia Bonspille Boileau acknowledges the central role women played and continue to play in re-writing history and positioning Indigenous identity as part of a much bigger narrative. Thus, at the very end of the film, we see the women in Sonia's family reunited at the cemetery, claiming the need to put her assimilated grandfather's remains back on the land, where he belongs.

In the same way, the APTN (Aboriginal Peoples Television Network) series *Princesses* and *Skindigenous*, in which Sonia participated as a creator (for *Princesses* and *Skindigenous*) and co-director (for *Skindigenous*), carve out spaces for Indigenous women who perpetuate tradition, all the while innovating and transmitting their knowledge to the next generations. In *Princesses*, directed by Angie-Pepper O'Bomsawin, a wide range of Indigenous women, from scholars to actresses, address the stereotype of the "Indian Princess." The stereotype was born and fed in books, paintings, and films, through the transformation of real-life characters of Sacagawea and Matoaka (Pocahontas) into Indigenous heroines who were famous for betraying their own people by helping the colonizers. Throughout the series, standards of beauty are confronted as individuals from different nations (cultures, languages) express their relationship to beauty, for example, citing criteria such as knowledge of one's culture and contributions to one's community as important ways of attaining beauty. The myth of the *celluloid maiden*[7] is revisited, as well as the invisibility of Indigenous women in cinema, who were mainly there as secondary characters played by non-Indigenous actresses. The series stresses the fact that not all Indigenous women are the same, and presents, as Alanis Obomsawin had done in her 1977 documentary *Mother of Many Children*, diverse portraits of Indigenous women artists, activists, athletes, lawyers, doctors, and teachers.

For its part, *Skindigenous* explores the art of traditional tattooing and its significance for various Indigenous nations around the world. Again, the filmmaker, along with co-directors Jason Brennan, Jean-François Martel, Randy Kelly, and Kim O'Bomsawin (who contributed one episode), was careful when choosing the protagonists and the order in which the episodes would be seen, so as to have a woman present at least one time out of two. In episode 1, a grandmother and granddaughter from the Philippines perpetuate the age-old hand tap tattooing technique inherited from their ancestors; in episode 10, Inupiaq scholar Marjorie Rathbone explains how important it is to know why and how their people use tattooing (for generational reconnection, cultural reappropriation, decolonization, and to situate themselves in a healing way). Whatever the place, culture, or people, *Skindigenous* shows us how cultural memory is kept alive through tattooing, and how the adhesion to one tradition usually brings individuals and communities to explore the culture, stories, and ceremonies surrounding those traditions. The filmmaker does not hesitate in filming her protagonists in contexts where they are viewed as playing more than just one role in their community. For example, in episode 11, filmed in Prince Rupert, Nakkita Trimble is shown breastfeeding her child, teaching in front of a class, and walking on the land. In episode 10, Marjorie Rathbone can be seen jumping off a bridge, picking fresh traditional plants, and practising Inupiaq dancing. Like the women of *Princesses*, the individuals filmed in *Skindigenous* show the complexity and well-roundedness of Indigenous women today, as well as the intergenerational connection that unites one generation to the next, which was confirmed by Bonspille-Boileau in the conversation below.

Interview with Mohawk Filmmaker Sonia Bonspille Boileau

KB: How did you get into cinema? What made you want to become a filmmaker?

SBB: I've always loved movies and theatre and characters and stories. When I was younger I used to do plays and make up stories and of course I loved to watch films, but honestly it probably became clearer after the Oka Crisis. I saw so many horrible things, I felt that I had something to say about that. So basically, I blended that experience with my love of cinema and the power that I knew documentary film had.

KB: Are there any films or filmmakers that have influenced your work?

SBB: This might sound like an easy answer but it's the truth. *Kanehsatake: 270 Years of Resistance* by Alanis Obomsawin was actually, honestly, one of the first documentaries I saw, because I was a teenager and I didn't really watch documentaries. My family were more into the blockbuster kind of thing and we didn't necessarily watch documentaries. And for me it was huge to get to see another side of a story that I actually lived, compared to what we found in the media. Not another side as in "I didn't see that," because I saw what was going on and that could be found in the movie – but what I witnessed in the media, about the Oka Crisis, was totally different from what I was living on a day to day basis, during the events. So, to see that there was a way for us to tell our own story, that was really, really inspiring.

KB: In your opinion is there a difference between Indigenous women's cinema and Indigenous men's cinema? Because most of the films that are made right now in Canada are made by Indigenous women. Why is that?

SBB: There are many layers to this answer. I come from a very matriarchal community and a very matriarchal nation, so I am not surprised that it is mostly women that are the storytellers and that are passing on the culture and the knowledge. I think the other side of that is we are the most marginalized population in this country, therefore there is a greater need for us to actually take the talking stick and go out and tell our stories by all mediums, like arts and social revolutions and all those things. We feel we have to do those things to stay alive, in a way, so that has something to do with it. And we've always been more on the cultural side of things. When you look at history we were the weavers and the beaders and so we were already in that sharing of culture, so maybe it's just a natural progression to be making films. There are a lot of great Indigenous men storytellers that make movies but I guess there is just ... I don't know ... this natural instinct from women that makes them want to share the culture.

KB: Coming back to the beginning of my last question, do you notice a difference, for example, between films made by Mi'kmaq filmmaker Jeff Barnaby, Inuit filmmaker Zacharias Kunuk, and the movies of Arnait Video Productions (a film collective consisting of Inuit women and Marie-Hélène Cousineau)?

SBB: There is definitely a difference where Jeff Barnaby's work is concerned. I think Jeff is way more into playing with horror and suspense. I guess there are not many Indigenous female filmmakers that go that route. It goes back to the need to express social injustices, so it's more on a sensitive side, and an emotional side and trying to get people to feel that way. Whereas Jeff is really a natural-born storyteller in the very pure, suspenseful way. For Zacharias and Marie-Hélène (from Arnait) ... The pacing is much faster for *Atanarjuat* (Kunuk's film) and more masculine in that sense, and heroes are men ... Except for *Rhymes for Young Ghouls*, the heroine is a young woman. Although, this being said, it is a boy that kills the bad guy, so we are still giving power to the boy, but he's also expressing his own reality growing up.[8]

KB: What is the role of storytelling and oral tradition in your work?

SBB: I think because I didn't necessarily grow up with culture being passed down, because my grandfather went to residential school, and after the Oka Crisis, my family had a hard time expressing who they were as Mohawk people. For me, my initial goal in the way I told stories, especially documentaries in the beginning, was actually an exploration of that lack of culture. I was exploring how I could reclaim a sense of pride. So for me it was kind of reversed; it wasn't about making film to transmit culture. I was making films to explore my own culture and reclaim it. I got to take a reversed path, if I compare it to many of my peer filmmakers. And with my fiction film *Le Dep* I actually explored another nation (the Innu) but I still based it on the similarities between my own past and the Innu community. I still use things from my own community, my own family, and put it in an Innu setting and based it on what we have in common, and not necessarily on the cultural aspects that make us different nations. There again, it wasn't in the hopes of sharing or passing down traditional knowledge – it was just exploring our similar tragedies, how colonialism affected us both as nations, what we had in common.

KB: We see many Indigenous women filmmakers using different genres (animation, experimental, documentary fiction) to communicate their stories. What film genres do you use to express yourself?

SBB: I think it depends on the subject I want to tackle. For me documentary has always been a tool for the exploration of who I am, but also to learn. I see documentary as a learning tool for me and if I can make something amazing out of it that people can relate to, then great, but that's how I go into it; wanting to know more, and I get to learn about different Indigenous cultures in various countries (for example with *Skindigenous*). I use fiction to connect to people on an emotional level. It's not a knowledge process, it's an emotional process. I want to get people by the gut and find what connects us as humans. Then there's the social aspect of it, being in an Indigenous setting comes in a subtler way, so that people don't even realize it but they get to understand the bigger picture. When I go into fiction I don't go in thinking I want to teach someone about this or that; I go in thinking I want someone to feel this, whereas in documentary I want to learn and therefore I'll teach them.

KB: Can you tell us a little more about your process when you are making films? Do you have a specific way of working, or an aesthetic that defines your style?

SBB: That's a really good question and I don't know. I'm in editing right now (for *Oracle*) and while I'm editing my producer and my editor both tell me things like: "Oh that scene is so you," and "If I saw this I would know that it's your work," but I don't see it. I guess you would have to ask someone else if I have an aesthetic. I don't think I do, honestly. I think each story has its own life. I am attracted to certain things; I like long scenes ... I like Steadicam, honestly, I have this affection with things that are shot on Steadicam because I like following people and letting them explore the space, all the while exploring the space with them. I really like that and I have used that in *Le Dep* – although we were shooting in 900 square feet so I couldn't do it all that much – but there are scenes where I'm just walking with the actress (Eve Ringuette) for the dream sequence in *Le Dep*, it was all one long Steadicam shot. For *Skindigenous*, I also used the Steadicam to introduce the protagonists I was interviewing, following them around. And in *Rustic Oracle* there are many of those shots too, when we're just following a kid. But still, I think each project has its own aesthetic. I should try working with new people. I have been working with the same people for many, many years, so I guess the aesthetic that comes out is connected to team work

Figure 4.2 Sonia Bonspille Boileau (centre) with actresses Carmen Moore and Lake Delisle on the set of *Rustic Oracle* (2019).

(my DOP, my editor, and I). My approach for documentary, my aesthetic, will be based on who the story is about. I like to get to know the person first and it's something I try to translate visually, i.e., who they are. I do that with fiction too because my fiction films are centred around a character. The main character that I'm building, I try to think of that person's sense of aesthetic and how I can translate that with an image.

KB: Is it important for you to portray strong female characters, either in fiction or documentary films?

SBB: I think about it all the time. Honestly, it's the main thing I think about, in any project that I do. At a point where I think that I'm annoying because if anything is too masculine I'll fight to bring it back to feminine, which I had to do quite a bit with *Le Dep*. A lot of people around me kept seeing the film as if the story it told was that of P.A., the brother, but for me, from the get go, it was the story of Lydia, the girl that's being held up. She's the one that had to take control of the story. I had to fight to keep her as the main focus, and in *Rustic Oracle*, I figured I'm not even gonna have to deal with that, so all of my main characters are female. They are all women, so no one can try to take up too much room with a male character. I'm good with that! Everyone else are just secondary characters. I think I do it naturally in documentary too. Personally, it's because I feel more compelled to represent women, I want to see them shine on screen, so I'll just give them more room. That's what interests me. I like movies that have a female vision, and when I say female vision it doesn't mean sappy or romantic, it's a misconception that many people have. It can be very strong, very bold, it can be action-packed. It's just something ... The female characters are often deeper, I find. They are multilayered when written or directed by a woman. I think I'm a bit of a feminist (laughs). Even for *Skindigenous* I had two episodes where the two main characters were men, and that was fine, but when we were trying to find the other protagonists, because I knew I was shooting four episodes and two of them were men, there was no negotiation; the other two would be women. Therefore, we put a lot of male characters on backburner for season 2, so that I could find women to balance it out. There was no way I was going to do four episodes with four dudes; there had to be women who were tattooing. I knew doing the research that in many Indigenous cultures it was the women doing the tattoos. So we had to find these women; it was non-negotiable. Fortunately, I had the producer to do that.

KB: Was it more of a personal decision to integrate female characters into your work, or was it partly because you wanted to change the stereotypical "Pocahontas" representation of Indigenous women that has been the norm in Hollywood for the last eighty years?

SBB: That's exactly it. That was the motivation at the beginning but now it just happens naturally, it's what I want to do. I wrote an entire series based on that. *Princesses* (available on APTN) was entirely about reclaiming our beauty as Indigenous women, redefining what the word "beauty" is and how to move away from all the stereotypes that are put on us. Right now we are close to Halloween and it's the time of the year when I get really upset because I see all these ads for Pocahontas costumes and it makes me sick. This is why I developed a series that I didn't end up directing, because I was doing *Le Dep* at the same time, but I still had hands in the project and I gave it to Pepper O'Bomsawin who's a great friend of mine and who did a great job directing it, but I developed it. The whole point of this series was to break the stereotypes associated with the Indigenous Princess, starting from episode 1 where we explain there is no such thing as an Indigenous Princess, there was never any royalty in Indigenous nations – so the concept of princess shouldn't even exist – and to explain how the Pocahontas myth has been hurtful to Indigenous women. People don't realize that she was a fourteen-year-old girl who was raped and kidnapped and who eventually died, very young. Even in cinema, especially American films – but in Canada too – there are only three female archetypes in cinema; the sexualized maiden (the squaw); the Indigenous woman that needed to leave the community to be with the white guy (the traitor), who needed to be "saved" by the white guy; or the old sorcerer, who's this twisted, often old, crazy lady with powers. All these archetypes had one thing in common: at the end they all died. When I realized that, I decided that the series *Princesses* was going to deal with that. After that, all the other things, when I'm working on the characters I don't necessarily say, "Oh I'm going to fight a stereotype." I just want to build a strong character that's multi-dimensional, that has personality and emotions and if you are doing that you're already breaking the stereotypes.

KB: What are the subjects or topics that are close to your heart? How do you go about choosing what you are going to do next? Can you tell us about your latest project, for example?

SBB: My latest project, *Rustic Oracle* (a feature-length fiction film), is about a missing Mohawk teenager that is told through the eyes of her eight-year-old sister and going into that. Obviously, so many people in the country, Indigenous people and many allies, have been deeply affected by and pissed off at the situation of Missing and Murdered Indigenous women in Canada. I've been to many gatherings and protests and all that, but when Maisie Odjick and Shannon Alexander went missing in 2008 in Kitigan Zibi, a community situated about two hours north of Gatineau, Quebec, that really hit close to home, mainly because physically it's very close, about an hour from where we live (in Gatineau), but it's also my partner's community; his little brother was friends with one of them, so it seemed too close for us to ignore the situation. Sometimes when you don't know someone personally it feels like a distant subject, it feels like you understand the bigger picture and you understand at a cognitive level that something's wrong but you don't necessarily feel anything beyond the normal feeling of "it's too bad." This really hit closer to home, and for weeks and weeks I had a hard time sleeping and I was haunted by the fact that I don't know Shannon that well but I know that Maisie has younger siblings, and I thought of them, who probably couldn't understand what was going on and who got glimpses of things, understanding words and situations, but it's harder for little kids to comprehend what just happened and why you don't have your sister in your home every night. That's where the idea for *Rustic Oracle* came from. It's not a political film because I don't do political films. It's not a comment on Canadian society.

Again, my objective was: if everyone could feel what these families go through, what mothers go through, what a mother feels, what a sister feels, regardless of their cultural background, then maybe they can better understand what thousands of families in Indigenous Canada are feeling, beyond the political issue, on a human level, connect with your heart, then maybe that will break down a few barriers. I guess I go into projects with that in mind, how to connect with a non-Indigenous audience to what we have in common instead of seeing how we are different. It sounds like a political answer but it's not!

KB: I know you shot your latest project, *Rustic Oracle*, in your community of Kanehsatake. Is your community involved in your work, and how do the people respond to your fiction and documentary films? Do you do what you do for yourself or is there a part of you that works for the community?

SBB: If you look at all the major projects that I've done, in my career, the only one I didn't do in my community was *Le Dep*. Everything else, *The Oka Legacy*, now *Rustic Oracle*, and the short that I shot last fall, *We'll Always Have Toynbee*, were all shot in Kanehsatake. This last one is also an homage to the women in my community, to the land defenders of my community, and the leaders. Even though I don't live there anymore, and even though I have one foot in one culture and one in another, and even if my family is culturally disconnected, I've always felt very, very supported by my community. They are the ones that actually pushed me to study in film. My education centre funded my trip to Paris, so I could study under the New York Film Academy. For a while I didn't really know if I wanted to go back to university, and they are the ones that said there was no way I was going to drop out. They are all women championing me, so I guess this is why I feel a responsibility to bring the work back home, especially for *Rustic*. I wanted it to be as close to me as possible. *Le Dep* was close in the theme but it was still another language (Innu Aimun), another identity that I was portraying. This one (*Rustic Oracle*), I wanted for it to be as close to me, to my identity, as possible. I also wanted to bring the financial opportunity of financing a film into my community. There was money involved and they were going to make money; renting the spaces to shoot, hiring local people to work on the crew and as extras in the film. That's one of the reasons why we shot in the community. And we gave the community a pretty decent amount of money. And I felt good about it! As far as the reception of this specific film, I have no idea how it's going to be received. They were really happy with my short, though

(*We'll Always Have Toynbee*). There is a big protest scene in the film, and a large amount of people in this scene actually lived this kind of situation, including the Oka Crisis, so for them it was really cathartic. They didn't know how to react at first, although they knew what the script was, but at the end they all told me how good it felt to do that scene, to scream out loud again "This is our land," and to reaffirm our role as land defenders, even though it was a fiction film.

KB: I'd like to know your thoughts on the new generation of Indigenous women filmmakers that came after women such as Alanis Obomsawin, Shelley Niro, and Loretta Todd, i.e., Lisa Jackson, Zoe Hopkins, Elle-Máijá Tailfeathers, Kim O'Bomsawin, Amanda Strong. Do you notice new ways of telling stories, new challenges for these generations?

SBB: It's all of that! I think one way it has evolved in a positive way is that we know we don't have only one shot at telling a story. We don't necessarily feel the responsibility of doing just one thing, which is denouncing colonialism. I think for the first generation of Indigenous filmmakers, such as Alanis Obomsawin, that was the goal. Cinema was a tool to show the rest of the world how unfair Indigenous people were treated. Not saying that it's not the case anymore, it's just that we can divide this up into themes instead of just having one major theme. I don't know if this has crossed Alanis's mind, because she has done fifty films in fifty years, but for me, when I was shooting my first documentary, I remember thinking, "If I only have one shot at doing this I'm going to make sure that I say everything I have to say," so it does feel more politically charged. Now, I feel I don't have to say everything in one project, which means I can be more creative. I think our creativity has evolved quite a bit in recent years.

For example, I just got back from the Indigenous film festival imagineNATIVE, and Lisa Jackson's VR project blew my mind. It's the same with Amanda Strong (who does animation). Her approach is unique and it goes way beyond social injustice. It does send out a message but it does so in new, artistic ways. I think there is going to be much more narrative and fiction, something we didn't have much of until recently, maybe because we couldn't access funding, and that's the other reality. The reason why we can do more projects, the reason why we can push the boundaries creatively, is because we can now access funding that will allow us to do that. For the longest time, no matter what the project was, if people knew it was an Indigenous project it was judged poorly by broadcasters other than APTN (Aboriginal Peoples Television Network) and by government funders. They automatically assumed we didn't have the experience to pull it off and that there would not be an audience for this kind of content. Some people actually told me this to my face. In my opinion, first of all, our stories shouldn't necessarily be labelled Indigenous stories, but rather a story that needs to be told. Because as soon as someone heard the word "Indigenous" they labelled it as something negative. Up until recently we had to scramble to find the funds to do these things and now because of lobbyists and people like (Indigenous filmmaker) Danis Goulet and Jesse Wente, who fought for us, things are changing. If you look at the opening and closing films for TIFF (Toronto International Film Festival) in 2018, the opening and closing films were Indigenous, directed by Indigenous women. The best Canadian feature was directed by an Indigenous woman, so our stories actually are appealing to wider audiences.[9] We are also transforming the medium, bringing new approaches, new ways of seeing. We see the medium of cinema as something more akin to a circle than a square; something round and flexible and organic so it does change the format, by putting an Indigenous imprint on it. Because we don't see things in a linear way, it pushes the boundaries of storytelling.

KB: Looking at the representation of Indigenous women in Quebec cinema, it is safe to say that they have been mainly invisible in Quebec fiction films until recently (with films like Michel Poulette's *Maïna*, for example). In this vein, the relationships between Québécois people and Indigenous peoples living in Quebec is very different than the relationship between English Canadians and First Nations and Inuit people. The Québécois forgot for a long time that they were not only colonized but they were also colonizers. There is also the fact that statistically speaking, the métissage (mixed-blood) rate is perhaps slightly higher in Quebec than anywhere else in Canada. Do you think this historical/social context has an impact on your work, or on the work of other Indigenous women filmmakers living in Quebec?

SBB: Yes, for sure there is! It's also a national debate. I always found it very ironic that the Quebec art world and the art world of Indigenous people in Quebec are things that are viewed as being separate, in terms of we don't identify one with the other and one sees the other as a threat when we are essentially fighting the same thing; we are fighting to keep our identity, our aesthetic, and our stories alive in a bigger colonial system. Why does there have to be such a big separation? I am Mohawk, and being Mohawk (so usually speaking English rather than French) means a bigger separation, even. In that sense, I am hoping that there will come a time when our own Indigeneity in Quebec can become part of the landscape, because we have amazing storytellers on both sides and Quebec has a beautiful aesthetic that the rest of the country doesn't have, and a *main d'oeuvre* that is exceptional. Can you imagine if we put those two identities together to build our national identity, how strong visually it would be! There are so many similarities; the identity quest and many other themes, like exploring our suffering. There is a similarity there and still one is a threat to the other, which I don't understand.

Notes

1 Lee Maracle, *I Am Woman* (Richmond: Press Gang, 1996); Leanne Simpson, *Islands of Decolonial Love* (Winnipeg: ARP Books, 2013); Gerard Vizenor, *Survivance: Narratives of Native Presence* (Lincoln: University of Nebraska Press, 2008), x.
2 Joséphine Bacon, *Un thé dans la toundra* (Montreal: Mémoire d'encrier, 2013); Natasha Kanapé Fontaine, *Manifeste Assi* (Montreal: Mémoire d'encrier, 2014); Manon Nolin, *Ma peau aime le Nord* (Montreal: Mémoire d'encrier, 2016).
3 Natasha Kanapé Fontaine, *Assi Manifesto*, trans. Howard Scott (Toronto: Mawenzi House, 2016).
4 Michelle Raheja, *Reservation Reelism* (Lincoln: University of Nebraska Press, 2010), 193–4.
5 Bill Marshall, *Quebec National Cinema* (Montreal and Kingston: McGill-Queen's University Press, 2001), 239.
6 The Kahnawake Warrior Society was formed in 1972 "as a means to carry out the resolutions of the Clans in Council and to serve as the defensive vanguard of the Longhouse ... assuring the defense and security of the people." No author, "Government: National Defence and Public Security," Haudenosaunee website: http://www.kahnawakelonghouse.com/index.php?mid=1&p=3 (accessed 29 January 2022).
7 Elise Marrubio, *Killing the Indian Maiden: Images of Native American Women in Film* (Kensington: University of Kentucky Press, 2006).
8 In an interview done at Queen's University in 2016, Mi'kmaq filmmaker Jeff Barnaby declared that the character of Ayla was inspired by the women in his family and his community.
9 *SGaawaay K'uuna / Edge of the Knife* (Gwaai Edenshaw and Helen Haig-Brown, 2018), *Falls around Her* (Darlene Naponse, 2018), and *Biidaaban* (Amanda Strong, 2018) were all shown at TIFF in 2018.

5

Le cinéma à l'estomac
Denis Côté and the New Wave of Quebec Cinema (2004-19)

Jean-Pierre Sirois-Trahan
Translated by Anna Pletnyova

Denis Côté is one of the most important and prolific filmmakers in the history of Quebec cinema. He was born on 16 November 1973, in Perth-Andover, New Brunswick. His parents moved to Longueuil when he was just eighteen months old. In his teenage years, he studied film at Ahuntsic College, Montreal. An independent cinéphile, he is one of those filmmakers – rare in Quebec, but numerous in France, where the New Wave enjoyed great success – who became known as a critic before turning to directing. Côté initially worked in community radio (in a duo with Sandro Forte) where his caustic tone quickly set him apart; then at the weekly free magazine *Ici Montréal*, which he presided over as a bureau chief. His eloquence, demanding aesthetics, and excellent knowledge of cinema made him one of the most prominent critics of his generation. In the meantime, he made his debut with short films. His vicious criticism of Jean Beaudin's *Nouvelle-France / Battle of the Brave* (2004), a French-Quebec co-production starring Gérard Depardieu, had him banned from press screenings by one of Montreal's most important distributors. Another distributor followed suit.

This latent censorship made his position as a critic untenable; as a result, he decided to switch to full-length feature filmmaking with *Les États nordiques / Drifting States* (2004). This film announced the arrival of a new generation of directors. In the opening shots, which show a crowd attending a wrestling match in the basement of a parish church, Côté pays tribute to the history of Quebec cinema, notably the significant Direct Cinema documentary *La Lutte / Wrestling* (Michel Brault, Marcel Carrière, Claude Fournier, and Claude Jutra, 1961). His films have always

Figure 5.1 Denis Côté.

oscillated between an awareness of a situated reality, borrowed from the aesthetics of Direct Cinema, and the cinematographic forms that put him into the context of independent international cinema. Côté presents the landscapes, customs, and especially the language of Quebec, with its accent and colourful expressions.

Combining the aesthetics of *arte povera* (filming with a small digital camera) and the punk ethic of Do It Yourself (films made at the author's expense, like his latest opus *Wilcox*), *Drifting States* ushered in a change of epoch. Participating from a distance in the Kino movement, an informal group of filmmakers who made movies with the means at hand, Côté was the first young director of this generation (simultaneous with Sophie Deraspe's *Rechercher Victor Pellerin/Missing Victor Pellerin*, 2005) to try his hand at full-length feature films. At that time, Telefilm Canada had changed its policy, introducing the famous funding envelopes, which privileged the production of "blockbuster" commercial films. Côté's films and those of the new generation acted as an antidote and would undoubtedly have a lot to do with the repositioning of funding agencies in favor of independent cinema.

By winning the Golden Leopard (for video) at the Locarno International Film Festival, Côté's first effort heralded a new aesthetic later called the *renouveau* (renewal, revival) or the "New Wave of Quebec cinema." This included filmmakers such as Stéphane Lafleur, Sophie

Deraspe, Maxime Giroux, Rafaël Ouellet, Myriam Verreault, Henry Bernadet, Xavier Dolan, Sébastien Pilote, Guy Édouin, Mathieu Denis, Simon Lavoie, Yves Christian Fournier, and Yvan Grbovic, among others.[1]

How can we, aesthetically speaking, define this group of filmmakers? Their works include an aesthetic of duration and a mise-en-scène that rejects the imagery and aesthetics of commercial film; a flexibility of production which can move from big (professional shooting crew) to small (light shooting unassisted by funding agencies); a certain puritanism and an absence of sexual glamour; an awareness of the irreparable and banal; a special focus on characters without qualities, lost in blank suburban and regional landscapes; a naturalism of representation that resembles what André Bazin called "the cinema of cruelty"; a subtle irony that tracks the absurd and the *punctum* (Roland Barthes), giving rise to derision in a sort of burlesque in slow motion; borrowings from genre cinema (fantasy, Western, horror, and even science fiction); and a way of expressing political ideas in the form of allegory rather than the militant discourse of "vouloir-dire" (Godard) and of "thesis films." These filmmakers tell stories that attach more importance to the relationships between characters and places, between individuals and spaces, than to any significant dialogue. As Sylvain Lavallée stresses, speaking about the mother's death in *Drifting States*: "Côté is not interested in the psychological effects of this premise, and the character is portrayed through his relationship to the place and to his environment rather than through a defined psychology with a narrative function."[2] We see already in Côté's first film, in its raw form, all that the aesthetic of this movement will become.[3]

Place and the Refusal to Portray It as a Postcard

What equally stands out in the works of *renouveau* filmmakers is the refusal to portray places as postcards. They film suburbs or villages as neutral backgrounds, taking into account their banality and, at the same time, their singularity, attentive to the spatial setting with which the mise-en-scène of the characters is merged. They depict their locations' undeniable ugliness, but also their paradoxical beauty, similar to contemporary photographers working close to cinema like Isabelle Hayeur[4] or Jeff Wall. At the same time, they are well aware that this anchoring in the natural can be somewhat exotic to a European or Asian viewer. In Côté's *Curling* (2010), a god-forsaken snowbound place is as exotic for the Locarno or Jeonju audience as a tiger in a jungle in Weerasethakul's movies is for us (and with a wink, Côté adds a tiger as a bonus). It is Côté who went the farthest in this direction. In *Nos vies privées / Our Private Lives* (2007), he films two Bulgarians on holiday in Quebec, enclosed in the proverbial "Canadian cabin." After we gradually become accustomed to this exotic situation, an *uncanny familiarity* establishes itself and Côté plants his pair of characters in the midst of the Sainte-Perpétue Pig Festival! To amuse the audience, the comedians Dominic and Martin go at it with their rather depressing antics while another man catches hold of the poor domestic pig. This is an implicit representation of all Quebec, presented to us as exotic, profoundly weird, and monstrous (you have to wait and see, or rather hear, the final shot). The "cabin" reappears in *Vic + Flo ont vu un ours / Vic and Flo Saw a Bear* (2013). After being released from prison, the protagonists take refuge from the world in a remote countryside. This is a liberation for Victoria, a Quebecer happy to cut herself off from society; but for Florence, an extroverted Frenchwoman, this life represents a new prison. The isolation of Quebec culture is an important topic in Côté's filmography, which can also be found in his recent movie *Répertoire des villes disparues / Ghost Town Anthology* (2019).

As often happens in naturalist representations, banal places are shown as part of the "monde originaire,"[5] which is like the reverse shot or the instinctual background of a civilized city. It makes us think of the forest in *Continental, un film sans fusil / Continental, a Film without Guns* (Stéphane Lafleur, 2007); of the woods and wastelands that close *À l'ouest de Pluton / West of Pluto* (Henry Bernadet and Myriam Verreault, 2008) and *Jo pour Jonathan / Jo for Jonathan* (Maxime Giroux, 2010); of the lake in *Vic and Flo Saw a Bear*; of the dump with a roaming pack of wolves in *Drifting States*; of Mount Royal (with its Carollesque rabbit), tidal flats of Montmagny, and Domaine Joly-De Lotbinière in Dolan's work; of the scrap yard of *Nos vies privées / Our Private Lives* (2007), also used in *Carcasses* (2009); of the woodlot with a tiger and dead bodies in *Curling*; and of snow-covered plains in *Ghost Town Anthology*. The edge of civilization is a place of animality, savagery, and the fantastic, which permeates most of these films (see the telekinesis in *Jo for Jonathan* and the man of the future from *En terrains connus / Familiar Grounds* by Stéphane Lafleur, 2011).

Exterior exile on the road or interior exile in "the abyss of dreams" ("The Ship of Gold" by Émile Nelligan) are a constant temptation for Quebec culture. There is also the collective utopia, but at a time when all our collective dreams are broken it seems that this is a dead-end of representation. Filmmakers are trying to find another way out – by showing confinement, but without making a destiny out of it. The matricide in *Drifting States* wants to shut himself off from society, exiling himself from the world of men on the northern frontier of Quebec, flirting with wild nature. Love will let him take a step back to society. His eventual arrest, which is not spectacular, appears – more than a final imprisonment – to be the seal of his return to humans (and their law). We can also see that the young woman in *Elle veut le chaos / All That She Wants* (2008) and the family in *Curling* end up leaving their confinement to return to life. It is in this situation that the ethic of the director resides, as Joachim Lepastier rightly pointed out in the *Cahiers du Cinéma*.[6]

Allegories of Quebec

In the works of the *renouveau* filmmakers, we can find passages, contacts, and meetings that articulate an interplay between the microcosm (a family, a group of friends, isolated individuals) and the macrocosm (society, human race, the universe). In *Drifting States*, Côté links the story of a matricide with the frontier myth and the colonization of Abitibi with big hydroelectric projects. In *Our Private Lives*, a love story between two strangers who meet on the internet allows the director to show a profound disconnection from Quebec's reality. In *All That She Wants*, there is a constant tension between the culture of Quebec and the cultures of other places (two Russian prostitutes, an exiled Frenchman, a German national team hockey jersey, Eastern European musicians). In *Curling*, the isolation of the Sauvageau family (what a name!) is nothing but the allegory of today's Quebec. When the father brings his daughter some books, he slips a history of Quebec in between a book of comics and a book of elementary math. "It's not complicated, you'll see," he says! When he goes curling for the first time – itself a metaphor for his family situation with a red "house" protected by guard stones – there are flags of Quebec and Canada on the wall of the gym, which we can also see on the wall of a women's prison. And when, at the end, the father fantasizes about his curling victory, the camera focuses on the flag of Quebec ...

In *West of Pluto*, when the teenagers are not dreaming about forming a rock band, they argue with each other about the national question, falling into silence when the discussion comes to a deadlock. Their personal situations reveal what is happening at a larger scale, connecting the family with the cosmos, as the movie title indicates. The magnificent final shot attempts to link these dimensions: the framed painting of the family is filmed in this non-human *monde originaire*, which is a wasteland, then the camera takes off to inscribe it in the space of the suburb and beyond it. It is the same figure, *mutatis mutandis*, as the closing shot of *Solaris* (Andrei Tarkovsky, 1972). In *J'ai tué ma mère / I Killed My Mother* (Dolan, 2009), the son dreams of matricide, which he will never commit: the mother, whom he simultaneously abhors and loves, personifies *kétaine* (tacky and corny) Quebec – we can no more kill our mother than our society, unlike our father. The film ends in a declaration of love, which will be refuted in the following film, *Les Amours imaginaires / Heartbeats* (Dolan, 2010), where two aesthetes speak harshly about the remote regions of Quebec, as if Dolan was taking a stance against his previous work. He is taking a really intimate approach there, as if he is looking for new possibilities of existence (another legacy of Jutra's *À tout prendre*, 1963). Among other current filmmakers, each individual story relates to the global situation (the aging of the population, idleness and young suicides, juvenile prostitution, etc.), without (and this is the most important point!) ever falling into the trap of a sociologizing discourse (Yves Christian Fournier's *Tout est parfait / Everything Is Fine* [2008] is exemplary in this respect). This is political cinema which, thanks to its elegance, appears as if it never meddled with politics. Rafaël Ouellet offers a sociological explanation of this phenomenon, linked to the fact that the filmmakers are all from generation X, except Dolan: "We are filmmakers, born, for the most part, in the 1970s and educated in the atmosphere of post-referendum cynicism. We approach politics obliquely, and our ways of doing things are similar."[7]

The Impossible Community

The impossible community, the inability to be "part of," is at the heart of Denis Côté's oeuvre. Far from being pointless or empty, as they are sometimes described by the blind critics, his films ask eminent political questions but at a fundamental level. Each time one ends up wondering what it is that unites human beings: his characters would like to belong to the tribe, but they are excluded from it, pushed back, despite themselves, to the limits of civilization and savagery. This animality might be the "off-camera" of humanity. Consider the pack of wolves in *Drifting States*, the ape-man and the pig rodeo of *Our Private Lives*, or finally the *montage interdit* (André Bazin) between the young Sauvageau and the big cat in *Curling*.

His characters are often caricatured as marginals, but it would make more sense to say that they are lost in a free zone between the human

Figure 5.2   Emmanuel Bilodeau in *Curling* (2010).

and the non-human, between the community and its exterior. It is no surprise that his work is haunted by the Western, a genre of which only the bones are left. In his first film, *Drifting States*, the mother-killer escapes to the far northern frontier (the open city of Radisson) in order to find his innocence again before the Downfall, while the garbage-picker of *Carcasses* lives in his earthly Paradise, which the "Indians" are demanding to share. In *All That She Wants*, his most stylized film – a kind of Spaghetti Western script as written by Sophocles, or a kind of white-trash *Rio Bravo* – an undefined territory shared by the heroes and villains is essentially outside the law, unmapped, almost on the fringes of society. Only a highway, visible in the background of many shots, recalls reality and itself suggests a possible line of flight from this ruthless world.

As we guessed, it is society that is not self-evident in Côté's films, and which he is constantly calling into question in a radical way: can one still hope to become part of the human world after committing the most heinous of crimes (*The Drifting States*)? What happens to the new sociability of the web when it is plunged into reality (*Our Private Lives*)? Isn't the exchange value attributed to things by society merely an arbitrary fiction (*Carcasses*)? *Curling*, his masterpiece (see figure 5.2), summarizes these topics, and moves beyond them. The father (in a masterful performance by Emmanuel Bilodeau, awarded Best Actor in Locarno) protects his little girl from the evil society of men, but cannot protect her from his own neuroses or from the Oedipal shadow underlying the fear of others. The metaphor of the title (*Curling*) sums up the challenges: he may want to protect his "house" with guard stones, but the continuous assaults of others by their never-ending "curls" make the task impossible. This film puts forward a new hypothesis that saves Côté's cinema from nihilism and ends up making it extremely moving – this hypothesis is nothing else but love. Love as opening-up, as off-camera, as a remedy against confinement.

Pierre Barrette called Côté "the most philosophical of our filmmakers."[8] We can't say if the director himself would like this label (he doesn't like labels ...), but, to a certain extent, it does him justice. In *Lignes ennemis / Enemy Lines* (2010), for example, he is always engaging in reflection at the most fundamental, almost anthropological, level, about an interplay between civilization and savagery. Thus, it is not surprising that he revisits the Western, a philosophical genre of a kind.

"I Hate People"

An award-winner at the Berlinale, *Vic and Flo Saw a Bear* marked a modulation in Côté's work. After being released from prison, the asocial and caustic Victoria (played by the wonderful Pierrette Robitaille) finds refuge in an abandoned maple grove because she "hates people." She is joined by her lover Florence (Romane Bohringer), an extrovert, who also seeks the company of men. The story unfolds in geometric shapes: in multiple centrifugal lines, Flo wishes to go towards others, whereas Vic, centripetal by nature, is trying to protect herself from the exterior world. The direction, alternating between still frames and graceful camera movements, reinforces these two opposing lines. Flo, the Frenchwoman, quickly gets tired of this "Canadian cabin" and starts looking for adventures as their passion withers. The compelling story of this lesbian couple is presented by the director as if it was the most commonplace thing in the world: even in the heart of the region, nobody finds anything wrong with it (we are far from the homophobic countryside of Dolan's *Tom at the Farm*, which was released the same year).

Another geometric storyline in the film is that of Jackie (played with delight by Marie Brassard), who is looking to break the other two lines and further tighten her trap. Alfred Hitchcock once said that the more successful the villain, the more successful the picture. This is the case here. Rarely can one find in Quebec cinema a figure of Evil that would not be a caricatural brute or a chintzy bad guy. Brassard, with her cunning and intelligence, creates one of the most convincing villains of our cinema.

The love story of Victoria and Florence (thwarted by Jackie) is undoubtedly the director's most touching film. It is moving to see, in the midst of extreme violence at the end, a moment of infinite peace, reminiscent of the ending of Ridley Scott's *Thelma and Louise* (1991). It is also touching to see Victoria realize that she and Florence will finish their life together, united for eternity. In Côté's films, love is warmer than death. Emotion also comes from the beautiful face, mineral and opaque, of Pierrette Robitaille, which, in certain moments, radiates pure feeling. We find in this a motif similar to *Curling*: a popular actor, moreover a comic and a TV star, is plunged into an unfamiliar universe, far from their own media ecosystem. This is Côté's way of playing with the viewers' expectations, going beyond appearances to experiment with an unknown world. Perhaps the only problem with the film is that it doesn't leave enough space – that it doesn't instill enough mystery outside of its well-oiled narrative mechanics. The film also ushers in a weaker section of films after Côté's more creative first period (let's say up until *Bestiary*).

Boris sans Béatrice / *Boris without Béatrice* (2016) is perhaps the director's weakest movie. Seductive, intelligent, and brusque, Boris Malinovsky is a successful businessman surrounded by women (his daughter, wife, lover, mother, and an au pair girl). But, as they say, the poor have only one problem, and the rich have plenty: his wife (Béatrice) becomes depressed, his mother and daughter will not see him anymore, his love conquests do not satisfy him, and his conscience is torturing him. A life full of vanity only leads to a feeling of emptiness. Less a criticism of capitalism than a moral fable on the dangers of arrogance, *Boris without Béatrice* offers a narrative arc in two parts. The reference to Greek tragedy is evident, but without catharsis it produces an artificial result: the transformation of the character is rapid, without real progression, leading to a happy ending with a Judeo-Christian morality. Normally preferring opacity for his characters, this time, Côté shows his limits in terms of psychology. Two men, the prime minister of Canada (played by filmmaker Bruce La Bruce) and a guru (Denis Lavant), play the role of his timely superegos who will bring Boris back on the right track. The scene where Lavant meets James Hyndman in a quarry at night, copied from the cowboy scene in *Mulholland Drive* (David Lynch, 2001), borders on the ridiculous. The charismatic but unconvincing acting of Hyndman contributes to bringing the movie down, whereas its three female leads (the remarkable Simone-Élise Girard, Isolda Dychauk, and Dounia Sichov) save it from sheer gratuitousness.

Released in 2018, *Ghost Town Anthology* marks a powerful comeback for the filmmaker. In a village lost in the greyness of winter, residents are preoccupied with the apparition of inexplicable "silhouettes." Phantoms, zombies, or products of an irrational phobia: the film never explains this question. The direction follows the best traditions of the horror genre: disturbing music, use of off-camera space, hand-held camera throughout the movie, and so on. Côté has always rejected the school of social realism (à la Sébastien Pilote): he departs from reality, overturning it with the intrusion of a flaw, a mystery, or a fantasy. What is original about the film is that it rejects all violence; the living dead are not dangerous – you should simply accept their presence and learn to live with them. The villagers who cannot do so just emigrate to a big city (Quebec or Montreal) where there are no intruders. François Truffaut said that a good movie should express both ideas about the world and ideas about cinema. *Ghost Town Anthology* is a film that reflects on its art. These silhouettes are also cinema images, figures that stand out on the snowbound background, representing the screen. Cinema's simultaneous death-and-life (*mort-vie*) is one of its founding myths, with the first commentators underlining that cinematographic images have the power to raise from the dead: "When these devices become accessible to the public, when everyone can take photographs of their loved ones, not in immobile form, but in motion, in action, with their familiar gestures, with words parting from their lips, death will stop being absolute. We will keep, as it were, a living memory of those whose loss we regret."[9] Now, 127 years later, cinema is populated with countless dead, some quite cumbersome; a quotation from Pasolini's *Teorema* (1968) is, without a doubt, Côté's way of saying that modern cinema has to reconcile itself with its history and its clichés.

The film also offers ideas about the world. Irénée-les-Neiges is an allegory of remote regions with their problems of aging populations, a lack of prospects, the idleness of the young, endemic suicides, and xenophobia, completely opposite from fairy tales like *La Grande Séduction* (Jean-François Pouliot, 2003). Cinematographer François Messier-Rheault's magnificent desaturated images evoke traditional Quebec paintings (recalling the late works of Jean-Paul Lemieux, and his vast flat tints of white and muddy brown half-tones), embedding the movie into a familiar Quebec territory from which horror could easily emerge. When the father dies (itself a variation on François Paradis in *Maria Chapdeleine*) we no longer know if it is an expression of irony or emotion. As in *Curling*, Côté creates a gallery of appealing characters (the mayoress, the two snowshoers, the phobic woman …), played by TV comedians, constantly switching between comedy and horror without ever insisting on either of them. This explosive mixture of *néo-terroir* (neo-rural) and a Quebec ghost story augurs well for the rest of Côté's oeuvre.

Arts poétiques

Côté's filmography can be divided into two very distinct parts: script-written movies made with professional actors and crews (*All That She Wants, Curling, Vic and Flo Saw a Bear, Boris without Béatrice, Ghost Town Anthology*) and more experimental films made on the cheap using documentary techniques (*Drifting States, Our Private Lives, Enemy Lines, Carcasses, Bestiary, Joy of Man's Desiring, A Skin So Soft*, and *Wilcox*).

Three of his films on a smaller scale, *Bestiaire / Bestiary* (2012), *Que ta joie demeure / Joy of Man's Desiring* (2014), and *Ta peau si lisse / A Skin So Soft* (2017), could be understood as *arts poétiques* (works of art that reflect more or less explicitly on artistic creation). In *Bestiary*, Côté tries his hand at animal documentary, a genre with many traps for a filmmaker, and reflects on the question of representation: how can we film animals without clichés? Through its analogy with prisons (see figure 5.3), zoos are shown to be charged places, where locked-up animals inevitably trigger a militant discourse and anthropomorphic reactions. Refusing to state the obvious, Côté gives viewers the freedom of their own positioning and commits himself to filming animals as if it was *for the first time*; as if he had to, in fact, compete with the wall paintings in Lascaux. The scene with the scared zebra, which mixes up incarnation and abstraction, makes us think of the horses in the Chauvet cave, with their great kinetic force. The scene in a studio where apprentices are drawing stuffed animals further convinces us that the film is a rumination on the topic of representation rather than an academic depiction.

The next movie, *Joy of Man's Desiring*, deploys a cutting style consisting of still frames and zooms into the machines, producing a sensuality that echoes the cream separator motif in Eisenstein's *Old and New* (1929; the Russian characters on the poster confirms this inspiration). But unlike the great Soviets, Côté does not make a propaganda movie. One is almost tempted to say that the film is a provocation: titled in the theological manner of Bernard Émond, it is centred on sociopolitical issues (workers, immigrants) and themed like an essay film on the alienation of mechanical labour. Upon this framework of a militant film, Côté adds just enough duration and ambiguity to blow up all preconceived

Figure 5.3 The zoo as a prison in *Bestiary* (2012).

discourses. Like a Rorschach test, everyone sees there what they want: a denunciation of exploitation, a formalist experiment, love for a job well done, an apology for the freedom brought about by work, and so forth. From this point of view, it resembles *Bestiary* a great deal. It could be seen as an exercise in style, but very few Quebec directors have filmed the reality of factory work with such attention and precision. These gestures, filmed with an uncompromising distance, are interwoven with fictional scenes with unrealistic diction, where monologues and dialogues are acted out like theatrical rehearsals. Politics is a theatre stage where individuals and their attitudes towards work matter less than their *masks* (girl mother, immigrant, etc.) in a revolutionary act. Côté questions these representations.

Another similarity between *Bestiary* and *Joy of Man's Desiring* lies in its meta-poetic discourse. In the latter, Côté proceeds no differently than in his other films: he asks himself complicated questions about representation (how to film animals? how to film work?), and tries to answer them with maximum singularity and with the conviction that these problems of mise-en-scène will end up revealing something new about the world. If, at the beginning, he presents the reality of factories, the more the film moves forward, the more Côté gets interested in small-scale manufacture where tailor-made items are created: he thus highlights the fact that he has always, even in his films more to the standards of the industry, preferred quasi-artisanal methods – "hand-made" films crafted in his little corner – to goods manufactured in factories (of dreams).

In *A Skin So Soft*, students under the supervision of an instructor are trying to paint a bodybuilder with well-defined muscles. Just like stuffed animals in *Bestiary*, this scene acts as a foil: how can we film bodies without falling into academicism? Throughout the film, Côté asks himself from what distance to show his characters: a strong man capable of pulling a long-haul truck and a handful of bodybuilders. The figure of the *strong man* is one of the most important myths of Quebec culture, recalling Louis Cyr and the Great Antonio, whereas the *bodybuilders* in the movie are definitely turned towards the American Dream and narcissistic internet culture (they take selfies, flexing their muscles for an Instagram pose). Isn't Arnold Schwarzenegger both a bodybuilding and a Hollywood icon? In this opposition between two cultures, the strong man is isolated. Côté treats the kitschy aspect of this (in the style of *Elvis Gratton*) with a perfect mixture of ironic distance and kind empathy. In the end, a rural getaway makes the men return to their natural state, playing shepherds in a kind of legendary Arcadia. The tension, constant throughout the film, is never really resolved. The closing titles show Eugen Sandow, the father of bodybuilding and a big rival of Louis Cyr, posing (*Sandow*, William K.L. Dickson, 1896) and wrestling with Greiner (*Ringkämpfer*, Max Skladanowsky, 1895), which convinces us that painting and digital imaging (one of the bodybuilders puts on a virtual headset) were not there by accident. Côté revisits one of the favourite subjects of early cinema and tries to make it innocent again, stripping from it its clichés of directing or of scriptwriting.

Portrait of the Artist as a Young Woman

One of the reproaches made of Denis Côté is his refusal to tell a story, a rejection within the tradition of modern cinema in the style of Antonioni. However, let's dare put forward a paradox: the story interests him as much as the mise-en-scène. Though complicated, punctured, or gutted, his scripts are narratives – a dysnarrative is nothing but a narrative. A former critic with a knowledge of the ins and outs of scriptwriting, he attempts to tell his stories in such a way that they do not have a taste of déjà-vu, aiming to disrupt the apathy of the viewer by unexpected clashes, poetic splices, puzzling gaps in narratives, and a certain formal openness that engages spectators in a strong experience commensurate with their own feelings of risk. Hence the state of perplexity into which he plunges the audience with his stories.

Auteur cinema since Truffaut has been based on the idea that a film should convey obsessions, be they conscious or unconscious, and the singular personality of the director. Even though Côté concentrates on the cinematic form as a mediation of the world – this discourse is a recurring theme in all of his interviews – his films are no less endowed with obsessional traits. For example, in most of his movies, we can find a corpse, so to speak, forgotten somewhere along the way. It is not introduced there by necessity of the narrative because death is a gap, a hole in the script, a breach of meaning. What idea is hiding behind such a strange figure? What to make of these corpses, whose meaning is concealed?

At first sight, Côté's movies, unlike those of Dolan or Stéphane Lafleur, are exempt from autobiographical references, even though he does seem to be interested in a certain type of world. Closest to Côté is perhaps *Maïté* (2007), the best of his short films, which tells the story of a young goth girl who leaves her village to go to the big city to see a black metal concert. The movie mixes fictional scenes with a concert filmed in documentary style, but the line between them is blurred when, after returning to her hotel room and thinking over the performance, she sees the musicians appear as goth phantoms. Although the character is female, could it be that Côté is reflecting on his own teenage years, as a suburbanite drawn to the big city and haunted by horrific figures?

He will use the same gender inversion in a strange text entitled "She Cried at the Disco," published in the *Nouveau Projet* magazine. The story traces the life of a young independent female filmmaker in the world of international festivals.[10] Côté seems to embrace a criticism that is often made of him: being a festival filmmaker. It is true that his success in the festivals, and his skill with the media, did not come without creating enemies. The text is astonishing; it seems to be a kind of self-portrait:

> For some time now, she has been drifting on the other side of the world. She has heard and read about crises and other problems that are shaking her society. But she has chosen to avoid them, shying away from mass movements. She knows she is a bad citizen. People like her have taken to the streets, chanting slogans and waving banners. Their capacity for indignation touches her, but she does not feel the need to add her voice to the concerto of the revolt. She listens from a distance without commitment or response. We could reproach her for it, but that's how it is, and it has nothing to do with laziness.

The melancholy tone with which the author seems to be willing to define his approach to art, as well as his amused criticism of small vanities and bustles of this *small world*, casts a new light on the aesthetics of the Quebec filmmaker. He defines himself as an unaffiliated artist, on the periphery of society but watching it closely thanks to that distance, and not without a form of despair that his nihilism would arouse (his company is called Nihil Productions).

À l'estomac

Côté is much reproached for his "little game of forms." It is true that he says nothing in interviews to attenuate this formalist side for which he is criticized, especially on the Left, and which would make him an *apolitical* filmmaker. Certainly, his films do not harbour cheap hopes. But how can we reconcile the criticism of the alleged gratuitousness of "art for art's sake" with his reputation as the most philosophical of our filmmakers? It is just that, for a filmmaker, the form, in other words directing, is always of primary importance. What we can say about cinema is not much different from what novelist Julien Gracq wrote about the French *belles-lettres* in *La Littérature à l'estomac*:

> When I say that "for a few years, literature has been the victim of formidable intimidation from the non-literary, and the most aggressive non-literary," I would only like to remind you that it is by the irrevocable commitment of putting thought into a *form* that life is breathed into literature day by day: in the realm of senses, this commitment is the very condition of poetry, in the realm of thoughts, it is called *tone*. Without a doubt, Nietzsche belongs to literature just as Kant does not belong to it. It is because we have slightly forgotten about this that we find ourselves threatened today by this unthinkable thing: the literature of *magisters*.[11]

Far from a cinema of *magisters*, Côté's commitment to the cinematographic form makes his cinema, through this primary requirement, a thought in action.

Notes

1   Elsewhere, I have termed this generational movement "la mouvée." See my article providing its overview ("La mouvée et son dehors: renouveau du cinéma québécois," 76–8) in a dossier about these filmmakers in *Cahiers du Cinéma*, no. 660 (October 2010). The current article continues and develops

parts of that article as well as parts of "Table ronde sur le renouveau du cinéma québécois" ("Round Table on the New Wave of Quebec Cinema"), organized by Bruno Dequen, *Nouvelles Vues*, no. 12 (spring–summer 2011).

2 Sylvain Lavallée in "Round Table on the New Wave of Quebec Cinema."

3 Of course, not every film of the *mouvée* shares the characteristics of the *Drifting States*, but most of the films do possess them. Pierre-Alexandre Fradet spoke of a "family resemblance" (Ludwig Wittgenstein): an extended family shares a certain number of physical characteristics even if each of its members may not necessarily have all of these traits (in general, a family may have a straight nose and brown hair, but one of its members may have a pug nose, another black hair). Cf. Pierre-Alexandre Fradet, "Entretien avec Rafaël Ouellet: le néoterroir au cinéma," *Spirale*, no. 250 (fall 2014): 37; *Philosopher à travers le cinéma québécois. Xavier Dolan, Denis Côté, Stéphane Lafleur et autres cinéastes* (Paris: Hermann, 2018), 93.

4 The photographer, not the filmmaker, her cousin of the same name.

5 Gilles Deleuze, *L'Image-mouvement* (Paris: Éditions de Minuit, 1983), 173–7.

6 Joachim Lepastier, "Les pas de Côté," *Cahiers du Cinéma*, no. 66 (October 2010): 79.

7 Pierre-Alexandre Fradet, "Entretien avec Rafaël Ouellet: le néoterroir au cinéma," 37–8.

8 Pierre Barrette, "Le refus du monde," *24 Images*, no. 149 (October–November 2010): 69.

9 Anonyme, "Soirée offerte à la presse. La photographie vivante," *La Poste*, 30 December 1895.

10 Denis Côté, "Elle a pleuré à la discothèque," *Nouveau Projet*, no. 3 (spring–summer 2013).

11 A "magister" in French is a schoolmaster and, figuratively, a pedantic or dogmatic person who professes the Truth. Julien Gracq, "Note," in *La Littérature à l'estomac* (Paris: José Corti, [1950] 2018), 74. In this pamphlet, Gracq, one of the most important French novelists of the twentieth century, analyzes the situation of post–World War II literature. His verdict is that there is a crisis of the novel, due to many factors. One the reasons is what he calls the "bonne presse" (good press, from a Catholic publisher who worked in the field of catechism and religious propaganda), by which he means "edifying" literature, be it Catholic or extreme leftist. He opposes these "thesis" novels, whose militant contents dominate any other consideration, and advocates for "individual literature," which concentrates on the form. It is not about creating a pleasing, inoffensive, and apolitical literature, but about making sure that thoughts and engagement in the world pass through singular, original work on the form or signifier. The untranslatable expression "à l'estomac" means to do something with audacity, courage, and, why not, a little bit of impudence.

6

Fluid Privilege

Reading "Canadian" Water in *Wet Bum* (2014) and *Sleeping Giant* (2015)

Jennifer VanderBurgh

Films often communicate culturally specific ideas. This chapter makes the case that although close reading seems to have fallen out of fashion as a method of engaging with films, it has value as an approach that can identify and articulate taken-for-granted ideas that circulate in national contexts. After the millennium, Canadian film criticism has resisted making generalizations about Canadian film. It has also resisted using "Canadian" as a descriptive term. Arguably, these are good developments that account for the diversity of Canadian films and reflect a healthy skepticism of the opinion that shared approaches and perspectives exist among a diverse group of filmmaker-citizens. While scholarly accounts of Canadian cinema have historically resisted totalizing discourses, in the first decade of the twenty-first century, the "national cinema" or "two solitudes" (English Canada/Quebec) approach that had dominated discussions about "Canadian film" from the 1970s to the 1990s was replaced with a more expansive conceptualization of "film in Canada."

Jerry White's edited collection, *The Cinema of Canada* (2006), for example, presented a triangular metaphor to account for "three distinctive cinematic traditions" in Canada that were identified as anglophone, francophone, and Aboriginal (now Indigenous).[1] While on the one hand, this framework usefully expanded Canadian cinema's traditional categories from two to three, the collection also self-reflexively acknowledged the limitations of its framework to account for other kinds of sub-national or hyphenated groupings of films and to reflect the actual identifications of the filmmakers that it represented. Notably, Atom Egoyan's preface to the collection points out that while the idea of Canada having three main cinematic traditions may be historically accurate, the "assumption of Canadian identity" as a "triangular reality" is "problematic."[2] Particularly with a mind toward representing Canadian cinema's future, Egoyan specifically wonders where immigrant filmmakers fit within a triangular conceptualization of Canadian cinema tradition, a question that could also apply to queer-, region-, gender-, and class-identified artists. Taking issue with the triangular model presented, Egoyan explains that he prefers Tom McSorley's metaphor of the cinematic hydra to conceptualize Canadian cinema, a creature whose proliferating heads evokes a concept that can both represent and adapt to Canada's changing cinematic complexities.[3]

As a more diverse articulation of Canadian cinema was developing, discourse leading up to the millennium also reflected a growing awareness that Canadian films were increasingly being shaped by micro- and transnational influences. Following the influential work of scholars such as Arjun Appadurai on the cultural anthropology of globalization, it came to be understood that Canada's cinematic hydra reflected proliferation not just in terms of filmmaker identifications, but also in terms of the range of industrial modes and genres of production it encompassed, its transnational and micronational funding structures (such as co-production agreements and tax credit programs used to augment Telefilm and Canada Council funds), and its increasing trans-medial distribution platforms.[4] All of these factors destabilized the primacy of a national framework for thinking about cinematic production in Canada, and raised the question, what did it mean to make a "Canadian" film?

While mining films for national essentialisms should remain a relic of the twentieth century, the opposite presumption, that films are expressions of freewheeling individual subjects or of groundless international markets, is arguably a twenty-first-century interpretive risk. Given the instability and erosion of "the nation" as an interpretive framework for cinema after the millennium, this chapter considers what, if anything, films that are made in Canada can collectively express. To what extent can films after the millennium be considered products of national environments? In what follows, I contend that while films can no longer be thought to speak of "Canada" or of "Canadian cinema" per se, they can still be considered to reflect located perspectives that are tied to particular places and lived experiences that are determined by national policies and strategies.

In what follows, I explore this idea by reading two post-millennial, "Canadian" coming-of-age films that are made in different parts of

Ontario, and deal thematically with how characters negotiate their agency and identifications in relation to water. I argue that both the treatment of water and the concept of fluidity-as-agency in these films is tied to specific and socio-economic understandings of place that, at least to an extent, are nationally determined. While neither film deals with cinema as such, the films' arguments about their characters' engagements with their identities and locations via water can be extrapolated to think about how cinematic expression is also inevitably (if inadvertently) tied to located experiences of place.

Wet Bum and *Sleeping Giant*

Wet Bum (Lindsay MacKay, 2014) and *Sleeping Giant* (Andrew Cividino, 2015) are two Ontario-based first features that present divergent and gendered approaches to water. *Wet Bum* (international title *Surfacing*) is shot on the outskirts of Toronto in southern Ontario.[5] It uses a suburban swimming pool as a location through which to express the contradictions inherent in protagonist Sam's female coming of age. Protected, chlorinated, and controlled, the community pool is a space where Sam receives both empowering lifeguarding lessons and incapacitating social bullying. The hard, tiled, physical and social spaces of the pool deck and changing room are contrasted with Sam's feelings of freedom in the water of the pool, a womb-like environment in which she experiences temporary transcendence through the sensations of floating, swimming, and diving. Unwilling to expose herself to others in the changing room for fear of ridicule, Sam wears her wet bathing suit under her clothes. While Sam refuses to shed her bathing suit as an assertion of control, the water seeping from her bathing suit, visible through her clothes, also evokes the involuntary urination of early childhood and the menstruation of early adolescence. In this way, water is used in the film to explore issues of agency and embodiment, as well as involuntary projected signs of female adolescent development.

Whereas *Wet Bum*'s suburban pool-based water metaphors for female adolescence are floating, swimming, leaking, and seeping, *Sleeping Giant* compares the threshold of male adolescence to a leap off of a tall, jagged cliff on the shores of Lake Superior. Shot in the communities of Shuniah and Thunder Bay in northwestern Ontario, the film's climactic event is a dangerous jump into water. *Sleeping Giant*'s portrayal of water as a metaphor for male adolescence is framed as a reluctant dare between cousins, and binary choice between stasis and the need for change.

At the same time that *Wet Bum* and *Sleeping Giant* present gendered differences in their portrayals of water as a metaphor for adolescent coming of age, viewed alongside other notable representations of water in postmillennial Canadian films such as *Atanarjuat: The Fast Runner* (Zacharias Kunuk, 2001) or *Water* (Deepa Mehta, 2005), their portrayals of water seem remarkably unified in expressing white, middle-class anxieties about adolescence that are primarily concerned with achieving personal agency and entitlement. In viewing the films' representations of water through the lens of ethnicity, class, and environment/region, we might consider the implications of the films' use of (clean, warm, unlimited, recreational) water to represent (middle-class, white) millennial experience as a "universal" struggle, and reframe it as an inadvertent expression of privilege.

Wet Bum

Wet Bum is a coming-of-age film about Sam, a fourteen-year-old girl, at a threshold stage of development. Water in this film is used as a metaphor for Sam's ambivalence about transitioning from childhood to adulthood. The film's opening sequence establishes the centrality of water to the film's narrative. It opens with a long shot of Sam, who stands fully clothed on the deck of an indoor swimming pool, looking despondent, facing the camera and addressing it directly. The words "Deep Area" are framed above her, suggesting a figurative connection between the physical space of the pool, and Sam's felt experience of emotional depth and existential angst. Sam's presence, standing at the water's edge, dressed in her outdoor clothes that echo the blue-grey colours of her surroundings, also suggests a connection between the physical space of the pool and Sam's personal struggles.

Throughout the film, the water of the pool, as Sam experiences it, suggests a womb-like, embryonic environment. Warm, highly controlled, and protected by lifeguards (one of whom is her brother), Sam appears to feel a sense of ease when she is submerged beneath the water. This idea is first introduced in the opening sequence in a moment of magical realism when Sam calmly closes her eyes, leans back, and instead of falling on the pool deck, appears to float suspended over the surface of the pool in her street clothes. Match cuts from this shot of Sam's body suspended in mid-air transition to shots of two elderly bodies, floating in similar positions, but in different settings, and who are later introduced in the film as residents of the retirement home where Sam works as a part-time cleaner. The seamless transition between

Figure 6.1   Water as metaphor in *Wet Bum* (2014).

Sam's youthful body and two senior bodies floating in the same position suggests that Sam's transition into adolescence is intended to be representative of broader commentary the film is making about the anxiety of life transitions.

Sam's body rotates and plunges feet-first into the pool. With a match cut on action and a costume change to a bathing suit, Sam now appears underwater. No longer in the magical realist mode, the duration of this shot, exaggerated in slight slow motion, emphasizes Sam holding her breath, a figurative representation of waiting or pause. Throughout, the film accounts for Sam's desire to be underwater by presenting the view that change is emotionally disruptive and unpleasant. This happens in many ways, but perhaps most obviously when, ten minutes into the film, Sam's classmate reads aloud from Mary Shelley's *Frankenstein*, that "nothing is as painful to the human mind as a great and sudden change." This passage, where Victor reflects on his wife's death at the hand of his creature, uses water imagery to explain his experience of pain. Sam's classmate reads from Victor's account that "tears streamed from my eyes. The rain had ceased for a moment, and I saw the fish play in the waters as they had done a few hours before; they had then been observed by Elizabeth." Being underwater appears to bring Sam relief from the suffering that she experiences as a girl maturing from childhood to adulthood. On land, Sam reinforces the emotional affect of this transition. In an effort to be left alone in her room, Sam cries out, using the poignant double entendre, "I'm changing!"

The built environment of the swimming pool where Sam takes lifeguarding classes expresses her ambivalence about transitioning to adulthood. It does this first by contrasting Sam's experience of the embryonic conditions of the pool water with the hard, slippery surfaces of the pool deck and the socially abusive conditions that are waiting for her at the end of each class in the girls' locker room. While Sam experiences water as a safe space – a place that supports her as she floats, and through which she can propel herself with confidence – on land she is characterized as a fish out of water. Not yet as physically mature as the other girls in her class, Sam avoids their ridicule in the changing room by refusing to expose her body to them, bucking convention by wearing her wet bathing suit under her street clothes. In this sense, Sam, quite literally, refuses to change. *Wet Bum* refers to this gesture in its title, since after her lesson, wearing her swim suit under her work uniform, Sam goes about her duties while water seeps out from under her clothes.

On the one hand, Sam's "wet bum" suggests fluids of adolescence – menstruation, and acknowledgment of newfound sexual excitement for her lifeguarding instructor – but it also maintains a connection with the idea of childhood. As one resident of the retirement home remarks, "it looks like you peed your pants." Indeed, the presence of Sam's wet bum and wet hair in the retirement home indicates her desire to maintain a connection to the pool-as-womb even outside of that environment, and suggests an unwillingness to mature. The nature of Sam's cleaning job at the senior's home further ties her to the pool, as she cleans the apartments with spray bottles filled with water.

At the pool and at work, Sam is visually tied to umbilical objects. A cord on a pay phone where she calls her mom and a cord on the vacuum cleaner that she uses to clean the retirement home are aspects of mise-en-scène that reinforce Sam's reluctance to mature. Sam also repeatedly refuses her instructor's request to graduate her swim stroke – to do the crawl in her swim practice rather than her preferred underwater breast stroke. As Sam's lifeguarding instructor reminds her, refusing to leave the breast (stroke) and graduate to the crawl will prevent her from moving faster in water, graduating the course, and maturing to the next level of her swim practice.

In *Wet Bum*, clean water imagery and the culture of the pool are used to represent points on Sam's journey toward maturity, which ultimately has her exiting the pool and transitioning from her cautious womb-like state. Her first experience of sexual desire with her lifeguarding instructor has Sam literally playing the victim, lying prone on the pool deck while her instructor demonstrates how to revive her by breathing into her mouth. At a party a few weeks later, held at a subdivision under construction – a housing development in a state of adolescence – Sam allows the same instructor to blow smoke into her mouth. Replacing life-giving air with drugs and desire, Sam moves toward initiating and inviting sexual experimentation. Ultimately, when the same lifeguard refuses Sam's wishes to "slow down" and attempts to rape her, Sam finds confidence in using her own voice to assert the pace at which she feels comfortable proceeding. No longer timid, or playing the drowning "victim," Sam learns that maturity, like water, is not a straight path, but fluid in nature. In learning how to navigate her maturity, Sam has the newfound agency to decide the pace at which she would like to move. When back in the pool, Sam swims over to her would-be rapist – doing the front crawl as instructed – and drags him into the pool, knowing that this defiant gesture will result in her failing the course.

Sleeping Giant

In *Sleeping Giant*, water features differently. Rather than a pool set in a suburban community, the film's featured body of water is Lake Superior, the largest in surface area of all freshwater lakes. As in *Wet Bum*, water is a constant presence in the film, but rather than characters finding solace by engaging with it, in *Sleeping Giant*, water is depicted as a site of challenge. Filmed in summer, and in good weather when the water appears to be welcoming and still, the lake's seemingly neutral presentation is deceptive. Throughout the film, wide establishing shots of the film's teen protagonists on the shore make use of scale to suggest a relative disparity between the size of the lake and the agency of the characters. Measured against each other, the lake visually dominates the teens, each of whom negotiates their existence in relation to the complex economic and social space that the lake provides.

Sleeping Giant is set in Shuniah, Ontario, a thirty-minute drive from Thunder Bay.[6] The film tells the story of three fifteen-year-old boys who are brought together by circumstance one summer as unlikely and strained companions. Nate is a troubled local who lives with his grandmother and has difficulty passing school. Riley, whose dad committed suicide, is visiting Nate, his cousin, for the summer. Adam, the film's main protagonist, is a bored, seasonal vacationer from the city. In their triangulated relationship, Riley is the go-between, torn between his loyalty to Nate and his attraction to Adam and his economically privileged family from away.

Water, in this film, is characterized as a complex site: as a vacation spot, and as a determining factor in the region's divided economy. The film's depiction of calm water becomes a slippery metaphor, evoking a sense that the location can be experienced as an inviting and welcoming environment for summer vacationers, but which can also be experienced as static and oppressive for the area's year-round residents. The connection between water and the idea of immobility is established in the film's introductory shots of a crumbling grain elevator and a single lake freighter, which remind the viewer of the booming economy that was once facilitated by the lake and its use as a trade pathway. In this sense, still water is a metaphor that conveys a sense of the region's economic austerity.

Adam's dad, as a privileged vacationer, is one character who has agency in relation to water. For pleasure, and with a cooler of beer, he glides across the surface of the lake in his speedboat, past islands that he claims are uninhabited. Using the community for its views and summer fun, his behaviour is not considered neutral, and he is characterized to a degree as a predator. Extreme close-ups of his eating mouth frame his consumption as violent and grotesque, particularly when he eats lake trout that is sold to him by a local fishmonger who makes her living from the lake, and with whom he is having an affair. In this way, Adam's dad is characterized as duplicitous and predatory in extracting his amusement from the location in summer, then returning to his home in the city.

The only other character who has a degree of agency in relation to water is Brad, the local drug dealer. On land, Brad sells drugs to kids out of his trailer without wheels – a vehicle that goes nowhere, but that functions as an island of debauchery in the community that allows Brad to marginally eke out a living. Brad's dealing affords him a certain degree of agency in the form of an aluminum boat with an outboard motor. Not as fast or fancy as Adam's dad's, Brad's boat has trouble starting, but it allows him to get out on the lake and take the kids to Todd's Cliff, the iconic location where Brad became the only person ever to survive the 120-foot jump into the water. While a videotape recording provides evidence of the feat, the teens debate the event's significance. While Nate refers to Brad as "a legend," Riley initially feigns interest, but ultimately minimizes the event, insisting that he just "jumped off of one fucking cliff." From Brad's point of view, the event offered a moment of transcendence, of flying like an eagle, and claims that it is not often that "people get the opportunity to prove something" like he did that day.

While Brad and Adam's dad have vehicles that get them out on the water, Adam, Nate, and Riley are aligned with the land. The boys are

Figure 6.2 The Sleeping Giant framed in the distance.

frequently depicted in wide shot at the shoreline, which makes them appear small in relation to the lake that laps gently at their feet and disappears over the horizon. Out of boredom or frustration, the boys often react to the lake's banal and constant presence in their lives with violence, attacking it by hurling rocks, golf balls, and fireworks at it. In one instance, the boys beat a dead seagull at the water's edge with a stick. By jumping into the lake from cliffs, they pierce the water with their bodies at high speed. The lake, however, easily absorbs these moments of violence, which appear to have no lasting effect on the environment that they perceive to be restricting them.

Perpetually framed across the water in the distance is a rock formation known as the Sleeping Giant. While the formation is never named in the film, Sleeping Giant, which is also known as Nanabijou, is a rock formation that resembles a reclining figure who appears to lie sleeping with hands folded on his chest. With no explanation in the film of the actual Indigenous (Ojibwe) knowledge that the landmark represents, Sleeping Giant, framed with the boys in the foreground, becomes a symbolic projection of their adolescent frustrations and anxieties. Dominating the landscape, the Sleeping Giant suggests both dormant power and a threshold time of adolescence before transitioning to the wakefulness and consciousness of adulthood. The Sleeping Giant is also a dominant formation on the landscape that is made out of rock cliffs. Looming in the background, it is a constant reminder of the physical challenge that the boys will inevitably encounter.

As a dare that becomes an act of solidarity, and as a statement that "something has to change," Adam looks on as Nate and Riley eventually follow in Brad's footsteps and jump into the lake from the top of Todd's Cliff. While Nate and Riley both initially appear to have survived the fall, the celebration is short lived. Nate quickly succumbs to internal bleeding, the result of his impact with the water. Despite the fluid appearance of the lake water, Nate, the one teen of the three who is a year-round resident, experiences it as a hard surface that kills him. Importantly, Nate is not motivated to jump because of hubris. Unlike Brad, he does not expect to fly. Nate jumps reluctantly and with foreboding only after Riley goes over the edge, insisting that the jump is necessary to bring about change. Whether or not the film intends to comment on Nate's class and place-based economic agency, it is interesting that Nate is the one incapable of making a transition.

After a night of processing Nate's death, Riley and Adam sit at the water's edge. The final shot of the film is positioned behind the boys, who are pictured looking out over the water in despair. In the morning light, the Sleeping Giant is framed between their heads and shrouded with mist. Now a figure on the horizon that is more suggestive of death than transition, the formation continues to assert its prominence over the landscape.

Place-Based Understandings of Water

Wet Bum and *Sleeping Giant* both use water as a way of exploring ideas about adolescence as a time of transition. While each film presents a gendered approach to its framing of water, both films present discourses that use water as a vehicle for exploring the agency of their characters. Arguably, these are specific, place-based understandings of water, since this connection between water and human agency is not understood or experienced universally.

In both films, water is portrayed as a clean, plentiful resource that is freely available for its characters to use. This, of course, is not a universal or even a universally "Canadian" idea. While the United Nations passed a resolution in 2010 that recognized drinking water as a human right, in 2016, Human Rights Watch reported that despite Canada being "one of the wealthiest" and "water-rich" countries in the world with "18 percent of the world's fresh surface water," drinking water advisories exist for 134 water systems, ninety in the province of Ontario.[7] Clean water advocate Maude Barlow reported in the *Globe and Mail* that "First nations homes are 90 per cent more likely to be without running water than the homes of other Canadians."[8] As a CBC news article framed it, "discrimination against First Nations people is a 'legal fact' in Canada when it comes to safe drinking water."[9] Add to this what Cameron Fioret calls the "advent of the commodification and privatization of water," and the result is an experience of water accessibility that is causing "strife and inequality amongst the most marginalized people in society."[10]

My point in mentioning this is not to somehow blame *Wet Bum* or *Sleeping Giant* for neglecting issues of water inequity, which is not the films' concern, but simply that it is not a neutral gesture to depict water as a plentiful medium for self-expression. Doing so inevitably marks the films as reflecting particular kinds of located, lived experiences in relation to others. Neither neutral or universal in their representation or address, both films arguably reflect discourses about water that are connected to long-standing legacies of Canadian governance. While these films don't claim to speak for Canada, they also can't help but speak about Canada, however inadvertently.

Considering that both films represent adolescence as a site of struggle, their representation of water-as-environment has political implications. Although these teen characters experience adolescence as emotionally tumultuous, their privilege is signalled, in part, by being surrounded by environments that are receptive to their bodies. In *Wet Bum*, the water of the pool is highly regulated and controlled to be receptive to Sam, even though her experience of the social space that surrounds it is strained. In *Sleeping Giant*, water is presented in summer when it is at a comfortable temperature for human bodies to experience. If characters experience discomfort in relation to water, it is because of a decision they have made. The extreme example is Nate's jump into water, which results in his death. A milder example is when the group of teenagers experience discomfort because they have plunged into the lake after having warmed themselves in a sauna. In this example, their experience of "cold" water is sought out as a momentary thrill. Compare this portrayal of water that is receptive to human bodies to the iconic, postmillennial scene from *Atanarjuat: The Fast Runner* (2001) of Atanarjuat running naked and barefoot across the ice. Here, the vulnerability of Atanarjuat's body in relation to frozen water has high stakes and presents an actual threat to his life. In contrast, when Sam's clothes are taken from the pool deck by the mean girls in *Wet Bum*, she simply picks up the phone and calls her mom.

While considered globally and contextually, both films present relatively privileged positions of being-in-the-world. At the same time, they also include small moments that reflect on their characters' privilege. In *Wet Bum*, Sam's moment of awakening comes when she is taken down a peg by Ed, a resident of the seniors home, who tells her, "you're a little brat who doesn't realize she's not the centre of the world." In *Sleeping Giant*, Nate tells Adam, the vacationer from the city, that there's something that "pisses him off" about him, but he's not sure what. As characters whose defining metaphor for their adolescent development is swimming in a pool, or being adjacent to a lake, water for Sam and Adam reflects the fluid nature of their agency and subjectivity. For both characters, water is a medium that supports their personal development. *Wet Bum*'s closing sequence, for example, features references to Sam in its closing song lyrics, that "the world rests on her shoulders ... she has a fear of flying, a fear or crashing down." The lyrics' advice to "just let it ride" implies that success (i.e., "flying") is as simple as not worrying about failure. This experience, one expects, is the global exception, not the rule.

Deepa Mehta's *Water* (2006) is one postmillennial Canadian film that presents a very different understanding of water than *Wet Bum* and *Sleeping Giant*. Water in this film is not tied to individual subjectivity, but rather to a communal understanding of shared everyday practices that are simultaneously related to both life and death. The film's understanding of water is linked to its setting at a widow's ashram next to the sacred Ganges River in Varanasi, India.[11] Water in this film is a complex signifier that brings relief in the form of rain and refreshment, as well as threat and death. The river is a site where "fleas and sins" are "washed away," where people wash clothes, and pray. It is a place where Kalyani, the main character, experiences her first kiss and also drowns. It is a threshold space that separates the houses of the rich from the poor, and where people must "learn to live like a lotus, untouched by the filthy water it lives in." This sentiment presents a different, place-based understanding of water, which relies less on what it can do for the individual subject than on its centrality in negotiating community relations.

Conclusion

In asking the question, what does it mean to be *from* somewhere after the millennium, the answer, as presented in these films, appears to be that it depends on who the person is and where they are from. In this sense, place still matters to the interpretation of film. Individual negotiations with water in *Wet Bum* and *Sleeping Giant* reflect specific place-based engagements that reveal ideas about the nature of citizenship and human agency – engagements with the world that can't be abstracted to a universal idea of "Canadian experience," but are arguably, and particularly, found in Canada. We might think of these films as being symptomatic artifacts that use the metaphor of water as a medium to think through the concept of identity.

While the experiences and ideas represented in *Wet Bum* and *Sleeping Giant* do not extend to all of Canada, they do reflect place-based Canadian experiences. Although totalizing discourses about Canada should continue to be avoided in postmillennial film scholarship, we should also avoid throwing out the proverbial baby with the bathwater. Canadian films, even after the millennium, express discourses of place, which can be understood and made observable through close reading.

Wet Bum and *Sleeping Giant* are two postmillennial Canadian films that use water as a visual aesthetic and figurative analogy to represent struggles that are associated with a particular conceptualization of adolescence and change. I have argued that since these conceptualizations of water and of adolescence are not universal, they can be read as cinematic expressions that also reveal (place-, class-, and identity-based) understandings of the world that are both taken for granted and ideological. These understandings are not unique to one place, and can be read as ways of seeing that help us to observe and articulate how art presents located views of the world.

Notes

1. Jerry White, "Introduction," in *The Cinema of Canada*, ed. Jerry White (London: Wallflower Press, 2006), 3.
2. Atom Egoyan, "Preface," in *The Cinema of Canada*, xiv.
3. Ibid.
4. A key text that outlines these trends is David Pike, *Canadian Cinema since the 1980s: At the Heart of the World* (Toronto: University of Toronto Press, 2012).
5. *Wet Bum*'s credits indicate that the film was shot on location in Guelph, Dundas, Ancaster, Stoney Creek, and Toronto, Ontario. It was funded by national and provincial funding bodies: Telefilm Canada and the Ontario Film Development Corporation.
6. *Sleeping Giant*'s credits indicate that the film was funded by national and provincial sources: Telefilm Canada, Canada Council for the Arts, Ontario Arts Council, and the Northern Ontario Heritage Fund Corporation.
7. Human Rights Watch, "Make It Safe: Canada's Obligation to End the First Nations Water Crisis," 7 June 2016, https://www.hrw.org/report/2016/06/07/make-it-safe/canadas-obligation-end-first-nations-water-crisis.

8 Maude Barlow, "'Do You Have Running Water? I Don't and I Live in Canada,'" *Globe and Mail*, published online 28 July 2011, updated 3 May 2018, https://www.theglobeandmail.com/opinion/do-you-have-running-water-i-dont-and-i-live-in-canada/article588465/.

9 CBC News, "Canada Violates Human Right to Safe Water, Says Report by International Watchdog," published online 7 June 2016, updated 11 June 2016, https://www.cbc.ca/news/canada/thunder-bay/human-rights-water-first-nations-1.3619218.

10 Cameron Fioret, "We Need Grassroots Activism to Ensure Water Access," *The Hamilton Spectator*, 9 January 2019, https://www.thespec.com/opinion-story/9117140-we-need-grassroots-activism-to-ensure-water-access/.

11 *Water* (2005) identifies as an Indo-Canadian film, and as a Canada/US co-production.

7

Toronto's New DIY Filmmakers

David Davidson

> If you're serious about doing anything it shouldn't be easy.
> Matt Johnson, "Interview with Cinephile Directors," *Toronto Film Review*, 21 July 2015

The Toronto DIY Filmmakers label is used to describe a regional development of grassroots initiatives among a new generation of Toronto filmmakers. Propelled by developments in digital filmmaking, they were able to put forward original narrative work about their experiences, engagement, and perceptions of the city. The label's emphasis is on the *do it yourself*, which is tied to the filmmaker's impulse to create work regardless of permission or the necessity to follow the lengthy and time-consuming steps to access state-subsidized media funding. The two proposed models for this approach are Matt Johnson and Kazik Radwanski, who created and encapsulate many of its recognizable qualities: a focus on outsiders, a style that is a hybrid between documentary and fiction, and a reticence towards state legitimization.

How the two filmmakers differ is important: Johnson's work is funny and engaged with popular culture, blending Toronto's comedic stand-up scene and independent music tradition. Radwanski's work is more social and meditative, more in line with contemporary art cinema trends and film festival curation. These differences are significant because of how prescriptive institutional discourses have since addressed the topic of the role of Canadian cinema. If it appears that there is more legitimate currency in independent Canadian film – via grants, programming allotments, and prizes – for social naturalist films and the administrative skills to acquire funding, how Johnson and Radwanski avoid these pitfalls is significant. Johnson's model with *nirvana the band the show* is one of joyousness and popular ambitions, while Radwanski's project with his Medium Density Fibreboard Films (MDFF) screening series remains one of grassroots community-building. Both Johnson's and Radwanski's success and public visibility has led to an emerging generation of young Canadian filmmakers breaking through and receiving more funding, programming, and media attention. This is why the Toronto DIY Filmmakers label is best viewed as a fluid entity rather than as a fixed idea. Its path and future are still open. It is up to this generation of filmmakers and the following ones to decide its trajectory.

The years between 2007 and 2013 can be seen as the emergence of the Toronto DIY Filmmakers movement. Though not without resistance, this period, through the short films and other works that were made, laid down the aesthetic and production framework for the feature films that would follow, like *Amy George, Tower, Krivina, Everyday Is Like Sunday, The Dirties, The Oxbow Cure, Sleeping Giant, Diamond Tongues, How Heavy This Hammer, The Waiting Room, Operation Avalanche, Never Eat Alone*, and *Fail to Appear*. This period is the start of a paradigm shift that has slowly opened up new possibilities of funding, production, distribution, promotion, and exhibition for these young filmmakers. These early years are decisive, and worth exploring to gain a better understanding of the circumstances that led to its creation. The present chapter will help define the four main characteristics of the Toronto DIY Filmmakers: a youthfulness and emergence into the Toronto film community, a desire to create and not be stifled by bureaucracy, a focus on new Toronto narratives told in a novel manner, and a resourcefulness and control of the means of production. This will be done by focusing on the movement's early years and addressing its originating impulse and context, looking at its predecessors and the groundwork laid in local film production schools, considering its oppositional qualities, and finally offering remarks on its possible direction.[1]

The origin of the label "Toronto DIY Filmmakers" comes from a special issue of *Cahiers du Cinéma* from September 2011 which featured (and labelled) a new generation of New York City filmmakers as *la génération do it yourself*. In its opening essay, Stéphane Delorme and Nicholas Elliot write: "The time is right to bring together these filmmakers from rather diverse trajectories – from which there are born New Yorkers and immigrants, autodidact cinephiles and former NYU students, traditional filmmakers and video artists. The cinema from New York is as diverse as the city that it emanates from … But if the films don't resemble each other, they still share the impression of being *Made in New York* due to their *homemade* qualities. The films are made in the filmmakers' own homes or in their neighbouring streets, are self-financed or made with the help of friends or online acquaintances."[2] The featured dossier included interviews with Ronald Bronstein, Josh and Benny Safdie, Ramin Bahrani, and Alex Ross Perry, who were representative of New York City's emerging independent film community.

In this period, there was also renewed filmmaking activity in Quebec. With Xavier Dolan and Jean-Marc Vallée at the forefront, Quebec filmmakers started to receive more festival programming slots, funding opportunities, and media attention.[3] Some of the more respected film magazines were starting to publish feature dossiers on the developments coming from the province. *Cahiers* featured a dossier on québécois cinéma with essays on Dolan's *Les amours imaginaires*,[4] Denis Côté,[5] and a general overview by Jean-Pierre Sirois-Trahan, "La mouvée et son dehors: Renouveau du cinéma québécois."[6] The Montreal film magazine *24 Images* had a special issue on the "Renouveau du cinéma québécois" (Rebirth of Quebec Cinema).[7] So the term "Toronto DIY Filmmakers" emerged to describe a similar rise of filmmaking activity taking place in Ontario's capital that was on the cusp of breaking out as its principal figures would soon start to make feature-length films.

A Generation with No Models

Matt Johnson reflects on the isolation he experienced as an emerging film production student in relation to the Toronto film industry during this period:

> There was no generation right above us. And the previous generation included people like Atom Egoyan and David Cronenberg. All of the Toronto New Wave filmmakers were already old and irrelevant with their best work behind them, and everybody knew it. So, there was no one to be hopeful about, no one to look up to and say, "I want to be like that person ..." It was tough to determine what was success, because there was the system and the industry, which was closed off. And you wouldn't want to be a part of it, because the work that was being made was completely irrelevant. That goes from film to television. And outside of that there was nobody working in the independent world that was doing anything interesting at all.[8]

Johnson's statement gets at some of the paradoxes of Canadian cinema in the new millennium: the Toronto film industry, which is perceived as the centre of English-Canadian cinema, is dismissed out of hand as

Figure 7.1 Left to right: Matt Johnson, Matt Greyson, Andy Appelle, Matthew Miller (back), Jared Raab, and Owen Williams on the set of *Operation Avalanche* (July 2014).

being irrelevant and uninteresting. The statement reaffirms that the Toronto film industry's initiative to participate in a global market ended up isolating itself from an emerging generation of Toronto film production students while simultaneously not being susceptible to periphery activity.

Though Johnson's claims might be somewhat unfair about the state of Canadian cinema in the new millennium – Canadian cinema has never been mainstream and its most interesting work is usually made at its margins, as TIFF's Canada's Top Ten, which started in 2001, can attest – his main point still rings true: there was a gap between the type of work an emerging generation of film production students admired and wanted to make, and the type of work that film schools and the industry were expecting from them. For Johnson, who was then taking film production courses as an undergraduate student at York University, there were no models. For Johnson, and the Toronto DIY Filmmakers, there needed to be new approaches that would be more in touch with the evolving media landscape to create exciting work in and about Toronto.

It Didn't Happen Overnight: Precursors

> The term *Independent* is quite useless, especially in this country where there is no studio system to be independent from ... The enemy of the would-be outlaw filmmaker lies first in themselves, and in the timidity of the community and industry in thinking there are rules they must follow. There ain't.
>
> Bruce McDonald, from his special Outlaw Edition of *Cinema Canada* (1988)

There were precursors leading up to the public acknowledgment of the Toronto DIY Filmmakers. As the above Bruce McDonald quote indicates, the term "independent" is harder to define in a Canadian context than it is in an American one. McDonald, in his own way, had contributed to an adventurous and renegade filmmaking culture in the eighties and nineties. By the early millennium this energy seemed to have stalled. But there were signs of innovation in English-Canadian cinema in the new millennium before the rise of the Toronto DIY Filmmakers. There were some quasi-independent Toronto films that had been moving into this direction. The precursors for the Toronto DIY Filmmakers included the in-between generation of filmmakers that came after the Toronto New Wave. Film school peers and filmmaker models would also be very important.

The three most relevant Toronto filmmakers of the in-between generation prior to the Toronto DIY Filmmakers were Simon Ennis, Daniel Cockburn, and Nadia Litz. Ennis had worked with Radwanski at Revue Video on the Danforth and had made some short films dating back to 2005, and a feature, *You Might as Well Live*, in 2009. Ennis would also make a documentary, *Lunarcy!*, in 2012, before going to work with Ron Mann. *You Might as Well Live* is a commercial comedy about a slacker played by Joshua Peace (who had a small role in Radwanski's *Assault*), who, after suffering from depression, decides to change his life. Daniel Cockburn is also an interesting case. In 2010, his first feature, *You Are Here*, played at TIFF before receiving a theatrical release at the newly opened Bell Lightbox. The film's trailer featured a positive quote from Atom Egoyan (who Cockburn would go on to profile in a short documentary for the NFB). It is a detective puzzle film full of intellectual non-sequiturs set in a purposefully geographically made-up Toronto. *You Are Here* would also receive a positive review in the Toronto film magazine *Cinema Scope* whose fall cover of that year went to Denis Côté's *Curling*.[9]

Cockburn's film starred the acclaimed Canadian actresses Tracy Wright and Nadia Litz. Litz was a successful actress whose career dates back to the mid-nineties. She had already played a myriad of roles in such works as *Due South*, Jeremy Podeswa's *The Five Senses*, and Reginald Harkema's *Monkey Warfare*. Litz fought to challenge the boring stereotype of English-Canadian cinema through her youthful and adventurous roles before making a DIY feature, *Hotel Congress*, in 2014 through Ingrid Verninger's 1K Wave project. She went on to make the big-budget film *The People Garden* (neither of these films is set in Toronto). These three filmmakers represent a changing and alternative approach to making Toronto films in the new millennium, and as such should be seen as precursors to the DIY Filmmakers.

But perhaps a better network of confluence for the Toronto DIY generation took place at the level of peers from film production schools and filmmaker models. According to Kazik Radwanski, "In film school, the industry is your cohort."[10] In the Ryerson film production program he would meet an important collaborator, the co-founder of MDFF and his producer Dan Montgomery. During their time at Ryerson, from 2004 to 2008, their professors included James Warrack, Michael Conford, Brian Damude, and Alex Anderson, who are all described as being encouraging of their artistic practice. During their program they made *Assault* in third year, *Nakuru Song* that summer in Africa, and *Princess Margaret Blvd.* in their fourth year. There they met the cinematographer Daniel Voshart (who filmed *Tower*) and editor Ajla Odobasic (who has worked on all of Radwanski's films).[11] Other peers included Jacquelyn Mills (*In the Waves*) and Brandon Cronenberg (*Antiviral*), who were also included in the 2008 TIFF Student Showcase. That is where Radwanski and Montgomery first met Antoine Bourges, who at the time was studying film production at the University of British Columbia, and would go on to join MDFF. The peers who met at film festivals would have the biggest and most direct influence on this generation of filmmakers. They would soon form a group and through these connections acquire a better understanding of how film festivals functioned; it was also the start of relationships with programmers and critics.

For Radwanski and Montgomery, it was by attending festivals that they started to understand the economy that they were participating in. Radwanski had three of his short films play at the Berlin film festival from 2008 to 2010: *Princess Margaret Blvd.*, *Out in That Deep Blue Sea*, and *Green Crayons*.[12] These were in the short film competitions and were taken seriously as they were contextualized in a longer cinematographic tradition. For Radwanski, "Seeing a Canadian film in this European context was pretty exciting. It felt like the stakes were higher."[13] For Montgomery, the festival circuit "got us thinking about audiences, and who would be interested in our types of film,"[14] and it led them to be comfortable working outside of the Toronto commercial film industry. According to Bourges, there is a dilemma after you graduate: "If you find work in the industry after film school, it's then harder to make your own films on the side. It's draining and time-consuming. So, I would rather have a part-time job and make my own work."[15] In this period, Radwanski worked for his uncle's construction company, Montgomery at the documentary company White Pine Pictures, and Bourges for the artist Jeff Wall in Vancouver from 2008 to 2012, before moving to Toronto.

An early filmmaker model that Radwanski regularly cites is Denis Côté. They first met in 2009, the year *Carcasses* played at TIFF after it had premiered at the Directors' Fortnight in Cannes.[16] Radwanski says of *Carcasses*, "It was exciting to see a Canadian film in that context, next to a Pedro Costa and a Lisandro Alonso film." In 2009, Radwanski also met Igor Drljača, Albert Shin, and Nicolás Pereda, who were from York University, as they had short films in the same program. Drljača is noteworthy, as a first-generation immigrant filmmaker, for setting his films in both his native Bosnia and Toronto. Pereda was also a good model: he had a minimalist and efficient approach and regularly premiered his new films at international festivals. At York there was also Luo Li, Hugh Gibson, Chelsea McMullan, and Simone Rapisarda; and in Montreal there was Brian M. Cassidy and Melanie Shatzky. So, the year 2009 is important because through these connections Radwanski would form a peer group that was both supportive and constructive. The group would also provide a useful model as they were prolific filmmakers who were fostered by more restrained Canada Council funding. They gave Radwanski confidence that his films could also exist in the film festival ecosystem.

Johnson has positive memories from his time at York University, though he had a more rebellious response towards the production model that was being proposed. Johnson's experience in film school was also formative in specific ways, notably through what he learned about film production and film studies in the courses offered by the professors John McCullough, Tereza Barta, and Steve Sanguedolce. Johnson remembers having to watch a lot of old films, many by the European masters, including discovering for the first time such classics like *Citizen Kane*, *The Wizard of Oz*, and *Nobody Waved Good-bye*. From these films he discovered the importance of personal resonance in the filmmaking process. Some collaborators from York that he would keep on working with include Jared Raab, Matt Greyson, Josh Bowles, Evan Morgan, and Josh Schonblum. Raab speaks highly of his peers Joyce Wong, Dusty Mancinelli, and Lindsay MacKay. There was also at York the yearly CineSiege undergrad student showcase, which goes back at least to 2003, and was important in uniting the different cohorts.

Johnson started out by making home movies and early film school projects.[17] He describes a noteworthy student film and what he was like back then: "we had to work on 16mm film. I made two films on this stock. One was a time-travel movie that starred my brother who sent radio signals into the past. In first year, I would always do that kind of stuff, joke around. I wasn't sure what to do. I was an immature idiot, but it was a good place to start."[18] Johnson's first noteworthy project was the original ten-episode *nirvana the band the show* web series and its extra-textual website and videos, which was made in close collaboration with its co-star Jay McCarrol and cinematographer Jared Raab. Then came Johnson's first feature *The Dirties* (2013), a high school shooting comedy, which really benefitted from his new producer Matthew Miller, who would go on to help him make his next film *Operation Avalanche* (2016) and the television show *nirvanna the band the show* (2017–18).

Miller was important as a peer and model who contributed a lot to the success of his and Johnson's production company, Zapruder Films. Miller graduated from York a few years earlier in 2003 and had made an independent feature, *Surviving Crooked Lake*, with his peers Sascha Drews and Ezra Krybus. Raab had volunteered on its post-production, which is how they had met. The key technological development that Miller highlights is the digital revolution; in contrast to analogue, it greatly changed the accessibility of filmmaking as it allowed for more improvisation and the possibility for mistakes. Filmmaking would now be a lot more manageable and affordable. This would help tear down economic barriers. This greatly influenced the *cinéma vérité* style that Johnson used. Miller is also the reason that Johnson submitted *The Dirties* to Slamdance after *Surviving Crooked Lake* had already played there. He would also bring some other core contributors from his time teaching at Humber College to Zapruder Films, such as Andrew Appelle, Curt Lobb, and Robert Hyland.

This was also a period when the visibility of emerging and visiting professor filmmakers was changing. Miller started to teach film production classes and then so would Johnson. This represented a shift in the types of guests that would visit undergrad production classes. They were

Figure 7.2 Dan Montgomery (left) and Kazik Radwanski.

no longer directors of Canadian television, but a younger and brasher generation that had a lot of things to say. Students in Toronto film production schools would soon find someone more relatable and would start to think that they could do this too.[19] Since then this tendency has only increased.

An Oppositional Cinema

Radwanski describes the hand-made, artisanal quality of his work in relation to the reasoning behind naming the production company Medium Density Fibreboard Films in 2007.[20] At Ryerson there was a debate between filming on analogue or digital. Deriving their production company's name from medium density fibreboard was their answer to this. All of their work was digital, and the company name conjured images of large sheets of synthetic material that, if properly used, could be really effective.[21] For Radwanski and Montgomery, the importance of having a production company was that it enabled them to package and promote their films while also identifying them with a particular aesthetic project. The production company became empowering as they could make the films that they wanted to and have the self-determination to not get stuck in development. This contrasted with the situation of some of their peers, such as other respected short film directors of their generation, who would get trapped in development which could last up to five years – and then their film would still not turn out as they would have liked.[22]

Radwanski also explains the reasoning behind the company name in relation to his family's construction background, and in particular his uncle's construction company; he sees his resourcefulness and independence as coming from his Polish side.[23] Construction is a motif throughout much of Radwanski's work, from *Assault* (2007), *Tower* (2012), *Cutaway* (2014), and *Scaffold* (2017). Radwanski likens his production model to a small construction crew: it is the idea of having a filmmaking practice that is sensible and practical. This was against the idea of some classmates who wanted to work with the bureaucracy of larger crews and increased funding. Radwanski preferred having smaller crews that benefitted from being able to afford more time for actual filmmaking, working on his own schedule, and having more time to work with his actors. It was the idea that filmmaking should be able to work around permits or only get them strategically. Through this model Radwanski learned his creative strengths.

Radwanski's work would be a collaborative process where a film would come to life through the process of filmmaking and working with the actors. At first, Radwanski's cinematographer was Dan Voshart (who first started working on *Princess Margaret Blvd.*), who helped define his style, but he now continues with Nikolay Michaylov, who has shot the more experimental short films *Cutaway* and *Scaffold*, the feature *How Heavy This Hammer* (2015), and *Anne at 13,000 ft* (2019). But Ranwanski and Montgomery see their production model as less oppositional and instead more pragmatic. They see their practice not so much as being against the industry, but more as an adaptation to their surroundings. The subjects, characters, and stories that they like to tell just come from the things that they know about, and their low-cost solution was just a logical response rather than a reaction to Telefilm. They have come to understand how their films are more in line with art-cinema practices, which Radwanski learned about from his time working at a video store. They are happy working on a smaller scale if they can keep their independence and find a place for their work in film festivals and cinematheques rather than on the business side of the industry.

In contrast, Johnson seems to revel in the excitement of breaking the rules: "Part of the thrill of making *nirvana the band* was that it was illegal. For every episode we tried to respond to what we heard in film school: you can't make this. Same thing with *The Dirties*."[24] The do-it-yourself approach involved getting away with ideas that were not supposed to be possible or legal: this included filming strangers on the streets, not having permits, and infringing on copyright material. If Radwanski's approach was more sensible and was used as a model to hold onto independence, for Johnson it was more about finding cracks in the system that could be exploited so that his work could stand out. This was in opposition to what he perceived to be the very controlled and rigid model that was already in place in the larger Toronto film industry. For example, the idea of *The Dirties* came from Josh Bowles's idea for Johnson to star in a remake of *Man Bites Dog* inspired by the Columbine shooting.[25] This, Johnson thought, was everything that was *not* being promoted in film schools.[26]

Johnson's filmmaking philosophy was "You go out with a camera and just film stuff. Just like kids in high school, which was the philosophy I was coming from. Shoot stuff and then figure it out later."[27] The idea of being more efficient with just a small and independent group of close friends is a shared characteristic between Johnson and Radwanski. For Johnson, this means having worked with Raab on all of his projects and regularly working with Jay McCarrol (the star of both *nirvana* and *nirvanna*, with a small role in *The Dirties*, and composer of the score for *Operation Avalanche*) and Owen Williams (*The Dirties, Operation Avalanche*). Johnson is loyal to the original guerrilla filmmaking idea behind the *nirvana* web series, which he brought to its reboot and his subsequent films. Johnson's resourceful methods include improvised stories, a rough plan, and filming a lot and then fixing up the story during the editing process. But at the same time, he was still able to grow and evolve with each new project as he added more people to the team when others left.

Many of the skills that Johnson would use early in his career would be developed and refined with each new project, especially appropriating fair use copyrighted material and filming in public. Johnson's production model was making films about neophyte filmmakers making their own films. Johnson likes to compare this approach to software design and its idea of turning bugs into features, as developed by Guy Kawasaki, Jonathan Blow, and Mark Rosewater. Johnson explains: "Taking the things that make you bad and then turning them into what makes you stand out."[28] For Johnson this meant taking what could be considered the drawbacks of independent student filmmakers – poor writing and dialogue, off-kilter performances, and limited resources and locations – and using them as assets. His use of textual poaching is also reminiscent of what Henry Jenkins has described as the converge culture of fan fiction.

Reaching for the Moon: *Operation Avalanche* and *How Heavy This Hammer*

Both Radwanski and Johnson are now in their thirties. Both of their production approaches – mixing documentary with fiction, independent and lengthy productions – continue into their present work and affect their narratives and style. For Radwanski, in *Tower* and *How Heavy This Hammer*, this means being able to step back and address unpleasant topics such as crisis, uncertainty, and inarticulateness. Their economic independence gives them the freedom of longer production periods that allows them to really get to know and work with their actors. This is this case with *How Heavy This Hammer*. The film tells the story of Erwin, who is unhappy in his marriage and retreats to the virtual world of computer games as he avoids any form of personal responsibility. The film is about the grey and miserable parts of life. The expressive depth of its lead actor Erwin Van Cotthem, in its extended scenes of inarticulateness and depression, has been described by Radwanski as only being possible by his process: through filming he is able to figure out what story he is going to tell. *How Heavy This Hammer* examined the placid and mundane quality of living in an unwelcoming Toronto. And it would find a public; both the Toronto and Berlin film festivals featured the film where it received good reviews, before it travelled to many other festivals and received positive reviews in publications like *Cinema Scope* and the *Globe and Mail*.

Johnson, since *The Dirties*, has gone on to make *Operation Avalanche* and two new seasons of *nirvanna the band the show* for Viceland. He describes how the process of making the films taught him to extrapolate from his original production model to the legal norms of industrial filmmaking. *Operation Avalanche* could be seen as a real breakthrough film for Johnson; shortly before its premiere at Sundance he gave an especially critical interview in *Now Magazine* where he denounced the complicity of Canadian film programmers and critics for supporting middling Canadian content. *Operation Avalanche* was Johnson's MFA thesis film from York, and it is quite incredible that it premiered at such a prestigious American film festival. It also received distribution from Lionsgate Films, an anomaly for contemporary independent Toronto films. It is a historical fantasy that stars Johnson (like in everything else that he does) as a CIA agent who needs to break into NASA to stop a Russian mole and eventually to fake the moon landing (he even recruits Stanley Kubrick to help him out). The film was well received and played in the United States to a positive *New York Times* review. But what is noteworthy is how Johnson used his position to be a vocal proponent for low budget filmmaking in Canada. He publicly criticized the bloated budgets and spending of Telefilm, whether on their expensive feature-length films or co-productions, all the while overlooking first-time filmmakers and their access to resources. Johnson publicly criticized them, sometimes violently, until they capitulated: Telefilm ultimately adapted its policies to include a welcome new Zapruder-initiated Talent to Watch program in 2018 (which was formerly their micro-budget production program) that had the goal of helping emerging and diverse voices make their first feature-length film. This program offered many grants to emerging filmmakers. The nomination process is directly tied to film schools and co-ops.

Conclusion

> I want to enlist your support to persuade Robert Lantos to produce my next and probably last film, *Coitus Interrupted* ... I know the characters are interesting and the material is rich and the story entertaining with a pretty lively last act. I sure would be grateful for a little help in bringing my work to an honourable conclusion. As for my talent, it is not only intact but greatly enriched by the work I have done as a painter and on my own inner life; I see more vividly and I'm more open and alert than ever.
>
> Don Owen, letter to David Cronenberg and Atom Egoyan, from an unrealized screenplay folder at the TIFF Film Reference Library

As this letter from the late Canadian filmmaker Don Owen suggests, the history of Canadian cinema can be quite cruel. The quotation is from a 2001 letter to Atom Egoyan and David Cronenberg, requesting their aid to help him finance a possible last feature film. The script of *Coitus Interrupted*, which is available at the TIFF Film Reference Library, is full of love and excitement, melancholy, and the troubles of everyday life. Spanning different time periods, the film is a documentation of how Toronto has changed over the last twenty-five years, and through the character of the ailing patriarch there is an impression of Owen dealing with his own mortality. But finally, what makes the script for *Coitus Interrupted* so great is its rich portrait of its characters and the celebration of life. In the archive there are no responses to Owen's letter; the film was never made. This is just one example of how the filmmaking industry in Canada has not sustained its talented filmmakers. It should be seen as cautionary sign, as there are countless other Canadian filmmakers who were not given the opportunity to blossom due to limited resources and an unsupportive infrastructure.[29]

Hopefully the Toronto DIY Filmmakers receive more luck. But as Johnson says, in the quote that opened this essay, "If you're serious about doing anything it shouldn't be easy." This is a great reminder that it is a lot of hard work to develop a movement and it demands perseverance. The accomplishments of the Toronto DIY Filmmakers are already a positive sign of how things are changing. MDFF and Zapruder Films are now closer to being institutional then when they began; it's exciting to see their model being used and adapted into a more institutional framework. It is a good sign of how the system can change. Neither Radwanski nor Johnson is holding back in his work, as they continue to be as lively and ambitious as ever. For example, the two-part season 2 finale of *nirvanna* took months to be released due to the ambition of their rule-breaking (stealing from a museum display at the ROM) that caused them many legal problems. Radwanski's latest feature was in the works for almost four years before it premiered at TIFF in September 2019.

It is useful to imagine this generation of Toronto DIY Filmmakers as a group, as a fluid entity readily able to grow and adapt. Prospective film students and filmmakers could share a DIY ethos and be freed from the constraints of the system and the industry. Within the Toronto film community these filmmakers are becoming public figures, creating conversations and confrontations, and hopefully increasing the stakes and overall quality of Canadian cinema in the new millennium. While the norm is to imagine this generation of filmmakers divided – all in competition for the shrinking programming allotments and funding opportunities – seeing them as part of a larger entity allows for the possibility of them benefitting from their position as a collective. The new Telefilm initiative Talent to Watch had the goal of supporting up to fifty projects by emerging directors each year. The changes in how media is funded, produced, exhibited, and distributed make it seem like a new frontier in Canadian media is being opened. There should be more risk-taking and original stories told throughout the film community. The lesson from the Toronto DIY Filmmakers is that there are still stories to tell, adventures to be had, and problems to overcome. And it is happening in Toronto. Its ethos is to imagine victory, instead of succumbing to defeat.

Notes

1. This research was aided through interviews with the two main production companies, Zapruder Films and MDFF. The author met with Matt Johnson, Matt Miller, and Jared Raab, and then with Kazik Radwanski, Dan Montgomery, and Antoine Bourges in early April 2018.
2. Stéphane Delorme and Nicholas Elliot, "À la rencontre de la nouvelle scène new-yorkaise," *Cahiers du Cinéma*, no. 670 (September 2011): 65. My translation.
3. For more about Dolan and Vallée, see Robinson's chapter in this volume.
4. Jean-Philippe Tessé, "Love, etc.," *Cahiers du cinéma*, no. 660 (October 2010): 72–3.
5. Joachim Lepastier, "Les pas de Côté," *Cahiers du cinéma*, no. 660 (October 2010): 79.
6. Jean-Pierre Sirois-Trahan, "La mouvée et son dehors: Renouveau du cinéma québécois," *Cahiers du cinéma*, no. 660 (October 2010): 76–8.
7. *24 Images*, no. 152 (June–July 2011). For more about the rebirth of Quebec cinema, see Sirois-Trahan's chapter in this volume.
8. Interview with Matt Johnson, Jared Raab, and Matt Miller (Zapruder Films), April 2018.
9. Adam Nayman, "The Antisocial Network: Daniel Cockburn's You Are Here," *Cinema Scope*, no. 44 (fall 2010): 10–13.
10. Interview with Kazik Radwanski, Dan Montgomery, and Antoine Bourges (MDFF), April 2018.
11. The cinematographer Rich Williamson was part of this and so were the Casey brothers (Lyndon, Dillon, Conor).
12. Alongside Bourges's *Woman Waiting*.
13. Interview with Radwanski, Montgomery, and Bourges.
14. Ibid.
15. Ibid.
16. Radwanski had received a screener of *Carcasses* from Adam Nayman who had positively reviewed *Princess Margaret Blvd.* in *Eye Weekly*. The Directors' Fortnight was then still being programmed by Olivier Père; Père would go on to program *Tower* at Locarno.
17. For the only public example of this side of Johnson's oeuvre there is *Lhotsky and Fisher: Honolulu Blue* from 2004, which is hidden on *The Dirties* DVD.
18. Interview with Johnson, Raab, and Miller.
19. Ibid.
20. At first their production company was only named MDF Productions, but in 2008 they discovered that there was already an MDF Productions in Toronto, so they changed it to MDFF.

21 There is a good special feature video on the MDF Trilogy DVD, which is made out of medium density fibreboard, where you see Radwanski and Montgomery working to create them.
22 MDFF interview.
23 Ibid.
24 Zapruder interview.
25 Another film that Johnson has cited that he wanted to use as a model was Peter Watkins's *Edvard Munch* for a proposed John A. Macdonald biopic.
26 York would be quite appreciative and supportive of Johnson and the Zapruder team: Kuowei Lee, the graduate program assistant, for a long time had a *The Dirties* poster on his office door. York sponsored a really nice launch of *Operation Avalanche*, Johnson's graduate thesis film, at CineCycle.
27 Zapruder interview.
28 Ibid.
29 Most notably John Paizs and his film *Crime Wave* from 1985 or other historical figures like Sidney J. Furie, who could not develop an industry in Toronto so had to move abroad, as would many others.

8

Northern Frights

Canadian Horror in the Twenty-First Century

Murray Leeder

In 2000, the Canadian horror novelist Edo van Belkom edited *Northern Horror* for Quarry Press's "Canadian Fiction" line.[1] In his introduction, van Belkom speaks to the relative legitimation of Canadian science fiction and argues that it is now horror's turn. Though his focus is on literature, van Belkom briefly mentions David Cronenberg as a Canadian horror icon.[2] Van Belkom says:

> If you think that because of their subject matter the stories assembled here are not worthy of being considered CanLit, count how many of them deal with such classical CanLit themes as survival and the search for identity.
> This is Canadian Horror.
> This is CanLit.[3]

The Giller Prize nomination for David Demchuk's *The Bone Mother* (2017), published by Canadian horror specialist ChiZine Publications, would seem to signal increasing willingness to embrace horror literature on the part of CanLit's tastemakers. Perhaps the same revolution of legitimization is underway for Canadian horror cinema, since the zombie film *Les Affamés* (2017) was nominated for Best Picture at the Canadian Screen Awards – though the most prominent Canadian horror films of recent decades (e.g., *Ginger Snaps* [2000], *Pontypool* [2008], and *Splice* [2009]) have received a smattering of nominations at best. The version of Canadian cinema championed by the likes of Katherine Monk as "challenging, cerebral, ambiguous, and decidedly offbeat films"[4] leaves relatively little space for horror. With the major exception of Cronenberg – often treated as an entity relatively unpinned from the generic traditions in which he works – Canadian horror has inspired only a few concerted scholarly treatments.[5] For instance, the major role of Canadian productions in the initial slasher film cycle has only received belated attention,[6] in part because films like *Prom Night* (1980) and *My Bloody Valentine* (1981) deliberately take place in non-specific North American locales.[7]

Nonetheless, horror has been a thriving business for the Canadian film industry. Most any horror subgenre has had its Canadian incarnations. Vampires? *Thralls* (2004), *La peau blanche* (2004), *Bloodsuckers* (2005), and *Suck* (2009). Zombies? *Fido* (2006), *Sick: Survive the Night* (2012), and *Ahockalypse* (2018). Ghosts? *11:11* (2004), *The Marsh* (2006), *They Wait* (2007), and *The Last Will and Testament of Rosalind Leigh* (2012). Found footage horror? *Grave Encounters* (2011), *Grave Encounters 2* (2012), *Crowsnest* (2012), and *Afflicted* (2013). Torture? *Live Feed* (2006), *The Chair* (2007), *Tortured* (2010), and *Les 7 jours du talion* (2010). Slashers? *Ripper* (2001), *Spliced* (2002), *Left for Dead* (2007), and *Girl House* (2014). Ecohorror? *Something Beneath* (2007), *The Thaw* (2009), and *Devil in the Dark* (2017). Nor is horror regionally bound: beyond the predictable hubs of Toronto, Montreal, and Vancouver, there have been horror films made in Winnipeg (the extensive *Maneater* series for Syfy Channel, *Wishmaster 3* [2003], and *The Editor* [2014]), Calgary (*Scar* [2007], *Kept* [2012], and *Red Letter Day* [2019]), Saskatchewan (*The Messengers* [2007], *Grace* [2009], and *Stranded* [2013]), Nova Scotia (*The Corridor* [2010]), Newfoundland (*Lovely Mummers* [2018]), Nunavut (*Slash/Back* [2021]), and even Northern Alberta (*The Corrupted* [2010]).

The twenty-first century has also seen the advent of Canadian production companies emphasizing horror (Foresight Features from Collingwood, Ontario, Winnipeg's Astron-6, Vancouver's Luchagore Productions, Toronto's Black Fawn Films, Ottawa's Brook Street Pictures), and a number of Canadian horror specialist directors like Jeff Barnaby, Vincenzo Natali, Cody Calahan, Adam MacDonald, David DeCoteau,[8] Lee DeMarbre, Roger Boyer, B.J. Verot, Maurice Devereaux, Jon Knautz, Jovanka Vuckovic, and the Soska sisters. There have also been dalliances with horror material by established Canadian directors like Guy Maddin (*Dracula: Pages from a Virgin's Diary* [2002]), Thom Fitzgerald (*Wolf Girl* [2001]), and Bruce LaBruce (*Otto, or, Up with Dead People* [2008] and *L.A. Zombie* [2010]). In addition, a number of foreign directors associated with horror have operated in Canada, including George A. Romero (a Canadian citizen from 2009 until his death in

2017), Guillermo del Toro, and the notorious Uwe Boll. There are also a plethora of Canadian horror co-productions, including *Silent Hill* (2006), *Martyrs* (2008), and *Ghostland* (2018) with France; *Pact with the Devil* (2004) and *Stranded* (2013) with the UK; *American Psycho* (2000), *Land of the Dead* (2005), *White Noise* (2005), *Orphan* (2009), *Lords of Salem* (2012), *Horns* (2012), and *The Witch* (2016) with the US; *The Moth Diaries* (2011) with Ireland; *Wolf Girl* with Romania; *Ang Pamana: The Inheritance* (2006) with the Philippines; and many, many more.[9]

This chapter traces some key developments in Canadian horror in the twenty-first century. It will discuss how Indigenous filmmakers have challenged and complicated narratives of Canadian horror, as well as the role of authorship since David Cronenberg backed away from the genre. It also identifies comedic and "cosmic" horror as strengths for Canadian cinema. Throughout, it will pay attention to the topic of legitimation: the increased recognition of Canadian horror in both academic and more popular realms in recent decades, to the point where horror is becoming increasingly difficult to ignore as a key product of the Canadian film industry.

The Wilderness Within, the Wilderness Without

What makes a horror film culturally, as opposed to institutionally, Canadian? The documentary *Nightmare in Canada: Canadian Horror on Film* (2004), produced for The Movie Network (TMN), is overtly recuperatory and celebratory. Its premise, articulated early on, is that neither Canadian film audiences nor horror fans pay enough attention to the specifics of Canadian horror films. So, what are those specifics? Through the documentary, interviewees position Canadian horror films as cerebral and character-driven, tending to be based around isolation, dread, and the wilderness. Their low budgets drive innovation, and they reinvent familiar archetypes in new and refreshing ways. Again and again, it is suggested that Canadian horror films resist American/Hollywood cinema's reliance on special effects, formula, and moralizing, and yet they often try to pass (with limited success) for American. The fact that *Nightmare in Canada* cannot seem to quite decide whether Canadian horror is shallow, pandering, and disposable or rich and intellectual is revealing in itself: Canadian horror is too diverse and varied for easy definition.[10]

Nightmare in Canada also implicitly evokes what has been more explicit elsewhere: the association of Canadian horror with the Northrop Frye's "garrison mentality," especially as explicated in Margaret

Atwood's *Survival: A Thematic Guide to Canadian Literature* (1972). In the introduction to their collection about Canadian horror cinema, Gina Freitag and André Loiselle propose "a theory of the Canadian horror film that locates the 'terror of the soul' in the interval between external threat and internal dread."[11] The idea surfaces in more popular criticism as well: an article appearing in the *National Post* shortly before Halloween in 2018 uses an Atwoodian framework to claim *Black Christmas* (1974) as "the quintessentially Canadian story" in which the apparent threat from without is actually *coming from inside the house*.[12] Of course, it's debatable whether the interplay of internality and externality and a dread of the wilderness are themes distinct to Canadian horror films as opposed to horror films in general.

Probably the two most acclaimed Canadian horror films of the twenty-first century – certainly those that have drawn the most academic interest – are *Ginger Snaps*[13] and *Pontypool*.[14] The former concerns two teenaged goth outsider sisters in a fictitious Canadian suburb who become infected by lycanthropy; its success led to a sequel, *Ginger Snaps 2: Unleashed* (2004), and a prequel, *Ginger Snaps Back: The Beginning* (2004), making for one of Canada's few horror franchises. *Pontypool* takes place in the real Ontario town of that name and involves a madness-induced apocalyptic contagion that spreads through the English language. Perhaps unsurprisingly, both *Ginger Snaps* and *Pontypool* lend themselves to being read through that Atwoodian approach, as both take place in a location with aspects of both the settled and the wilderness and concern invasion by an external force that quickly becomes internal. Both have also earned international followings among horror fans presumably less invested in their "Canadianness" than their innovative variations on familiar subgenres (the werewolf and zombie invasion film, respectively).

Atwoodian themes of wilderness and survival play out dramatically in *Backcountry* (2014), by actor-turned-director Adam MacDonald.[15] *Backcountry* echoes previous eco-horror films and especially killer bear movies like *Grizzly* (1976), *Prophecy* (1979), and *The Edge* (1997), as well as innumerable "lost in the woods" films, including the Canadian classic *Rituals* (1977). In *Survival*, Atwood wrote: "You'd think that the view of Nature as Monster so prevalent in Canadian literature would generate, as the typical Canadian animal story, a whole series of hair-raising tales of people being gnawed by bears, gored to death by evil-eyed moose, and riddled with quills by vengeful porcupines. In fact this is not the case; fangs and claws are sprouted by mountains and icebergs."[16] *Backcountry* looks to correct the lack of bear-gnawings.

Backcountry begins with young white urbanite Alex (Jeff Roop) taking his girlfriend Jenn (Missy Peregrym) hiking in an Ontario provincial park while deliberately leaving behind both a map and a cellphone. Alex means to propose to Jenn, but by the time she slides the engagement ring onto her finger, he is dead, torn apart by a ravening black bear in an extremely vivid sequence. Early in the film, a park ranger (a cameo by Nicholas Campbell) warns Alex not to go to his destination, Blackfoot Trail, which is closed for the season: "there were some yahoos tramping around there and disrespecting everything. This is a treasured site ... and Parks and Recreation want to keep it that way." The ranger also warns him that they could each be fined if they are found there. Alex ignores this warning and does not tell Jenn about it. Later, he "whitesplains" the meaning of Blackfoot Trail to Jenn: "The local tribes called it that because when the trail ends it circles around this really small lake, and the earth around the lake is black, so when they hunted they followed animal tracks in the black earth and called it 'Blackfoot Trail.'" His authority is quickly undermined when Jenn asks the name of the lake and he admits he does not know it. A distinct loser even by the standards of Canadian film protagonists, Alex responds to the presence of a bear in his camp pathetically by crouching in his tent and trying to wish or pray it away.

Only seen on signs, the fictional setting of *Backcountry* is named "Nibookaazo Provincial Park." "Nibookaazo" is Ojibwe for "he/she pretends to be dead,"[17] a bear-attack avoidance technique that the characters do not attempt. Alex's failure as an outdoorsman is also a failure as a Canadian; instead of finding harmony with the wilderness or mastering it, the wilderness rises up and conquers him. *Backcountry*'s third act is a survival horror film about the badly injured Jenn's attempts to evade the bear and escape. In the end, she follows a caribou that leads her back to the couple's rented canoe, painstakingly paddles across the lake, and ends up passing out in the camp parking lot in sight of a group of tourists. Her fate is ambiguous but certainly is presented as preferable to Alex's undignified death; her untrained instincts mark her as having access to a form of Canadianness superior to Alex's putative expertise.

A subtext in *Backcountry* concerns colonialism, appropriation, and erasure, holding only a bit short of the "old Indian burial ground" trope. Alex is punished for deliberately transgressing a sacred First Nations site, in violation of both Indigenous and white laws; Jenn, relatively innocent of that transgression, escapes the wilderness to reach the nearest outpost of white civilization, the parking lot. First Nations are repeatedly referenced but in vague, allusive ways ("a treasured site," "the

Figure 8.1 Jenn collapses at the end of *Backcountry* (2014).

local tribes" that Alex probably cannot name), with no Indigenous characters appearing. *Backcountry* thus appears to allegorize both the attempted erasure of the Indigenous peoples of Canada, attached to names of places but their meanings lost and twisted, and to rehearse that same erasure. Alex is constructed as a "bad settler" who is horribly punished for his deliberate transgressions, while Jenn is a "good settler" who transgresses out of simple ignorance and thus is spared, with the caribou intervening almost supernaturally to guide her to that Indigenous-derived symbol of outdoorsy Canadianness, the canoe.[18] The film's shift of audience identification towards Jenn implies a "move to innocence"[19] designed to exculpate the general audience of guilt over colonialism.

Canada figures prominently in the increased global presence of Indigenous-made horror films, in which familiar horror themes play out quite differently.[20] Mi'gmaw director Jeff Barnaby's zombie film *Blood Quantum* (2019) takes place on the fictional Red Crow Reserve. This was also the setting of Barnaby's previous feature *Rhymes for Young Ghouls* (2013), a generically mixed work that moves into the representational space of the horror film (the zombie film, especially) to allegorize the real-life horrors of the Indian residential school system. Earlier, Barnaby made the stunning short *File Under Miscellaneous* (2010), in which a Mi'gmaw man (Glen Gould, also of *Rhymes for Young Ghouls*) in a futuristic *Blade Runner*–style dystopian city undergoes a gruesome surgery to be converted into whiteness. The process of cultural assimilation is represented through a body horror idiom, including his tongue literally being ripped out (an echo of Barnaby's earlier short *From Cherry English* [2004]), at which point the Mi'gmaq narration is replaced by English. His tattooed skin is graphically torn away, replaced by an anonymous black suit, and he sits in a hazy theatre watching a huge monitor with an

Figure 8.2 The process of cultural assimilation is represented through a body horror idiom in *File Under Miscellaneous* (2010).

Orwellian giant head – transformed, assimilated, and de-individualized, all ostensibly voluntarily.

The horror genre and the historical horrors of Indigenous experiences in Canada are put together differently in Anishinaabe director Lisa Jackson's short film *Savage* (2009). Set in the 1950s, it shows a young Cree girl in the backseat of a car. She watches the landscape zoom by, obscured by a partially open window. Her transportation is intercut with her mother singing a Cree lullaby in an empty kitchen and growing increasingly distraught. We see brief shots of the girl's hair being cut and of her wearing a uniform in the cold, institutional halls of a residential school. *Savage* plays within the idiom of social realist filmmaking until the following sequence punctures this mode with an intrusion of horror. From the back of a classroom, we see rows of children at their desk with pencils in hand, heads lowered as the teacher writes on the chalkboard. She suddenly leaves the room and a reverse shot shows that the children have pale zombie-like makeup reminiscent of Michael Jackson's "Thriller" (1982) – the first girl we see in close-up has inhumanly blue eyes. Their heads lurch forwards and they hop from their seat and engage in an intricately choreographed dance sequence. At first, they move as a mass, but individual children get "featured" solo routines. At the sound of the returning teacher's footsteps, they return to their seats and continue as if nothing had happened. The short closes with a symmetrical composition of the exterior of the residential school, framed from a low angle like a looming haunted house. As Jackson has explained, the zombie dance simultaneously represents the deadened state of the children as a consequence of residential schooling and provides an expression of resilience and survival.[21]

Perhaps more easily affiliated with science fiction or urban fantasy but invoking similar horror themes is Cree-Métis director Danis Goulet's *Wakening* (2013).[22] It takes place in a dystopian future Canada controlled by a military dictatorship referred to as "the Occupiers." A Cree woman (Sarah Podemski) stalks through a landscape of urban decay carrying both a futuristic gun and a bow, and penetrates a cavernous, ruined theatre where a few patrons are trapped with their feet in bear traps.[23] The theatre is occupied by Weetigo, the fearful spirit of Cree lore, here visualized as a hulking antlered monster; the woman explains that Weetigo does not realize it, but he has in fact been imprisoned there by the Occupiers.[24] After lamenting that its power is diminished since "the forests are all dead," Weetigo soon identifies her as Weesageechak, the trickster hero; though the two are ancient enemies, Weesageechak enables Weetigo's escape, slaughtering two SWAT-like soldiers on the way. In redirecting Weetigo's anger and power against the Occupiers, she is deploying a pre-colonial monster against colonialism itself.

Wakening resembles *File Under Miscellaneous* in its use of a hyper-urban, authoritarian future to comment on the present state of Indigenous peoples under colonialism, and also links with *Savage* in its invocation of monstrosity as a form of resistance. In all three, and markedly in contrast to the Atwoodian model favoured by a film like *Backcountry*, the source of horror is estrangement from the landscape and the cultures and traditions it implies.

An Empty Throne: The Horror Auteur in Canada

One of the institutional advantages of horror films is their ability to find an audience without major stars or a big budget. In the Hollywood of the 1960s, the making of inexpensive horror films became a viable "proof of skill" for emerging filmmakers, even for directors who would not become noted as "horror directors" per se (e.g., Francis Ford Coppola with *Dementia 13* [1963] and Peter Bogdanovich with *Targets* [1968]). It is much the same in Canadian cinema today. A good example is *La peau blanche*, a variation on the vampire film (technically about succubi) replete with commentary on race relations in Montreal. Its director, Daniel Roby, won the Claude Jutra Award for best first feature at the Genies in 2004, and then went on to direct two historical dramas about Quebec history, *Funkytown* (2011) and the highly successful *Louis Cyr* (2013).

Somewhat different is the horror auteur, whose public "brand" emphasizes horror even if he or she occasionally makes films of other sorts (when Wes Craven died in 2015, few obituaries emphasized his lone Oscar-nominated film, the Meryl Streep vehicle *Music of the Heart* [1999]). As mentioned earlier in this essay, David Cronenberg has a singular status in the history of Canadian horror as the "acknowledged" and firmly canonized horror auteur. From the 1970s through the 1990s, Cronenberg reigned as the undisputed "King of Canadian Horror," owing to his unique brand of vivid and visceral yet also intellectual horror. Though often controversial, Cronenberg was an eloquent and thoughtful presence, willing to meet and debate his critics in public forums. His influence on Canadian horror is incalculable; certainly, it is easy to detect his legacy in the fondness for medical/scientific themes and settings that unites films as otherwise diverse as *Sur le seuil* (2003), *La peau blanche*, *Splice*, *Grave Encounters*, *American Mary*, and *The Void* (2016). Yet Cronenberg has increasingly departed from horror, arguably since his move towards more overtly "arty" fare with *Dead Ringers* (1988); his commercial output in the twenty-first century has favoured crime films and dramas. This is not to say that certain of his late-career films, like *A History of Violence* (2005), *Eastern Promises* (2007), and *Maps to the Stars* (2014), lack echoes of his earlier horror films; they continue to work through his authorial preoccupations with embodiment, sexuality, and transformation. But just as surely, he has moved outside of the horror genre as a cultural/industrial entity, abdicating, as it were, that long-held kingship – although *Crimes of the Future* (2022) may change that picture.

Who will claim the throne? The aforementioned Jeff Barnaby is surely staking a claim. Meanwhile, the Cronenberg horror brand continues through his son, Brandon Cronenberg, whose directorial debut *Antiviral* (2012) mixes science fiction, horror, and social commentary. It takes place in a near future where celebrity worship has reached visceral new heights, including restaurants where diners eat the cultured flesh of celebrities and deliberately inject themselves with their diseases. In prime Cronenbergian fashion, *Antiviral* mixes sterile, clinical environments and a plethora of fleshy, abject substances. Eight years later, his sophomore feature, *Possessor* (2020), was another violent and vivid science fiction/horror hybrid; Cronenberg *fils* works within the milieu established by his father but is developing his individual stamp on it.

Another candidate for the definitive twenty-first-century Canadian horror auteur who is also decidedly influenced by Cronenberg is Vincenzo Natali. A dozen years after his well-received debut *Cube* (1997), Natali scored a great success with *Splice* (2009). *Splice* brings the *Frankenstein* mythology of overreaching science into the era of genetic engineering as effectively as any twenty-first-century film, and adds the unforgettable Dren (Delphine Chanéac) to the canon of sympathetic movie monsters.[25] Natali's next feature was *Haunter* (2013), a clever mix of time travel and ghost film that follows the perspective of Lisa (Abigail Breslin), the ghost of a murdered teenage girl in Northern Ontario. Natali has also been an in-demand director of "quality television" series like *Hannibal* (2013–15), *American Gods* (2017–), and *Westworld* (2016–), and directed an adaptation of the Stephen King/Joe Hill novella *In the Tall Grass* (2019) for Netflix, starring Patrick Wilson.

But perhaps the time has come for a Queen of Horror – or more than one. Female-directed horror has been a growing trend worldwide, with Canada making significant contributions. The most prominent are the Vancouver-based twins Jen and Sylvia Soska, who bring a feminist edge to gory, grindhouse-style filmmaking. Their debut was the ultra-low-budget *Dead Hooker in a Trunk* (2009), in which they also starred, distributed by IFC. It was followed by the acclaimed horror film *American Mary* (2012); they subsequently directed the slasher sequel *See No Evil 2* (2014) and the 2019 remake of Cronenberg's *Rabid* (1977). Their key film thus far is *American Mary*, which stars the closest thing to a Canadian horror star, *Ginger Snaps*'s Katharine Isabelle. Mary is a trainee surgeon who, in need of money, falls in with an underworld of radical body manipulation. After being horrifically raped by one of her supervisors, Isabelle's Mary extracts a brutal revenge by transforming him into a living practice dummy for extreme medical procedures. Featuring actual members of the body modification community in small roles, *American Mary* foregrounds its subcultural sensibility while also providing a new spin on the rape-revenge narrative of films like *I Spit on Your Grave* (1978) and *Ms. 45* (1981). The Soska sisters also host the game show *Hellevator* (2015–), produced by American horror specialists Blumhouse Productions, and have authored comic books. The Soska sisters' vivid, confrontational directorial style is matched by their off-screen persona as the "Twisted Sisters," on display in many provocative photo shoots where they often appear clutching chainsaws and swords or smeared with fake blood.

Another Canadian horror director to emerge in the twenty-first century, Jovanka Vuckovic, has had a notably different career trajectory. An award-winning visual effects artist, she went on to spend six years editing the Toronto-based horror culture magazine *Rue Morgue* before directing the impressive short *The Captured Bird* (2012).[26] Produced by no less than Guillermo del Toro, *The Captured Bird* features gorgeous cinematography that mixes formal elegance and terrifying imagery. It shows a young girl in a white dress drawing with chalk on a stone walkway, even as her parents cradle a new baby. From a crack in the ground, a mysterious black liquid oozes forth, and she is drawn into the fantasy world of a huge Victorian manor. Her experience becomes increasingly horrific as she encounters scores of maggots piling out of a drain and then a tentacled monster. As with many of del Toro's films, *The Captured Bird* is perched between fantasy and horror but veers starkly to the latter by its end. As the girl flees from five hovering insectoid aberrations that have suddenly manifested, she claps her hands over her eyes, rather like Danny (Danny Lloyd) in *The Shining* (1980). The suspenseful music drops off on the soundtrack, replaced by tinkling reminiscent of a music box. The implication is that she will be spared from further terrors by imagining them away. But as she begins to peek through her fingers, a reverse POV shot shows the monster still hovering before her. She screams and we see no more of her, but the hideous creatures continue to stalk the house before flying out in a rosy landscape as a cacophony sounds. Lavish and gorgeous in its visual aesthetic despite its disturbing content, *The Captured Bird* seems to announce the arrival of a major talent. Vuckovic went on to contribute a segment to the American horror anthology film *XX* (2017) alongside four other female directors, and made her feature debut with the alternate history gang film *Riot Girls* (2019).

Other female Canadian horror directors include Mary Harron (best known for *American Psycho*, Harron later directed the vampire film *The Moth Diaries*), Karen Lam, Patricia Chica, Nyla Innuksuk, and Maude Michaud. Women-directed horror films are a trend across the world at present, and Canada has proven to be key to that development. Due to the degree to which it has expanded, Canadian horror cinema is not likely to again be dominated by a single auteur's name and sensibility. Cronenberg's empty throne is not waiting to be filled but has been fractured – to the genre's overall benefit, as countless distinct voices emerge instead.

The Comic and the Cosmic

Two other trends in Canadian horror bear examining; one is very old and the other fairly new. The first is the blending of horror and comedy. Horror scholarship in general often ignores or outright disparages horror-comedy, favouring horror that is grim and serious.[27] In Canada, horror-comedy has a lengthy history, going back at least to Ivan Reitman's early feature *Cannibal Girls* (1973). In the twenty-first century, Canadian horror has produced a host of films that range from gently comedic to full-blown farce. One of the more successful examples is *Fido* (2006) by Andrew Currie. Using the prism of the zombie film to deliver social satire, it takes place in an alternate version of 1950s America where humanity has survived a zombie uprising and now use the dead as domestic labour. Mixing Sirkian melodrama with Romero-esque horror in a campy package, *Fido* has received academic attention for its engagement with patriarchy, race, and conformity.[28] It is not even the only Canadian "zom-com"; others include *Graveyard Alive: A Zombie Nurse in Love* (2004), *Otto, or, Up with Dead People*, *Eddie: The Sleepwalking Cannibal* (2012), and *A Little Bit Zombie* (2012).

A very different sort of horror-comedy film, *Jack Brooks: Monster Slayer* (2007), takes its cues more from the 1980s splatter films, especially the works of Sam Raimi (*The Evil Dead* [1981], *Evil Dead II* [1987]) and Peter Jackson (*Bad Taste* [1987], *Brain Dead* [1992]). The title character is a version of the Canadian loser male protagonist reworked into heroism; Jack Brooks (Trevor Matthews), a "rageaholic" plumber who eventually channels his aggression into fighting colourful monsters, comes off as a kind of lower-grade Canadian version of *Evil Dead*'s Ash (Bruce Campbell). The cheerfully gruesome *Jack Brooks: Monster Slayer* contains the kind of 1980s throwback practical effects that appeal to the nostalgia streak among horror fans and allows horror icon Robert Englund an overtly comic role as the villain, a demon-possessed math professor. Director Jon Knautz followed *Jack Brooks: Monster Slayer* with *The Shrine* (2010), a more serious mix of supernatural horror and torture porn (particularly borrowing from the remote European setting of *Hostel* [2005]), the psychological drama *Goddess of Love* (2016), and the thriller *The Cleaning Lady* (2018).

The Editor, directed by Adam Brooks and Matthew Kennedy of the Winnipeg-based collective Astron-6, pays homage to a different strand of the horror film: *giallo*, the Italian-made horror/thriller cycle of the 1960s and '70s. Though full of gore and nudity, its broad silliness (the characters speak the kind of artificial, clipped English dialogue typical of dubbed *giallo*) makes it impossible to see *The Editor* as anything but a spoof, or perhaps a travesty of Peter Strickland's mind-bending *giallo* homage *Berberian Sound Studio* (2012). Swinging even further into farce is *Jesus Christ Vampire Hunter* (2001) by Lee Demarbre, in which the kung fu–fighting messiah returns to protect Ottawa's lesbians from the ravening undead.

Canadian films have also proved among the stronger entries in the peculiar subgenre of "cosmic" or "weird horror."[29] This ill-defined category draws from the thematic preoccupations of H.P. Lovecraft and the authors who followed him. It tends to dwell pessimistically on the insignificance of humanity in the context of the universe; it deals more with a fear of madness and transformation into the unhuman than with death. Though certain of John Carpenter's films, notably *Prince of Darkness* (1987) and *In the Mouth of Madness* (1994), are often associated with Lovecraftian "cosmic dread," there is a persistent sense that it is a difficult mode for cinema to capture. Yet several Canadian films have taken up the challenge, including *Beyond the Black Rainbow* (2010) and *The Void*, two films united, curiously enough, by the image of an ominous glowing triangle. Directed by Panos Cosmatos, *Beyond the Black Rainbow* is set in an alternate 1983.[30] It concerns a 1960s experimental institute devoted to psychedelic mind expansion that has degenerated into a horrifying medicalized prison for Elena (Eva Allan), a young woman with psychic powers. With its glacial pace, the film presents a science fiction-horror variation on the art house constellation of "slow cinema" – an intoxicating trip that sacrifices narrative momentum in favour of conspicuous style, a repressive modernist aesthetic reminiscent of *2001: A Space Odyssey* (1968) and *Altered States* (1980).

Where *Beyond the Black Rainbow* is oppressively studied and formal, Steven Kostanski and Jeremy Gillespie's *The Void* is more messy and chaotic. It has a rural American setting, with its characters trapped in a remote hospital by rampaging cultists and twisted, trans-dimensional monsters. Like *Jack Brooks: Monster Slayer*, *The Void* can be seen as a piece of 1980s nostalgia horror that leverages practical effects as an authenticating strategy, but its tone is considerably more serious, with a breathtaking finale that offers a glimpse of an alternate universe dominated by a huge black pyramid. Neither comedy-horror nor cosmic horror is precisely Canadian horror's contemporary "brand" – it does not have and perhaps does not need one – but Canadian filmmakers have carved a place in both on the international scene.

The Unapologetic

One could investigate contemporary Canadian horror cinema from countless other angles. These might include the renewed importance of the anthology film format in the twenty-first century, shifting distribution platforms and the role of television, or the role Guillermo del Toro has played as a nurturer of Canadian talent and the significance of his Art Gallery of Ontario exhibit "At Home with Monsters." Fan conventions (including Toronto's Horror-Rama and the Calgary Horror Con) and festivals, like Toronto After Dark, the Rue Morgue Festival of Fear, the Blood in the Snow Canadian Film Festival, Dead North, Northern Frights, the Bloody Horror International Film Festival, and the Fantasia Film Festival, also seem ripe for study.[31] Throughout this essay I have drawn attention to short Canadian horror films – these, whether exhibited alone or in the anthology format, could prove a special topic of interest. One might also draw attention to moments in films of other genres that incorporate horror imagery and themes; for example, the serial killer plotline in *Bon Cop, Bad Cop* (2006) has imagery owing more to *Saw* (2004) than *Lethal Weapon* (1987), and an army of monstrous gang members in the style of *Assault on Precinct 13* (1973) parades through the centre of *Treed Murray* (2001).

One thing that seems certain is that Canadian horror is more voluminous than ever before, and if horror ever truly was on the fringes of the Canadian film industry, it is now close to its core, and becoming more acknowledged as such. In 2018, Adam MacDonald (director of *Backcountry*) published an essay on the official page of the Academy of Canadian Cinema and Television defending the vitality and importance of the contemporary Canadian horror film. MacDonald basically takes the same stance about horror cinema that van Belkom did about horror literature eighteen years earlier: that it *is* Canadian cinema. The essay is titled "No Need to Apologize," and film scholarship ought to take the same attitude where the Canadian horror film is concerned.

Notes

1 Special thanks to André Loiselle, Caelum Vatnsdal, Rhett Miller, Gina Freitag, and Heather Igloliorte for their help with various stages of this chapter. I borrow the name "Northern Frights" from the line of horror anthologies edited by Doug Hutchison.
2 Edo van Belkom, "Canadian Horror Comes of Age," *Northern Horror* (Kingston: Quarry Press, 2000), 8.
3 Ibid., 9.
4 Katherine Monk, *Weird Sex and Snowshoes: And Other Canadian Film Phenomena* (Vancouver: Raincoast Books, 2001), 5.
5 Notably Gina Freitag and André Loiselle, eds., *The Canadian Horror Film: Terror of the Soul* (Toronto: University of Toronto Press, 2015); Caelum Vatnsdal, *They Came from Within: A History of Canadian Horror Films*, 2nd ed. (Winnipeg: ARP Books, 2014); see also Gina Freitag and André Loiselle, "Tales of Terror in Québec Popular Cinema: The Rise of the French Language Horror Film since 2000," *American Review of Canadian Studies* 43,

no. 2 (2013): 190–203; David Christopher, "Discourse of the Damned: On Canadian Horror Cinema," *Horror Studies* 6, no. 2 (2015): 283–303; Scott Preston, "The Bloody Brood: Canadian Horror Cinema – Past and Present," in *The Oxford Handbook of Canadian Cinema*, eds. Janine Marchessault and Will Straw (Oxford: Oxford University Press, 2019), 331–66.

6 Richard Nowell, *Blood Money: A History of the First Teen Slasher Film Cycle* (London: Continuum, 2001), 149–86; Rose Butler, "Faces of Rage: Masks Murderers, and Motives in the Canadian Slasher Film," in *Fashioning Horror: Dressing to Kill on Screen and in Literature*, eds. Gudrun D. Whitehead and Julia Petrov (London: Bloomsbury, 2018), 195–214.

7 The cheap and exploitative horror films of the "tax shelter era" (1975–82) are increasingly being repositioned as objects of valorization, as in Xavier Mendik's documentary *Tax Shelter Terrors* (2017).

8 The highly productive DeCoteau is known as the "undisputed king of contemporary homoerotic horror"; Harry M. Benshoff, "'Way Too Gay to Be Ignored': The Production and Reception of Queer Horror Cinema in the Twenty-First Century," in *Speaking of Monsters: A Teratological Anthology*, eds. Caroline Joan S. Picart and John Edgar Browning (New York: Palgrave Macmillan, 2012), 133.

9 There is also Kevin Smith's curious duo of American-made horror films about Canada, *Tusk* (2014) and *Yoga Hosers* (2016).

10 An understated ghost story with an urban setting, *The Changeling* (1980) fits neatly into almost none of the characteristics ascribed to Canadian horror by *Nightmare in Canada*, and yet it is probably given more time than any other single film.

11 Frietag and Loiselle, *The Canadian Horror Film: Terror of the Soul*, 4.

12 Justine Smith, "More Than Horror, *Black Christmas* is the Quintessential Canadian Story," *National Post*, 21 October 2018, https://nationalpost.com/entertainment/movies/more-than-horror-black-christmas-is-the-quintessential-canadian-story.

13 For a selection of the scholarship on *Ginger Snaps*, see Bianca Nielsen, "'Something's Wrong, Like More Than You Being Female': Transgressive Sexuality and Discourses of Reproduction in *Ginger Snaps*," *Thirdspace: A Journal of Feminist Theory and Culture* 3, no. 2 (March 2004); April Miller, "'The Hair That Wasn't There Before': Demystifying Monstrosity and Menstruation in *Ginger Snaps* and *Ginger Snaps Unleashed*," *Western Folklore* 64, no. 3/4 (summer–fall 2005): 281–303; Sunnie Rothenburger, "'Welcome to Civilization': Colonialism, the Gothic, and Canada's Self-Protective Irony in the *Ginger Snaps* Werewolf Trilogy," *Journal of Canadian Studies* 44, no. 3 (fall 2010): 96–117; Ernest Mathijs, *John Fawcett's Ginger Snaps* (Toronto: University of Toronto Press, 2013).

14 For scholarship on *Pontypool*, see Aalya Ahmad, "Gray Is the New Black: Race, Class and Zombies," in *Generation Zombie: Essays on the Living Dead in Modern Culture*, eds. Stephanie Boluk and Wylie Lenz (Jefferson: McFarland Press, 2011): 130–46; James Jason Wallin, "Representing and the Straightjacketing of Curriculum's Complicated Conversation: The Pedagogy of *Pontypool*'s Minor Language," *Educational Philosophy and Theory* 44, no. 4 (2012): 366–85; Andrea Subissati, "Viral Culture: Canadian Cultural Protectionism and *Pontypool*," in *The Canadian Horror Film: Terror of the Soul*, 30–43; Sharon J. Kirsch and Michael Stanliff, "'How Do You Not Understand a Word?': Language as Contagion and Cure in *Pontypool*," *Journal of Narrative Theory* 48, no. 2 (2018): 252–78.

15 Macdonald's subsequent feature was the supernatural horror film *Pyewacket* (2017), which shares *Backcountry*'s remote Ontario setting and interest in the wilderness as a site of horror.

16 Margaret Atwood, *Survival: A Thematic Guide to Canadian Literature* (Toronto: McClelland and Stewart, 1972), 87.

17 My thanks to Maeengan Linklater for the translation.

18 Bruce Erickson, *Canoe Nation: Nature, Race, and the Making of a Canadian Icon* (Vancouver: UBC Press, 2013).

19 Eve Tuck and K. Wayne Yang, "Decolonization Is Not a Metaphor," *Decolonization: Indigeneity, Education and Society* 1, no. 1 (2012): 1–40.

20 Indigenous directors of horror films not otherwise discussed here include Nyla Innuksuk (Inuit), Roger Boyer (Saulteaux/Ojibwe), Cowboy Smithx (Blackfoot), and Doreen Manual (Secwepemc/Ktunaxa). For more on First Nations horror in Canada, see Gail de Vos and Kayla Lar-son, "Cowboy Smithx's *The Candy Meister*," in *Horror: A Companion*, ed. Simon Bacon (Oxford: Peter Lang, 2019), 175–80. For more on Indigenous horror more broadly, see Joy Porter, "The Horror Genre and Aspects of Native American Literature," in *The Palgrave Handbook to Horror Literature*, eds. Kevin Corstorphine and Laura R. Kremmel (Houndmills, Basingstoke: Palgrave Macmillan, 2018), 45–60.

21 Kristin L. Dowell, *Sovereign Screens: Aboriginal Media on the Canadian West Coast* (Lincoln: University of Nebraska Press, 2013), 112–13.

22 See Salma Monani, "Feeling and Healing Eco-Social Catastrophe: The 'Horrific' Slipstream of Danis Goulet's *Wakening*," *Paradoxa* 28 (2016): 192–213. I am borrowing Monani's spellings of "Weetigo" and "Weesageechak," both names that have been transliterated in a variety of ways. Goulet subsequently made the post-apocalyptic feature *Night Raiders* (2021).

23 Weetigo's prison is "played" by Toronto's Elgin and Winter Garden Theatre, also featured in del Toro's *The Shape of Water* (2017).

24 For more on Wendigo/Weetigo see Shawn C. Smallman, *Dangerous Spirits: The Windigo in Myth and History* (Victoria: Heritage House, 2014).
25 Lars Schmeink, "Frankenstein's Offspring: Practicing Science and Parenthood in Natali's *Splice*," *Science Fiction Film and Television* 8, no. 3 (autumn 2015): 343–69.
26 *Rue Morgue*'s editor prior to Vuckovic, Rodrigo Gudiño, is also a filmmaker, having directed the ghost film *The Last Will and Testament of Rosalind Leigh*.
27 Murray Leeder, *Horror Film: A Critical Introduction* (New York: Bloomsbury, 2018), 106–8.
28 See Michele Braun, "It's So Hard to Get Good Help These Days: Zombies as a Culturally Stabilizing Force in *Fido* (2006)," in *Race, Oppression and the Zombie: Essays on Cross-Cultural Appropriations of the Caribbean Tradition*, eds. Christopher M. Moreman and Cory James Rushton (Jefferson: McFarland Press, 2011), 162–76; Michael C. Reiff, "Better Living through Zombies: Assessing the Allegory of Consumerism and Empowerment in Andrew Currie's *Fido*," in *The Laughing Dead: The Horror-Comedy Film from Bride of Frankenstein to Zombieland*, eds. Cynthia J. Miller and A. Bowdoin Van Riper (Lanham: Rowman and Littlefield, 2016), 187–200.
29 For a discussion of the weird in cinema, see Brian R. Hauser, "Weird Cinema and the Aesthetics of Dread," in *New Directions in Supernatural Horror Literature*, ed. Sean Moreland (New York: Palgrave Macmillan, 2018), 235–52.
30 Cosmatos would later direct the cultish Nicolas Cage revenge movie *Mandy* (2018).
31 See Preston, "The Bloody Brood" (360–2), for notes on many of these festivals.

PART TWO
Documentary and Experimental Filmmaking

9

Beauty Day and the Crises of Self-Directed Work

Mike Meneghetti

Initially received as another entry in the catalogue of Canadian "hoser" films, Jay Cheel's feature-length documentary *Beauty Day* (2011) clearly shares several surface characteristics with cult movies like *Strange Brew* (Rick Moranis and Dave Thomas, 1983) and *Hard Core Logo* (Bruce McDonald, 1996) – continuous beer drinking, idiosyncratic expressions, a focus on hyperactive and comically self-defeating egocentrism, and so on.[1] According to the film's director, however, *Beauty Day* was not conceived or created solely within such a Canadian framework. On the contrary, as he worked in the relative remoteness of Ontario's Niagara Region, Cheel referred instead to American cinematic resources, and *Beauty Day*'s evident lack of interest in positioning itself exclusively as a Canadian work grew naturally from the broader circumstances of its production in 2009–11. Indeed, *Beauty Day*'s indifference to a narrowly imagined Canadian-ness is perhaps more usefully understood in relation to the period's rapidly changing documentary ecologies. The film's frequent allusions to a broad range of American nonfiction and fiction artifacts, for example, speak directly to the increasingly easy availability of assorted audiovisual media at this moment, and Cheel's concurrent work as a podcaster and blogger reveals a corresponding immersion in the era's internet-driven access to movies of all kinds.[2] The attendant flattening of common categories such as "national cinema" or "national culture" is evident in *Beauty Day*'s equivocal investment in Canadian cinema, but more importantly, the film's multiple exchanges with these other resources also inevitably direct it to the widely shared themes and techniques of present-day American documentaries.

Beauty Day describes the volatile professional history of Ralph Zavadil, the creator/star of *The Cap'n Video Show* (1990–95) and a near-mythic figure to the program's lingering band of enthusiasts in the Niagara Region. Essentially isolated in the small city of St Catharines, Zavadil dedicated his local cable program to intentionally unsophisticated – and frequently dangerous – physical stunts for his weekly audiences: the "pool plunge," "rooftop tobogganing," "clothesline skiing," and "instant razor in a bottle" are only a few of these aptly named precursors to *Jackass* and other shows of its kind. In a sense, Cheel's documentary seeks to commemorate Zavadil's TV program by compiling representative moments from *The Cap'n Video Show* and its behind-the-scenes creation. *Beauty Day*'s introductory sequences therefore simply describe Zavadil's decisive escape from the drudgery of factory work and discovery of a self-expressive brand of video-making. In these early passages, spectators are immersed in Zavadil's newfound sense of freedom, and the film aligns itself fully with this figure's subjectivity and experiences as an independent producer.

But *Beauty Day*'s memorial first act, composed mainly of Cheel's archival sifting and present-day interviews with Zavadil, is supplanted by the very different approach of its final movement. *Beauty Day*'s concluding passages strategically deploy a more familiar observational technique, and the film's shift to the style and associated themes of American direct cinema discloses an unexpectedly instructive deliberation on precarious work. As we'll see, *Beauty Day*'s narrative is split between its commemoration of Zavadil's modest historical achievements and a more judicious observation of his chaotic present-day production, and this division is a key to grasping the film's subtle revelations about so-called "creative work" in the contemporary world. Suspended between a summary of Zavadil's self-directed labour in the early 1990s and a more closely observed portrait of its present-day unsustainability, *Beauty Day*'s recourse to the methods and themes of direct cinema ultimately reveals the diminishing rewards and increasing vulnerability of autonomous labour today.[3]

Monotony and Autonomy in *Beauty Day*

Beauty Day's introductory act briefly summarizes *The Cap'n Video Show*'s humble origins in the Niagara Region. Unhappily employed as a millwright at General Motors, Zavadil describes his earliest working experiences in the common terms of alienation: he felt despondent and powerless at GM; his working life was meaningless, and his growing sense of isolation and self-estrangement soon led to periodic bouts of drug abuse and alcoholism. After a liquor-fuelled professional crisis and lengthy suspension by GM in 1989, Zavadil definitively abandoned his factory job for the relative autonomy of small-scale video production, and *Beauty Day*'s opening scenes accordingly narrow their focus to an account of this figure's newly obtained freedom. *The Cap'n Video Show*, Zavadil recalls, immediately became a vehicle for self-expression; it was a salve after so many agonizing experiences at GM, and an escape from the daily strain of his life in St Catharines. During these early segments, the film sifts through a wide range of clips from *The Cap'n Video Show* and combines them with present-day interviews to reveal an invigorating period of creative work and continuous risk-taking. By contrast, *Beauty Day*'s middle section is marked by a series of intensifying catastrophes, both professional and personal. We witness the rapid erosion of Zavadil's autonomy as drugs, alcohol, and a generally dissipated comportment make him an increasingly unreliable television entertainer. A drug-related arrest threatens to derail his career, and his show is abruptly cancelled in 1995 after an ill-conceived stunt involving puppies and chocolate sauce. However, although his work as a self-sufficient producer appears to end with the cancellation of *The Cap'n Video Show*, *Beauty Day*'s empathetic final act chronicles Zavadil's present-day attempts to resuscitate his long dormant video-making practice and create a twentieth anniversary episode for his local cable station. His efforts end predictably in frustration and failure, but the film's generous concluding images establish a fitting – if only fleeting – memorial for *The Cap'n Video Show*'s former existence.

Such a summary of *Beauty Day*'s narrative risks making it appear too diagrammatic. The film's well-worn three-act construction produces an individualized documentary portrait, and it is composed of recognizable crises and resolutions. In this respect, it resembles several popular documentary predecessors: *Crumb* (Terry Zwigoff, 1994), *Grizzly Man* (Werner Herzog, 2005), and most importantly *American Movie* (Chris Smith and Sarah Price, 1999) are all resources for Cheel's envisioning of this "character piece."[4] But *Beauty Day*'s initial intrigue – or rather, spectators' immediate intrigue – with Ralph Zavadil is not derived solely from Cheel's shaping of a familiar character study. On the contrary, the opening act's objective is to provide a commemorative examination of Zavadil's inventive and peculiar possession of his everyday world through *The Cap'n Video Show*; that is, the film's introductory passages focus on the creative mingling of this figure's consciousness with an ordinary environment of limited possibilities, and the resulting

Figure 9.1 *Beauty Day*'s narrative is split between its commemoration of Zavadil's modest historical achievements and a more judicious observation of his chaotic present-day production.

commemoration of Zavadil's subjectivity is also implicitly a tribute to his labour as an independent video producer. In select sequences from *The Cap'n Video Show*, we watch Zavadil transpose the tactile dimension of millwrighting to his unusual brand of televisual production, and in the process, we get to witness his persistent reorganization of a lived relation to the everyday world. *Beauty Day*'s opening act thereby provides perceptible and palpable images of Zavadil/Cap'n Video in various states of work and physical exertion, but more importantly, the film seeks to immerse its spectators in this equation of individualized work with self-realization. In other words, *Beauty Day*'s introductory examination of *The Cap'n Video Show* directs one to an empathetic comprehension of Zavadil's self-sufficiency because it is, at least in the film's retrospective images and interviews, distinct from the daily despair of factory work.

According to Cheel, the main model for Zavadil's conception of the unruly and unsophisticated Cap'n Video character was *Sesame Street*'s Grover: always shouting in a hoarse voice seemingly directed at children, Cap'n Video's energetic approach to his otherwise dangerous physical stunts indicates the pliability and indestructability of a puppet.[5] Moreover, and perhaps more significantly, this general flexibility is complemented by a sense of social ineptitude. Continually ill at ease in his small world (at least initially), Cap'n Video is attentively engaged with the perplexing contents of his house in each of *The Cap'n Video Show*'s sketches. How do people normally eat, shave, ski, or remove the covers from their pools? By contrast, how does the resourceful Cap'n Video do these same things? This inventiveness is what distinguishes Zavadil from near-contemporaries like Tom Greene or Johnny Knoxville. Greene and Knoxville are, like Zavadil, comically unskilled; but Cap'n Video's daily projects demand that he concentrate completely on the world before him and discover a manner for dispatching its objects unpredictably, imaginatively. The emphasis upon tactility in this relation is fundamental: the possibilities for self-realization in such a close correlation between figure and world is the primary meaning of Zavadil's work in *The Cap'n Video Show*.

In this respect, Zavadil's invention of the Cap'n Video character resembles the contemporaneous work of another Canadian comedic actor: Jim Carrey. In her examination of Carrey's various comic exertions, Vivian Sobchack writes approvingly of his "microanalysis" of "gesture and voice," his thinking about their place in the formation of personality, and their importance to the creation of "nuanced social and cultural meaning."[6] Carrey's comic film performances, derived in part from an analysis (and very broad elaboration) of meaningful everyday behaviour, encourage viewers to inspect "how our [own] bodies shape and 'perform' our intentions in the world."[7] In other words, Carrey's physical exertions constitute "critical judgment[s]" – about his own comedic exaggerations, but also their wider sociality – and can therefore be said to constitute a form of thinking about the world.[8] Carrey's conspicuously telegraphed enactment of intentions brings their social and cultural determination into sharper focus for viewers, and like Zavadil's Cap'n Video, his rudimentary, inventive labour indicates a reconfiguration of the everyday world according to unconventional precepts.

Beauty Day's commemorative introductory act immerses viewers in a similarly subjective dimension of Zavadil's work: when perceiving objects in the world before him, Zavadil/Cap'n Video makes sense of them, but in a critically different sense, his vision takes possession of these things and redeploys them for entirely different ends. The philosopher Maurice Merleau-Ponty describes such substantive involvement in perception as a "strange possession" of the world, and *Beauty Day*'s opening section repeatedly reveals a Zavadil/Cap'n Video who is in a constant state of strange possession.[9] With few exceptions, Zavadil worked by himself on his roughhewn cable program, and each episode is purposely set within the constricted spaces of his home and yard. Clearly, though perhaps not consciously, evoking the physical comedy of early silent film comedians like Charlie Chaplin, Buster Keaton, and their vaudevillian antecedents, Cap'n Video is noticeably puzzled by his everyday relation to the world of objects, but this confusion is quickly transformed into an animation of his simple possessions, a recasting of things according to their significance for him. Daring stunts thereby become the externalization of Cap'n Video's assorted thoughts about his world and tasks: lighter fluid is the elementary medium for shaving when one is burdened with an unbearable hangover; in the context of contemporary life's exhausting pace, raw eggs can be inhaled as an "instant breakfast"; a steep, poorly constructed rooftop is suddenly the place for winter tobogganing; an unstable clothesline becomes a collapsing ski slope; an abandoned and archaic television set is converted into a poor man's fireplace or televisual womb; and so on. The actor's pliability becomes the prototype for a more generalized malleability: everything can potentially shift in these reciprocal exchanges between Cap'n Video and his ordinary world. In this respect, comportment in *The Cap'n Video Show* implicitly discloses a manner of interacting with the social world, while everyday relations reveal this one figure's meaningful intentionality. It is "the senses that remember," Fredric Jameson writes in a different context, "not the 'person' or personal identity," and one should say something comparable about Ralph Zavadil and *The Cap'n Video Show*. Once the tangible dimension of Zavadil's labour as a millwright is moved to another task, namely, his weekly TV production, the resourceful Cap'n Video can somehow become newly conscious of the ordinary world around him.

In this way, *Beauty Day*'s opening segment memorializes Zavadil/Cap'n Video's imaginative comic comportment. However, it also tacitly valorizes the wholly individuated (or "independent") labour that produced the original *Cap'n Video Show*. Such a narrowly conceived commemorative impulse is especially evident in the film's own deportment. *Beauty Day*'s first section seeks to be more than a simple compilation of Zavadil/Cap'n Video's stunts, and its celebratory view of this world's disposition is eventually extended uneasily to subsequent portions of its narrative, that is, to those scenes set in a present-day Niagara Region. The film's frequent shifts in aspect ratio, for example, reveal a willingness to readjust its vision of Zavadil's environment to fit a more broadly commemorative objective. When deploying sequences from *The Cap'n Video Show*, *Beauty Day* preserves the square aspect ratio of the era's television sets, but these images are continually supplanted by the film's expressive widescreen views of the contemporary Niagara setting. The expansive sight of Zavadil paragliding through the air as he prepares a new segment for his twentieth anniversary show memorializes his former career as an autonomous producer, and the closing images of an incongruous contemporary iteration of the Cap'n Video character riding his motorized scooter alongside Lake Ontario's waterfront are equally salient. The empathetic tenor of Cheel's widescreen compositions generously reconfigures Zavadil's often disordered personal and professional history in commemorative terms.

And yet, although *Beauty Day* immerses its viewers completely in Zavadil's subjective experience of self-realization and celebrates his modest achievements as an independent producer, its final act ultimately discloses a substantially different narrative, one which casts the commemorative assemblage of clips from *The Cap'n Video Show* in a new light. Indeed, the film becomes especially instructive once the fallout from Zavadil's mid-1990s professional crises makes itself fully evident, and the concluding movement's tale of mounting frustration and failure resituates the notion of autonomous labour within a much more discouraging contemporary actuality. Crucially, *Beauty Day*'s final section is devoted to a new present-day undertaking, the production of a twentieth anniversary episode of *The Cap'n Video Show*, not past achievements. As a result, the tactics of compilation and retrospective interviews are exchanged for a more judicious observational approach, and the film is thereby able to survey Zavadil's incompatibility with a changing present-day media environment. This shift to an observational mode also – and perhaps unavoidably – incorporates the themes of American direct cinema, but as we'll see, their repositioning in this contemporary setting produces several unexpected disclosures. American direct cinema's customary emphasis on the narrowly self-seeking scope of a "creative" working life is now emptied of its purportedly liberating qualities and is instead framed as a dismal obligation and source of insecurity for the film's main subject.

Individualization and Self-Directed Production: *Beauty Day* and Direct Cinema

Beauty Day's first and second acts focus on the unruly finished products of Zavadil's seemingly self-sufficient creative endeavors. By contrast, the film's concluding segment takes viewers behind the scenes to witness the realities of contemporary independent video production. More importantly, however, *Beauty Day*'s final act implicitly directs viewers to consider the meaning of various transformations to cable television since the cancellation of *The Cap'n Video Show* in 1995, and its informally observed passages subtly disclose the consequences of these changes, for both Zavadil *and* the very idea of autonomous production. For example, Zavadil remains committed to the *Cap'n Video Show*'s knowing, do-it-yourself ineptitude, and he defiantly – and humorously – insists upon using his archaic camera and editing suite to produce his twentieth anniversary episode. (At one moment, he pivots slowly with his analogue video camera, staring intently through its viewfinder while the lens cap remains fastened to the lens.) Although he is evidently knowledgeable about digital media production (he casually refers to pixelation, for instance), he dismisses it in favour of his previous, expressively focused, solitary approach to creative work. But Zavadil's iconoclasm results in a series of unanticipated confrontations with the noticeably altered domain of present-day media production, and *Beauty Day*'s analysis of his newly commissioned anniversary show proves to be more meaningful than its explicitly commemorative schema suggests. Indeed, it produces value-laden knowledge about the plight of so-called "creative workers" today.

Such shifts to the analytical, observational approach are increasingly common in contemporary reality-based media. As critics have noted, we are at present experiencing "a moment when documentary seems back under the thrall of all things cinéma vérité."[10] The meaning of this phenomenon, however, has remained elusive. Film theorists and scholars have long recognized the legacy of observational filmmaking in "reality TV" and today's culture of surveillance, but many present-day documentaries have returned purposefully to the techniques and themes of American direct cinema. Why? Why have filmmakers rediscovered the usefulness of these well-known observational forms and their concentration on "person-sized spaces?"[11] One feels tempted to link such developments to a cultural preoccupation with cataloguing everyday life on social media platforms, but the pervasiveness of observational methods is at odds with many assessments of the twenty-first century's media regime. If new documentary ecologies are said to increase generative, collaborative user experiences, the reinvigoration of direct cinema, with its repeated implication of a reflective and deliberative spectator, suggests an effort at engaging with present-day realities differently. In this respect, *Beauty Day*'s adoption of an observational approach is instructive: it resuscitates – and resituates – classic direct cinema's obsession with solitary producers, self-expression, and a self-directed form of work, but this in turn exposes the growing uncertainty of these endeavours in today's world. Interpreting the significance of *Beauty Day*'s recourse to the style and themes of direct cinema should lead us to the real meaning of its final act: its account of the increasingly grim destiny of today's "new model worker" finally recasts the film's commemorative aims in much more elegiac terms.[12]

Scholarly accounts of American direct cinema have focused on its critical analysis of traditional media and the latter's obfuscation of the public sphere. According to Jonathan Kahana, for example, *Primary* (Robert Drew, 1960) "seeks to teach its audience something about how popular images are constructed and how they function in the democratic process,"[13] and like Jeanne Hall and Paul Arthur, he rightly highlights the self-validating drive behind this variety of pedagogical image-making.[14] "*Primary*'s argument," Kahana observes, "consists largely of [a] critique of image; against the various manifestations of technologically induced charisma, the film posits the cinema's ability to present a true picture of personality."[15] This demystifying filmic rhetoric and the attendant valorization of authentic personalities are consistent with the period's Cold War posturing, its liberal ideological disposition, and direct cinema's original journalistic aims; but the films made by Richard Leacock, D.A. Pennebaker, and the Maysles brothers after their break with Robert Drew establish noticeably different emphases. Digging more intensively into a variety of intimate spaces and their potential to reveal "true pictures of personalities," these films offer contradictory sights of solitary figures interacting with their workplaces, even if such settings are often sites for public performances by musicians, actors, or politicians. *Salesman* (Albert Maysles, David Maysles, and Charlotte Zwerin, 1969), for instance, provides an outline of fundamentally competitive individualism amongst its door-to-door Bible peddlers, and it discloses the negative effects of its central figure's dwindling network of customers and supports. The film deepens and modifies the Maysles's earlier focus on public figures significantly, devoting itself instead to an observation of working-class life, and in so doing, it knowingly redirects the observational film's attention to different types of interaction between these subjects and their immediate surroundings.

Matt Stahl has demonstrated how other exemplars of American direct cinema in the 1960s, the rockumentary foremost among them, are no less concerned with the vagaries of workplaces and their solitary occupants. According to Stahl, rockumentaries "model and prescribe"[16] a distinctly modern understanding of work, though the films' musicians appear to achieve a level of self-expression and self-realization that would have been inconceivable to *Salesman*'s Paul "the Badger" and his cohort. In films such as *Dont Look Back* (D.A. Pennebaker, 1967) or *Woodstock* (Michael Wadleigh, 1970), competitive imperatives are clearly internalized (as they are in *Salesman*), while a heroic self-realizing deportment underlies social interactions, both onstage and behind the scenes. Bob Dylan's comportment in *Dont Look Back* is in this sense an archetype for direct cinema: his dedication to self-invention and its accompanying autonomy exemplifies self-directed work, and it would be a model for musicians throughout the following decades. Dylan's apprehensive movement between the ideal of 1960s cohesion and a contradictory commitment to competitive individualism is particularly evident throughout *Dont Look Back*. In his condescending response to Donovan's humble tribute, for example, Dylan is surrounded by devoted beatniks and fledgling hippies, yet his competitiveness quickly transforms the general sense of solidarity into a lopsided contest between these singer-guitarists. At such moments, one can see how direct cinema contributes to "the production and proliferation of new and future working subjects that articulate this odd tangle of self-actualization, discipline, responsibility, responsibility for oneself, freedom and authenticity."[17]

Like many present-day observational documentaries, *Beauty Day*'s final act embraces the procedures of classic direct cinema to activate these themes, yet with a critical difference. Modern musicians are prototypical figures in Stahl's analyses because their everyday experiences make disclosures about the vagaries of "work and social mobility in the neoliberalizing world,"[18] but the story of increasingly insecure "creative work" extends beyond the purview of rock music. Direct cinema has created a durable form for the figuration of work, especially in its intensifying neoliberal manifestation, and the present-day return to observational forms can be understood as an effort to meet the task of representing such individualized, precarious labour.[19] When Zavadil begins production on the twentieth anniversary episode of his *Cap'n Video Show*, *Beauty Day*'s shift into an observational register allows spectators to witness his tellingly different comportment, complete inability to advance in these altered professional circumstances, and failure to negotiate the current cable TV industry's contradictory demands for self-direction and supplication. Direct cinema's seemingly self-sufficient protagonists, situated in informal labour environments that are predecessors to Zavadil's self-described "editing studio," were routinely engaged in a form of value-added symbolic production (again, very much like Zavadil). And if the flexible labour on view in these films was once seen as part of the sixties counterculture's constructive revolt against monotonous work, such liberating or self-realizing exertions have since degenerated in the hands of assorted corporate managers.[20] At key moments in *Beauty Day*, Zavadil shares his own bitter, if inchoate, complaints about these epochal transformations, but the film's concluding movement invites spectators to observe and assess this figure's unsuccessful attempt to navigate a new and unfamiliar terrain.

Dissonant Feats and Self-Contained Production

As I indicated above, Chris Smith and Sarah Price's *American Movie* is *Beauty Day*'s most significant precursor, and its scrutiny of Mark Borchardt's single-minded quest for his "American Dream" establishes a template for Cheel's study of Zavadil and his work as an independent video producer. *American Movie* follows Borchardt, a social outsider and aspiring filmmaker from Menomonee Falls, Wisconsin, as he undertakes the production of his lifelong dream project, the feature-length *Northwestern*. Although the filmmakers' observation of Borchardt's dedicated pursuit of his "American Dream" registers as both admiring and occasionally mocking, *American Movie* provides an informative examination of this self-directed producer. Like Zavadil after *The Cap'n Video Show*'s cancellation, Borchardt is disconnected from any meaningful institutional and financial supports; he lacks access to the network of valuable contacts required for success in the movie business; and, evidently burdened by his disfigured American aspirations, he undertakes the production of *Northwestern* with no genuine hope of completing it. At several moments in *American Movie*, Borchardt finds himself sitting in front of a television set, watching intently but continually seething with anger. The TV's uninterrupted transmission of heroic American success stories is a source of self-alienation for Borchardt, and his sense of frustration and bitterness becomes increasingly palpable across these sequences. In one especially striking scene, Mark and his mother watch the Super Bowl with his best friend, Mike Schank, but the evening eventually deteriorates into drunken accusations. We see Mark pacing angrily around a small kitchen as he searches for beer, simultaneously berating his mother and everyone else for submissively accepting the daily misery of their working lives. If Mark's inebriated boastfulness about his film work appears hollow (it is, he insists, the sole salve against despair), especially in relation to the Green Bay Packers' on-field exploits, his loutish denigration of factory employment reveals a profound misapprehension of his immediate surroundings. Mark accepts the ordinary – though disintegrating – distinction between the autonomous self-expression of his filmmaking and his family's menial labour, but the distance between Brett Favre's Super Bowl triumph and Borchardt's dull destiny couldn't be greater: the performance of such feats of self-realization are desired but unachievable for someone in Mark's position, and the resulting sense of powerlessness is both deflating and destructive. The discomfiting scene ends abruptly with Mark's drunken exit and guarantee to "never" succumb to the working-class fate of everyone else around him.[21]

Like Borchardt, Zavadil's self-understanding vacillates between immodest proclamations (he compares himself to Nikola Tesla) and flashes of genuine insight about his present-day existence (his aging body now feels "creaky," he admits), but his retrospective interviews return repeatedly to a thoroughgoing preoccupation with self-expression and his lingering disenchantment with the entertainment industry. Zavadil is older than Mark and has the benefit of hindsight when reconsidering his modest success as a video producer in the early 1990s, yet he shares Borchardt's overriding sense of frustration and disillusionment. The commemorative agenda in *Beauty Day*'s first act alleviates Zavadil's occasional bitterness by explicitly celebrating his achievements: the sense of diminishing possibilities in his ruined hometown of St Catharines is counterbalanced by his video-making

Figure 9.2 Zavadil unearths his ancient video camera and editing suite, and we see him devise a new set of stunts for his imagined audience.

exploits and accomplishments. In *Beauty Day*'s concluding act, however, present-day actualities continually impinge upon the film's otherwise celebratory tone, and Zavadil's willingness to produce the twentieth anniversary tribute to *The Cap'n Video Show* forces him to confront an unexpected set of contradictory and insupportable demands in today's altered world of media production. In these scenes, *Beauty Day* provides indispensable knowledge about precarious work in the neoliberal world. We watch as this figure unearths his ancient video camera and editing suite, and we see him devise a new set of stunts for his imagined audience. Zavadil's commitment and enthusiasm initially dispel one's doubts about his long-deferred revivification of *The Cap'n Video Show*, but Cheel's circumspect observation of this present-day undertaking soon reveals Zavadil's powerlessness within his new professional circumstances.

Zavadil's former working relationship with his local cable television station ultimately proves to be meaningless. Although he still possesses the connections required to pitch his plans for an anniversary episode, he is eventually forced to assume the entire financial burden for its creation. Unsurprisingly, his commemorative show is rejected because of the very attributes he prizes: the production values are no longer consistent with current digital standards, he is told; and the Cap'n Video character's complete irreverence, the heart of the original program and a key to Zavadil's sense of self-realization, is now seen as a potential legal liability. Cheel provides surreptitiously recorded audio of Zavadil's brief meeting with the cable company, and its rejection of his work is unequivocal and demoralizing, even if the evidence onscreen had already predicted its inevitability. Zavadil emerges from the meeting a dejected and incongruous figure. In his giant poncho, long and thinning hair, and vintage Volkswagen van (the "hippy van" according to its licence plate), Zavadil appears to have returned from the dead, a ghostlike remnant from some distant era. Having long ago been dislodged from any meaningful professional network of contacts within the television industry or its related institutions, his "autonomy" now makes him defenceless, so he immediately resolves himself to accepting the fate of countless other precarious producers today. He'll put the rejected video on YouTube, he announces, with the slim hope of somehow striking it rich on the Internet. Cheel rewards Zavadil's present-day efforts with several deliberately composed, elegiac images of an aging Cap'n Video riding his motor scooter alongside the Lake Ontario waterfront, but the preceding segment's harshest lessons linger even as *Beauty Day* comes to an end. The previous possibilities for self-realization simply no longer exist for Zavadil in this contemporary context.

Discordant Accomplishments in Documentary Cinema

Beauty Day is an especially relevant example of the contemporary resuscitation of themes and methods derived from classic American direct cinema because, like Zavadil's proposed twentieth anniversary episode, it was financed and produced by the filmmakers, and its fraught relationship with the risk-averse movie business explains its uncommonly empathetic observation of Zavadil's frustrating experiences.[22] *Beauty Day*, however, is not the only recent documentary to explore the ongoing neoliberal transformation of labour. *Tony Robbins: I Am Not Your Guru* (Joe Berlinger, 2016) examines life coach Tony Robbins as the mainstream supplier of "positive thinking" platitudes and a duplicitous discourse of "self-help." The multi-millionaire Robbins repeatedly disavows his exceptional status as "guru," but he does so solely to peddle a self-serving concept of "self-actualization" and individual autonomy, and the assorted images of this strange colossus at work, both onstage and (especially) behind the scenes, indicate a complete reconfiguration of one's life according to these terms. If Mark Borchardt's and Ralph Zavadil's lives reveal the mounting desperation of autonomous self-realization in the neoliberal world, Robbins by contrast presents himself as a model of self-sufficiency and accomplishment. As a result, however, *I Am Not Your Guru* inadvertently provides a valuable lesson about Robbins's steep and elusive path to achievement: the exceptional, unbridgeable distance between Robbins's self-sufficiency and his supplicants' despair exposes the remoteness and improbability of such autonomous success. Josh Kriegman and Elyse Steinberg's *Weiner* (2016), on the other hand, simply observes its subject's crisis-ridden, disorganized private and professional lives, but this too proves to be instructive: Anthony Weiner's inharmonious comportment is finally framed as the true source of his persistent public failure. And even unconventional examples such as *The Wolfpack* (Crystal Moselle, 2015) manage to reveal how the processes of individualization have become the essential integuments to neoliberalism's conception of labour. Its concluding images of victorious creative enterprise are entirely consistent with its subjects' disconcerting libertarian dismissal of all institutions, society, and general welfare. In this respect, the contemporary observational documentary's representations of various forms of precarious labour establish an informative counterweight to the prevailing – and politically suspect – confirmations of individualization and subjectivity in so much present-day nonfiction media production. *Beauty Day*'s modest survey of these same matters uncovers the grim neoliberal purpose in self-directed work, and its tribute to Ralph Zavadil exposes real limitations in the widespread equation of work and self-realization.

Notes

1. See Linda Barnard, "*Beauty Day*: Meeting the Original *Jackass*," *Toronto Star*, 9 June 2011. The film's title, *Beauty Day*, is derived from one of its subject's many distinctive utterances ("It's going to be a beauty day," he says before performing his stunts), but "beauty" is also a very common Canadian expression. *Strange Brew*'s Bob and Doug Mackenzie, for example, respond to almost every situation with an exclamatory "beauty," and one can assume that *Beauty Day*'s Ralph Zavadil has taken these figures as models in his creation of the "Cap'n Video" character.
2. The Niagara Region's proximity to the US border is surely another factor in *Beauty Day*'s complete immersion in American filmic resources and popular culture. The film's allusions are wide-ranging – *Vernon, Florida* (Errol Morris, 1981), *Rocky IV* (Sylvester Stallone, 1985), *Crumb* (Terry Zwigoff, 1994), *American Movie* (Chris Smith and Sarah Price, 1999), *Grizzly Man* (Werner Herzog, 2005), and *The Wrestler* (Darren Aronofsky, 2008) are only a few examples. While Cheel's *The Documentary Blog* is no longer active, he continues to co-host *The Film Junk Podcast*. Started in January 2005, it is "the longest running film podcast on the internet."
3. My critical description of these assorted phenomena (individualization, self-realization, and so on) is derived from Axel Honneth, "Organized Self-

Realization: Some Paradoxes of Individualization," *European Journal of Social Theory* 7, no. 4 (2004): 463–78. See also David Hesmondhalgh and Sarah Baker, *Creative Labour: Media Work in Three Cultural Industries* (New York: Routledge, 2011), 33–4.

4 Cheel's contemporaneous online film criticism often expresses an interest in documentary "character pieces."

5 Cheel shared this information during a post-screening conversation in November 2011.

6 Vivian Sobchack, "Thinking through Jim Carrey," in *More Than a Method*, ed. Cynthia Baron, Diane Carson, and Frank P. Tomasulo (Detroit: Wayne State University Press, 2004), 278–9.

7 Ibid., 279.

8 Ibid., 286.

9 Maurice Merleau-Ponty, *The Primacy of Perception*, ed. James M. Edie (Chicago: Northwestern University Press, 1964), 166.

10 Jeff Reichert, "How to Smell a Rose," *Reverse Shot* (11 August 2015).

11 I am using the phrase "person-sized spaces" as Matt Stahl does in *Unfree Masters: Recording Artists and the Politics of Work* (Durham: Duke University Press, 2013), 71. The objective of direct cinema, he writes, "rushing out to examine the experiences and lives of individuals who were often at crossroads or in crises, was to create person-sized 'spaces' in otherwise inaccessible social situations into which audiences could imaginatively insert themselves."

12 Stahl, *Unfree Masters*, 84. For a very useful summary of debates about the so-called new model worker, see Greig de Peuter, "Beyond the Model Worker: Surveying the Precariat," *Culture Unbound* 6 (2014): 263–84. See also Andrew Ross, *Nice Work If You Can Get It: Life and Labor in Precarious Times* (New York: New York University Press, 2009), 1–10.

13 Jonathan Kahana, "The Reception of Politics: Publicity and Its Parasites," *Social Text* 58, 17, no. 1 (1999): 101.

14 See Jeanne Hall, "Realism as a Style in Cinema Verite: A Critical Analysis of 'Primary,'" *Cinema Journal* 30, no. 4 (1991): 24–50 and "Don't You Ever Just Watch?" in *Documenting the Documentary: Close Readings of Documentary Film and Video*, eds. Barry Keith Grant and Jeannette Sloniowski (Detroit: Wayne State University Press, 2014). See also Paul Arthur, "Jargons of Authenticity (Three American Moments)," in *Theorizing Documentary*, ed. Michael Renov (New York: Routledge, 1993).

15 Kahana, "The Reception of Politics," 102.

16 Stahl, *Unfree Masters*, 74.

17 Ibid.

18 Ibid., 66.

19 See Mike Meneghetti, "The Paradoxes of Precarious Labour in Direct Cinema Today," *New Review of Film and Television Studies* 18, no. 2 (June 2020): 190–213.
20 On the corrosive influence of "corporate managers," see Ross, *Nice Work If You Can Get It*, 5. See also David Harvey's *A Brief History of Neoliberalism* (New York: Oxford University Press, 2005). It is worth nothing here that Zavadil refers to his ancient Volkswagen van as the "hippy van." His personal revolt against routine factory work is very loosely derived from the 1960s counterculture and its bohemian ideals, though it is also obviously mixed with a different sense of small-town frustration.
21 The resemblance between *American Movie* and *Beauty Day* speaks to more than the former's significant influence on Cheel's work. It also indicates neoliberalism's global reach and the widespread conundrums of individualization, labour, and precarity. *American Movie* and *Beauty Day*'s countries of origin are ultimately of small consequence, at least if one is considering the post-1990s realities being documented in each film.
22 *Beauty Day* was eventually produced by Primitive Entertainment and distributed by Films We Like, but Cheel had already assumed the primary financial risks of producing, shooting, and editing his documentary.

10

Mythologizing Manitoba
The Negated Truth of *My Winnipeg*

Miriam Siegel and Charlie Keil

Our only truth is narrative truth, the stories we tell each other and ourselves – the stories we continually re-categorize and refine.
     Oliver Sacks, *The River of Consciousness*

When I tell stories, it's important that the stories must be psychologically and emotionally plausible, that they tell a version of the truth, the way people are or the way people think and feel … the way a good fairy tale feels psychologically sound no matter how perverse it gets. And so I guess that's my version of truth-telling.
     Guy Maddin, interview with Charlie Keil

By 2003, Guy Maddin, Canada's resident bad-boy fantasist, had amassed a formidable oeuvre in the first twenty years of his career, building a reputation as a resolute iconoclast who revelled in recasting antiquated genres as fever-dream narratives. From *Tales from the Gimli Hospital* (1988) to *The Saddest Music in the World* (2003), Maddin's features traded in silent-film imagery and melodramatic plot contrivances with surrealist shadings, even as his cast lists became starrier and the budgets more sizeable. But the same year as *The Saddest Music in the World*'s release, Maddin's work took an expressly autobiographical turn with *Cowards Bend the Knee*, the first of a "Me Trilogy" that would feature protagonists named "Guy Maddin." The improbable final chapter in this trilogy was a commissioned documentary entitled *My Winnipeg* (2007). As Maddin has explained it, he eschewed the standard approach to nonfiction filmmaking, as he was unprepared to engage in conventional research; instead, he proposed making "a documentary about my feelings about the place [i.e., Winnipeg] … all of the research would be conducted in my memory and in my heart."[1]

Accordingly, the power of the stories that make up *My Winnipeg* derives less from their accurate relationship to the facts of the city or even of Maddin's own life, and more from their relationship to other aligned stories. As Maddin has put it, "I was trying not to depart so much from my previous films as the task of documentary would seem to call for."[2] With stories at the centre of *My Winnipeg*, the truth-telling potential of documentary (even if the film's categorization as such is a label Maddin accepts reluctantly) cannot be disentangled from its suitability for storytelling. The truth Maddin is aiming for, as he describes it, is at once "emotional" and "psychological": "the title gives me permission to ... hide behind the claim that everything I am discussing is more a feeling than a fact."[3] Maddin's *My Winnipeg*, then, is an account that is avowedly personal at the same time that it defies any standard of reliability; Maddin has characterized its seeming prevarications as "an absolute version of the truth ... if I put a negation in front of something and make it a lie, it's still the same thing as when you're telling the truth."[4] In presenting the "negated truth" of Winnipeg, Maddin fashions a myth of the city that fuses with the film's autobiographical tendencies.

Myths, for Maddin, are those stories that – whether or not they are literally true – have been exaggerated and repeated to the point that they become essential to how we define ourselves. To attempt to verify whether George Washington actually cut down a cherry tree, to employ one of Maddin's examples, would simply be to miss the point that stories of this kind "are more important as stories" than as facts of the past. And such stories function to affirm a nation's sense of its own identity. Canada, "being in the shadow of the greatest self-mythologizers in world history,"[5] may well lack the impulse to create myths, so Maddin uses *My Winnipeg* as an opportunity to turn the stories he tells about Winnipeg into the type of mythic totems he suggests the city lacks. In the process, he opens a space to allow what he narrates to be taken as both truth and fiction, as both fact and story. On the surface, this could create a narrational impasse of sorts: a fundamental aspect of the documentary's tacit contract with its viewer entails the rejection of such equivocation, which would seem to prevent a filmmaker from knowingly engaging in lies. To present fabricated stories about the city as documentary "facts" would amount to little more than uttering a series of falsehoods. To offer these stories as a series of fictional tales about Winnipeg, on the other hand, would not give them the air of facticity that Maddin associates with myth. A documentary dedicated to relating the civic history of Winnipeg should seemingly admit little middle ground between fact and fiction.

The same, however, cannot be said for personal histories, which are free to exploit an inherent ambiguity in autobiographical narration. Typically, the "autobiographical pact" is similar to the one that governs the documentary in its provisional guarantee of truth, with the added assurance that the author is identical with the narrating "I."[6] The autobiographical documentary combines these assurances by emphasizing both the "identity of name between author/filmmaker, voice-over narrator and on-screen subject," and the truth value of the stories being told.[7] The use of family photos and home movies and of narration in the filmmaker's own voice – particularly when it makes highly personal or confessional statements – serves to authenticate both the personal nature and truth-value of the film.

Fictiveness, however, does not necessarily preclude autobiographical truth. As Susan Lanser notes, fictional narratives rendered in first person are always potentially equivocal and *"rely for their meaning on* complex and ambiguous relationships between the 'I' of the author and any textual voice."[8] We may take the narrator to be purely fictional, to be a fictional evasion of the autobiographical, or some combination of the two, depending on a host of textual and extra-textual markers. We may similarly take the events narrated to be wholly fictional, true occurrences rendered in a fictional mode, a combination of fictional and real events, or even fictional events that nonetheless are designed to reveal an autobiographical truth. While fiction film tends to lack anything resembling a coherent narrative voice, as there is no evident "I" of either author or narrator, the same ambiguity nonetheless marks "personal" works by filmmakers who employ actors to play themselves within autobiographical or semi-autobiographical narratives. In spite of any demurrals that such works are "only fiction," they seem to invite us to conflate character and filmmaker, and therefore to parse the narrative for what it might reveal about the latter.

Autobiography and Fabrication in *My Winnipeg*

Maddin had already been working in this mode of autobiographical fiction in the other two films in his "Me Trilogy," *Cowards Bend the Knee* and *Brand upon the Brain!* As Maddin recalls this moment in his career, "If I started confessing to all of my most embarrassing and lurid humiliations, then I was suddenly supplying myself with a narrative worthy of Euripides for my screenplays – for me to write autobiographical sketches and then shoot them, it was so exciting, and I really seemed to hit my stride as a filmmaker once I vomited up all of this autobiographical stuff."[9] However, in *My Winnipeg*, the equivocality these kinds of stories tend to trigger is complicated by the inclusion of Maddin's voice-over narration, a typical feature of autobiographical documentaries. We first hear Maddin's voice in the film's cold open, where it is associated with a particular kind of documentary truth. A clapper board marked with the film's title gives way to a close-up of Ann Savage (who plays the director's mother in the segments depicting his family's interactions) as Maddin feeds her lines from somewhere out of frame. The clapper, the difference in sound quality between Savage's voice and Maddin's, the filmmaker's attempts to shape Savage's performance, and the cuts indicating multiple takes all suggest that the Maddin we hear is serving in his real-life role as director, and that we are watching the type of raw footage typical of behind-the-scenes or making-of documentaries. That we are watching an actor in the process of creating a scene serves to authenticate Maddin's voice as that of the "real" filmmaker by setting it against an obviously fabricated fiction. Yet these seemingly clear indicators of the divide between fact and fiction, actor and character, are undercut by the nature of the scene we are watching. In opening with such outtakes, *My Winnipeg* also announces its indebtedness to the techniques of fiction filmmaking, even as the status of this "Guy Maddin" (through his offscreen voice) complicates our sense that we are observing a set of purely fictive moments.

If the opening seems to signal an overall indebtedness to the resources of fiction by highlighting the very act of crafting such fiction, Maddin further underlines the possibilities of fabrication after a credits sequence that employs archival footage, a standard assurance of documentary authenticity. In the post-credits scene, Maddin presents us with a series of shots of a sleepy figure inside a train carriage. Compared to the archival footage that precedes them, these shots seem marked as fancifully fictionalized, by a host of indicators ranging from the editing – which gives the impression of a moving train by cutting between the engineer at work and mobile shots of Winnipeg passing by that were clearly taken from a moving car – to the mise-en-scène – a half-eaten sausage hangs from the train carriage ceiling near a broken window that seems to have been mended with duct tape. Maddin's voice returns, but now with the clarity, directness, and highly personal tone of an autobiographical narrator. The manner in which the shots isolate the unidentified passenger, the voice-over's description of what passes by the window of the train as he looks out, and the repeated use of personal pronouns while eschewing the past tense suggest both that the voice belongs to this man, and that the actions on the train and

Figure 10.1   A fancifully fictionalized shot of a sleepy figure inside a train carriage in *My Winnipeg* (2007).

the voice-over's narration are occurring at the same time. We know the voice to be Maddin's from the initial sequence and from the typical documentary assurance of identity between filmmaker and speaker. Yet, because the scenes on the train are obviously fabricated, with an actor playing "Guy Maddin," and because the voice-over lacks the retrospection we expect of autobiography, the strong sense of identity between speaker and on-screen subject that typically obtains in autobiographical documentaries is lacking. But the film does not suggest that the scenes are entirely fictional either, since they offer a visual representation of the voice-over's stated desire to escape. As a result, the relationship between the two performances, between the two "Maddins," remains somewhat unreconciled. Maddin could be performing the inner voice of the fictional "Maddin" just as much as the fictional "Maddin" could be a stand-in for Maddin on the image-track, performing the filmmaker we hear on the sound-track.

That this confusion between the autobiographical and the fictional will be essential to Maddin's depiction of Winnipeg is established in the first story about the city the filmmaker offers. His rendering of the city's founding myth creates an intimate connection between

Winnipeg's birth and the filmmaker's own through similar slippage: the metaphorical lap of the city created by the confluence of the Red and Assiniboine Rivers becomes the literal lap of Maddin's mother. The connection between these two points of origin, however, is not simply one of visual similarity; they also share an intimate connection with the supernatural. The voice-over informs us that a First Nations legend suggests that "there are subterranean forks, two secret rivers meeting, directly beneath the Assiniboine and Red, this double pairing of rivers being extra supernaturally powerful." Mother is later described as being "as supernatural as the Forks themselves," and as more than usually psychic in a city already possessed of great "psychic possibilities" due to its proximity to the Forks. By linking the city's origins to his own under a single myth, Maddin's accounts of the city and of his personal history become intimately interdependent. One story, it seems, cannot be told without the other.

The scenes on the train, however, also establish a general narrative framework for the film: Maddin's desire to escape Winnipeg. All the stories Maddin tells are therefore subsumed under this avowed goal to leave the city that has served as his home for his "entire life." The confessional tone of the narration suggests that this desire belongs to the filmmaker, but it is "Maddin" that we see making his way out of the city. We may therefore be inclined to take this "Maddin" as a convenient fiction, a means of representing the filmmaker's desire to leave. Yet, this also suggests that the stories Maddin tells may similarly be convenient fabrications, a way to work through "everything [he has] seen and loved" in order to make his way out.

The story of the annual Canadian Pacific Railway treasure hunt, for example, is perhaps the most straightforwardly rendered tale in the film. While the voice-over takes on a somewhat conversational tone, it also adopts some of the markers of documentary authenticity, eschewing the first person in favour of a more detached description of a putatively historical event. The story is also authenticated by the use of archival footage of city streets, happy Winnipeggers, and public officials overseeing an event and then ostensibly awarding prizes. Yet, while the archival footage seems to serve as evidence of the veracity of the story, the tale itself acts to support the voice-over's contention that the city is difficult to escape for those who know it well. The story is framed by two declarations that the narrator is dedicated to leaving for good, while also providing the first indication of the potential avenue of escape at the centre of the film. While the prize for winning the hunt – a "one-way ticket on the next train out of town" – is a means of leaving the city, the primary goal of the contest is actually to encourage Winnipeggers to stay, "the idea being that once someone had spent a full day looking this closely at his own hometown, he would never want to leave." Maddin, however, inverts the terms of the hunt, suggesting that engaging deeply with the city may finally allow him to leave. Whether or not the story is true, therefore, is beside the point, since it provides Maddin with both a means of escape and of structuring the film.

Archive and Authenticity

In addition to encouraging us to willingly conflate author and character, truth and fiction, the film also systematically undermines the standard cues we rely on to make a determination about a documentary's truth value at any given moment. In literature, the equivocation between truth and fiction is easier to trigger, since fictional, first-person narratives and autobiographical narratives both make use of the same set of storytelling resources, centring on the presence of the narrating "I." As a result, all other things being equal, we have no way of making a determination from the text alone. In film, however, the situation is somewhat complicated by our association of certain stylistic markers and narrational modes with documentary filmmaking, and others with fiction. While Maddin tends to clearly mark his footage as belonging to one type of filmmaking or the other, not only do the stories Maddin tells in the film rarely make use of one without the other, but both kinds of images hardly ever function in the same way across stories. As a result, the presence of a particular formal marker offers no guarantee of the truth value of any given story.

For example, while Maddin calls on archival footage as a typical means of demonstrating the veracity of the treasure hunt, the status of these and other seemingly authenticating resources is frequently undercut by the filmmaker's tendency to create a host of different associations between these "real" images and footage that clearly demonstrates its status as a fictional construction. Occasionally, Maddin seems to signal the truth status of his stories by setting obviously fabricated images against shots that equally signal their documentary authenticity. The filmmaker's description of Winnipeg's unusually high rate of sleepwalking, for example, initially plays over images that seem designed to display their fictiveness: the sleepwalking figures are costumed in old-fashioned attire; the shots are carefully composed using an overpass as an internal frame to create an aperture effect; the figures move unnaturally, often toward the camera; and the image is overlaid with a patently artificial snow effect. When the voice-over informs us of the law allowing sleepwalkers to enter old homes, the footage even includes an optical point of view shot rendering the experience of someone sleepily wandering into a house. Yet, Maddin also uses documentary-style footage to suggest the continued prevalence of sleepwalking that is just as strongly marked as "real": the image quality is poor; the figures seem unaware of being filmed; the shots are less carefully composed, suggesting that they were simply captured by chance; and the figures' actions appear less deliberate, even accidental. The Winnipeggers Maddin captures making their way through the city's snowy streets, however, bear little resemblance to his fabricated sleepwalkers. As a result, they simultaneously give the lie to Maddin's story and suggest his desire to transform reality by conflating it with a more poetic fiction.

In the sleepwalking example, Maddin provides two distinct image streams, each signifying its own reality, while refusing to reconcile their mutual exclusivity. In telling other stories, however, he inverts the relationship between the two types of footage, so that the fabricated images seem to connote a truth value while nonetheless still being clearly marked as fabricated. Maddin's description of his childhood at 800 Ellice, for example, again adopts a confessional tone, as the filmmaker admits to his simultaneous embarrassment over and love for the strangeness of his family home, before musing on the effects that living in a hair salon might have had on him. In addition to the highly personal nature of the narration, the purportedly autobiographical status of the sequence is reinforced by its exclusive reliance on family photos and home movies, the type of authentic images that autobiographical documentarians are expected to employ to represent their past selves. Maddin's description of his experience in the hair salon similarly makes use of personal and archival photos. Yet, while these images previously seemed to document Maddin's experience of his home, here their sheer concatenation and typicality – the images seem to depict a series of period-appropriate salons and hairdressers, rather than the specific spaces and people from Maddin's childhood – weakens their connection to that experience. His description of the smells and sounds of the salon is instead conveyed using a series of "fictional" shots composed to resemble the other fabricated instances in the film. His suggestion that the air was "fuzzy with sprays," for example, plays over a hand isolated in close-up emptying a can of hairspray into the air against a plain black background clearly designed to ensure that the resultant cloud can be seen in relief. His description of the constant snipping of scissors is similarly accompanied by close-ups of hands wielding scissors in black and empty spaces. The almost assaultive nature of these close-ups, intensified by the pace of the editing, which mimics the staccato rhythm of the narration, offers an approximation of the overwhelming sensory experience being described. As a result, they seem to come closer to the truth of that experience than do the archival photos that should nonetheless possess an inherent truth value.

Maddin renders the episode with the school girls of St Mary's Academy in a similar fashion. While the sequence makes use of home movies depicting Maddin happily playing as a toddler, the encounter itself is rendered using fabricated images of the solicitous girls. Again, rapidly cut together close-ups of legs, hands, and looming faces moving in for kisses serve to suggest the overwhelming nature of the experience while also pointing to the "truth" of the implicitly threatening sexuality of the girls. The fact that this incident could not have been filmed also serves to forgive the use of fabricated images as little more than an expediency. We are free, in other words, to take this sequence as true even while knowing that the events it depicts have been narrativized rather than captured.

The animated images are similarly ambivalent. Like the live-action footage, some seem to simply serve as stand-ins when "authentic" images are lacking. The brightly coloured animated images of Winnipeggers visiting Happyland and enjoying the amusement park's rides, for example, are inherently lacking in photographic evidentiary value. Yet, they are also validated by a series of colourized archival photos – one of the few uses of archival or documentary materials in colour in the film – that possess a similar artificiality: the stark contrast between the vibrantly coloured skies of the animated footage and the black silhouetted figures and rides is answered by the vibrant skies, grass, and clothing against the uniformly white structures of the archival photos. Both forms of representation have the appearance of being worked over, an attribute readily associated with animation, but not typically with photographs, especially those of an archival origin.

Nowhere are the tensions between a recorded past and a transformed memory more striking than when Maddin plumbs his own childhood. Maddin's tendency to confuse truth and fiction even when the artificiality of the stories he tells is overtly acknowledged permeates his purported attempt to recover and then analyze his childhood memories by staging re-enactments in his old home. The voice-over narration informs us that Maddin has hired actors to play his siblings and enlisted his girlfriend's dog, Spanky, to stand in for the "long dead"

Figure 10.2 Mother is imbued with the fantastic power of the buffalo in *My Winnipeg* (2007).

Chihuahua Toby. Each of Maddin's three siblings is introduced with a pair of images: a family photo and a shot of the corresponding actor in the reconstructed Maddin living room. These equations between Maddin's real family members and the actors playing them rely on a similar logic as the association that conflates the two Guys on the train. While here the relationship between actor and character is explicitly stated, the seemingly secure boundaries between fact and fiction are nonetheless troubled by the narration's insistence that Maddin's mother is being played by the woman herself.

Even if we are unaware that the role of Mother is actually being played by Ann Savage, the film has continually insisted on her status as a fictional, occasionally fantastic, construct. In addition to her appearance as a performer in the film's opening moments, Mother materializes impossibly on the train or outside its windows. When the narration informs us of her incredible strength, that she is "as perennial as the winter," "as ancient as the buffalo," and "as supernatural as the Forks" of the Assiniboine and Red Rivers, she appears isolated against a screen displaying each element in turn as if in response to the narrator's imagined conception of her. Moreover, she is often framed against the black spaces that dominate Maddin's fabricated footage, placing her within an imagined space rather than the real spaces depicted in the filmmaker's documentary footage.

During the re-enactments, however, the narrator seems to commit to the lie that Mother is playing herself. The confusion is redoubled when Mother appears as the lead actress in the apocryphal *Ledge Man* television show alongside Darcy Fehr, the actor who stands in for Maddin on the train, still playing the role of son to Savage's mother. Yet, televised Mother's ability to talk this second, fictional son down from the window-ledge from which he threatens to jump nonetheless suggests the impossibility of escaping Maddin's mother, on which the narration has consistently insisted. As Dave Saunders argues, "the parallels with Maddin's struggle to escape the clutches of his hometown, and his mother's apron strings, are abundant," as "Ledge Man's leap into the unknown world … is constantly prevented by his mother's hectoring and infantilising."[10] In spite of the dizzyingly layered series of performances, then, the television show speaks to a truth of Maddin's experience by translating it into an archetypal narrative of repeatedly thwarted escape.

The re-enactment of the family's continually frustrated attempts to straighten the hall runner under Mother's equally persistent harangues has a similarly contradictory effect. The narration is careful to remind us of the fabricated nature of the scene, commenting on the "limp performance" put in by the actors. Yet, their lack of "affect" itself serves to produce the same feeling of frustration for the director that he is attempting to depict in recreating this episode from his past. While the narration insists that the re-enactment is a failure, it therefore also succeeds more fully than the other recreated scenes from Maddin's family history in actually reproducing something of the "dynamic" he is attempting to expose.

The hall runner scene, the narration informs us, does have the beneficial effect of getting Mother to be "in the moment" despite her previous resistance to Maddin's experiments with re-enactment. We are therefore reminded to "never underestimate the tenacity of a Winnipeg mother." In addition to once again insisting on Mother's strength, this admonition serves as something of an abstract for the ensuing tale of the defense of the Wolseley Elm by a determined group of "elderly neighborhood women." Like the story of the treasure hunt, therefore, the two tales – the purportedly real incident from civic history and Maddin's depiction of the dynamics of his personal history – become conflated, with both seemingly supporting the truth of the tenacity of

Winnipeg's matrons. As a result, the Elm defenders attain some of the fantastic strength associated with Mother, while she is afforded some of the factual solidity that, in spite of the film's continued attacks on their veracity, still inheres in the archival photos that depict the women.

Myth, Memory, and Place

The integrative logic of the film, the relationship it creates between personal and civic history and between real and faked materials, is particularly evident in its depiction of the destruction of the Winnipeg Arena. This central incident in the film, as William Beard notes, contains "two narratives" that are "inextricably intertwined at certain points: the 'objective' history of hockey in the arena, the storied past, full of heroes, and Maddin's childhood history, with his absorption of those legends, his integration of them into his own direct experience ... and finally the connection between all this and Maddin's sense of his father."[11] While Maddin's real father worked in the arena, the filmmaker reinforces his autobiographical links with the building by turning the entire structure into his "male parent." Yet, this poeticized rendering of the truth of the importance of the arena to Maddin is immediately met by an entirely faked connection, as the filmmaker claims that he was "even born" in the dressing room. This myth of origin therefore matches the founding myth at the beginning of the film by again conflating a supernaturally charged space with one of Maddin's parents. The mythic quality of this story of Maddin's birth is reinforced by a shift to the film's fabricated image style. The appearance of a male baby in a black void surrounded by hockey sticks is the first feigned image in a sequence that makes use of all of the heterogeneous materials that have been employed to relate the other stories in the film.

Perhaps because it is the one event that Maddin himself recorded as it occurred, the initial images of the arena being destroyed seem dedicated to dispassionate documentation. Shot on colour video tape, these images resemble television news footage and stand in stark contrast to the black and white archival photos Maddin employs to introduce the arena's fabled past. Again, however, it is the fabricated images that carry the truth of Maddin's experience. The trio of smells – urine, breast milk, and sweat – that mark Maddin's memories of the arena are rendered in a frenetic series of black-backgrounded shots of mothers feeding their babies and players showering after games. Maddin's tribute to the arena similarly relies on a further fantastic twist to the representational logic of the re-enactments. The filmmaker's imaginary hockey team, made up of players from various squads throughout the history of the sport in Manitoba, again employs actors to represent real people in an event that the narration acknowledges is feigned. And like the insistence that Mother is playing herself, the narration implicitly asserts that these players are the genuine article. Yet, while the re-enactments ostensibly represent attempts to replay incidents from Maddin's childhood, the game is pure fantasy, relying on the logic of "what if" to create an event that is necessarily impossible. Like the re-enactments, however, the sequence relies on some vertiginous ontological sleight-of-hand. Maddin cannot possibly deny the imaginary nature of the game: the palpably surreal images of aged hockey players carrying on as the arena is destroyed around them – a demolition that is rendered through the equally palpably artificial technique of shooting the men in front of screens displaying the building's destruction – seems to continually acknowledge that fact. But Maddin also wants to claim the team as a representation of the truth of the arena's status as a repository of memory and history. To do so, the narration simultaneously gives up and maintains the game: the voice-over both suggests that we are seeing the players and acknowledges that this could possibly be not the case. The narration tells us that "it's even rumoured that the heavily-bandaged goaltender ... is the late Terry Sawchuck," only to remind us, "but that's impossible of course." Even this is a sly evasion, since Sawchuck's presence is only a "rumour," a story not of the narrator's own making, but one that he refuses to either confirm or deny. The voice-over's suggestion that "no one knows why [the team] formed" similarly places the squad members within the realm of a collective fable, legend, or myth, rather than treating them as a personal fantasy.

The importance of the arena, however, does not rest solely in its ability to act as a space in which both truth and myth can seemingly coexist without contradiction, but also in the fact that it represents the ultimate loss for Maddin. The imagined game momentarily redeems the arena and the stories it houses from being erased from both the Winnipeg landscape and memory, but because place and memory are so intimately connected, the destruction of the arena also represents an unforgivable act of forgetting. The building, the narrator informs us, "will be ripped into oblivion, and soon too, will the great careers of these wonderful souls." The destruction of Eaton's represents a similar failure of memory; the store's centrality to Winnipeg life is implicitly lost with the razing of the building. Yet, the fact that the narrator seems less betrayed by the demolition itself than by the "civic government" failing to "dream up an inventive second life for the old store" also suggests the importance the film attributes to the material traces of memory and history.

One can certainly make the case that *My Winnipeg* serves as a plea to typically "stupefied" and "sleepy" Winnipeggers to be more cognizant of the history, and therefore the mythic potential, of their own city. Nonetheless, it is a potential, like so many other aspects of the film, that relies on a contradiction. In addition to a conflation of truth and fiction, the film implies, myths also depend on belatedness. The stories we tell must always come from a time that is "not now," and is therefore inaccessible save for the material traces and memories that are left behind. If, as Ian Robinson argues, the film proposes that "in order to understand the city, its history and geography must be reimagined and reinvented," it also suggests that its attempts to "obscure, mystify and transfigure the city through image and narrative" can only be carried out by working on what has already been partially obscured by being inherently past.[12]

The Winnipeg of the film is made particularly ripe for mythologization because it is full of absences. Practically all the stories Maddin tells focus on losses ("I've submerged myself in loss," Maddin has said).[13] As if searching for a point of rupture when Winnipeg's history should have become myth but was instead simply forgotten, the film enacts a series of potentially determinant breaks. In addition to the loss of Happyland, Eaton's, Whittier Park, the Wolseley Elm, the lower levels of the Sherbrook Pool, and the Winnipeg Arena, the film laments Winnipeg's decision to join the NHL and the erasure of an entire history of professional hockey that the decision represents, even before the loss of the Jets.[14] It also muses on forgotten practices like the Golden Boy Pageants and the séances and exorcisms that suggested Winnipeg's connection to illicit sexual desires and to the supernatural, respectively.

The losses that seem to particularly trouble Maddin, however, are those that foreclose the possibility for narrativization by erasing any material traces. Some of Maddin's attempts to mythologize the city are premised on reading these traces with an eye toward their fantastic potential. For example, the narrator takes his fellow Winnipeggers to task for not recognizing the mythic provenance of the Golden Boy statue on the roof of the legislature: "That's the Greek God Hermes atop our dome, disguised as the Golden Boy by an armful of wheat, our sleepy eyes never suspecting his fearsome pagan power and unlikely presence in modern North America." The narrator also insists on the more illicit provenance of the city's feminine street names, suggesting they originally belonged to "great women" who ran Winnipeg's "illustrious brothel collectives." Maddin transforms the Paddlewheel Club on the top floor of the Bay department store into another trace of the city's illicit desires – as the centre of Winnipeg's "thirst for betting" after the destruction of Whittier Park, and therefore the origin of "modern Winnipeg nightlife." The narrator's fear for the store, that it will be demolished like Eaton's before it, is therefore a fear for the loss of the potential for narrativization that sites such as these hold. Similarly, until the new arena built on the site of the demolished Eaton's can "accumulate" its own "memories," its own potential to generate stories, the MTS Centre is simply "MT," the S obligingly blinking out to indicate that the building is inherently "em[p]ty" without narratives of its own.[15] The mythologizing imagination, it seems, must have something to work on. Save for the memories preserved by Maddin, however, Eaton's, the arena, Happyland, and the Wolseley Elm are simply gone.

As a result, it is only when Maddin can imagine a way to redeem all these sites and hand over custody of "all of [Winnipeg's] regrets" that the narration suggests he will be able to leave the city. With Citizen Girl, Maddin dreams up a figure capable of recognizing and preserving the city's past, someone who can "undo the damage done during Winnipeg's first trip through time," and therefore "look after this city" as its "new lap." The imagined reconciliation of Maddin's mother and brother Cameron offers a similar redemptive resolution for his family's history. Like his exploration of the city, Maddin's rendering of his personal history is founded on a search for a single determining moment in which his own history turned into the enervating memories that the film seeks to uncover. The re-enactments become a means of externalizing these memories, so that they can be worked on in the same way that the film transforms the city's spaces through fabulation. The time Maddin's sister struck and killed a deer with the family car, for example, is transformed into a melodramatic episode that evidences both the barely concealed illicitness of the mundane in the city and Mother's supernatural perspicacity in being able to reveal them. Mother is able to read the blood and fur on the fender as evidence of a sexual encounter in much the same way that Maddin encourages Winnipeggers to recognize the interpretive potential of the city.

Rather than providing a series of "facts" about Winnipeg, then, Maddin offers a means of understanding it, a way the city can be imagined that affords more meaning and power than a historically accurate account could. It is a means of understanding that the film itself demonstrates in transforming the material at its disposal into the constituent elements of a mythic civic and personal history. Archival footage and photos, fabricated images, and shots that capture the city in documentary fashion become fodder for mythic narrativization just as much as the filmmaker's own memories. If the film is therefore about Maddin's Winnipeg, as the title suggests, it is also about the creative process Maddin calls on to construct that image of his home town. As he has said, "I discovered an odd thing about my lying. You curate so much and with so much variety. I've turned out to be a lie curator ... I was curating the lies and the lies I chose to tell revealed as much about me as if I were telling the truth the whole time. I preferred a certain kind of lie, and I realized that I might as well be telling the truth ... My lies are ultimately the same as my facts, because I'm just talking about my feelings."[16] Even if the stories Maddin tells in *My Winnipeg* appear to be false, these negated truths are ultimately the only ones worth telling.

Notes

1 Charlie Keil, interview with Guy Maddin, Toronto, 9 March 2020.
2 Ibid.
3 Ibid.
4 Ibid.
5 Kurt Halfyard, "Guy Maddin Talks *My Winnipeg*, Self-Mytologizing, Psychological Honesty, and Even *The Host*," ScreenAnarchy, 2 October 2007, https://screenanarchy.com/2007/10/guy-maddin-talks-up-my-winnipeg-self-mythologizing-pyschological-honesty-an.html.
6 Philippe Lejeune, *On Autobiography* (Minneapolis: University of Minnesota Press, 1989).
7 Igor Krstić, "A Foreigner in One's Own Tongue: Jonas Mekas, Minor Cinema and the Philosophy of Autobiographical Documentary," *New Cinemas: Journal of Contemporary Film* 15, no. 1 (2017): 103.
8 Susan S. Lanser, "The 'I' of the Beholder: Equivocal Attachments and the Limits of Structuralist Narratology," in *A Companion to Narrative Theory*, eds. James Phelan and Peter J. Rabinowitz (Malden: Blackwell, 2005), 210.
9 Keil, interview with Guy Maddin.
10 Dave Saunders, *Documentary* (New York: Routledge, 2010), 160.
11 William Beard, *Into the Past: The Cinema of Guy Maddin* (Toronto: University of Toronto Press, 2010), 337.
12 Ian Robinson, "The Critical Cinematic Cartography of *My Winnipeg*," *Canadian Journal of Film Studies* 23, no. 2 (fall 2014): 102.

13 Keil, interview with Guy Maddin.
14 The Winnipeg Jets have had a tumultuous history as a nationally based hockey team. One of the original franchises in the World Hockey Association (founded in 1971), the Jets enjoyed initial success, anchored by defecting NHL star Bobby Hull. When the WHA disbanded in 1979, the Jets became part of the NHL, until the franchise was sold and moved to Arizona in 1996, becoming the Phoenix Coyotes. Rather confusingly, the Winnipeg Jets resurfaced as an NHL team in 2011, reborn through the purchase and relocation of the Atlanta Thrashers, originally formed in 1997, almost the same time the original Jets ceased to exist under that name.
15 The very naming of this building has entailed a series of replacements, denying the establishment of a stable identity. Envisioned as the True North Centre during the planning stages, once constructed in 2004, the building was known as the M(anitoba) T(elecom) S(ervices) Centre. A renaming occurred in 2017, when it was renamed Bell MTS Place, acknowledging Bell's acquisition of MTS. By 2021, naming rights had been sold to Canada Life, resulting in yet another moniker: Canada Life Centre.
16 Ibid.

11

Indigenizing the Archive
Souvenir and the NFB

Gillian Roberts

An archive can be dangerous if it is the final resting place of a story.
Warren Cariou, "Who Is the Text in This Class?"

In 2015, the Aboriginal Pavilion at the Pan Am Games in Toronto featured a series of short films comprising "repurposed" National Film Board footage, entitled *Souvenir*.[1] The series included three short films by Indigenous artists: *Etlinisigu'niet (Bleed Down/Vidés de leur sang)* by Jeff Barnaby (Mi'gmaq), *Sisters & Brothers / Soeurs et frères* by Kent Monkman (Cree), and *Mobilize/Mobiliser* by Caroline Monnet (Algonquin).[2] These films were made with footage from the National Film Board's archive, representing NFB films from the 1920s to the 1990s. The original NFB films featuring Indigenous people were primarily made by non-Indigenous filmmakers, and were repurposed by Barnaby, Monkman, and Monnet to produce new film critiques of both Canadian settler colonialism and the NFB's role in producing – and reproducing – the settler-colonial gaze. Despite the temporal span of the footage – covering most of the twentieth century – the films that constitute *Souvenir* address twenty-first-century concerns. Footage of residential schools, which features in both Barnaby's and Monkman's films, makes a very different statement in a post–Truth and Reconciliation Commission context (the TRC's work formally concluding in 2015, the year of these films' exhibition at the Pan Am Games). Monnet's film, the only one of the three films in colour, uses the figure of a single Indigenous woman in an urban environment in ways that underscore Indigenous modernity. In making use of NFB materials for their own work, these Indigenous artists enact a kind of repatriation of a digital archive. As Marc André Fortin observes of non-material forms, these "cannot simply be 'returned' as a traditional object is returned."³ Further, even the notion of a "digital return"⁴ is somewhat misleading in *Souvenir*'s context, as the peoples documented in the NFB footage do not necessarily correspond to the Indigenous nation of the artist, and the work of *Souvenir* is not physically to return film stock to individual Indigenous nations.⁵ Rather, *Souvenir* enacts a kind of pan-Indigenous confrontation with and reclamation of the NFB archive, refusing the archive as the "final resting place" of these images, as they are recontextualized and reanimated by Barnaby, Monkman, and Monnet using Indigenous non-diegetic soundtracks by Inuit throat singer Tanya Tagaq and hip-hop group A Tribe Called Red.⁶

The *Souvenir* films highlight the fact that "for most of the twentieth century, Indigenous peoples were situated in front of, not behind, the lens."⁷ Barnaby's *Etlinisigu'niet* opens with the title "The Red Man in Canada," made by Conquest Pictures, copyright 1918, by Thomas A. Edison, Inc. The inclusion of this image calls the settler-colonial archive to account for its racist discourse, the gross oversimplification of Indigenous peoples in the territory now claimed by the Canadian state, and the ways in which Western filmmaking feeds off the settler-colonial project, as the name "Conquest Pictures" and its implication of the imperial gaze suggest. In the context of the NFB archive in particular, as Zoë Druick writes, for much of the board's history, "the production of films about First Nations followed federal Indian policy closely," and "from the outset, NFB films romanticized native customs as vanishing folkways."⁸ As Dallas Hunt (Cree) writes, "In the archives of settler nation-states like Canada, Indigenous peoples are often either absent, depicted as ciphers of the real individuals they are meant to represent, or represented as always already disappearing from the landscape."⁹ Settler-colonial filmmaking has often functioned, historically, to "preserve" Indigenous cultures considered destined to disappear; as Diana Taylor argues, "the 'preservation' argument ... barely conceals a deep colonial nostalgia," a notion akin to Rosanne Kennedy's idea of the "*perverse* archive" that encapsulates the state's record of violence against Indigenous peoples for which the state itself is responsible.¹⁰

If Barnaby's *Etlinisigu'niet* begins with an invocation of the settler-colonial notion of the "Red Man," the film's repurposing of archival footage testifies to the white man's violence. Accompanied by Tanya Tagaq's "Tulugak," the film opens with images from Colin Low's *Circle of the Sun* (1960), representing the Kainai Sun Dance, including drumming, dancing, the community gathered around a fire, and tipis. As Paul Williams observes, "Low's film about the Blood Indians of southern Alberta, while beautifully crafted, is made by and for English Canadians with the native [*sic*] voice reduced to a running commentary of images of the Bloods' performing certain rituals."[11] Indeed, Pete Standing Alone, "a young Blood" who provides voice-over narration about his community, is framed by the additional narration of settler Stanley Jackson, who characterizes Standing Alone as someone "who doesn't really belong in the old order of things, and isn't entirely at home in the new," emphasizing the fact that despite the presence of Standing Alone's voice in Low's film, *Circle of the Sun* is a settler film for a settler audience. Standing Alone's "running commentary" is, itself, subject to Jackson's running commentary. Thus, the recontextualization of the footage in Barnaby's film is all the more significant.

In *Etlinisigu'niet*, following the *Circle of the Sun* footage, shots of men in headdresses meeting a white man act as an analogy for the colonial encounter, with images of the settler-colonial state's institutions proliferating thereafter: a white man speaks at a podium into a CBC microphone; First Nations children arrive at a residential school, where they all have identical haircuts, testifying to the white supremacist state's enforced uniformity. The children are inspected by a doctor; in another shot, they are made to pray. Shots of children going to bed in a crowded dormitory invoke the spectre of sexual abuse that has come to be horrifyingly commonly associated with residential schools (which the original NFB footage would certainly never have suggested). The state violence of the residential school project and its cultural dispossession, the film suggests, go hand in hand with territorial dispossession and state resource extraction. Shots of smokestacks, a field of animal skulls, waste pipes, and bitumen precede those of Indigenous women and children being inspected by white doctors in a clinic and a hospital, a clear critique of the extractivist state's poisoning of Indigenous territories and people.

Footage of surgeons operating, with close-ups of incisions being sutured, precedes the final image of the film, a sign that reads:

A TRIBUTE TO THE GOVERNMENT OF CANADA
HERE LIE THE REMAINS OF WHAT WAS ONCE THE CUTLER ACID PLANT – 9000 TRUCKLOADS OF CONTAMINATED WASTE. OWNED AND OPERATED IN CONSECUTIVE ERAS BY NORANDA MINES AND CIL. THE PLANT SHUT DOWN IN 1963. LEAVING US WITH THIS GREAT LEGACY. DIA NEGOTIATED THE LEASE ON BEHALF OF THE BAND AND SETTLED IT WITHOUT INCLUDING US.
THE PEOPLE OF THE SERPENT RIVER INDIAN BAND DEDICATE THIS SITE TO THEM IN RECOGNITION OF THEIR RELENTLESS PURSUIT OF GOOD ON OUR BEHALF.
GOD SAVE THE QUEEN

Both the sign and the film testify to the poisoning of Anishinaabe territory through this pointed accusation of state violence. The film itself becomes an ironic "tribute," in the spirit of sign, to both the NFB archive and the settler-colonial state, the lie of "on our behalf" exposed by the charge that the Department of Indian Affairs negotiated "without including" the Serpent River First Nation. The "great legacy" of contaminated waste is anything but. The reference to a great legacy also invokes the archive; if archival contents "remai[n] dormant," in Saidiya Hartman's conceptualization, Barnaby's film "retriev[es]" them in order to forge a different legacy from this footage altogether.[12]

Whereas residential schools form part of the narrative arc constructed in Barnaby's assemblage of the NFB footage, Monkman's *Sisters & Brothers* focuses more squarely on this issue while also comparing the settler-colonial state violence of residential schools with the extermination of the buffalo. Like Barnaby's film, Monkman's begins with imagery constructed as potentially pre-contact, with shots of a river preceding those of white men on horseback, looking through binoculars at buffalo. The intercutting of shots of buffalo with shots of First Nations children at a residential school underscores the film's comparison of two forms of state violence, both of which were fundamental in the dispossession of Indigenous peoples. The juxtaposition of children running along the side of a road with a buffalo herd running makes this comparison especially clear. A shot of buffalo being penned in precedes footage of children bidding families farewell at a train station. The superimposition of one buffalo onto the image of four children walking in two pairs (see figure 11.1) encapsulates the settler-colonial state's genocidal policies.

Images from within the residential school are largely mundane, revealing children being taught to sew, mopping the floor, boys standing in a row in a kitchen, girls setting food down on a table. The emphasis on domestic tasks demonstrates the extent to which Indigenous children were used as labour in residential schools, denied the kind of education non-Indigenous children received. As with Barnaby's film, Monkman's uses footage of children going to bed, followed by several cycles of repetition of the images of sewing, mopping, the boys standing, the girls setting down food. The repetition of these shots following the footage of the children in the dormitory, as in Barnaby's film, alludes to sexual abuse perpetrated against children in residential schools, with the rapid reuse of the mundane actions suggesting the trauma of that abuse.

After this point, *Sisters & Brothers* seems figuratively to unspool, revisiting earlier shots in the reverse order in which they initially appear

Figure 11.1 Superimposition of children and buffalo in *Sisters & Brothers* (2015).

in the film. What changes, however, is the soundtrack. The only film of the *Souvenir* series not to use a Tanya Tagaq piece for its non-diegetic sound, *Sisters & Brothers* is set to A Tribe Called Red's "The Road." The fact that this track was released in December 2012, as a tribute to the Idle No More movement, demonstrates how Monkman's film uses archival footage to address the twenty-first-century present, particularly with respect to Indigenous resurgence. As Monkman's film "rewinds," as it were, returning to images from the film's beginning, the sounds of the "The Road" cut off, giving way to the sound of a running buffalo herd, accompanying not only shots of buffalo but also of Indigenous children running, until the film finally returns to the initial images of bodies of water.

The final titles that close out the film, a quotation from Justice (later Senator) Murray Sinclair, who chaired the Truth and Reconciliation Commission, read, "We have recorded the deaths of over 6,000 children [while in residential schools] ... Many were not returned to their families and most were buried in unmarked graves." Following the juxtaposition of children removed from their families and subjected to state-sponsored violence at residential schools with the buffalo, this quotation reminds the viewer that the residential school project was not simply one of cultural genocide: as the TRC discovered, children at residential schools had less chance of surviving these institutions than Canadian soldiers did of surviving the Second World War.[13] Recent uncoverings of unmarked graves at residential school sites in 2021 bear out this earlier statement by Sinclair. Thus, through the comparison of Indigenous children subject to residential school policy with the buffalo, deliberately exterminated by the state so as to deny Indigenous people subsistence in the drive to expedite the settler-colonial project in the west, the film exposes the intentions of the white supremacist state. If an archive in itself can be described, in the words of Hartman, as "a death sentence,"[14] Monkman reframes NFB archival footage to illustrate the state's own orchestration of death sentences for Indigenous nations.

Caroline Monnet's *Mobilize* breaks with Monkman's and Barnaby's films in both its subject matter and its aesthetic, examining different contexts and mechanisms of Indigenous motion through the use of NFB colour footage. Whereas Barnaby and Monkman's films begin by positing ostensibly pre-contact premises through imagery of the natural world that is then interrupted by footage of settler-colonial intrusion, Monnet's film sustains its focus on Indigenous motion throughout, first in the bush and then in urban settings. Like Barnaby's beginning with traditional First Nations lifeways, Monnet's film opens with the image of hands stringing snowshoes, intercut with shots of snowshoes in motion on snowy terrain. The focus on snowshoes gives way to images of canoe construction, such as the separation of bark from a birch tree trunk and the lowering of ribs into position (see figure 11.2).

Although the film includes footage of two canoes on a lake, as well as of a man and a child on a speedboat, much of the film focuses on a single canoeist in a green plaid jacket, Sam Blacksmith from Tony Ianzelo and Boyce Richardson's 1974 film *Cree Hunters of Mistassini*, expertly paddling through rapids, with occasional jump cuts suggesting an accelerated motion. Other images include houses in winter, with long washing lines full of laundry extended over the snow, a man on a snowmobile, a child playing on a carousel, and two children playing cat's cradle with pieces of string. At this point, resolutely urban imagery enters the film through footage of Mohawk ironworkers walking along the beams of New York construction sites and the movements of cranes, taken from Don Owen's 1965 film *High Steel*. The film leaves the urban setting with footage of the corner of a house being laid, Sam Blacksmith in a canoe, underwater plants and fish, and the drying of pieces of meat on wooden poles. This departure from the city setting insists on a coexistence of traditional and modern lifeways, rather than a linear

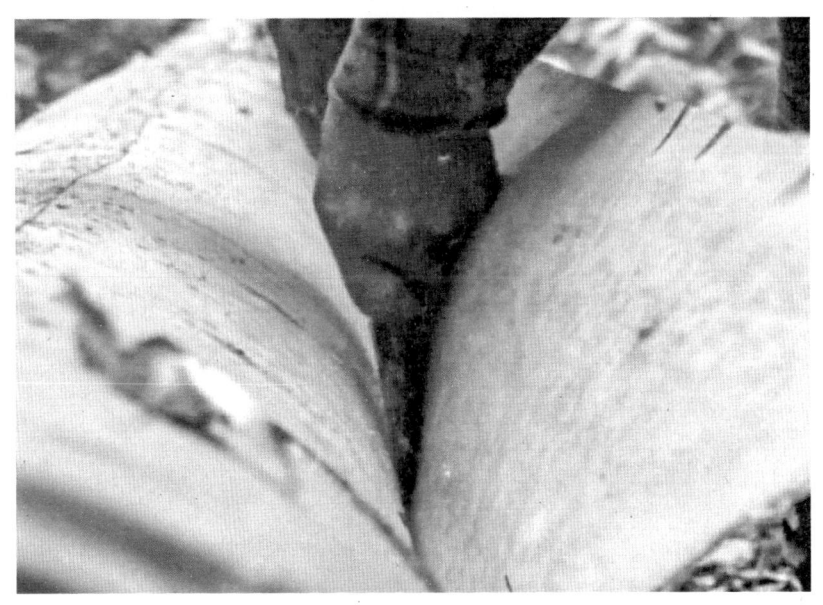

Figure 11.2 Separation of birch bark from the trunk in *Mobilize* (2015).

trajectory from the bush to the city (suggested by the original context of the urban footage, as Owen's film, according to Druick, positions the Mohawk as "curious subjects of modernity").[15] Similarly, footage of Sam Blacksmith canoeing reappears, intercut with shots of a seaplane at various stages of take-off and flight. Shots of the surface of water give way to more urban images, including a city skyline, subway trains, and New York construction sites. Another intersection of traditional and modern lifeways appears in the form of a typewriter with syllabics on the keys, and a page in the process of being typed in syllabics. At this point, the film begins to focus on a First Nations woman in a green dress, walking through the city: Janice Lawrence (Okanagan), one of the "hostesses" at the Indians of Canada Pavilion at Expo 67, as featured in the NFB film *Indian Memento* (dir. Michel Régnier, 1967). Shots of Lawrence are intercut with shots of construction workers building skyscrapers, city traffic, subway trains, and the typing of syllabics. Although Lawrence does not return the camera's gaze, she is shown smiling in profile. The film ends with Lawrence walking along the street.

Monnet has said of her film, "I wanted to show how skillful we are as Indigenous peoples, how Indigenous people are not stagnant, but vibrant, working people"; "I wanted to use the archives to speak about the future; usually archives are nostalgic but, on the contrary, I wanted to talk about the future."[16] Jacques Derrida writes, "the question of the archive is not ... a question of the past. It is not the question of a concept dealing with the past that might *already* be at our disposal or not at our disposal, *an archivable concept of the archive*. It is a question of the future, the question of the future itself, the question of a response, of a promise and of a responsibility for tomorrow."[17] In using – or indeed, mobilizing – the archive to plot a future-oriented trajectory, Monnet orients her film towards an ongoing responsibility. Set to the music of Tanya Tagaq's "Uja," *Mobilize* rescues the NFB archival footage from the kind of nostalgia that Taylor diagnoses. Tagaq's music in itself, blending traditional throat singing with electronic sounds, suits *Mobilize*'s projection of a coexistence of traditional lifeways and the modern world.

Monnet's selection of footage from *Indian Memento* underscores this coexistence: Régnier's film was produced by the Department of Indian Affairs, bearing out Druick's characterization of the NFB as "the eyes of Canada."[18] *Indian Memento* initially turns the settler-colonial lens on mountains and waterways, featuring trains carrying logs, both "according with the Canadian Pavilion's emphasis on industry and its narrative of progress"[19] and insisting that the future of Indigenous territory is resource extraction. The film shifts to footage of Lawrence in her community in British Columbia, in which she folds laundry, climbs trees, swims, and rides horses. We mostly see her wearing cut-off denim shorts and a striped T-shirt, until the film cuts to her standing outside the Indians of Canada Pavilion at Expo 67, wearing her uniform tunic and speaking to white visitors. After several sequences in which we see Lawrence explaining Indigenous cultural objects in the pavilion for a largely white audience, *Indian Memento* shows her off-duty in Montreal, wearing a stylish green dress, having a drink with a white man before leaving to go window shopping. Régnier's film thus privileges a singular trajectory of Lawrence as an exceptional figure (signalled by her selection as a hostess in the first place),[20] away from her community and its associations with the natural world to the urban space of Montreal in the cosmopolitan context of Expo 67. Further, this DIA-produced film about the Indians of Canada Pavilion masks the conflict between Indian Affairs and the Indian Advisory Council in the pavilion construction and content, given Indian Affairs' desire for "a venue in which to present a positive image of its policies and their results," as opposed to the Indian Advisory Council's "belie[f] we were going to plan our own pavilion," only to discover, as George Manuel (Secwepemc) recalls, that "the Department saw to it that Indian people had the same voice in our pavilion that we had in our own lives. Scaled down to size."[21]

Monnet excises the pavilion itself from her film, focusing instead on the figure of Lawrence away from the context of her labour at Expo; neither do we see her drinking with the white man or window-shopping in *Mobilize*. Thus, Monnet disrupts the pavilion-centred trajectory that *Indian Memento* presents for Lawrence's life story in particular and, by implication, for Indigenous people more generally, away from traditional territories to urban, capitalist contexts, by insisting in *Mobilize* on movements back and forth between urban and non-urban spaces. That Monnet focuses on Indigenous forms of motion under the title "Mobilize" politicizes them, the imperative of the title constituting a rallying cry for the future.

If Monnet's film addresses the future through footage of the past, the *Souvenir* series itself, of course, now forms part of the NFB archive. As Druick writes of the NFB documentaries of the celebrated Abenaki filmmaker Alanis Obomsawin, "As a politicized aboriginal artist, Obomsawin brings a particular advocacy to her role as filmmaker; but since her films are made through the government agency, they also tacitly become part of the national dialogue about the place of aboriginal communities in Canadian society."[22] Similarly, the *Souvenir* films both contest the NFB archive and now reside within it. At the same time, that archive is not just made up of films by white directors. Not only does the NFB archive feature the politicized films of Obomsawin, but it also includes documentaries by Indigenous filmmakers, films that furnish some of the footage for *Souvenir*, such as René Siouï Labelle's (Wendat) *Kanata: Legacy of the Children of Aataentsic* (1999), shots of which appear in Monnet's *Mobilize*. Monnet's film also includes footage from *Cree Hunters of Mistassini*, directed by white "outsider-filmmakers"[23] Boyce Richardson and Tony Ianzelo, which presents the hunting patterns of this Cree community in an ethnographic manner, complete with white-settler, voice-of-god narration. Yet, as Druick explains, the film was circulated amongst Indigenous communities with the express intent of informing them about the threats to their traditional lifeways posed by the James Bay Hydro-Electric project; thus, its circulation firmly embeds the film in an activist context that only the final voice-over by Richardson suggests: "In 1972 the James Bay Indians and Inuit began a legal battle against the James Bay Hydro-Electric project in what has become Canada's longest and most complex Indian land case, still unresolved when this film was finished. They have argued that the project will destroy their way of life." Thus, the ethnographic mode of the original film, typically colonial, is at odds with the film's politicized circulation.

In the case of the film *César et son canôt d'écorce/César's Bark Canoe* (1971), directed by the white Québécois filmmaker Bernard Gosselin, which also features in *Mobilize*, the original film captures the making of a canoe by César Newashish, a Tête de Boule Cree, without any settler-colonial narration, only sporadic, brief, lower-case titles in Cree, French, and English that inform the viewer of what materials are being used when, such as "making stem pieces / cedar wood." This film, even by a non-Indigenous director, attempts the representation of this traditional practice with little to no interference by the director. Yet the NFB website presents the film as a salvage narrative, proclaiming, "Building a canoe solely from the materials that the forest provides may become a lost art, even among the Indigenous peoples whose traditional craft it is,"[24] when the film itself arguably presents the making of a canoe as very much a living tradition. Thus, the archive itself is neither monolithic nor coherent, but the ways in which it is still presented to prospective audiences replicates colonial discourse, even where the films themselves might appear to diverge from such an explicitly colonial framework.

The series' bilingual title, *Souvenir*, also illustrates the ambivalence of the archive. Rhéanne Chartrand, curator of the exhibit *Gazing Back, Looking Forward*, of which *Souvenir* was a part, has stated, "The name in itself is a double-edged sword ... For so long, Indigenous culture was seen as kitsch, as a souvenir, a remnant of the past. But with this film, the artists took the archival footage, claimed it and made it a tool of empowerment."[25] The exoticist keepsake of the English meaning of "souvenir" resembles the notion of "memento" in Régnier's *Indian Memento*. However, this version of "souvenir" also coexists with the word's French translation: to remember. As Monnet's film makes especially clear, however, this remembering works in the service of the future. The choice of soundtracks, too, with both Tanya Tagaq and A Tribe Called Red making use of electronic sounds, not only diverges sharply from classical documentary's voice-of-god narration, especially the "omniscient" settler narration in films about Indigenous people, but also frames and steers our viewing towards the present-day production of the *Souvenir* films, rather than leaving us with and re-consolidating the contexts in which the original footage was shot.

Watching the *Souvenir* films both inevitably returns us to the original footage and exceeds the parameters of its contexts. On the one hand, as Crystal Fraser (Gwichya Gwich'in) and Zoe Todd (Métis) remind us, "it is essential that we continue to recognise archival spaces, especially state archives, for their original intent: to create national narratives that seek to legitimise the nation state by excluding Indigenous voices, bodies, economies, histories, and socio-political structures."[26] Furthermore, Hunt observes, "It is not lost on me that the onus for unsettling colonial narratives is often placed on Indigenous peoples."[27] On the other hand, if Warren Cariou (Métis) "worr[ies] that, once a story becomes a document, a location in an archive, it no longer has the capacity to change, to become relevant to a new situation, a new audience,"[28] the films of Barnaby, Monkman, and Monnet mount an intervention in the colonial archive, reclaiming and figuratively repatriating images of Indigenous peoples in ways that not only indict the settler-colonial gaze as preserved in the archive, but also mount powerful challenges to settler-colonial visual culture in the present.[29]

Notes

1 Jovana Jankovic, "Repurposing the Archive: 4 NFB Films by Contemporary Artists at the 2015 Aboriginal Pavilion," 13 July 2015, https://blog.nfb.ca/blog/2015/07/13/repurposing-archive-4-nfb-films-contemporary-artists-2015-aboriginal-pavilion/ (para. 11).

2 A fourth film, *Nimmikaage (She Dances for People / Elle dans pour son people)* by Michelle Latimer, accompanied the three films by Barnaby, Monkman, and Monnet in the *Souvenir* series. In December 2020, a CBC news story reported that doubts had been raised about Latimer's claims to Indigenous identity, noting that her "clai[m] to be of 'Algonquin, Métis and French heritage, from Kitigan Zibi Anishinabeg (Maniwaki), Que.'" had not been upheld by "Kitigan Zibi members who began questioning her family connection to the community" (Ka'nhehsí:io Deer and Jorge Barrera, "Award-winning Filmmaker Michelle Latimer's Indigenous Identity under Scrutiny," *CBC News*, 17 December 2020, https://www.cbc.ca/news/indigenous/michelle-latimer-kitigan-zibi-indigenous-identity-1.5845310). Although in the context of the original NFB films, from which Latimer takes images of Indigenous women and girls, *Nimmikaage* might be said to foreground and problematize the colonial gaze, it is not appropriate to include substantial discussion of Latimer's film in this essay as an example of Indigenizing the archive.

3 Marc André Fortin, "'Ought We to Teach These?': Ethical, Responsible, and Aboriginal Cultural Protocols in the Classroom," in *Learn, Teach, Challenge: Approaching Indigenous Literatures*, eds. Deanna Reder and Linda M. Morra (Waterloo: Wilfrid Laurier University Press, 2016), 464.

4 Jennifer R. O'Neal, "Going Home: The Digital Return of Films at the National Museum of the American Indian," *Museum Anthropology Review* 7, no. 1–2 (2013): 180n1.
5 See Hearne for examples of different forms of repatriation of ethnographic footage, particularly Edward Curtis's 1914 film *In the Land of War Canoes* (first titled *In the Land of the Head Hunters*), which "was repatriated when in 1967 Bill Holm and George Quimby showed the footage to Kwakwaka'wakw audiences," with some members "contribut[ing] to a new soundtrack for the film in 1972"; Joanna Hearne, "Telling and Retelling in the 'Ink of Light': Documentary Cinema, Oral Narratives, and Indigenous Identities," *Screen* 47, no. 3 (2006): 319.
6 A Tribe Called Red announced their change of name to The Halluci Nation in April 2021. This essay will continue to use their previous name given the timing of the *Souvenir* films' production.
7 Wendy Gay Pearson and Susan Knabe, "Globalizing Indigenous Film and Media," in *Reverse Shots: Indigenous Film and Media in an International Context*, eds. Wendy Gay Pearson and Susan Knabe (Waterloo: Wilfrid Laurier University Press, 2015), 16.
8 Zoë Druick, *Projecting Canada: Government Policy and Documentary Film at the National Film Board* (Montreal and Kingston: McGill-Queen's University Press, 2007), 102.
9 Dallas Hunt, "Nikîkîwân: Contesting Settler Colonial Archives through Indigenous Oral History," *Canadian Literature* 230/231 (2016): 26.
10 Diana Taylor, *The Archive and the Repertoire: Performing Cultural Memory in the Americas* (Durham: Duke University Press, 2003), 24; Rosanne Kennedy, "Indigenous Australian Arts of Return: Mediating Perverse Archives," in *Rites of Return: Diaspora Poetics and the Politics of Memory*, eds. Marianne Hirsch and Nancy K. Miller (New York: Columbia University Press, 2011), 90.
11 Paul Williams, "Obsomsawin, Alanis," *Senses of Cinema* 22 (October 2002), https://www.sensesofcinema.com/2002/great-directors/obomsawin/ (para. 2).
12 Saidiya Hartman, "Venus in Two Acts," *Small Axe* 26 (2008): 2.
13 See Daniel Schwartz, "Truth and Reconciliation Commission: By the Numbers," 2 June 2015, https://www.cbc.ca/news/indigenous/truth-and-reconciliation-commission-by-the-numbers-1.3096185.
14 Hartman, "Venus in Two Acts," 2.
15 Druick, *Projecting Canada*, 109.
16 Quoted in Jennifer David, "A Different Kind of Souvenir," 6 February 2018, https://www.gallery.ca/magazine/in-the-spotlight/a-different-kind-of-souvenir (para. 7).
17 Jacques Derrida, *Archive Fever: A Freudian Impression*, trans. Eric Prenowitz, (Chicago: University of Chicago Press, 1996), 36.

18 Druick, *Projecting Canada*, 182.
19 Jane Griffith, "One Little, Two Little, Three Little Canadians: The Indians of Canada Pavilion and Public Pedagogy, Expo 67," *Journal of Canadian Studies* 49, no. 2 (2015): 198.
20 Thirteen Indigenous women were hired to be hostesses at the Indians of Canada Pavilion at Expo 67, out of 220 applicants. Yves Theriault, head of the Cultural Affairs Section of Indian Affairs, stated, "We should spend a great deal of attention towards making these hostesses the very embodiment of what an Indian can be"; this transformation occurred through Expo hostesses "receiv[ing] instruction in 'makeup, grooming, posture, and walking'" (Myra Rutherdale and Jim Miller, "'It's Our Country': First Nations Participation in the Indian Pavilion at Expo 67," *Journal of the Canadian Historical Association* 17, no. 2 [2006]: 162, 163).
21 Rutherdale and Miller, "It's Our Country," 156; George Manuel and Michael Posluns, *The Fourth World: An Indian Reality* (Minneapolis: University of Minnesota Press, [1974] 2019), 174, 177.
22 Druick, *Projecting Canada*, 174.
23 Ibid., 154.
24 National Film Board, "César's Bark Canoe," https://www.nfb.ca/film/cesars_bark_canoe/ (accessed 31 December 2021).
25 Quoted in David, "A Different Kind of Souvenir" (para. 2).
26 Crystal Fraser and Zoe Todd, "Decolonial Sensibilities: Indigenous Research and Engaging with Archives in Contemporary Colonial Canada," *Internationale Online* (2016), http://www.internationaleonline.org/research/decolonising_practices/54_decolonial_sensibilities_indigenous_research_and_engaging_with_archives_in_contemporary_colonial_canada (para. 10).
27 Hunt, "Nikîkîwân," 39.
28 Warren Cariou, "Who Is the Text in This Class? Story, Archive, and Pedagogy in Indigenous Contexts," in *Learn, Teach, Challenge: Approaching Indigenous Literatures*, eds. Deanna Reder and Linda M. Morra (Waterloo: Wilfrid Laurier University Press, 2016), 473.
29 I would like to express my gratitude to Nicole Périat at the NFB for her invaluable assistance in locating the original films used by the artists of the *Souvenir* project.

Filmography

César et son canôt d'écorce. Directed by Bernard Gosselin. Canada: National Film Board, 1971.
Circle of the Sun. Directed by Colin Low. Canada: National Film Board, 1960.

Cree Hunters of Mistassini. Directed by Tony Ianzelo and Boyce Richardson. Canada: National Film Board, 1974.

Etlinisigu'niet (Bleed Down). Directed by Jeff Barnaby. Canada: National Film Board, 2015.

High Steel. Directed by Don Owen. Canada: National Film Board, 1965.

Indian Memento. Directed by Michel Régnier. Canada: National Film Board, 1967.

Mobilize. Directed by Caroline Monnet. Canada: National Film Board, 2015.

Nimmikaage (She Dances for People). Directed by Michelle Latimer. Canada: National Film Board, 2015.

Sisters & Brothers. Directed by Kent Monkman. Canada: National Film Board, 2015.

12

I-doc and My-doc

Bear 71 and *Highrise* as Canadian Documentaries

Seth Feldman

Starting Posts

In a recent review of books on "postcinema," Lisa Åkervall identifies two periods in the emergence of the technologies and practices associated with the term: "In the late 1990s and early 2000s, theorists warned of the end or the death of cinema – a great rupture – in the face of a supposedly new and threatening digital cinema. In the past ten years, by contrast, scholars turned specifically to the term, 'postcinema,' usually identifying it with shifting relations to traditional cinema. The older emphasis on rupture has given way to an interest in the dislocation and recomposition of cinematic assemblages."[1] Åkervall's historical schema points to John Corner's year 2000 identification of a "post-documentary" occasioned by "the widespread dispersal (and, in part, perhaps dissipation) of documentarist energies."[2] For Corner, documentary had suffered from ever-expanding means of production and dissemination. What was once a calling had become the habit of those billions of people newly outfitted with easy-to-use means of production. If capturing the extra-cinema reality became ubiquitous, it would inevitably become formless.

There is a third phase of digital communication that, like the earlier two phases, impacts directly on cinema and documentary. Digital communication has become something of a poisoned chalice that runneth over with fake news, fake people, threats to net neutrality, rampant commercialism, and attacks on privacy (or what's left of it) – all under the auspices of trillion-dollar corporations too big to regulate. Nor is there an easy way out. Technological societies that have made themselves totally dependent upon digitally controlled systems have come to realize just how vulnerable those systems are. One hacker can bring down a nation or a civilization.

Within cinema as a whole the poisoned chalice has inspired both recidivism and weariness. A safer world of pre-digital filmmaking is evoked both in the physical (e.g., a minor revival in the use of film stock) and the stylistic (e.g., the interest, particularly among documentarians, in the uses of pre-digital, archival images). Another relevant trend here is the multi-part forensic documentary, exemplified by *The Staircase* (Bryan Gildner, 2018), *Wormwood* (Errol Morris, 2017), or the inspired satire of the genre, *American Vandal* (Tony Yacenda, 2017). All these works present a loose assemblage of often contradictory evidence that points to the futility of self-proclaimed, truth-seeking technologies. The weariness with the digital is also apparent within a growing sense that CGI has hit a wall. The genre in which digital imagery plays a large if not determining factor has devolved into a competition between CGI providers, a medium-encompassing trade show to be viewed with expensive popcorn. The gap between blockbuster franchise filmmaking and films about human relationships has never been wider (e.g., the Academy of Motion Picture Arts and Sciences' failed attempt to establish a prize for popular films).

Interactive documentary (a.k.a. "i-doc") has developed in the last two decades within the trends noted above. Appearing amid the fear of "dispersal" and "dissipation" Corner described, it has grown in the milieu of "recomposition" described by Åkervall. If conventional documentary has been overwhelmed by the emergence of new technologies and is reacting against them, i-doc appears to offer a means of reversing the "dissipation" that, at the same time, utilizes the technologies responsible for it. I-doc has performed the role of mediator not simply between the limitations of conventional documentary and the threat of digital media, but also between the authorship that can be claimed by humans – the maker and the viewer – and that which emerges from the technologies that connect them.

I-docs also represent a way of thinking about documentary that has long been part of Canadian practice. From at least the 1930s, when Albert Tessier shot his widely seen home movies of Quebec frontier settlement and Gordon Sparling made documentary shorts at the film lab where he happened to work, the amateur documentarian and the low-budget project have demonstrated their importance to the nation's cinematic memory. At the other end of the spectrum, John Grierson's founding and directing of the National Film Board and his service as the first film commissioner injected a world-class professionalism to Canadian documentary. Grierson, while heading the NFB, insisted on differentiating between his documentary ideal and its pursuit through any one technology. Discussing the success of his documentary movement as a "public cause," Grierson wrote: "These facts should have made it clear that the documentary idea was not basically a film idea at all, and the film treatment it inspired only an incidental aspect of it. The medium appeared to be the most convenient and most exciting available to us. The idea itself, on the other hand, was a new idea for public education: its underlying concept that the world was in a phase of drastic change affecting every manner of thought and practice, and the public comprehension of the nature of that change vital."[3]

Grierson practised a bit of what he preached when he created the NFB's Still Photography Division in 1941, which, among its other accomplishments, incorporated the long-established practice of documentary photography into Canadian documentary practice.[4] Within film, Grierson's recruiting of animation into the documentary agenda occasioned not the pursuit of animated documentary (that would come later), but rather another form to serve documentary's purpose. Perhaps most importantly, the idea of incorporating changing styles and technology into the pursuit of the documentary ideal continues to be part of the NFB's mandate. Its history of innovation includes Unit B and the French Unit in their development of direct cinema; the Expo-era films with which the NFB and its personnel were involved; Challenge for Change; the various instances of drama-documentary; and, as will be discussed here, the "documedia" that Peter Wintonick wrote of in "New Platforms for Docmedia: 'Variant of a Manifesto.'"[5] With a Vertovian stridency, Wintonick predicted that conventional documentary was dead at the hands of a new wave of media tools.

Wintonick also practised a bit of what he preached. Working at the film board, he and Katerina Cizek (the future designer of *Highrise*) made a film entitled *Seeing Is Believing: Handicams, Human Rights and the News* (2006) about the repercussions of the Rodney King video. While not made with "documedia," the film was concerned with their potential. At the same time, the film board was investigating digital platforms for the distribution of its films. As early as 1997, the NFB producer Gerry Flahive (the future executive producer of *Highrise*) conceived of what could have been the first streamed film, his documentary *The Man Who Might Have Been* (John Kramer, 1998). Because of technical limitations, this became the streaming that might have been.

The event that brought the NFB into the world of documedia was producer Tom Perlmutter's appointment as film commissioner in 2007. Perlmutter came to the post having already forged an ambitious digital agenda. He was determined to stream as many as possible of the 13,000 films the NFB had made to that time. The process was slowed by the need to clear intellectual property rights for aspects of those films not owned by the board and it has taken more than a decade to put 5,000 titles online. Yet the achievement is remarkable in that the films have not only been digitized and in many cases made downloadable but have also been cross-referenced in a database. Users became informed participants in the use of archival film for the purposes of understanding history and culture. Robert Lower's *Shameless Propaganda* (2014) demonstrated archival based-filmmaking by editing clips from the board's 500 films made during World War II to present a portrait of Canada during that period.

Perlmutter also had a plan for producing digital documentary. The board opened an English Digital Studio in 2008, and a French Digital Studio the following year. Both the digitization and production of digital documentary came with a high cost, though one that Perlmutter was willing to pay. As commissioner, he redirected between 4 and 5 per cent of the board's budget into digital. Eventually 20 per cent of its English language production funds went to digital productions.[6] Perlmutter's commitment to digital was facilitated by the NFB's long-standing tradition of adapting its work to new technologies. Selling DVDs or asking viewers to visit one of the very few "mediatheques" at NFB offices was clearly not effective at a time when most Canadians were online. Their replacement in production and distribution would go hand in hand.

The two Emmy-winning works to be discussed below have roots in the NFB's interests and practices. *Bear 71* (Leanne Allison and Jeremy Mendes, 2012) takes on an issue of perennial importance in Canadian culture: the wilderness and Canadians' representations of it. On a more technical level, it demonstrates a continuation of interest in voice-over and its variations that has been present since the first works produced by the board. For its part, Katerina Cizek's *Highrise: The Towers in the World, the World in the Towers* (2010–15)[7] is a consciously planned extension of Challenge for Change, particularly in its emphasis on community participation and the recognition of documentary subjects as co-creators. Unlike *Bear 71*, the issue it explores – urban and suburban vertical housing – has had far too small a role on the national or international agenda. *Highrise* provokes the needed discussion through a maximized interactive challenge to the viewer who, following its many possibilities, earns the title of "user."

Bear 71

Bear 71, in the non-VR version currently available in the NFB's online catalogue, premiered at the 2012 Sundance Film Festival in a manner that hasn't been seen since. As the festival catalogue describes it: "Participants explore and engage with the world of a female grizzly bear via animal role play, augmented reality, webcams, geolocation tracking, motion sensors, a microsite, social media channels and a real bear trap in Park City."[8] The microsite remains active and the virtual reality version of *Bear 71* came online in March 2017.[9] Yet despite these augmentations and despite its being listed as an interactive documentary in the National Film Board's online catalogue, *Bear 71* is more correctly seen as a very well-made documentary short with a strong interactive component.[10] Seen as a "linear" film, there is a perfectly coherent story with a beginning, middle, and end. An even more anti-interactive characteristic of the work as we see it today is its fixed time limitation. The opening graphic tells us that what follows is exactly twenty minutes long. Immediately a countdown clock begins.

This said, the interactive core of *Bear 71* does play a role in both its genesis and in establishing its meaning. At the film's core is an archive of Banff National Park trail camera surveillance footage accessible to the user via a schematic map of the park. Users click on map locales where the cameras have seen particular animals. They see what the camera saw, captioned with a snippet of information about the animal species being observed. From this point of view, these users identify with the naturalists studying the wildlife roaming the park.

The trail cam images are compelling for many of the same reasons that interactive documentaries as a whole engage their users. They are randomly organized, not only because they are accessed randomly by the user, but also because the surveillance cameras capture the images of passing animals by happenstance. The animals that accidentally walk within the cameras' range are totally unaware of being filmed. They are "caught" in the same way that humans – or, as we see them more frequently, humans behaving in an atypical or criminal manner – are caught by surveillance cameras. There is also a sense within the pictures of how infrequently the cameras find the animals. Seeing the animals in daylight, at night, in summer and winter, lingering and dashing past, tells us that this is the best material from a very long and patient observational process. The user gets a sense of how unnatural it is to see these animals without their awareness of humans watching them.

Figure 12.1   Poster for *Bear 71* (2012).

We are crossing an existential boundary to look at that tree in the forest that no one sees or hears falling.

That we are being made aware simultaneously of both the animals and the surveillance of them reflects the genesis of *Bear 71*. Leanne Allison, one of the two co-designers, began working on the project when she gained access to the archive of Banff trail camera footage. Allison's co-designer, Jeremy Mendes, saw in that footage not just the images but the surveillance that produced them: "I thought, this is the CCTV cameras in Times Square, this is post 9/11 security, observation, privacy issues of the day. It's about technology. It's about us."[11] Or, to expand upon Mendes's construct of the footage, the constant surveillance under which we live post-9/11 violates not only our privacy but also our "nature." Rather than the independent agents we might think ourselves to be, we, like the animals in the park, have become that which is being watched.

Pointing us to the surveillance footage and to this interpretation of it is Bear 71 herself. She makes herself known at the beginning of this largely linear work. The first images we see have nothing to do with the interactive schematic map of the park. Instead, we see a montage of conventional film shots in which a bear is snared, tranquilized, and has a radio transponder clamped around her neck and tags stapled to her ears. The sequence is narrated by the bear not only with a human voice but, thanks to the script by J.B. MacKinnon and Mia Kirshner's performance of it, with the wry assurance of a very well-informed observer. Transformed into Bear 71 by the naturalists who have tagged her, she acquired the naturalists' knowledge of the process. Her first words in the film are: "That snare had a breaking strength of two tons. The dart was full of something called Telazol, brought you to by Pfizer, the same people who make Zoloft and Viagra. Next thing I know, I'm wearing a VHF collar and have my own radio frequency. They also gave me a number. Bear 71."

This opening sequence ends with the naturalists releasing Bear 71 amid a barrage of fireworks that sends the terrified animal running full speed into the woods. Cut to the schematic of the park – designed by the Toronto firm J3 – where an expanding dotted line traces Bear 71's escape. Soon other creatures are seen making their way through the schematic, including one identified as a human tourist. All the while Bear 71, with her consciousness seemingly awakened by the tranquilizer dart, guides us through the complexities and contradictions of her world. Citing the surveillance tools distributed throughout the park, she tells us that she thinks of that world in exactly the way the park is shown in the schematic, as "the grid."

While the user navigates through the interactive grid, the physical grid in which Bear 71 lives is described by her as being equally artificial. Grizzlies, she tells us, evolved on the prairies and were forced out of their habitat. Their expulsion is so recent that they have not yet learned to climb trees. Nor can they make optimum use of their sensitive sense of smell. Thanks to the ubiquitous tourists, the park smells of "deodorant, dog food, hash browns and anti-freeze." The bears' privacy has been taken from them not only by the surveillance apparatus but also by the towers that broadcast its images – and a virtual tour through the park – to anyone in the world with a computer. As Bear 71 tells us: "it is hard to say where the wired world ends and the real one begins."

Although tourists come to Banff to see the wildlife, the actual encounters are hardly gratifying and certainly not part of "nature" (a term that is, as Bear 71's monologue continues, reduced to a myth or sales pitch). Bear 71 tells us about an encounter with two tourists who came too close to her cubs. She would have attacked them had she not realized they were young women. The young women run off with a tale they will tell for the rest of their lives, that sort of tale being the park's premium product. Other contacts with humans have less happy endings. Bear 71 tells of thoughtless tourists leaving the lids open on the ever-tempting bear-proof garbage containers. Encounters with the park rangers have ended with the sting of rubber bullets, the technical term for which is "aversive conditioning." Other human interaction with bears goes beyond the awkward or painful to the potentially lethal. The highway running through the park has necessitated building overpasses and underpasses to keep animals from being hit by cars. The animals learn to use them, another modification of their "natural" behaviour. This anthropomorphizing of nature is made more explicit by images of animals and then of human tourists using an underpass. A greater danger comes from the railroad tracks running through the park. The trains are hauling boxcars that leak grain. Bears, Bear 71 tells us, are attracted to the grain. While standing on the tracks eating it, they become casualties of the speeding trains at, so far, the rate of one dead bear for each five miles of track. It is a poignant statistic that combines, in our unnatural narrator's recital of it, human machinery and numbers with torn animal flesh.

From these and other experiences Bear 71 has derived the most important lesson she has learned in her humanized habitat: "never do what comes naturally." This bit of advice is the sum of what is learned through *Bear 71*'s design and content: there is nothing "natural" about the outdoor habitat that humans have created in Banff. It is then altogether apt that our guide to this unnatural (or, if we dare say it, "post-natural") world is herself a fabricated being. Not only is she an all-knowing, talking bear, but as we learn in Bear 71's climax, she is narrating in the first person deceased. She and her cubs ventured onto the railroad tracks to collect the spilt grain. A train appeared and, in an instantaneous lapse, Bear 71 acted naturally. She rose up on her hind legs to protect her cubs by roaring at the oncoming train. In so doing, she became, as she said earlier in her description of the railroad threat, "a statistic." This too is shown in a montage, one that echoes the opening sequence of Bear 71 being fitted for surveillance. While we do not see her actually being hit by the train, we do see the tracks as filmed from the front of the approaching locomotive. Its camera, as we were told earlier, is there to protect the railroad from liability in the event of accidents. Bear 71's last moment, like most of her life, has been monitored for human purposes.

The device of Bear 71 (for, with her death in the story's climax, she has shed any remaining illusion of being something other than a device) is the product of another sort of evolution: that of the documentary voice-over. This is particularly true of the National Film Board, whose wartime origins were characterized by voice-overs that, if anything, exaggerated the conventions of their time. The voice-over was authoritative, backed by strident music and capable of transforming the images from indexical representations of the extra-cinematic world into icons of larger concepts. Many of the best-known films produced later at the film board worked to undermine the voice-over's gravitas. *Paul Tomkowicz, Street Railway Switchman* (Roman Kroitor, 1954) used the thoughts (if not the actual voice) of its protagonist as a world-weary narrator. *City of Gold* (Colin Low and Wolf Koenig, 1957), voiced by Pierre Berton as himself, turns the gold rush photographs on which it is built into icons of contradiction and oddity. *Corral* (Colin Low, 1954) was an exercise in missing narration. Direct cinema and the film board's Labyrinth Pavilion at Expo 67 (Colin Low, Roman Kroitor, Hugh O'Connor) are largely defined by that same absence. In this context, Bear 71, with a script as well written and presented as that of any classic NFB voice-over documentary, goes even further. Its dead bear narrator argues against the deception of presenting a "natural" landscape and its inhabitants. Her "unnatural" voice is intrinsically subversive, intent on undermining a facile presentation of imagery rather than verifying, much less elevating, what we see.

What is most successful in Bear 71 is its function as an addition to Canadian culture's enduring concern with the natural world. The wilderness shapes consciousness in Northrop Frye's notion of garrison mentality, in Margaret Atwood's "survival" and her adaptation of *The Journals of Susanna Moodie*. A bit closer to the present case, Marion Engle's *Bear*, in its own scandalous way, balances the human corruption of nature against nature's corruption of the human. Then there is the selling of the Canadian wilderness as a site for a safe and even luxurious rendezvous with the natural world that is on display in the decades of advertising by the Canadian Pacific Railroad for its frontier hotels (including, of course, Banff). Very early Canadian cinema played a part in this advertising. *Back to God's Country* (David Hartford, 1919), a milestone in Canada's silent film industry, starred Nell Shipman who both on screen and in real life kept company with a pet bear. The film board, perhaps because it is committed to the image of Canada as a technologically advanced, world-class civilization, has consistently dealt with the global perception of a wilderness nation. *Bear 71*'s depiction of a high-tech wilderness seen through the eyes of a technologically modified animal continues this undertaking with an evolved understanding of technological oppression as seen, at least in part, through equally evolved technology.

Highrise

One of commissioner Tom Perlmutter's objectives for digital production was to explore a revival of the NFB's Challenge for Change/Société nouvelle program, which had been a textbook case of progressive filmmaking in the late 1960s and through the 1970s. Adapting the principles of Challenge for Change to emergent digital tools would entail putting cameras in the hands of people, co-creators, who would normally be documentary subjects. Secondly, it meant establishing a structure through which these co-creators could share their sound and image recordings with each other and ultimately with those responsible for alleviating their conditions. This was the Challenge for Change model based on Colin Low's Fogo Island process. Low had filmed statements from the people of a Newfoundland outport that appeared to be unsustainable. He then showed these films to officials in St John's and in so doing established lines of communication that ultimately convinced the provincial government not to shut down Fogo, as it had so many other outports. This, at least, was the general impression of Fogo as a model for Challenge for Change as a whole. In reality, the processes the Fogo model and Challenge for Change employed were far more eclectic. Marit Kathryn Corneil has written of the Fogo Island Project as "an approach to documentary that contained a multiplicity of practices: aspects of narrative, *cinéma direct*, performance, participatory and reflexive modes, as well as interview and testimony ... By extension, the multiplicity of ethical and aesthetic approaches conceived under the umbrella of [Challenge for Change], that in fact ranged all the way from pre-screenings, to training citizens groups in production, to citizens

Figure 12.2   Production still from *Highrise* (2010).

writing and performing in fictions, demonstrates the rich legacy of the program as an experiment in a new political use of documentary."[12] In reviving Challenge for Change, digital tools would offer additional options for what was already a hybrid process.

Perlmutter shared his Challenge for Change idea with Katrina Cizek, the NFB's filmmaker-in-residence who along with producer Gerry Flahive had already made a documentary short on medical activism in Africa, *The Bicycle: Fighting AIDS with Community Medicine* (2005).[13] With Perlmutter's idea in mind, Cizek and Flahive approached Toronto's St Michael's Hospital with a proposal to tape the hospital's psychiatric crisis intervention staff working with the police to defuse potentially dangerous situations on the street. As per Challenge for Change, this footage was shown to doctors and administrators at the hospital. Cizek and Flahive also used some of their footage to make a conventional documentary short about the incidents they had filmed: *The Interventionists: Chronicles of a Mental Health Crisis Team* (2006). Other documentary expressions grew out of their work with St Michael's. *I Was Here* was a workshop that used digital cameras to allow homeless parents to talk about their lives. Cizek's *Street Health Stories* engaged formerly homeless photographers to document the lives of the homeless through photography and audio recordings. *Drawing from Life* (2008) combined animation and live footage to document twenty-eight attempted suicide survivors.[14]

The St Michael's work served as a proof of concept for what would become the much larger *Highrise* project in its four major manifestations. Cizek decided upon the subject of the *Highrise* project when she learned that approximately 1 billion people worldwide live in high-rise apartment buildings, that most of these buildings are rapidly deteriorating, and that the issue had very little public discussion. Further research – in conjunction with urban studies scholar Roger Keil – brought the realizations that Toronto was a prime example of a city rapidly expanding its stock of vertical housing and that the older high-rise towers in the city's inner suburbs were being occupied by disadvantaged populations. The state of the high-rise living could then be formulated as both a local (or as it was to be explored in one of the *Highrise* projects, a "hyper-local") and a global issue.

The first of the *Highrise* projects, *Out My Window*, was, in Cizek's words, "a whirlwind global tour of 13 cities."[15] Upon entering the site users chose images from the windows of a virtual apartment block that took them to short documentaries from places such as Bangalore, Montreal, São Paulo, Amsterdam, and other locations chosen as a representative sample of high-rise living. In each apartment, users were greeted by a pastiche of still images that could be seen as a 360-degree circle. Moving the cursor along the circle would take the user from the inside of the apartment to the view outside its window and back again. The people living in these apartments, speaking in their native languages, would tell the stories (or, in one case, perform a rap) about their apartments, their communities, and the lives being lived within these spaces. There were links within the 360-degree pans that connected to other aspects of the apartment or the community. In all, the apartment dwellers told forty-nine stories, each with its own musical signature. Throughout, Cizek had a singular intent: "I was interested in the minutiae. The everyday. The objects they look at time and time again. I wanted to explore documentary storytelling that mimics the way we get to know one another when we visit one another's homes. The small stories we tell about that painting on the wall, that lamp over there, the places we sit and think. That object right outside the window. These are the triggers for stories in our lives. We point to these artefacts to invite each other into our imaginaries."[16] *Out My Window* won the 2011 International Digital Emmy for Non-Fiction, the first of many awards to be won by the *Highrise* series.

For their next project, *The Thousandth Tower* (2011), Cizek and Flahive turned to a single apartment block in the Toronto suburb of Etobicoke. They spent two years with tenants collecting ideas about the tower's shortcomings and possible fixes. They then used basic media tools to compile a presentation. As Cizek wrote: "In *Thousandth Tower*, the residents we worked with … combined photographs, text and audio to describe their experiences of living in the buildings. Although they all had different ideas of home, each revealed a strong connection to their cultural roots. In these particular high rises 97% of the people were born outside of Canada. Themes that arose from their photos were dichotomies of belonging and loneliness, comfort and insecurity, success and struggle."[17]

Thousandth Tower evolved into *One Millionth Tower* (2011), a far more complex work around the shortcomings of the high rise as identified by five tenants and a layered process for addressing them. Cizek described it as "hyper local."[18] *One Millionth Tower* began when she took the *Thousandth Tower* presentation and the people who contributed to it to Toronto City Hall. There they met the architect, Graeme Stewart, who suggested that he and other architects design solutions to the problems the tenants had identified: making over a tennis court, a large unused space, the possibility of a garden, introducing colour to the apartment block. The architects took on their own consultative process, spending long periods of time developing their ideas with the tenants. For her part, Cizek discovered a means of using computer-generated 3D effects to insert the architects' plans into the images of the two high-rise towers. A 3D program developed by Helios Design allowed animators to work within the browser with which they retrieved the original high-rise images and the architects' designs. *One Millionth Tower* offered a "virtual landscape" that ranged from the photographic to the abstract. Users could explore that landscape, see how it was generated, export it, and find other high-rise buildings in cities of every nation. *Wired* magazine put *One Millionth Tower* on its front page, connected to it through its online site, and declared: "To tell the story of Canadian high-rise residents reinventing their homes in the sky, the makers of new film *One Millionth Tower* reinvented the documentary format."[19]

A Short History of the Highrise (2013) was, like *Bear 71*, a work originating in an archive. It began when Cizek was invited to work with the *New York Times* Op-Docs, a series of short documentaries accessible through the newspaper's online edition. The original idea was to make an Op-Doc on New York high-rises through the use of photographs in the newspaper's archive. Cizek eventually selected 500 of these photographs. With additional images found by Elizabeth Klinck and Jivan Nagra, the help of the *Times*' in-house interactive designers and, again, a collaboration with animators and Helios Design, Cizek made four three-to-six-minute films.[20] *Mud*, narrated by Feist, traces the history of the high-rise from ancient times. *Concrete*, narrated by Cizek, is about the ideologies behind high-rise living from the late nineteenth century to the present. *Glass*, narrated by Cold Specks, set in the present, relates the tensions between disappearing public housing and the rise of the condo. Narration in each of the first three films is in rhyme while minimally animated paintings (and some photographs) are reminiscent of *The Romance of Transportation in Canada* (Colin Low, 1952). In their interactive mode, each of the films offers sets of links to the sub-topic on screen at any given moment. Both sides of the *New York Times* photographs are scanned, not only helping to identify their subject matter but also showing the photo editor's notes and transforming the photographs from images into objects. The fourth film, *Balcony*, is made exclusively of photographs submitted to the *Times* for the project. Its links are to other submitted photographs that share their main features (e.g., "children," "fog"). *Balcony* ends the historical progression in the present, only occasionally (and poignantly) taking the user back to the history discussed in the three previous films.

Universe Within: Digital Lives in the Global Highrise (2015) offers a set of stories about the "hidden digital lives" of internet users in high-rise apartments. The project began when a survey of the tenants in the high-rise block seen in *Out My Window* revealed that 80 per cent of them were online. That finding was pursued through a joint research venture, *Digital Citizenship in the Global Suburbs*, undertaken with Deborah Cowen and Emily Paradis of the University of Toronto. Among its findings were examples of people in high-rises using the internet in an assortment of innovative ways. Cizek and her researchers continued finding these stories on their own. *Universe Within* was designed as a means of accessing several dozen of them. Entering the site, the user chooses between three virtual hosts: a nine-year-old girl, a First Nations woman, and a male actor (all of whom self-identify as algorithms). The three hosts raise issues that lead to sub-topics, such as Can the Internet Transcend: Hate; With Beats; With Laughs; Spiritually. The user can then click on one of these sub-topics in order to hear a story. The stories, told in the speakers' native languages, concern subjects such as praying in far-off temples online, organizing an international peace movement, or reconnecting to family after a long prison sentence.

Universe Within was, intentionally, the last of the *Highrise* productions. By the end of the project, *Highrise* had provided a model for multi-year, varied, and innovative i-docs. Cizek had achieved a reputation as "perhaps the foremost proponent of co-creation within interactive documentary."[21] If there was a problem with *Highrise*, it was that of knowing when and how to stop. Cizek cited the problem in her director's notes: "it's an exciting and troubling place to leave off. For our species, both the digital and vertical are becoming inescapable. We race toward more digital integration with Artificial Intelligence, virtual reality, surveillance, big data and robots, along with often rampant vertical development of our cities that shuffles and displaces millions of people. Whom do these processes exclude? Who wins? Who loses? And how might we harness these new technologies to improve our collective future? It's up to us; it's up to you."[22]

Another problem is less Cizek's than those who might wish to write about *Highrise* in some critical or scholarly fashion. For not only is *Highrise* never really over but its interactive structure makes it very difficult to define the exact subject matter under discussion. Offering infinite variations to the text is not a side effect but rather one of the designer's prime objectives. It is possible, as is done here, to focus largely on the design of the work, parsing the text as process rather than product. This would seem inconsistent with documentary's focus on content, those depicted circumstances in the extra-cinematic world leading to the documentary's production. The opposite strategy might be to describe the content of one or a small number of possible "remixes," perhaps with the assumption that some of these remixes are more likely than others. Yet this produces a high likelihood of the writer describing one text while the reader sees another. A third possibility would be to critique i-docs in a non-linear writing format, taking advantage of the sorts of hyper-text platforms used by the writers of computer fiction. Here, though, the product would be a shadow work whose most appropriate locale might well be within the work it is critiquing. None of these solutions is very satisfying. But, as Cizek writes, it is up to us.[23]

"A Troubling Place to Leave Off"

The new era of the poisoned chalice may well make it harder to view the i-doc and even harder to believe it. It may be lost in the digital cacophony. On the other hand, the i-doc may offer a model for the mediation of online information. Cizek insists that while she is a designer and encourages co-creators, she remains a director. She, along with her executive producer, will take responsibility, will give provenance to facts, and will have the last say as to the contents of the final work. Behind that authority lies the credibility of the National Film Board's reputation, a large part of the legacy of Canadian documentary. It is this sort of stabilizing framework that might well be necessary in order for i-docs' continuation of the documentary's work. This in turn leads to a more general consideration of the i-doc's place in the performance of social and political ideas. A political demonstration, for instance, is an interactive event in which very large numbers of people respond to a particular occurrence or other prompt. It is also, in the digital age, the making-physical of the social media wars. The i-doc has an as-yet-undetermined place in a spectrum of interactive performance that begins with cybernetic interplay and ends with real-world change.

Notes

1 Lisa Åkervall, "Reviews," *Screen* 59 (2018): 132–3.
2 John Corner, "What Can We Say about 'Documentary,'" *Media, Culture and Society*, vol. 22 (2000): 687.
3 John Grierson, "The Documentary Idea: 1942," in *Grierson on Documentary*, ed. with an introduction by Forsyth Hardy (New York: Praeger, 1971), 250.
4 See Renate Wickens, "National Film Board of Canada: The Still Photography Division," *History of Photography* 20, no. 3 (autumn 1996): 271–7.
5 Peter Wintonick, "New Platforms for Docmedia: 'Variant of a Manifesto,'" in *The Documentary Film Book*, edited by Brian Winston (London: BFI/Palgrave Macmillan, 2013), 376–82.
6 Jeff Beer, "How Canada's NFB Became One of the World's Hippest Digital Content Hubs," *Fast Company Newsletter*, 10 February 2012, https://www.fastcompany.com/1679850/how-canadas-nfb-became-one-of-the-worlds-hippest-digital-content-hubs.
7 I am using throughout the NFB's spelling of the project, *Highrise*, to refer to the project itself. The *Oxford English Dictionary* hyphenated spelling is used to refer to a high-rise building.
8 Layla Revis, "4 Inspiring Examples of Digital Storytelling," *Mashable*, 31 January 2012, http://mashable.com/2012/01/31/digital-storytelling/#OX9xxqpdZSq3.
9 *Bear 71* Microsite, http://bear71.nfb.ca/.
10 National Film Board of Canada Online Resources, https://www.nfb.ca/interactive/.
11 Robyn Smith, "Does a Bear Pose in the Woods?" *The Tyee*, 2 May 2012, https://thetyee.ca/ArtsAndCulture/2012/05/02/Bear-71/.
12 Marit Kathryn Corneil, "Winds and Things: Towards a Reassessment of the Challenge for Change/Société nouvelle Legacy," in *Challenge for Change: Activist Documentary at the National Film Board of Canada*, eds. Thomas Waugh, Michael Brendan Baker, and Ezra Winton (Montreal and Kingston: McGill-Queen's University Press, 2010), 402.
13 Although made in 2005, *The Bicycle* was not released until 2010.

14 A discussion of the Filmmaker in Residence program at St Michael's Hospital appears as "Interview with Katerina Cizek by Liz Miller" in *Challenge for Change*, 427–42.
15 Katerina Cizek, "Director's Note," http://highrise.nfb.ca/onemillionthtower/1mt_webgl.php.
16 Katerina Cizek, "Director's Statement," *Out My Window*, http://outmywindow.nfb.ca/#/outmywindow.
17 Katerina Cizek, "Director's Blog," http://highrise.nfb.ca/tag/out-my-window/.
18 Katerina Cizek, "Director's Statement," *One Millionth Tower*, http://highrise.nfb.ca/onemillionthtower/1mt_webgl.php.
19 Angela Watercutter, "Premiere: One Millionth Tower High-Rise Documentary Takes Format to New Heights," *Wired*, 5 November 2011, https://www.wired.com/2011/11/one-millionth-tower-2/.
20 Katrina Cizek, "*Highrise* and the *New York Times*," http://highrise.nfb.ca/2013/03/highrise-and-the-new-york-times/.
21 Mandy Rose, "Not Media About but Media With: Co-Creation for Activism," in *I-docs: The Evolving Practices of Interactive Documentary*, eds. Judith Aston, Sandra Gaudenzi, and Mandy Rose (New York: Wallflower Press, 2017), 50.
22 Katrina Cizek, "Director's Notes," *The Universe Within*, http://universewithin.nfb.ca/desktop.html#boy_q3.
23 I would like to thank Katrina Cizek and Gerry Flahive for their valuable input to this discussion of *Highrise*.

13

Diasporic Sights
Trauma and Representation in Recent Canadian Poetic Cinema

Dan Browne

As the recent Syrian crisis and abuses at the US-Mexico border demonstrate, the refugee will be a central figure of the twenty-first century, one that necessitates new forms of solidarity in a world dominated by interconnected ecologies of culture and information. This central role will be accentuated by the encroaching severity of climate collapse, a factor that will instigate increasingly widespread diasporic conditions as displacements due to environmental instabilities become a new normal. As ecological tipping points are reached with growing frequency, land stresses caused by extreme weather, social stresses caused by resource shortages, and territorial contestations resulting from these factors will cause many populations to become itinerant, destroying homes, cultures, and communities.[1] In 2017, more than a million people were displaced by extreme weather events in North America; this figure is predicted to rise to hundreds of millions worldwide within the next three decades, potentially encompassing one quarter of the planet's population by mid-century, should initiatives to limit emissions fail or prove insufficient.[2] These issues pose an array of urgent questions for culture as well as social and political thought, for they will impact the meaning of all art produced not only in our time, but also in that of every subsequent generation.

In *The Great Derangement: Climate Change and the Unthinkable*, Amitav Ghosh contends that the lack of engagement with climate collapse in contemporary fiction represents a failure within the modern capacity for narrative itself. As Ghosh writes, "the climate crisis is also a crisis of culture, and thus of the imagination."[3] This claim runs parallel to similar ideas advanced by the Canadian filmmaker and critic

R. Bruce Elder in his essay "The Cinema We Need," which draws upon George Grant's forceful critique of technology to argue that narrative forms leave viewers implicitly biased towards modes of technocratic thought, paradigmatically expressed by the will to mastery.[4] In a fashion similar to Elder, Ghosh views narrative as maintaining an inherently gradualist and bourgeois worldview; by contrast, Ghosh proposes, "to think in the Anthropocene will be to think in images."[5] Building on this insight, I contend that it is through poetic forms that a clearer understanding of the character of our troubled era may be found, and that cinema is preeminently suited for such a task due to its capacity to act as a site of collage for experience. In this chapter, I explore these themes by drawing together works by Canadian filmmakers who reflect upon personal histories of displacement through experimental collage. Utilizing techniques of fragmentation and decay, these artists invoke an awareness of media as a shaping environment to generate a catharsis of the imagination. Through this exploration, I articulate a paradigm of *diasporic sight* that reflects an aesthetic of trauma, crisis, and loss, by considering how these makers utilize absence as a structuring force and foreground embodiment in order to reintegrate traumatic experiences.

Many of the crises that lie ahead for inhabitants of developed countries have already been encountered and assimilated by those directly impacted by conditions of diaspora. To this extent, works dealing with these conditions fulfill what Marshall McLuhan, quoting Wyndham Lewis, argued to be an essential role of vanguard art: to offer "a detailed history of the future."[6] Experimental poetic models can offer greater insights into moments of crisis than narrative forms because the latter inherently reinforces closure and resolution, rather than emphasizing crisis as an unfinished, ongoing state. By contrast, poetic forms are typically open-ended and ambiguous, deploying radical juxtapositions to generate metaphors and perspectives not bound by linear causality and thus able to transcend the limits of logic. As Anne Carson observes, "If prose is a house, poetry is a man on fire running quite fast through it."[7] In the era of the Anthropocene, we must come to the realization that all of us are on fire today.

The model of diasporic sight developed in this chapter is grounded in my observation of the prevalence amongst filmmakers who have been personally affected by cultural displacement to utilize hybrid, collage forms to provoke meaning, often through disruptions that point towards absent presences, generative transmutations, and distances between symbols and the material world. The use of symbolism in such works reflects the etymology of the term "symbol" itself: from the Greek term *symballein* (συμβάλλω), meaning "to throw together," it suggests a collision whose violence evokes and seeks to re-integrate the fragmentation of diasporic experience. An additional factor of influence is the recent contemporary technical diaspora prompted by the rise of digital formats: technical instabilities resulting from this crisis have forced many filmmakers to question and revise their own approaches, leading to increased interest in hybrid forms that draw upon diverse assemblages of media languages and image processing that merge analog and digital forms. The hybrid materialism of these collage forms can act as a potent critique of the invisibility of media environments, in addition to serving as a metaphor for the fracturing of identity through forced relocation, generational disruption, and trauma.

The prevalence of collage techniques within works of diasporic sight can be viewed as an inherent response to displacement and trauma, for collage is an approach that offers the potential to construct significance from loss, wherein elements preserved or retained are constituted in a fragmentary form. In the context of diasporic experience in which personal and cultural histories have been disrupted and a multiplicity of cultures and languages become superimposed in hybrid configurations, an aesthetic aligned with the modernist notion of purity through the use of only a single medium is unable to resonate with the experience of the maker. Instead, the detritus of *whatever remains* is invested with the breath of imagination and aligned with an interior landscape. This mode reflects McLuhan's recognition of the hybrid,[8] interface status of counter-environments as a site of resistance in which cultural forms are deconstructed,[9] as well as the "third space" articulated by Homi K. Bhabha regarding postcolonial migrant experience,[10] and Mikhail Bahktin's conception of linguistic hybridity, an evolutionary state wherein language can become "pregnant with potential for new world views."[11] Diasporic sight thus refers not only to a form of reconstructed post-traumatic vision, but also to a *site* – a space or spaces both exterior and interior, held together by scraps assembled into constellations of meaning. Consequently, works that evoke diasporic sight reconstitute the crisis of medium instability as their source of strength. They offer an aesthetic of failure and limitation, one which accepts the inability of the signifier to truly convey the weight of what is signified. In their recognition of the finitude of signs, the materiality of language is embraced in these works, offering a space for re-integrating fragmented sensory experience through the prioritization of the body. Aesthetic and political concerns are merged through an embrace of decay and limitation as potent strategies for representing trauma and other modes of experience that are otherwise difficult to render in visual terms.

Representing Trauma: Haptic Visuality and Poetic Forms

Trauma is a challenging subject to articulate in visual terms, for it is both invisible and immaterial, and can only be expressed as a form of relation or effect. Because it exists within the context of embodied experience, trauma eschews the confines of language. As a result, despite its omnipresence, trauma remains a challenging subject for an era in which the real is often defined by its capacity to be visualized.[12] As Cathy Caruth observes, "trauma precludes all representation because the ordinary mechanisms of consciousness and memory are temporally destroyed."[13] Similarly, Elaine Scarry describes the experience of pain as resistant to the shaping force of language; it can only become an intentional state when integrated with the imagination, a process that transforms it "from a wholly passive and helpless occurrence into a self-modifying and, when most successful, self-eliminating one."[14] Caruth's and Scarry's analyses demonstrate that representations of trauma cannot be founded within a simple correlative. As E. Ann Kaplan and Ban Wang argue, this challenge can render it as "untouchable and unreachable," resulting in "profound doubts about the viability of historical writing and its vehicles: narrative and image."[15] Representations of trauma therefore necessitate a transformative address that is critical, self-reflexive, and grounded in concerns of embodiment.

It is in response to the challenges posed for representation by trauma that the aesthetic of diasporic sight can be best understood, for it offers an alternative visual paradigm that seeks to re-inscribe the materiality of touch within vision, and embrace the fragile, flesh-like qualities of language. This paradigm is defined astutely by Laura U. Marks's model of "haptic visuality."[16] Building upon the phenomenological analyses of Henri Bergson and Maurice Merleau-Ponty, Marks observes that sense experiences outside the realm of sight are "capable of storing powerful memories that are lost to the visual."[17] Haptic images use traces, gaps, and absences as carriers of meaning that reverse the traditional visual figure/ground relationship, understanding vision within a broader matrix of tactile experience that is co-constituted by an interplay between subject and object. Haptic forms offer a "form of vision that yields to the thing seen, a vision that exceeds cognition," whose resonances can evoke a transgressive eroticism.[18] As such, haptic imagery often reflects critiques of patriarchy also encountered in écriture féminine, in addition to critiques of imperialism through its deconstruction of "the alliance between dominant narrative form and official history."[19]

Haptic images evoke traumatic experience through their visceral qualities, which prioritize the body as a site of meaning and conflict upon which the forms of language and media play out. However, as Marks notes, they can never fully restore the sensation of touch, and so often express "a mournful quality ... for as much as they might attempt to touch the skin of the object, all they can achieve is to become skinlike themselves."[20] This quality reinforces an aspect of loss that is inherent to representation itself: images ultimately must always remain bounded within a frame and separate from the world. The paradox of haptic images, in seeking to reconstitute the spectator as an integrated figure, is therefore homologous to attempts in diasporic artworks to reconstitute a lost psyche or place.

Given that trauma affects the body even when it exists only in the psychological realm, a model of cinema that engages terms of embodiment is crucial to an address of traumatic themes. As Jennifer Barker observes, most narrative techniques "mark an insurmountable difference between film's body and [the] viewer's body."[21] Consequently, narrative cinema is constrained in its expressions of embodiment, often using tactile images to overwhelm, and even inscribe, trauma, rather than offering a connection that can re-integrate forms of trauma. By contrast, poetic models of cinema elicit multisensory engagement and produce juxtapositions that mirror the associative patterns of memory and imagination. As Dirk de Bruyn observes, the repetitive forms evoked within many experimental films reflect the structure of traumatic memories.[22] In addition to juxtaposition and repetition, poetic experimental films also utilize techniques of fragmentation and superimposition to evoke mental processes and establish a sense of alienation or unity between the ego and the world. These qualities are present in the examples I now turn to, which cover a diverse terrain of experience and techniques, yet remain linked by a desire to re-integrate traumatic experience through the blending of perspectives to imply the accumulation, retrieval, and even repression of absent places, people, and energetic forces.

Girl from Moush and *Stone Time Touch*: Gariné Torossian

In the films of Gariné Torossian, who immigrated to Canada at the age of nine as a refugee of the Lebanese Civil War, her homeland of Armenia is conjured as an idealized site through a collage of interwoven formats, a practice she observes as extending a maternal tradition of knitting and quilting techniques.[23] Torossian's first film about Armenia, *Girl*

Figure 13.1 *Stone Time Touch* (2007, 72 minutes, digital video), dir. Gariné Torossian.

from Moush (1993), was inspired by an invitation from Atom Egoyan to design the poster for *Calendar* (1993), a film about a photographer documenting Armenian churches. *Girl from Moush* (1993) reuses these images and complements them with frames from Sergei Parajanov's *The Color of Pomegranates* (1968), which Torossian felt to be closest to her mental conception of her homeland. While nearly every image in *Girl from Moush* originates as a still photo, all are reworked into constant dynamic movement via their translation into a quilt of Super 8 frames collaged within 16mm leader, producing a trembling and fractured patchwork of formats that evokes the itinerant conditions noted by Hito Steyerl in her conception of the "poor image."[24] This use of different gauges literalizes Torossian's issues of registration and translation as an immigrant to a land where she could not speak the dominant language, and her attempts to recall a homeland she had never visited. The scratches, dirt, glue, splices, video static, and scan lines that overwrite Torossian's images embed as much significance as the content they distort – their traces emphasize the artist's labours in her reconstruction of sight/site, and the challenges induced by these complex forms compel viewers towards a reciprocal visual labour.

Torossian's intensive methods of construction in *Girl from Moush* produce images whose temporality is fleeting in their rapidity and flicker, and her sculptural conceptualization of the film as a quilt lends a quality to the images that transcend a sensation of linear screen-time. The film's conception of eternity is enhanced, not suppressed, by the constrictions of its ephemeral fleetingness, which point to alternate forms of duration such as the timelessness reflected in the landscapes and sacred architecture of Armenia. The recurring visual patterns of *Girl from Moush* propose a cyclical temporality in which vision serves as a mode of ecstatic revelation, and which evokes a devotional attitude reflected in the repetitive manual labour through which the film was made. The soundtrack, composed of Armenian music and layered with a phone call made by Torossian to her imagined homeland, furthers this sense of invisible energetic transmission. Her voice is distorted by the apparatus as it broadcasts towards a location simultaneously in the past (a pre-diasporic Armenia) and the future (the viewer), with neither position able to offer a response. *Girl from Moush* finds a sense of identity and home within its tapestry form, which views culture as an embodied, devotional practice rather than a physical place. As Torossian states, "wherever I go, I am always in Armenia."

Torossian's concerns with visual culture as a tactile and intimate exchange, in which exterior space is understood in interior psychic terms, are extended in *Stone Time Touch* (2007), a feature-length documentary of her first visit to Armenia that extends her engagement with haptic forms within the format of digital video. A present-tense journey whispered in first-person narration, *Stone Time Touch* interweaves images from across the country and the perspectives of women who reflect on their engagements with the land and its history. The film incorporates and layers photographs, architecture, maps, fifteenth-century manuscripts, fabrics, landscape, and handwritten inter-titles into a complex tapestry that evokes a palimpsest, a form which Sigmund Freud drew upon as a model for the function of memory through the analogy of the "mystic writing pad" – a device which can be written on and easily erased, but retains a trace of its previous impressions.[25] The film's elements are often densely arranged in layers that compete for the viewer's attention, producing a fragmented experience in which multiple perspectives are continuously overwriting each other. By contrast, when images are singular, they present close-ups or dynamic movements that record the bodily resonance of Torossian's camerawork as much as the external landscape.

The filmmaker's body serves as a ground for many of the images in *Stone Time Touch*, as a self-portrait in a mirror is repeatedly layered and returned to, merging observer and observed. Markings and texts inscribed in stone serve as an anchor for the identity the filmmaker seeks to access through the medium of touch – both literally, with her body, and through her layering of images. This abstraction serves a devotional function: images re-presented on monitors are dissected in close proximity until their content becomes iconic formations of pixels; digital icons are juxtaposed with ancient religious mosaics, paintings, and statues, conveying their affinity to an extended tradition of spiritual transmission. One of the central images of the film is a church whose roof is an open circular space. The absence at its centre reflects both the broader search of the filmmaker and the losses of the Armenian people. However, the open church roof is also a receptive container into which light enters, much like the iris of the camera. With this image, *Stone Time Touch* comes to a complex understanding of presence as only understandable through absence, an insight deeply relevant for our era of ecological collapse. This paradox is drawn out further as Torossian recognizes over the course of her trip that, as she comes to know her country better, she feels that she knows it less. A simple formulation of place or identity is challenged and exposed as an oscillation between revelation and doubt; this limitation can only be understood by the interventions of juxtapositions and split perspectives. Torossian's questioning – which is sometimes ecstatic, and sometimes anguished – allows her to engage with her subject in a meditative process that is constantly challenged, and in which every seam is exposed and every crack mined for the light that lies within it. Through the languages of media, Torossian reflects on the personal effects of the displacement of her heritage, as well as what the depths of Armenian cultural traditions, which precede modernity, can offer us today. By conjuring these elements through a maelstrom of images, she relates her own fragmentation of identity, while ultimately overcoming this state by demonstrating how cinema can unite vision through the embrace of every potential fragment. As Torossian declares at the end of *Stone Time Touch*, "Now I am a part of it." Through the intimate honesty of her filmmaking, this experience is likewise opened up to the viewer. The solution to diasporic loss is thus embraced not as an arrival at a fixed place or territory, but in the recognition of a set of traditions embedded within experiences and people. By exposing her process in coming to this insight, Torossian imparts to the viewer the struggle and alienation of displacement, producing a document of internal experience that cultivates a sensitivity to how history manifests and imprints itself.

my I's and *Echo*: Izabella Pruska-Oldenhof

Izabella Pruska-Oldenhof's *my I's* (1997) uses a palimpsest-like structure to explore the landscape of her childhood home in Poland through family movie excerpts embedded within footage of her contemporary return. The film's layers produce a continuously modulating flow of imagery that evokes states of consciousness, conveying a tension between archival fragments and a present that is constantly reconfigured through camera movements, optical distortions, and superimpositions that overwrite each other. *my I's* opens with a shot of the artist as a child in a rural landscape running towards the camera, with the image beginning in freeze-frame, drawing attention to its nature as an artifact. This reading of this footage as a document or testimony is enhanced as the shot begins to loop, but its cohesion soon degrades as the repetitions progress, giving way to a collage of landscapes superimposed against the artist's face, her eyes closed. The film concludes with another repeating image of the girl in nature with her mother, this time interwoven with her image as an adult. Pruska-Oldenhof notes that *my I's* develops the maternal relation that shapes her vision, suggesting in the film's description that it acts as "a substitute umbilical cord" constructed from light. The relation between the identity construction of the child and vision of the adult is mediated by the suggestion that her ability to connect with history cannot rely on any stable document, but must dive into the trance-like rhythms encountered within streams of memory and proprioceptive experience. This emphasis on the body recurs in many of Pruska-Oldenhof's other films, which depict nudes via gestural camerawork (*Her Carnal Longings* [2003], *Scintillating Flesh* [2003], *Pulsions* [2007]), or use handmade photograms that testify to the engaged presence of the maker's body (*Light Magic* [2001], *Song of the Firefly* [2002], *The Garden of Earthly Delights* [2007]).

Pruska-Oldenhof returns to her homeland a decade later with *Echo* (2007), a work inspired by another childhood artifact: a recording of the artist singing a Polish folk song, two years prior to her emigration. *Echo* is a further reflection on themes of ancestry; however, it differs considerably from *my I's*, as well as from all of Pruska-Oldenhof's other films, by departing from a focus on present-tense embodied experience to instead rely on three distinct sections of isolated image, sound, and

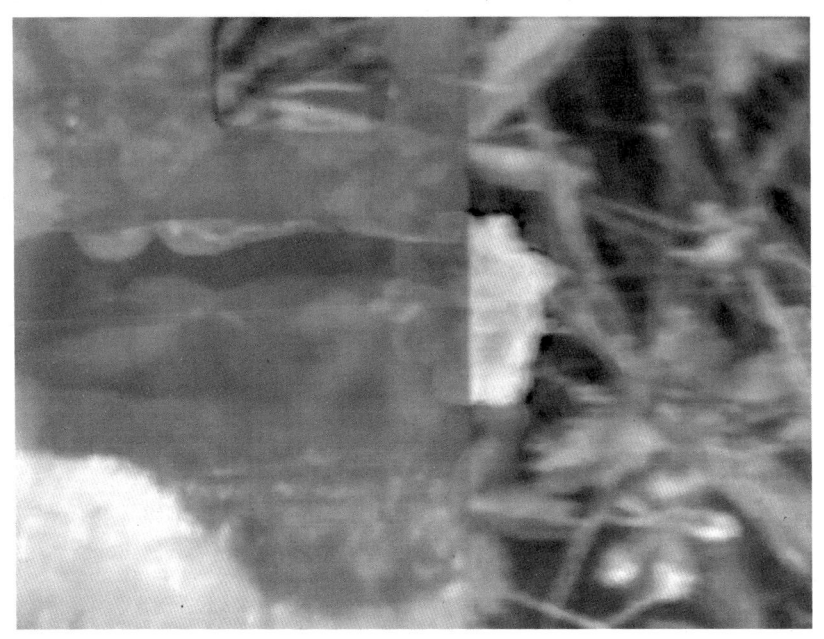

Figure 13.2 *Echo* (2007, 10 minutes, 16mm), dir. Izabella Pruska-Oldenhof.

text. In the first, images of the Polish countryside are layered over the filmmaker's mouth speaking words that cannot be heard. Following this, the audio recording is played over a black screen, after which the song's lyrics appear in handwritten inter-titles in the final section. The separation of these three passages delays the film's meaning within a gradual progression that evokes different sense modalities, from an embodied vision that is kinetic but mute, to an experience of sound isolated from vision, and finally to the written lyrics, translated into English to reveal the song's significance. This fragmentation can be read as a comment on identity development: in the first stage, we are immersed in a world of sensation for which there are no words; in the final section, language generates meaning, but at the cost of direct access to the world. This separation of elements gives *Echo* a tragic sensibility, one that is reinforced by the separation between the landscapes and the artist's body. These elements are superimposed in the first section out of a longing for synthesis. Yet, when this tension is resolved through the playback of the song, in which body and word are united, the event is understood as an artifact of the past, accessible only as a mediated fragment. While the lyrics concerning the beauty of the Polish landscape acquire a melancholy dimension amidst the filmmaker's yearning towards the light of these spaces from the darkened interior of the cinema, a notion of home is again understood as bound within the structures of memory and culture. In this respect, *Echo*'s fragmentation reflects a tension also evident in the work of Torossian: in her longing for reconnection, Pruska-Oldenhof seeks to reunite the senses, but the tragedy of *Echo* comes in her acknowledgment that experience, once lost, can never be fully reconstituted despite the promise of mediation. This is perhaps why Torossian is paradoxically able to achieve a closer synthesis of her homeland, on account of her lack of prior experience of it. This condition forces Torossian to enter more deeply into the idealized reveries of imagination, while Pruska-Oldenhof's reflections bear the weight of her memories of displacement, which she conceptualizes as akin to the myth of Eden, in which humans are cast from a holistic nature into the fragmentary realm of language.

perhaps/We: Solomon Nagler

Themes of absence, invisibility, and the weight of words similarly permeate Solomon Nagler's *perhaps/We* (2003), which offers a meditation on the intergenerational trauma of the Second World War and the Shoah. Photographed during a two-year period in which the filmmaker lived in Warsaw in an attempt to connect to his familial history, Nagler's images conjure esoteric themes of cabalism and alchemy, as withdrawn figures find intimate relations within cyclical montage and hand-processing techniques. The film opens with a cabalistic symbol from a book belonging to Nagler's grandfather, who survived the war but swore himself to silence, leaving his family alienated from his experience. Many scenes are tinted in cool tones that create flat landscapes foreclosing connection (represented by images of television antennae and satellites) in an urban environment consumed by darkness. Yiddish inter-titles that are left untranslated further a sense of alienation from language, which the film does not provide any initiation towards or reconciliation with. Nagler's use of hand processing and tinting generates flickering, unstable images that evoke a long-lost unearthed artifact whose significance has become eroded. This theme is literalized in a passage in which the camera moves rapidly across dead plants in a cemetery, resting briefly on a Star of David atop a tombstone, as blotches and scratches merge with the images to reveal a world in an advanced state of decomposition.

The decayed state of the natural world depicted in *perhaps/We* is further imprinted upon the bodies and language depicted in the film.

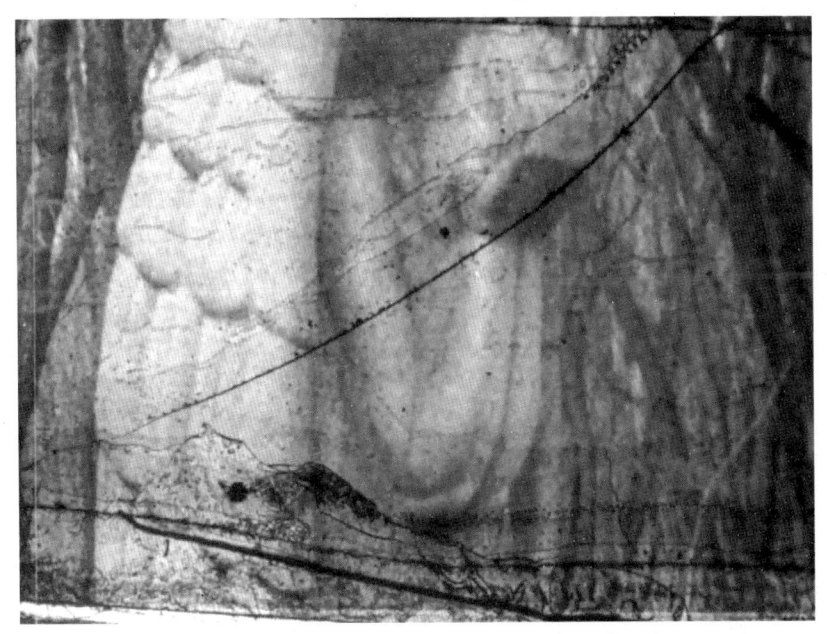

Figure 13.3 *perhaps/We* (2003, 11 minutes, 16mm), dir. Solomon Nagler.

In a recurring scene, a sleeping man is multiplied through superimposition, implying a split between body and soul that is echoed by a poem, written by the filmmaker and delivered in voice-over. In another passage, the turning pages of a book whose content is washed out is layered with a nude figure, connecting the vulnerability of flesh to the book, as well as the film strip itself, and evoking a process of un-writing or trace recovery. The presence of this nude is double-edged: while the figure is sensuous and evocative, nakedness was an essential component of the dehumanization of the Nazi camps,[26] converting humans into "bare life" ready to be exterminated.[27] The link between the nude and the pages of blank text reflects the removal of identity not merely through the body, but through language itself. *perhaps/We* evokes this history as inscribed on the vulnerabilities of the body, yet the fragility and mortality evoked by the film's decaying images also elicits a sensitivity that provokes an orientation towards care. In channelling destruction through the testimony of his film, Nagler encourages us to remain open and sensitive – to retain our ability to feel the depths of meaning that originates from the fragility of the body's flesh.

Towards the end of *perhaps/We*, the letter Aleph is drawn multiple times, a cabalistic invocation that serves as an origin point. Aleph is the first letter of the Hebrew alphabet but lacks sound; for Nagler, this signifies an erased presence.[28] *perhaps/We* offers a vision of the Shoah in which the subject is never explicitly identified. As such, its absences can be read as a response to Theodor Adorno's contention, "To write poetry after Auschwitz is barbaric."[29] This question of unrepresentability is at the centre of Nagler's film, which meditates on what poetic forms can exist in a foreclosed world living under a shadow, seeking to uncover what compensations are possible. Nagler's visions are eroded and obscured, but linger as traces to be reconstituted, intimating that meaning can potentially be rebuilt, but only through the care and vulnerability of witnessing.

Childhood Tales: Cecilia Araneda and Francisca Duran

Witnessing is also a central theme in the works of two Chilean-Canadian filmmakers, Cecilia Araneda and Francisca Duran, who use found footage in their respective practices as sources of testimony through which the political dimensions of mediation are reflected upon and questioned. In the works of both makers, a range of media sources are combined with text, voice, and material interventions to generate complex webs of relation that challenge official narratives.

Blending diaristic and archival approaches by integrating found footage with family photos and personal narration, Araneda reflects on the violence of the 1973 Chilean coup that forced her family to leave the country in *What Comes Between* (2009). For Araneda, memory of this childhood event is embedded and intertwined within the media artifacts that form its residue, providing a connective link to her former identity. Filmmaking serves as a means for Araneda to activate her memories, and to delve deeper into the historical contexts that inform her personal history. This is remarkably articulated in the film's least autobiographical moment, in which Dwight D. Eisenhower's 1961 speech about the dangers of the military industrial complex is reworked and disfigured through a series of interventions that distort its registration, responding to the speech's warning of a monolithic ideology by turning it into a material event that breaks the frame into shards. Araneda returns to the subject of the coup and her childhood displacement in *The Space Shuttle Challenger* (2017), in which a circular temporality links a diffuse series of media events, including the 1986 Challenger disaster, Omar Khadr's detention in Guantanamo Bay, and a cameraman who filmed his own death as military forces took the streets of Santiago in 1973. Combining analog and digital decay to address the implication of the

Figure 13.4 *What Comes Between* (2009, 6 minutes, 16mm/digital video), dir. Cecilia Araneda.

Figure 13.5 *Retrato Oficial (Official Portrait)* (2003, 1 min, 16mm), dir. Francisca Duran.

coup on both a personal and cultural level, Araneda deconstructs the materiality of images (as photographic emulsion, broadcast signal, and digital information) to consider the role of media in shaping political expression. The degraded images of the film and Araneda's recurrent juxtapositions between formats reflect the challenge of depicting trauma through any simple or singular form – an approach that opposes single-dimensional readings of images or language, implicating this approach as linked to fascist and totalitarian politics, in which critical readings are marginalized. Araneda seeks to counter this form of state-sponsored communicative violence, reflected in the mass distribution of images that collapse perspectives into a single narrative, by deflecting its force onto the images themselves, whose heterogeneity and ambiguity serve as foundations for an ideological resistance.

Similarly, Duran's *Cuentos de mi niñez (Tales from My Childhood)* (1991) reflects on the violence of the 1973 coup by juxtaposing her exiled home of Toronto with images from Chile in an associative montage that renders distinctions between the two spaces increasingly enmeshed. The landscapes of the sites that constitute Duran's split identity are framed through intrusions of media: flickering screens, maps, newspaper clippings, handwritten inter-titles, and first-person voice-over blends generational stories to achieve a greater universality. Duran's subsequent work has moved increasingly towards found footage as a strategy to address collective cultural and historical consciousness: in two films entitled *Retrato Oficial (Official Portrait)* (2003, 2009), images of the Chilean dictator Augusto Pinochet and nineteenth-century revolutionary Bernardo O'Higgins are deconstructed through screens. In *Even if my hands were full of truths* (2012), declassified telegrams sent by a US diplomat prior to the coup are read aloud while their text is distorted until the words become abstracted pixels, while in *8401* (2017), a collage of images sourced from Google offers a fragmented portrait of a former torture site. In her most recent works, *Traje de Luces* (2018) and *It Matters What* (2019), Duran uses analog techniques of hand processing, tinting, toning, solarization, and reticulation to transform found footage images into decaying forms with a shimmering vibrancy. In *Traje de Luces*, a bullfight is used to reflect on questions of politics and the dual status of the photograph as a document and aesthetic object. In *It Matters What*, amateur footage of a woman holding a dead owl becomes a central form against which Duran explores notions of death, extinction, and temporal foreclosure in the era of the Anthropocene, invoking an essay by Donna Haraway as a counterpoint against sequences of phytograms (impressions created by exposing film directly to light with plant matter on top to produce patterns without the use of a camera) and Letraset text (also applied directly to the film strip without a camera), both of which expose the kinetic embodied momentum of the film strip.

Significantly, Duran, Araneda, and Nagler all developed their materialist approaches towards analog film through their engagement with Phil Hoffman's Rural Imaging Retreat (or "Film Farm"), an annual summer workshop held since 1994 in Mount Forest, Ontario, in which artists explore handmade filmmaking practices in a partially outdoor lab housed in a barn.[30] The approach towards cinema cultivated at this retreat reflects a communal, back-to-the-land ethic, in which, as Hoffman relates, "sharing is not limited to the exchange of knowledge between people and communities but also relates to a symbiotic relationship with the world, a kind of empathy with natural forces."[31] Hoffman emphasizes natural forces as acting "in partnership with the making of film work" by asking participants not to bring ideas for projects, but rather have them emerge in the context of the environment of the retreat, and influences of this ecological conception of filmmaking can be noted in the subsequent works of many participants.[32]

her silent life: Lindsay McIntyre

The tendency noted in many of these works towards deconstructing fleeting instances of personal experience – a structure in which maker and viewer must attentively meet the material halfway, and in which the artist must establish intimacy as a precondition of making – plays a crucial role in Lindsay McIntyre's *her silent life* (2011). *her silent life* attempts to reconstitute the fractured lineage of McIntyre's family, centred around the departure of her Inuk great-grandmother from her community in Baker Lake, Nunavut, in 1936. The film draws together interviews, family photographs, and images filmed in the isolated northern landscape of Baker Lake. This material is reinterpreted through the use of first-person subtitles, which present McIntyre's voice while simultaneously displacing it as an absence – a strategy of negation that is repeated on multiple additional levels. Stark, black-and-white hand-processed images rest on details, such as her grandmother's hands, and landscapes in which figures are mostly absent. Intimations of violence remain obscure, powerfully evinced in a scene where a transition to a black screen is used as a placeholder for the revelation of information between family members that is too sensitive to be shared with a wider audience.

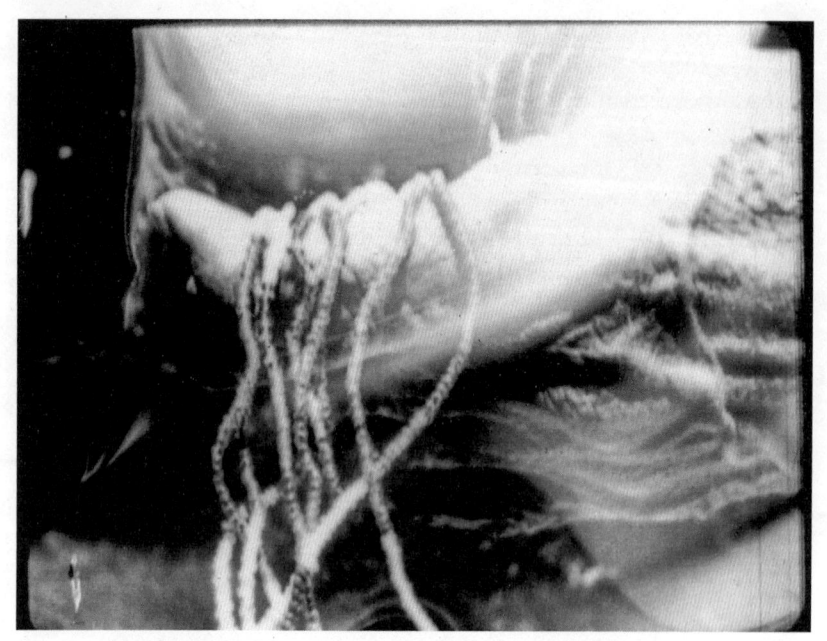

Figure 13.6 *her silent life* (2011, 31 minutes, 16mm/digital video), dir. Lindsay McIntyre.

her silent life presents a gradation of intimacies. It focuses upon McIntyre's personal relation to her family's trauma and the role that the act of documentation plays for her (notably, the footage of McIntyre's grandmother was photographed on the day they first met). But it also deals in equal part with how ethical questions of representation and witnessing play out within a broader social goal of cultural reconciliation. The film repeatedly returns to a central image of McIntyre's grandmother's hands parsing a beaded necklace, which corresponds to the continuity of tradition that McIntyre seeks to re-enact through her collection of fragments in the film. By linking moments in a structure that allows multiple elements to overwrite one another, McIntyre paradoxically invokes a consciously mediated distance to achieve greater intimacy. The slow pace and poetic division of words within the subtitles necessitate a close, attentive reading on the part of the viewer; counterpoints of image and sound, including music and speech, divert the viewer's attention from the content of the text, further obscuring a clear reading. In the only passage presented in colour – a present-tense moment that precedes McIntyre's grandmother revealing a secret of the family's history – the image is split into a triptych, seemingly asserting that the truth of this moment can only be encountered through a multiplicity of perspectives.

Conclusion

All of the works outlined in this chapter propose a mode of vision that is hybrid, tactile, partial, and imperfect, utilizing these qualities to retain a critical perspective on mediation that acknowledges the body as a crucial site of engagement. Today, all culture is necessarily hybrid and mosaic. Understanding how traditions are impacted through displacement can encourage models of cultural hybridity and fluidity that may be able to preserve traditions while responding to the pressures of contemporary environments. Such works help us to better appreciate the role of heritage within a transformed world, as something consciously evoked by a people rather than being associated with a fixed place. Poetic models of language can aid such insights through their compression and revitalization of meaning into the energetic discharge of artwork.

The works I have surveyed offer images that exist in constant states of flux, that are always on the verge of crumbling into absence. They invoke a realm of sight beyond the visible that reflects the invisible status of the refugee, just as their maelstrom of sources channel sites/sights that have been lost or never known.[33] While these works are intensely personal, their address is far from insular: their microcosms speak to issues that affect our society as a whole. In doing so, they suggest it is a misconception to consider trauma as primarily related to individual psychology and only secondarily to societies and texts.[34] We must instead come to an understanding of trauma as a broader cultural phenomenon, for this understanding will be a key to the overwhelming experiences and losses with which the contemporary era will beset us all. Trauma and grief are modalities we cannot avoid, and poetry – which, as Frye observes, is the root of language itself – provides us with a means for doing so. The idea is nothing new, but nonetheless bears repeating, for, as William Carlos Williams wrote more than half a century ago,

> It is difficult
> to get the news from poems
>   yet men die miserably every day
>   for lack
> of what is found there.

Notes

1. See Thomas Homer-Dixon, *Environment, Scarcity, and Violence* (Princeton: Princeton University Press, 1999); Harald Welzer, *Climate Wars: What People Will Be Killed for in the 21st Century* (Cambridge: Polity Press, 2011); Robert A. McLeman, *Climate and Human Migration: Past Experiences, Future Challenges* (New York: Cambridge University Press, 2014).
2. Norman Myers, "Environmental Refugees: A Growing Phenomenon of the 21st Century," *Philosophical Transactions of the Royal Society London: Biological Sciences: Series B* 357, 1420 (2002): 609–13; François Gemenne, "Why the Numbers Don't Add Up: A Review of Estimates and Predictions of People Displaced by Environmental Changes," *Global Environmental Change* 21, no. 1 (2011): S41–S49; Anouch Missirian and Wolfram Schlenker, "Asylum Applications Respond to Temperature Fluctuations," *Science* 358, no. 6370 (2017): 1610–14, https://doi.org/10.1126/science.aao0432; Chang-Eui Park, Su-Jong Jeong, Manoj Joshi, Timothy J. Osborn, Chang-Hoi Ho, Shilong Piao, Deliang Chen, et al., "Keeping Global Warming within 1.5°C Constrains Emergence of Aridification," *Nature Climate Change* 8, no. 1 (2018): 70.
3. Amitav Ghosh, *The Great Derangement: Climate Change and the Unthinkable* (Chicago: University of Chicago Press, 2016), 9.
4. R. Bruce Elder, "The Cinema We Need," *Canadian Forum*, no. 44 (February 1985): 32–5. See also George Grant, *Technology and Empire* (Toronto: House of Anansi Press, 1969). Elder's critique of technology also bears influence from the ideas of Jacques Ellul and Martin Heidegger (as does Grant's).
5. Ghosh, *The Great Derangement*, 83.
6. Marshall McLuhan, *Understanding Media: The Extensions of Man* (New York: Signet, 1964), 70.
7. Quoted in Kate Kellaway, "Anne Carson: 'I Do Not Believe in Art as Therapy,'" *The Guardian*, 30 October 2016, https://www.theguardian.com/books/2016/oct/30/anne-carson-do-not-believe-art-therapy-interview-float.
8. Marshall McLuhan, "The Relation of Environment to Anti-Environment," *The University of Windsor Review* 2, no. 1 (1966): 1–10.
9. See also P.P. Ajayakumar, "McLuhan, Media, and Hybridity: A Revaluation in the Postcolonial Context," in *At the Speed of Light There Is Only Illumination: A Reappraisal of Marshall McLuhan*, eds. John Moss and Linda A. Morra (Ottawa: University of Ottawa Press, 2004), 147–52.
10. Homi K. Bhabha, *The Location of Culture* (Abingdon: Routledge, 2004).
11. Mikhail Bahktin, *The Dialogic Imagination: Four Essays* (Austin: University of Texas Press, 1981), 360.

12 Shoshana Felman and Dori Laub, *Testimony: Crises of Witnessing in Literature, Psychoanalysis and History* (New York: Routledge, 1992); Dominick LaCapra, *Representing the Holocaust: History, Theory, Trauma* (Ithaca: Cornell University Press, 1994); Susannah Radstone, "Trauma and Screen Studies: Opening the Debate," *Screen* 42, no. 2 (2001): 188–93; Joshua Hirsh, *Afterimage: Film, Trauma, and the Holocaust* (Philadelphia: Temple University Press, 2004); Janet Walker, *Trauma Cinema: Documenting Incest and the Holocaust* (Berkeley: University of California Press, 2005).

13 Cathy Caruth, ed., *Trauma: Explorations in Memory* (Baltimore: Johns Hopkins University Press, 1995), 152.

14 Elaine Scarry, *The Body in Pain: The Making and Unmaking of the World* (New York: Oxford University Press, 1985), 164.

15 E. Ann Kaplan and Ban Wang, eds., *Trauma and Cinema: Cross-Cultural Explorations* (Hong Kong: Hong Kong University Press, 2004), 8.

16 See Laura U. Marks, *The Skin of the Film: Intercultural Cinema, Embodiment, and the Senses* (Durham: Duke University Press, 2000) and *Touch: Sensuous Theory and Multisensory Media* (Minneapolis: University of Minnesota Press, 2002).

17 Marks, *The Skin of the Film*, 130.

18 Ibid, 191. See also Marks, "Video Haptics and Erotics," *Screen* 39, no. 4 (1998): 331–48; Jennifer Barker, *The Tactile Eye: Touch and the Cinematic Experience* (Berkeley: University of California Press, 2009); Kim Knowles, "Blood, Sweat, and Tears: Bodily Inscriptions in Contemporary Experimental Film," NECSUS: *European Journal of Media Studies*, no. 4 (autumn 2013).

19 Marks, *The Skin of the Film*, 26.

20 Ibid, 192.

21 Barker, *The Tactile Eye*, 117.

22 Dirk de Bruyn, *The Performance of Trauma in Moving Image Art* (Newcastle upon Tyne: Cambridge Scholars Publishing, 2014).

23 Mike Hoolboom, "Gariné Torossian: Girl from Moush," in *Inside the Pleasure Dome: Fringe Film in Canada*, 2nd rev. ed., 148–55 (Toronto: Coach House Printing, 2001), 151.

24 Hito Steyerl, "In Defense of the Poor Image," *E-Flux Journal* 10 (November 2009).

25 Sigmund Freud, "A Note upon the 'Mystic Writing Pad,'" in *General Psychological Theory: Papers on Metapsychology*, ed. Philip Rieff (New York: Simon and Schuster, [1925] 2008), 207–12.

26 Tsvetan Todorov, *Facing the Extreme: Moral Life in the Concentration Camps*, trans. Arthur Denner and Abigail Pollak (New York: Holt/Owl Books, 1996); Sandra M. Gilbert, *Death's Door: Modern Dying and the Ways We Grieve* (New York: W.W. Norton and Company, 2006).

27 Giorgio Agamben, *Homo Sacer: Sovereign Power and Bare Life*, trans. Daniel Heller-Roazeni (Stanford: Stanford University Press, 1998).
28 The use of this symbol draws parallels to Wallace Berman's *Aleph* (1956–66), which presents similar juxtapositions between sacred and soiled forms in which energetic resonances transcend their opposition into a unity. Similarly, R. Bruce Elder's *Illuminated Texts* (1982) considers the experience of concentration camps through a shattered visual plane of moving fragments accompanied by disjointed text and synthesized speech, suggesting the end of history. In each instance, purification is sought through decay and representation is understood as metaphysics.
29 Theodor Adorno, "Culture Criticism and Society," in *Prisms*, trans. Samuel and Sherry Weber (Cambridge, MA: MIT Press, [1967] 1981), 34.
30 The number of contemporary film artists who use hand-processing methods that have attended the Rural Imaging Retreat is extensive; it is not an overstatement to suggest that a majority of North American filmmakers engaged in such practices have visited at some point in its twenty-five years of operation. For more, see Scott MacKenzie and Janine Marchessault, eds., *Process Cinema: Handmade Film in the Digital Age* (Montreal and Kingston: McGill-Queen's University Press, 2019); a full list of participants is available at https://philiphoffman.ca/category/film-farm/.
31 Philip Hoffman, "Vulture Aesthetics: Process Cinema at the Film Farm," in *Film in the Present Tense: Why Can't We Stop Talking about Analogue Film?*, eds. Luisa Greenfield, Deborah S. Phillips, Kerstin Schroedinger, Björn Speidel, and Philip Widmann (Berlin: Archive Books, 2018), 40.
32 Ibid.
33 There are several other Canadian filmmakers – including Madi Piller, Ajla Odobašic, Taravat Khalil, and the collaborative trio of Faraz Anoushahpour, Parastoo Anoushahpour, and Ryan Ferko – whose works correspond to principles of diasporic sight I have outlined, but whom I have been unable to engage with here due to considerations of length. It is also worthwhile to note that several other Canadian filmmakers have linked diasporic conditions to contemporary forces of media, supporting McLuhan's claim that, in the context of electronic media, "all of us today are dispossessed people"; "Electric Revolution: Revolutionary Effects of New Media," in *Understanding Me*, eds. Stephanie McLuhan and David Staines (Cambridge, MA: MIT Press, [1959] 2003), 2. Among the most notable examples of these are Christina Battle's *buffalo lifts* (2003), which evokes parallels between media and environmental displacement; Leslie Supnet's *In Still Time* (2015), which deconstructs images of catastrophe by translating them onto 16mm film via a laser printer; and Karl Lemieux and David Bryant's *Quiet Zone* (2015), which offers an unconventional take on diasporic subjects

through its depiction of "wave refugees" who have left their homes due to electromagnetic hypersensitivity. It is also important to note that this aesthetic is not limited to Canadian filmmakers – for instance, US-based filmmakers such as Nazlí Dinçel, Basma Alsharif, Ephraim Asili, and Sky Hopinka have also produced works that evoke similar aesthetic strategies. The recurrence of diasporic sight among North American filmmakers reflects the conditions of Canada and the United States as settler states composed of immigrant and refugee populations, while Indigenous nations remain internally displaced due to the ongoing impacts of colonialism.

34 See LaCapra, *Representing the Holocaust*.

dominique t. skoltz and New States of Cinematic Matter

Melanie Wilmink

Advancements in technology have ensured cinema's ubiquity in daily life. As the moving image leaves the theatre to enter the privacy of our homes, and even follows us around in our pockets, the material forms of cinema have diversified. Artists have further expanded the semblance of cinema through their own explorations, producing gallery-based artworks that emerge from the traditions of media-installation art as well as the expanded cinema movement in the 1960s.[1] The gallery's reputation as "neutral ground" influences its selection for media installations, as a space that can be subsumed in favour of the art and where viewing remains critical. In contrast, criticism against cinema commonly points to its immersive qualities, where the viewer ignores their bodily and critical positioning in favour of the ideological gaze structured by the camera and screen.[2] While the notion of the gallery's neutrality is just as much a fallacy as the passive nature of the theatre, the intersection of the two modes of viewing does offer an opportunity to disrupt the often-unseen conventions of both simultaneously. In this tension, the viewer must reconsider their spectatorial role and thereby forge new physical and mental relationships to both the traditional aesthetic forms of the gallery and of the cinema. It is this emergent dynamic that Montreal-based artist dominique t. skoltz leverages toward powerful aesthetic effects.[3] By creating slippages and disruptions between the two exhibition contexts, skoltz deconstructs the elemental components of the exhibition experience in order to construct new states of cinematic matter inside the art gallery.

While there is a long history of moving images in the gallery, there is an important distinction between works made in a cinematic tradition versus that of video art. Filmmaker Anthony McCall describes cinema as a "social institution" that is not connected to a specific medium, but rather a set of contextual rituals.[4] Over the course of three gallery-based exhibitions, skoltz reconfigured her single-channel short-film *y2o* (2013) into a variety of moving image, photographic, and sculptural forms. In these expansions, the cinematic quality of the work lies not only the fact that the film is shot on a high-definition digital camera and premiered at film festivals in theatrical settings, but also in the way that skoltz treats the set design, costuming, actor choreography, narrative arcs, and the durational relationships between a single frame, a scene, and the whole film. Drawing on the "social institution" of cinema, skoltz deconstructs filmic matter as linear and non-linear storytelling, human and mechanical experiences of time, as well as the social conditions of viewing.

Because video art from a gallery tradition carries different social conventions, the insertion of cinema into the gallery can be problematic, diminishing the specific ontology of the form in favour of the rules and traditions of what Brian O'Doherty dubbed "the white cube." As with cinema, visual art objects are defined more by the "social institution" of the gallery than by the materials used in their construction. An art object can take any form, but it is its placement within the context of "art" and labelling as such that determines its value as an aesthetic object. O'Doherty's foundational text *Inside the White Cube: The Ideology of the Gallery Space* points out that because the architecture of the gallery developed alongside modern art in the early twentieth century, the relationship between the spectator and object in the gallery is structured by a modernist interest in defining art as separate from everyday life.[5] This means that art objects are often seen to have autonomous – even philosophical – value as unique artifacts that should be considered with critical conceptual distance, creating a false dichotomy between the viewer's embodied experience of the work, and their conceptual interpretation.[6] As part of this mind/body split, the conceptual experience is prioritized. The architecture of the gallery, with its white walls, large open spaces, and brightly lit environment, is meant to direct attention solely toward the art object, which contains an intrinsic meaning that must be read and interpreted by the viewer in a one-to-one relationship with the object. In this way, the gallery operates pedagogically: to teach respect and appreciation for objects of national and cultural value, and raise the viewer's social cachet.[7] In fact, no matter what the form the art object takes, argues O'Doherty, "we have now reached a point where we see not the art but the *space* first ... [the white cube] more than any single picture, may be the archetypal image of twentieth century art."[8] Because the art gallery holds such well-established conventions about the aesthetic encounter, it is nearly impossible to read an artwork without incorporating these ideas into subsequent interpretations.

This becomes a problem for cinematic work, which holds completely different conventions shaped by its own architectures of viewing. The movie theatre developed alongside the white cube art gallery first as objects of technological curiosity in fairgrounds and later as part of multi-disciplinary variety shows.[9] What we now recognize as a standardized cinema architecture developed from this context of playful, light-hearted (and lower class) entertainment, and has also been imbricated with the commercial conditions of the Hollywood production system. Whereas early theatrical experiences were less formal, with more audience mobility and interaction between both the screen and other audience members, eventually the theatrical architecture developed into the fixed seating in a darkened auditorium that is commonly criticized as passive.[10] In the art gallery – where the viewer is expected to take up a mobile, critical position – the placement of cinema presents a problem. It is not possible to stage the durational and focused cinematic experience in the gallery, because the viewer enters into that space expecting to be mobile, and in control of their own durational encounters with work. Monitors are placed on pedestals in brightly lit rooms where the spectator is expected to stand, or, alternately, secluded into a dark room with a single bench, where the film plays on a loop. The time and space for longer and linear viewing is not supported under these conditions, and the social atmosphere of collective viewing is also lost within the individual viewing dynamics of the gallery.[11]

In skoltz's work, installation elements do not shroud the gallery in immersive darkness, but rather bring the structures of cinema into the light, pushing beyond the darkness, projection, and scale that is most commonly introduced as "cinematic" to materialize temporality instead. This is not to say that skoltz does not draw on these usual qualities of cinema, but rather that she adopts them differently. Whereas other artists use cinema to transform space into something new – to hide the gallery and spectatorial bodies – skoltz employs the viewer's movement through space to make visible the relationship between spectator and the moving image. The works also accomplish this without losing their essentially "cinematic" qualities to the bright light of the white cube, as skoltz adopts the convention of both the gallery and the cinema to stage a tension between the living body of the viewer and the intangible images of the screen. This is not a novel idea – other artists like Tacita Dean, Michael Snow, and Christian Marclay have all famously presented cinema as an auratic object in the gallery space by highlighting the spectator's ability to circumnavigate space and time at will. The *y20 dualités_* exhibition embraces this same mobility, but takes it a step further, breaking down the temporal constraints of the single-channel film and treating the moving image as an object to be deconstructed and manipulated. For skoltz, cinema is not only material in its presentation – the quality of light and surfaces that are incorporated into the projection – but also in its temporal, visual, and sonic form, which can be taken apart and put back together in ways that are the same-but-different than the original single-channel format. These works remain cinema but are simultaneously encountered as sculpture, photography, and performance.

I was privileged enough to view two different versions of skoltz's exhibitions with Arsenal gallery, first in Toronto and then in Montreal. As former warehouses, both venues are in many ways ideal gallery spaces, with just enough industrial touches to add charm to the atmosphere, but maintaining the concrete floors, white walls, open spaces, and high ceilings that are the epitome of the white cube. Culminating in the *y20 dualités_* exhibition at Arsenal's Montreal location, skoltz has deconstructed and reworked her short film *y20* for several years. Like the art objects themselves, the different versions of the exhibition expanded the form of the original film in various ways. Alongside an extensive international festival run, excerpts from the single-channel film showed as a loop at the Musée d'art contemporain de Montréal's Série Projections: Vidéomusique in 2013, and the first multi-screen version of the work was later presented at Phi Centre (Montreal, 7 February–16 March 2015). The next exhibition ran from 9 September–3 October 2015 at Arsenal's Toronto location, introducing more sculptural installations of the film; finally, from 6 November 2015–7 May 2016, *y20 dualités_* showcased the film in single and multiple-screen formats, alongside still photography, sculptures, and audio installations. Each of the works from these exhibitions elaborated on the same images and conceptual material of the film, presenting "the journey of two individuals submerged in the troubled waters of their own physical and emotional pulsations."[12]

The *y20* film stages all of its action within a large tank of water. In this tank float a man and a woman. Their long hair and loose clothing drift

Figure 14.1 *y2o dualités_* at Arsenal Toronto (2015).

around them weightlessly, as they push and pull against one another. Comprising nine chapters, the twenty-nine-minute film traverses the emotional arc of a romance through the dance-like movements of the two performers. As they are submerged for most of the film, there is no dialogue (there is an ambient soundtrack), but the figures' gestural interactions serve to convey the tone of their relationship through each chapter. Starting with passionate embraces, the film traces the decay of the relationship until the final moments when the tank drains and the figures are left standing dripping wet and facing – but not touching – one another. In the catalogue for *y2o dualités_*, critic and curator Bernard Schütze writes that throughout the film, water acts as an affective force, connecting the figures together. He notes that "affect is not so much something that is in the protagonists, it is they who are enveloped in it, just as they are submerged in water ... tellingly, the binding water is precisely what is drained away in the video installation's final movement titled [empty] in a sequence that signals the relationship's dissolution and a return of each to an individual, solitary sphere."[13] This push and pull between singularity and connectivity is what links the film and all of the artworks that are derived from it. Where water is visualized as an affective medium in the film, within the gallery installation this same connectivity is portrayed through the spatial relationships between artworks and the spectator.

In the Toronto installation of the *y2o* show, a darkened gallery highlights the cinematic luminosity of the work. Upon entering the exhibition space, a large self-supporting white wall confronts viewers – the kind that would usually separate a gallery space into separate zones and might feature introductory text about the exhibition. This wall doubles as a screen that showcases the full-length, single-channel version of the film; however, the surface of the divider is not subsumed by the image, as might ordinarily be the case with a screen. Instead, the wall is almost three feet thick, staging a monumental form of the image as a three-dimensional object. Additionally, the large ladder mounted on the side of the wall seems to invite the viewer to climb up and enter the virtual tank of water projected onto the side. Beyond this divider, the multiple-screen installation of the film stretches out along the far wall. In this work, each of the nine chapters occupies a single screen playing simultaneously – queued up through space instead of a linear filmic timeline. This installation is one of the first ways that skoltz breaks down the cinematic image into a sculptural form that references an entanglement between the theatrical context of a film, and the gallery context of visual art installations. By deconstructing the larger narrative of the single-channel film into its component parts, skoltz highlights cinematic tropes of serial storytelling and montage that connect disparate shots or events within a linear temporality. In this artwork, the artist removes the disparate parts from their linear relationship and spatially separates each chapter as a distinct enclosure. Instead of disguising the connections between the scenes inside the constant forward momentum of the film, the chapters spread out like a film strip. Each scene relates to all the other action simultaneously, creating tension between the durational scenes and longer timeline that is now visualized as a sequential arrangement.

The final work in the Toronto exhibition continued this sculptural expansion of the screen. Sandwiched between the aforementioned divider and the nine-channel work on the far wall of the gallery, *y2o Huis clos* (2015) was positioned inconspicuously. The work consisted of an LCD screen that played the single-channel film while enclosed in a medium-sized aquarium. By placing the screen inside the clear cube of the aquarium, *y2o Huis clos* mimicked the watery enclosure from the film. The glass box also articulated volume around the flat-screen monitor, implying an extension of the flat screen-space into the void of its aquarium container. Like Bernard Schütze's description of *y2o*'s water as an affective medium, the air in the aquarium took on a mediating quality; significantly, this air is not virtual, but rather takes up space

Figure 14.2 *y20 Huis clos* (2015) at Arsenal Montreal (2016).

in the real world, insinuating that it might affect the physical environment it shares with the spectator. Additionally, where the nine-channel installation fragmented the narrative into distinct intervals that have the potential for re-arrangement, *y20 Huis clos* stretched the twenty-nine-minute length of the original film into three hours. The result is an image that barely moves, which dwells on the materiality of shots that pass by rapidly in the film's normal duration. On her website, skoltz writes that that in *Huis clos*: "time has been transformed into an infinite commodity, where the story line vanishes to be replaced by an endless succession of movements and utterances ... Suspended outside reality, spectators are invited to lose themselves in touches, emotions and micro movements."[14] Like Roland Barthes's punctum, which momentarily frames time and allows it to be both experienced and considered simultaneously, skoltz draws out the subtle moments that are often unseen within usual pace of cinematic narrative.[15] In essence, she removes the intervals of time from the usual flow of human activity while also refusing the sequential dialectic of cinema from the images, so that chapters and scenes become one. The scenes are at once part of a mechanical experience of time, and yet not that of what we would ordinarily recognize as "cinema."

Shown in both Toronto and Montreal, alongside the other expansions of *y2o*, skoltz makes it obvious that time itself can function as a creative medium. In the Montreal installation of *y2o dualités_*, these same works transferred to the bright space of the white cube. Although it was contained in its own area, skoltz's solo exhibition shared partial walls, ceiling space, lighting, and audio transmissions with several other Arsenal exhibits. In this space, the nine-screen series and aquarium existed alongside other photographs and sculptures related to the *y2o* film. The one concession to cinematic darkness was the presentation of the single-channel film in a small, darkened room that was segregated from skoltz's main space by the lobby containing a group show of Arsenal's in-house collection. In this darkened room, the film filled an entire wall, and in addition to the obligatory bench seating, the space also contained a large pool of water that took up an amount of space similar to the projected image.

This new iteration of the exhibition stepped beyond the cinema screen to bleed fully into the gallery space. Where the first version in Toronto began to materialize the screen by distributing a single narrative over the space of nine screens, and by expanding the physicality of the LCD screen into the cavity of an aquarium, this exhibition transformed the projected image itself into an object. The addition of the pool of water to the single-channel projection focused attention on the space in front of the screen and highlighted sensual differences in the quality of the filmic image on the screen surface versus the water surface. In the darkened room, the reflection was slick and oily (an effect aided by the black plastic liner curling out from the edge of the pool; see figure 14.3). It was possible to see and feel the depth of the water, as the plastic lip curved into a shallow pond – yet the projection also covered this depth with the flat reflection of light. The surface of the water acted like a mirror, displaying a twinned image of the performers floating in their own watery container. As a reflection, the images necessarily moved together; they were the same, yet palpably different, as the quality of the water produced a sharper and more contrasted image than the one projected on the wall. In the pond, the spectator's overhead position and the texture of the water distorted the image,

Figure 14.3 *y2o* single channel (2015) at Arsenal Montreal (2016).

which in turn distilled attention. In drawing and painting, mirrors are often used to see objects anew – to flip perception so that it becomes possible to notice things that might have been previously overlooked because of the artist's assumptions about the object. When something seems familiar, our brains rely on pre-existing ideas to recognize objects quickly. This means that perception is often impacted more by our expectations than reality.[16] By turning the object upside down, the artist must look more closely because they can no longer rely on their habitual perceptual shorthand. This produces observations that are closer to the reality of the object, rather than relying on what we expect to see. skoltz's mirror image similarly operates as an unfamiliar double, which moves in reverse and takes up space in an unusual way in order to stimulate closer examination of the original image.

In his attempts to move past the traditional ideology of the gallery, Brian O'Doherty suggests a postmodernist "double mechanism of display" that references the material object and context of exhibition simultaneously. Published in 1976, his essays on the gallery describe something that is now common in performance art, including institutional critique, installation art, and other postmodern artistic practices.

In this discussion, he presciently notes that these interventions are fragile, since any new intervention into traditional forms only briefly denaturalizes conventional aesthetic practices. Over time any new gestures are inevitably subsumed into tradition and themselves become naturalized and ignored.[17] If O'Doherty's supposition is accurate, it may be true that an aesthetic that places the spectatorial context at the foreground of meaning-making has already been subsumed into the ideology of the white cube. So, if it is not enough to expose how the context of the gallery shapes reception, what might the next stage of intervention look like?

skoltz's interventions are additionally complicated because they reveal not only the context of the gallery but that of the cinema as well, which come together in what architectural theorist Sylvia Lavin describes as a "kiss" between media and architecture. For Lavin, this meeting describes a new form of artistic practice, which intermingles moving image and architecture, but also "a new sensibility – post-feminist certainly, but more acutely one of intense affect" that disrupts both the disciplines.[18] In this approach, denaturalization occurs not simply through a gesture that turns against familiar traditions, but rather through an embrace that brings the boundaries of form so close as to make them indistinguishable. For Lavin, this new approach insists upon the materiality of the surface, while simultaneously dissolving the distinctions between various surfaces.[19] It is a push-and-pull between the distance of the critical, impartial mind, and the incarnate and implicated body. Crucially, these two positions do not entirely collapse into one another, but rather fluctuate between closeness and distance, accumulating ideas and sensations that layer over top of one another.[20]

For Lavin, this form is particularly interesting because the multi-dimensionality of architecture is flattened and deepened by the projected image, while the cinematic projection is fragmented and dispersed in a way that interferes with the frontal mode of address that is normally established by a theatrical setting (or, for our purposes within the discussion of the gallery, the frame or pedestal of visual art). The play between the illusionistic depth of the cinematic image, and the flat, solid surfaces of architecture create a tension that cannot be resolved. The inability to resolve this dynamic leads to constant fluctuation between interior and exterior, as well as surface and depth. Lavin explains that "rather than being concerned only with meaning and images that demand close analytic attention, these surfaces work to provoke strong synesthetic responses in the viewer and therefore to make architecture participate in a culture of interactive receptivity instead of imposed signification."[21] With this synesthesia, images become further complicated by implicating the viewer as part of the artwork. The boundaries between artwork, architecture, and spectator blur to stimulate a dynamic form of meaning-making.

Both of skoltz's installations for the single-channel version of *y2o* disrupt the surface and depth relationship between the gallery environment and the image in this sensual manner. The traditional flat, white screen is unsettled (but not dismantled) by sculptural elements including the thick wall with its ladder and the pool of water that spills out to meet the viewer's feet, drawing the spatial range of the image out not only on a single, flat, vertical axis, but also horizontally. In this way, skoltz expands the dimensions of the image to confront the upright, straight-on positionality of the normal gallery spectator; however, instead of immersing the viewer's body inside the artwork, skoltz maintains the usual spectatorial distanciation. The Montreal installation with its pool of water is particularly interesting, because the pool delineates a large section of space where the spectator was not allowed to tread. In most galleries, there are unspoken rules about how close a spectator is allowed to come to a work of art: such policies may be labelled with tape on the floor, alarmed sensors, or even a security guard. The pool literalizes a protective zone for an image that would not ordinarily require such a space (a projected image does not require the same safeguards as a physical object), and simultaneously references the restrictive layout of a theatre, where audiences are constrained to their seats and cannot interact with the screen-image.

By revealing the architectures that structure the viewer's physical relationship to the image in both the gallery and cinema, skoltz underscores the distinct bodies of artwork and spectator, as well as the rapport between the two. Like the floating figures in her film, the spectator is implicated in a push-pull of affective meaning-making; it is possible to interact with but not control the other party within a kiss that temporarily comes close but does not blur distinctions. This dynamic becomes particularly obvious in the white-cube portion of her Montreal installation, where the peripatetic situation of the gallery moved to the foreground. As mentioned previously, the Montreal iteration of *y2o dualités_* includes a solo exhibition of skoltz's sculptural, photographic, and video work, presented within the bright, open space of the white cube. Walking into the space for *y2o dualités_*, spectators take in the whole space at once, seeing the variety of photographs hung on the walls, with three sculptures, and the *y2o Huis clos* aquarium distributed equally around the room.

In several large-scale photographs, the film's costume design translates into still-life shots of fabric corsets, plastic tubing, and water, which echo the female performer's wardrobe in *y2o* but are not a literal reworking as seen in the moving image displays. Instead, the new artworks draw inspiration from the other visual qualities of the film, including: textures, colour-timing, costuming, the dancer's movements, and key narrative moments. Other photographs included stills from the film, and a series of rusted audio speakers that were crumpled using high-pressure conditions, which were echoed by the three other speaker-related sculptures.[22] skoltz continues the romantic theme – this time envisioned through audio equipment – as she explores the tensions between words and actions, as well as the promises made and broken in the course of being with another person.[23] In each of these images, skoltz draws analogies between the filmic images and narrative, and the new art objects that approach the subject matter through their own disciplinary conventions. The photographs obviously lack the duration of the film but capture the decay of the relationship through frozen moments of time, enabling close attention on the textures of rusted metal, diaphanous fabric, and rubbery tubes. They are textural objects that clearly relate to human activity, but lack the representation of actual bodies, thereby conveying the sense of isolation and loss that is depicted through the narrative of the film. The photographs were also presented in large, shadow-box frames that pushed a distance between the protective glass and the mounted image, in a display choice that references the screen of the TV monitors, as well as the glass void of the aquarium tank. It is a gesture of display that draws an explicit connection between the materiality of the cinema screens and the still images, and links them as part of a continuum that functions in a variety of temporal rhythms.

There is a sensual juxtaposition between the photographs, with their unattainable tactility, and the sculptures, which are literally haptic but also exhibit the same clean lines, smoothness, and colouring of the film's digital images. This paradox of distance and closeness is particularly present in the sculpture *Face à Face* (2015), which creates an interplay between the viewing body and the sculpture while refusing to collapse the distance between the two. Positioned in the centre of the gallery, the large metal sculpture (223.5 × 274.3 × 121.9 cm) consists of what looks like a bellows – or more accurately two megaphones set face to face – structuring a hollow sculpture with two opposing viewing portals set at approximately eye-level for the average standing person. On her website, skoltz writes that this sculpture enables two visitors to speak through the structure, creating "a ludic space where words take on their full potential. It is a counter-moment to our instantaneous communications that are always in movement. This work resonates with the physicality and interiority of words."[24] The sculpture develops a tension between the peripatetic movements expected of gallery viewing, which are set against the large, static artwork that invites the viewer to stand still, to speak through, and even touch it. As the spectator rubs their fingers against the cool metal surface of the sculpture, they can lean into the void and speak. Their voice resonates in the chamber until it becomes deep and ringing, and although the stage had been set for a face-to-face meeting, the metal medium creates sonic drag and reverberations as the words pass from one side to the other. It is mediated and altered communication, not direct.

When there is no other human partner, the sculpture itself becomes the relational entity. Created at a human scale, the metal object automatically sets up a frame of reference with the viewing body, and the ability to touch and peer into its form also establishes a sensual interactivity between viewer and work. One's own voice and breath echoes through the metal interior, returning to the spectator's hearing altered by the body of the work. Most poignantly, when peering through the portals, *Face à Face* perfectly framed the *y20 Huis clos* aquarium, or the centre screen from the *y20* nine-channel installation, respectively. With this positioning the moving images of *y20* took up the place that a human speaker would ordinarily occupy, creating an analogy between human and object that brings the viewer and the filmic images into relationship with one another. In this way *Face à Face* implies an ongoing conversation between *y20 Huis clos* and the nine-channel *y20* installation when there is no viewer present to block their trajectory. This gesture recognizes the temporary nature of the viewing encounter, because the relational dynamics continue even when there is no human there to observe them. By creating active attention towards these effects, the installation disrupts conventions of viewing just enough to reveal the processes behind them.

Although it may seem as if these relational effects are only available in the bright, mobile space of the gallery, skoltz also deploys the time of cinema to prove otherwise. Cinema has long been dogged by the accusation that its static positioning and enveloping darkness automatically create a passive experience. In *Camera Lucida* – a text that famously argues for the material and affective qualities of the photograph – Roland Barthes denies moving images this same emotional power. He declares that cinema's constant flow of images lacks the punctum or the emotional shock of photography's freeze-framing, because the images are caught up in a constant forward momentum.[25] For Barthes, the emotional affect of the image is tied to a disruption of time: of holding a special moment out from the usual flow of human experience. Ironically, Barthes also suggests an alternative means for this affect to occur in a different essay entitled: "Leaving the Movie Theatre." In this text, he reiterates the idea that cinema seduces and hypnotizes the spectator with narrative flow, but also offers a potential solution by suggesting that viewers should let themselves be "fascinated *twice over*, by the image and by its surroundings – as if I had two bodies at the same time: a narcissistic body which gazes, lost into the engulfing mirror, and a perverse body, ready to fetishize not the image but precisely what exceeds it: the texture of the sound, the hall, the darkness, the obscure mass of other bodies."[26] Like O'Doherty's "double mechanism of display," Barthes calls for spectators to recognize the ideological effects of cinema's contextual architecture. For Barthes, when the viewer sees both the film and the surrounding architecture of the theatre, the spectatorial body is located in the actual space of the auditorium so that one might recognize the illusion of the virtual image. The intervention lies in a disruption of cinematic time in favour of the spectator's lived time. Yet, skoltz's artworks do not merely call attention to the exhibition environment as a frame for the work: they include the spectator within the durational flow of experience. Her installations express Barthes's punctum not in the photographic ability to draw an object out of the past, or in the distracted attention toward the material environment of exhibition; instead, skoltz creates a punctum by linking the present, ever-flowing temporality of the moving image with the same lived momentum of the spectatorial experience, as well as the spatial ability to step back into a panoptic position outside of duration.

In skoltz's work, the viewer must live in their own time, and in the time of the film simultaneously. It is a back and forth of attention between the subjective experience of the viewer and the constructed experience of the moving image, which oscillates so that the viewer is at once seeing – and also recognizing – the apparatuses that shape how and what they see. The act of being "fascinated twice over" requires both the durational flow of the live body experiencing, and also the critical act of making meaning. skoltz skillfully produces this effect by complicating the divisions between the material object and virtual narrative, since she treats the ephemeral material of the filmic narrative as an object that can be disassembled and reconstructed in a variety of material forms. By iterating the *y2o* chapters across multiple screens, inserting television monitors into aquariums as sculptures, and leaking the projected image off the screen and onto water or other gallery-objects, she transforms the light and time of cinema into something tactile and interactive. At the same time, cinema imbues the object-artifacts of the gallery with the duration and reproducible qualities of the moving image. The photographs and sculptures exist as individual segments that are part of a broader whole, with a narrative that links each object diegetically, and as demonstrated by *Face à Face*, the artifacts also gain a temporal quality that enables them to *perform* with the viewer.[27] They take up time as well as space, and require the viewer to enter into a durational conversation that is grounded in the live co-presence of the viewer with the artwork.

Through each iteration of *y20*, skoltz dismantles and reassembles the institutions of cinema and visual arts to create tension between lived and constructed experience. As a single-channel film, the work immerses the spectator through the visual and temporal conventions of the screen-image. Viewers cannot touch the performers floating in their watery enclosure, but the colour, texture, and movement of the cinematography connects our eye to the image while effacing our bodies. With the migration to the gallery, this sense of potential touch shifts from an abstraction to a real possibility, and the works suddenly require the viewer to position themselves in a physical relationship as well as mental. Here, we are not part of the image, but standing in relation to it, trying to forge a connection that flows both ways. Spectator and image-object dance forward and back, drawing close and stepping away, until the moment when the two brush up against one another in a "kiss." Within this gesture, there is not only the moment of encounter, but the before and after of the relationship, always ebbing and flowing as duration pushes onward. Through *y20 dualités_*, skoltz embodies her narrative of romantic entanglement within the dynamic between the spectator and artwork, making visible how we navigate the "troubled waters" of our "own physical and emotional pulsations."[28]

Notes

1. This is largely due to the flexible display environment of the gallery as well as the economic reality that these expensive and difficult-to-collect works often find funding only in visual arts exhibition systems.
2. Erika Balsom notes that the gallery is presumed to "save" cinema from its passive and commercial connotations, and discuses the tension

between mobile and passive spectatorial positions in *Exhibiting Cinema in Contemporary Art* (Amsterdam: Amsterdam University Press, 2013), 31. Historical writing on the ideology of the cinematic apparatus includes: Jean-Louis Baudry and Alan Williams, "Ideological Effects of the Basic Cinematographic Apparatus," *Film Quarterly* 28, no. 2 (winter 1974): 39–47; Stephen Heath, *Questions of Cinema* (Bloomington: Indiana University Press, 1981); Christian Metz, *Film Language: A Semiotics of the Cinema* (Chicago: University of Chicago Press, 1990); and Laura Mulvey, "Visual Pleasure and Narrative Cinema," in *Media and Cultural Studies: Keyworks*, eds. Meenakshi Gigi Durham and Douglas M. Kellner (Hoboken: Wiley-Blackwell, 2006), 267–74.

3   skoltz formats her name in all lowercase, and I will maintain that style.
4   Anthony McCall quoted in Paul Young, *Art Cinema*, ed. Paul Duncan (Köln: TASCHEN, 2009), 11.
5   Brian O'Doherty, *Inside the White Cube: The Ideology of the Gallery Space* (Berkeley: University of California Press, 2000).
6   For more information on the development of the gallery, see Charlotte Klonk, *Spaces of Experience: Art Gallery Interiors from 1800 to 2000* (New Haven: Yale University Press, 2009); Julia Noordegraaf, *Strategies of Display: Museum Presentation in Nineteenth- and Twentieth-Century Visual Culture* (Rotterdam: NAi Publishers, 2004); Suzanne MacLeod, ed., *Reshaping Museum Space: Architecture, Design, Exhibitions* (Abingdon: Routledge, 2005).
7   See Tony Bennett, "The Exhibitionary Complex," in *Thinking about Exhibitions*, eds. Reesa Greenberg, Bruce W. Ferguson, and Sandy Nairne (Abingdon: Routledge, 1996), 81–112.
8   O'Doherty, *Inside the White Cube*, 14.
9   See Tom Gunning, "The Cinema of Attraction: Early Cinema, Its Spectator and the Avant-Garde," in *Early Cinema: Space, Frame, Narrative*, eds. Thomas Elsaesser and Adam Barker (London: BFI, 1990), 56–62.
10 See Edwin Heathcote, *Cinema Builders* (New York: Wiley-Academy, 2001); Andrew V. Uroskie, *Between the Black Box and the White Cube: Expanded Cinema and Postwar Art* (Chicago: University of Chicago Press, 2014).
11 For more discussion of the two contexts, see Melanie Wilmink, "Moving through Images: Spectatorship in Interdisciplinary Art Environments" (PhD diss., York University, 2020).
12 Arsenal contemporary art contemporain, "*y2o duality*," Arsenal contemporary art contemporain, n.d., Wayback Machine, accessed 12 December 2019, https://web.archive.org/web/20170106132624/http://www.arsenalmontreal.com/en/exhibitions/y2o_duality.
13 Bernard Schütze, "Resonances of an Affective Field," *y2o catalogue* (Montreal: dominique t. skoltz, 2015), 5.

14 dominique t. skoltz, "Huis clos," dominique t skoltz~, n.d., accessed 12 December 2019, www.dominiquetskoltz.com.
15 Roland Barthes, *Camera Lucida: Reflections on Photography*, trans. Richard Howard (New York: Hill and Wang, 2010), 57, 96.
16 This shorthand is like the phenomenon of recognizing misspelled words, or even ignoring common words, because readers derive meaning from contextual phrasing rather than individual words. See Natalie Wolchover, "Breaking the Code: Why Yuor Barin Can Raed Tihs," *Live Science*, 9 February 2012, https://www.livescience.com/18392-reading-jumbled-words.html; Keith Rayner et al., "Eye Movements and Word Skipping during Reading: Effects of Word Length and Predictability," *Journal of Experimental Psychology: Human Perception and Performance* 37, no. 2 (2011): 514–28, https://www.ncbi.nlm.nih.gov/pmc/articles/PMC3543826/.
17 O'Doherty, "Gallery as Gesture," in *Inside the White Cube*, 87–107.
18 Sylvia Lavin, *Kissing Architecture* (Princeton: Princeton University Press, 2011), 4.
19 Ibid., 30.
20 Ibid., 36
21 Ibid., 101.
22 skoltz, "Collision no 01 & 02," www.dominiquetskoltz.com.
23 skoltz, "Union de Fait," www.dominiquetskoltz.com.
24 skoltz, "Face à Face," www.dominiquetskoltz.com.
25 Barthes, *Camera Lucida*, 89.
26 Roland Barthes, "Leaving the Movie Theatre," *The Rustle of Language*, trans. Richard Howard (New York: Hill and Wang, 1986), 421.
27 skoltz also incorporated live dance into the exhibition opening night at Arsenal, Montreal.
28 Arsenal, "y2o duality."

PART THREE
Canadian Film Contexts, Festivals, and Industries

15

A Taxing Culture

Reconsidering the Service Production

Charles R. Acland

The Canadian film and television scene has had a historically fraught relationship with international productions. It has been the conventional view of nationalist critics that foreign involvement in our media is detrimental to the growth of Canadian cultural expression. But there are those who embrace such projects, often referred to as service productions, as advantageous and welcome paths to the development and sustainment of our media industries. Producer Don Carmody, when asked about what advice he relays to film students in the US, replied that he tells them what a welcoming environment Canada has for film and television production. In his view, with many jurisdictions competing to be "film-friendly" to attract production work, Canada is among the friendliest.[1] Carmody would know. For more than forty years, he has worked at the heart of the Canadian film industry, producing over a hundred movies, including both Canadian and foreign projects shot in Canada. From David Cronenberg's early works to the *Resident Evil* franchise, Carmody's career has consistently put the lie to the assumption that Canadian movies, co-ventures, and co-productions are not popular: *Meatballs* (1979), *A Christmas Story* (1983), *Good Will Hunting* (1997), *The Boondock Saints* (1999), *Orphan* (2009), *Goon* (2011), *Pompeii* (2014). He has won the Golden Screen Award, which honours each year's highest-box-office-grossing Canadian feature film, an unprecedented nine times.[2] *Polytechnique* (2009) was invited to the Director's Fortnight in Cannes. And his co-produced film, *Chicago* (2002), won the Academy Award for Best Motion Picture.

The impact of high-profile popular films on the Canadian film industry cannot be overestimated, even if the films are not recognizable as specifically Canadian cultural expressions. When Clint Eastwood's *Unforgiven* (1992) won the Oscar for Best Picture, there was a spike in production in Alberta where the film was shot. Twenty-five years later, the Best Picture Oscar win for Guillermo del Toro's Toronto-made *The Shape of Water* (2017) yet again confirmed the exceptional quality of the Canadian production infrastructure. Like both of those Best Picture Oscar winners, *Chicago* is not a Canadian movie; it is an American movie, but made with majority Canadian crew and talent, location, policy incentives, and technological resources. And movies such as these work as worldwide billboard advertisements for the Canadian film and television production sector, even as they redirect talent away from domestic projects.

An infrastructure of sound stages, versatile location management, and highly skilled crew are required to make productions viable anywhere, and there are many countries and cities that compete to offer the very best facilities and personnel. The availability and assessment of production incentives for international production is a completely regularized aspect of contemporary production. The acclaimed *Call Me by Your Name* (2017) actually begins, before any other credit appears, by thanking named tax-credit programs that allowed this Italy-Brazil-France-US film of an American novel by an Italian director and shot in Italy to be made at all. Canada, though, has an especially long and active history of landing international shoots; there is a good deal of experience managing all productions big and small.[3] A number of established firms exist ready to bid for production contracts, and the relative proximity to the epicentre of the global media business in the United States doesn't hurt either, especially with Vancouver in the same time zone as Los Angeles. As a result, Canada is a seasoned host to international fly-by-night movie shoots and multi-season American television production. Think of it as the "panda theory" of Canadian film and television production: eats, shoots, and leaves. Beyond the experience with such endeavours, as Carmody told it, American students' jaws drop when he describes the financial incentives available for international shoots in Canada. Incredulity is the standard response among these young American filmmakers. Prospects and programs – federal, provincial, and municipal – exist to make productions financially viable in Canada that simply would not be possible in the US.

For a national cinema culture bent on maintaining an impression of underdevelopment and lost potential, evident successes and advantages are a troubling counterargument. The struggles to expand participation in film and television industries from underrepresented communities, to enliven diverse representational modes, and to make work available remain essential objectives. But whatever action is taken to advance on these fronts takes place in the context of a sizeable media production sector, an elaborate festival circuit, and enough innovative auteurs to feed cinephiles world-wide. According to world feature film comparative data from UNESCO Institute for Statistics, Canada produced ninety-two features in 2017, making it one of the top twenty countries with the highest rate of production.[4] As consumers of filmed entertainment, Canada is one of the ten largest markets by revenue.[5] Nevertheless, for many critics and audiences, the cinema we have has never been "the cinema we need," as the formative series of essays on the topic put it in 1985.[6] This chapter looks closely at this apparent contradiction – truly rooted in competing notions of what "success" in media culture looks like – by taking seriously some of the mechanisms designed to develop a viable production sector in this country.

Nowhere are the contradictions of cultural underdevelopment more evident than in the apparent invisibility of much production in Canada. Certain features construct a media culture drained of apparent specificity: Canadian talent and technology deployed to realize the work of another country, productions that do not prominently announce the Canadian contribution to the work, and Canadian locations disguised and dressed to look like somewhere else or nowhere at all. For every point of pride, for every key work that is seized upon as an exemplar of what we might accomplish – and the Quebec scene enjoys this uplift far more regularly than the rest of the country – there is the habitual incredulous double-take of "really, that's Canadian?" (e.g., the *Resident Evil* franchise) or "that American hit was made in Toronto?" (e.g., *The Shape of Water*) or "that American flop was made in Montreal?" (e.g., *Mother!* [2017]). The most basic feature of this discussion is the everyday way in which a distinction is understood between "Canadian film and television" and "film and television made in Canada." This distinction was not considered in 2018 when Heritage Minister Mélanie Joly negotiated a deal in which Netflix would spend $500 million over five years for production in Canada. Many critics unfamiliar with the intricacies of the film and television business were impressed by the raw size of the integer and consider this a major breakthrough success in wrestling with the international streaming giant. But it soon became apparent that the deal was not as valuable as it first appeared. The figure was likely not more than what they had been spending or planning to spend anyway, and possibly less. There were no metrics or enforcement measures for the deal, and no concrete commitment to productions in both official languages. And there were no definitions for what would count as a qualifying production – Canadian work or works made in Canada. Far from innovative, the meat of the deal consisted of the age-old gristle of Canadian cultural policy dilemmas. Whether you like it or not, we find ourselves again and again in the uncomfortable and inevitably fractious territory of designating some topics, approaches, and representations as more Canadian than others, which has historically been a force for exclusion and marginalization of diverse voices. As we will see below, some jurisdictions and cultural policy do exactly that by design.

To assess any policy framework, it is important to grasp the scope of the affected sector. It may be surprising to some, but Canadian cultural industries are a major source of employment, investment, and economic activity. Consider, for example, that in 2018, there were 7,826,000 Canadians who work in the expansive information, culture, and recreation sector, more than double the 3,453,000 who work in the forestry, fishing, mining, quarrying, and oil and gas sector.[7] Narrowing this to audiovisual and interactive media, which includes film, video, and broadcasting, the number was a significantly smaller but still substantial 144,811 workers in 2016.[8] The Canadian Media Producers Association's *Profile 2017* for film and television production reports the full-time job equivalent as 171,700 for 2016–17, which was a 27 per cent increase from the year before. The CMPA reported production volume of $8.38 billion, representing a year-over-year increase of 24 per cent. With $4.67 billion coming from foreign investment, which was a tremendous 41 per cent increase over 2015–16 figures, the sector accounted for $12 billion gross domestic product, an increase of 24 per cent.[9] A basic point, then, is that we are talking about an active arena of work, finance, and expression, one that relies on investment from abroad to function at this high level. Household and business economies alike depend on the regularity of employment in the sector, and both critical and policy apparatuses must never forget this.

Cultural policy involves providing transparent guidelines to enable and encourage certain modes of expression and practice over others. As Justin Lewis and Toby Miller put it, "cultural policies produce and animate institutions, practices, and agencies. One of their goals is to find, serve, and nurture a sense of belonging, through educational institutions and cultural industries. Such regimens are predicated on the insufficiency of the individual (for whom culture offers possibilities

Figures 15.1 and 15.2 Canadian or service production? Posters for *Resident Evil: Afterlife* (2010) and *The Shape of Water* (2014).

of a more complete self) alongside the generally benevolent sovereign-state."[10] Cultural policies are platforms that invite activity with the overall goal of individual and social amelioration. By definition not all possible cultural expressions and practices are equally invited. Policy frameworks provide incentives to some and can outright exclude others. It's not exactly that winners are chosen, though this could be the case. Still, cultural endeavours that are thought to have more advantages – for social development, democratic expansion, individual growth, creative innovation, representational diversity, profitability, economic possibility, and so on – come to be valued and supported, necessarily creating categories of marginal or debased works and practices. We may easily enough find widespread agreement about many underlying claims that guide policy decisions. Yet, we are nevertheless uncomfortably fixed on the ideological terrain of "common sense," meaning the fact that a cultural category is taken for granted as valuable doesn't make it true or fair. Like many cultural/economic policy initiatives, incentives flow toward activities that match an idea of desirable and valuable forms of cultural practice, continuing the "ethical" orientation of policy toward some amelioration of citizen and country. The appended ideological operation means that a process of evaluation pushes some works and practice to the centre and others to the side. Cultural policy is, in the end, a direct and operationalized arena of hierarchies of culture, which, as Pierre Bourdieu has exhaustively demonstrated, are hierarchies of class and unequal distribution of power.[11]

Nationalist cultural critique operates with cultural hierarchies that don't always match those of our cultural policy establishment. A reality check and a foundational contradiction in film and television: Canadian cultural criticism has relied upon the acceptance of an imaginary boundary that marks the international production as apart from our national home while our policy frameworks have muddied that distinction. The truth is that international productions are entirely and fully at home here, and they enjoy a familiar place in the everyday life of citizens and residents. Such is the case of service productions, that is, international projects that arrive here to take advantage of Canadian labour and technological resources, but whose financial beneficiaries and key creative personnel are, for the most part, not Canadian. They are indeed made locally, but then leave, to be imported as film and television shows that may also be embraced domestically by Canadian audiences. Multiple layers of belonging include such experiences of mobile cosmopolitanism, which are hallmarks of contemporaneity for the art connoisseur and the trash genre fan alike. Globally circulating culture is an ordinary part of everyday life. The deep integration of media production with the currents and systems of other national scenes mirrors a similarly complex and fluid affective connection with cultural products from virtually any international point of origin. Neither Canada, Canadians, nor our film and television sector are in any way unique in this respect. Yet Canadian cultural critics have tended to treat service productions primarily as missed opportunities and talent parasites.

Challenging this critical common sense, service productions need to be understood as a consistently vital feature of the media production environment in Canada. After all, they have been a long-standing policy target and have been valued by Canadian cultural agents and subsidiary service firms as necessary to their viability. Some of the challenges on this count that I pose here have been considered by others. The entwinement of Canadian talent with the American business complicates the expectations of where Canadian stardom is supposed to reside. Some have made cases that American films like *Wayne's World* (1992) and

Juno (2007) are para-Canadian texts, with considerable input at major creative points in each work and with slyly coded Canadianisms evident to the attentive northern viewer. Jennifer VanderBurgh effectively explored the limits of the Canadian Audio-Visual Certification Office (CAVCO) and the point system for the Canadian designation of a work by looking at the partial compliance of the Hollywood film *Ghostbusters* (1984).[12] Peter Urquhart has impressively taken on the national-cultural orthodoxy by reassessing select films from the late-1970s/early-1980s "tax-shelter boom," which has mostly been understood as a time of cinematic embarrassment with little redeeming value to Canadian cultural life. Instead, he showed us that the work of the Canadian Film Development Corporation (the precursor to Telefilm) and the 100 per cent Capital Cost Allowance policy produced not only substantial work for Canadian film crews but films that used popular film conventions to explore Canadian characteristics and debates.[13]

VanderBurgh and Urquhart both point in different ways to cultural policy and to our critical conventions that assess such policy. For the rest of the chapter, I focus on one of the more contentious but massively impactful features of our cultural policy environment: tax credit incentives for international film and television productions. I argue that there is a need to navigate a critical stance between two conventionalized positions, one that attacks such incentives for being insufficiently beneficial in an economic sense (typically the right-wing anti-interventionist position) and one that challenges them for being too economically invested (usually associated with that of the left-wing cultural nationalist).

Counting Credits

The Canadian Film or Video Production Tax Credit (CPTC) has provided reimbursements for some of the salary and wage expenses on Canadian productions since 1995. The tax credit is to support Canadian production, to build a viable production sector, and to stabilize production financing with a mechanism that could be applied regardless of the specific production. The CPTC replaced the 100 per cent Capital Cost Allowance, which more broadly provided an incentive to film investment.[14] Instead, the CPTC targeted labour, with the reasoning that helping boost employment in the film and television sector was more beneficial than tax breaks to investors where the impact on employment was not guaranteed. For the first eight years, qualified labour expenses generated a 25 per cent tax credit, with labour capped at 48 per cent of all production costs. In other words, the credit maximum was 12 per cent of the production budget. In November 2003, this credit was made more generous and the maximum increased to 15 per cent of the total production budget (or, more specifically, 25 per cent of salaries and wages up to 60 per cent of the total production budget).[15]

Heritage Canada conducted an impact audit of the CPTC after a decade in effect. At the time, in 2008, the CPTC represented the largest federal contribution to film and video production, worth $180 million annually. The impact of the policy varied depending on genre and region, but overall it contributed to a significant number of productions, with television programming accounting for the majority supported. The goal of providing increased financial stability was somewhat realized, and most production companies, many of which were small and continued to operate on a project-by-project basis, saw the credit as one of a number of instruments that made projects viable.[16]

The CPTC provides support for Canadian productions, not all productions in Canada. As such, the CPTC fundamentally requires a definition of Canadian production. It uses a point system that counts the citizenship of key creative participants (director, cinematographer, lead actors, screenwriter, etc.), an accepted qualifying criterion for cultural programs in this country. Versions of this point system are found elsewhere in our media policies; they are a standard feature of contemporary Canadian cultural bureaucracy, and variations are common in other countries. On a ten-point scale, a project with over six points is officially a Canadian production. Note the particularities of such a measure: a production with half the key participants, and conceivably with most of the other personnel Canadian, is not a Canadian production, but one with six of ten is a Canadian production. Other rules require a certain amount spent in Canada, that the copyright is owned by a Canadian entity, and that 75 per cent of labour costs go to Canadians, so there is an expectation that Canadians outside those key creative positions will always also be engaged. Nonetheless, there is considerable wiggle room, and the policy framework, steering clear of content and thematic requirements, embraces a measure in which "Canadian enough" (6/10 points) and "maximum Canadian" (10/10) are both Canadian productions. A ten-pointer may enjoy additional financial and broadcasting incentives, where "insufficiently Canadian" (5/10) is equal to non-Canadian, regardless of how many citizens and residents work on these types of productions.

In many respects, this approach reasonably presumes that works with major Canadian creative influence in the production, as captured by the point system, deserve financial support through this mechanism in the service of a full and vibrant creative sector, without consideration of what is being expressed or the mode of expression. It basically keeps cultural bureaucrats out of the content moderation business. But there are complications. For instance, Canada was an early, and enthusiastic, adopter of co-production treaties. At various times, Canada had more co-production treaties with other countries than any other national jurisdiction. What such treaties do is allow partnering between two or more countries to manage the expenses associated with production and distribution, providing access to different national funding structures that would otherwise be inaccessible, and hence providing a path to production viability. Co-production treaties work by relaxing certain nation-specific restrictions, with the assumption that over time there will be a balance of access between countries. Put differently, our status as one of the most highly developed co-production countries means we are among the most willing to relax our own rules, operating on the faith that Canadian producers will benefit comparably from access to the cultural incentives and markets found abroad. An Irish-Canadian co-production may be treated as "Canadian" for funding or broadcast content matters, even though on the point system it rates below the six-point threshold in "insufficiently Canadian" territory. Another work made through the same treaty may be majority Canadian in key personnel, but still access Irish state funding as would an exclusively Irish production. Peter Lester explores a detailed example of exactly this in his contribution to this volume. The CPTC does not, and nor is it intended to, support all production in Canada; it supports productions that have satisfied a metric that confirms they are, at least minimally, a Canadian contribution, a metric that is flexible under co-production agreements. On an individual case basis, if there is no co-production treaty with a particular country, Telefilm can be approached and may grant exemptions as though such a treaty was in effect.[17] Thus, the boundaries needed for nominally "Canadian" status in order to benefit from financial mechanisms to enhance production budgets can shift and slide. The definitional clarity provided by the point system can be blurred, making "Canadian" a provisional designation even within the very structure designed to offer certainty.

From 1995 through 2006 – the first twelve years of the CPTC – ten-pointer productions accounted for 76.7 per cent of the projects supported, which equalled 53.1 per cent of production volume (meaning the budget amount). Those with between six and nine points for creative personnel accounted for 12.9 per cent of the projects and 29.8 per cent of the production volume. However, a minority of the productions that benefitted from this instrument – 10.3 per cent of projects, or 17.1 per cent of production volume – were those emerging from international co-production treaty projects.[18] In short, a major tax credit, designed as an incentive for Canadian productions, assists minimally "Canadian" projects as well as works that do not meet the point threshold for "Canadian," as is permitted via international co-production treaties.

While subject matter and stylistic approach does not officially factor in the decision-making process for the CPTC, there are excluded genre categories. Talk, game, reality, pornography, telethons, awards, corporate, advertising, sporting, and news programming are all ineligible, as are all non-documentary productions made up largely of stock footage. In effect, this list of genres outlines the contours of what is outside the "cultural," and while it may be easy to come to an agreement about advertising and corporate material being categories rooted in promotion and persuasion rather than creative expression, other genres – say, sexually explicit or fiction compilation films – may well be explored to innovate or extend the representational range. One may argue that these excluded genres tend to be financially sustainable all on their own, so incentives are not as crucial. But the excluded categories seem particularly connected with dominant genres of television (news, awards, sports, talk, telethons) and "lower" forms (pornography, reality and game shows), betraying a taste hierarchy.

As with any measure that relies on the point system, the mere fact of nationality has not resulted in participation from a representative slice of the population. The openness to anyone with Canadian status has advantaged some over others, making it apparent that passive and nominally "neutral" approaches to cultural incentives can result in the fortification of existing divides and biases. Without specific programs, as expected of structural sexism and racism, women are not employed or paid equally, and people of colour remain marginalized on screen and off. Other measures targeting diversity and inclusivity aim to respond to these structural problems, including the Canada Media Fund's Francophone and Anglophone Minority envelopes, the Northern Production Incentive, the Indigenous program fund, and the Pilot Program for Racialized Communities launched in 2021. Welcomed by many, these actions have not yet disrupted the dramatic barriers to full participation and remuneration of diverse underrepresented communities. On this front, our cultural scene benefits from the funding, information, and advocacy work of the Indigenous Screen Office, Women in Film and Television, and BIPOC TV and Film.

On the standardized terms of policy assessment, the relative success of the CPTC was encouraging, though it was clear that it only handled some of the production that transpired in Canada. Whatever pride may stem from work on a maximally Canadian ten-pointer, the actuality of continuous employment doesn't always offer such choices to film and television talent. For this reason, in 1997, the Film or Video Production Service Tax Credit (PSTC) was launched for productions that do not meet the criteria of the CPTC, often those missing some component required for "Canadian" certification. The PSTC provides tax credits for 16 per cent of qualifying labour costs on production service in Canada, without any cap, which makes this mechanism especially appealing for big-budget productions. The PSTC can be used by either a Canadian- or foreign-owned entity engaged primarily in production, though in either case, it must have a permanent office in Canada, which means it is beholden to all domestic tax requirements. The same genres excluded from eligibility of the CPTC are likewise excluded here, but added are budget minimums of $1,000,000 for film, $200,000 for television episodes, or $100,000 for half-hour television episodes, all to be spent within two years of the start of principle photography. While these may be seen by media producers as reasonable budget minimums, they do pose barriers to those who do not command access to such financing. Though they are technically available to anyone at any stage of their career, the budget minimums rule out micro-budget projects. For this reason, these incentives effectively boost an already existing industry structure, its participants, and its standards.

But wait, there's more.

The federal program to attract production dollars sparks other Canadian jurisdictions to compete with one another to be the ultimate landing pad for shoots, services, and their associated expenditures. Provincial tax credits for production service provide additional incentives. British Columbia has a tax credit for 28 per cent of qualifying labour expenses, with no maximum, as well as extra amounts for shooting away from Vancouver and for digital animation and visual effects. Ontario has a more expansive 21.5 per cent tax credit for all production services expenses, including but not limited to labour, with no cap and with additional credits for digital animation and visual effects. Quebec's 20 per cent credit is similarly expansive with bonuses for digital effects, animation, and dubbing. BC and Quebec's credits are refundable. BC, Quebec, and Ontario's programs have the same budget minimums and genre exclusions as the federal one. Though these three provinces make up the majority of domestic and international production in Canada, other provinces have comparable mechanisms to support both homegrown projects and attract international media production spending. An added twist, or an irony, in our political framework is found in the fact that provincial service production tax credits compete for foreign productions as well as those from other provinces. Where the federal service production incentives operate with an understanding of a national domestic production infrastructure, the supplementary incentives from provincial jurisdictions bolster a more localized labour economy against those of other parts of the country. Sub-national competition, at root, cares less for a national cultural scene, counting, instead, on the gospel of state-supported competition in the labour market to invigorate domestic media production.

The contribution of the foreign production to the Canadian film and television industry, advantaged as it is by the PSTC, is considerable. For 2016–17, there was $3.76 billion in direct investment in service production for a total of 418 foreign projects, consisting of 183 films, 149 television series, and 86 television movies, miniseries, and pilots. This volume represented a 17.7 per cent increase from the year before; the investment was a whopping 42.1 per cent increase, making it a record high. The concern that Canada has grown into a branch of the US industry has merit, though this claim has been a standard element throughout Canadian moving image history. In 2016–17, a full 73 per cent of foreign productions (304 projects) originated in the US, with the copyrights of those works being held and exploited there, while 9 per cent were British and 5 per cent French. Consider this: among foreign location and service productions for that year, 5.5 per cent (twenty-three projects) originated in Canada and between 5 per cent and 10 per cent of the copyrights are held by Canadians. This narrow category where foreignness *and* Canadianness intersect includes films or television programs from Canadian producers, made in Canada, for international audiences or international co-productions made outside co-production treaties.[19] Where we may criticize the weight of the PSTC providing breaks to American projects, we must acknowledge the fact that Canadian labour *and* productions benefit.

The Ideological Horizon of Economic Incentives for Culture

Media production tax credits emerge from an economic model of cultural life; but be aware that economic analysts are not necessarily their champions. Free-market state minimalists embrace the view that entrepreneurs will, eventually if left to their own devices, produce the cultural scene we need, or deserve. Adhering to a conventional libertarian economic bias, such economic state minimalists think of tax credit programs for labour as market distortions. For this position, any policy that emboldens an investment culture is valuable and helps demonstrate and support their view that publicly supported culture is a policy dead-end. But, left cultural critics have been just as successful as the right in challenging what is simplistically seen as the statist drive of public institutions, leaving few to defend state-supported, but technically money-losing, cultural propositions. Steve Globerman's *The Entertainment Industries, Government Policies, and Canada's National Identity*, from 2014, is a case in point.[20] Prepared for the state-minimalist Fraser Institute, an influential think-tank that has generated arguments for privatization for the last forty years, the report offers the recommendations one expects to see from this venue: outside very specific applications, government efforts to increase production and consumption of Canadian entertainment are ineffective, as are policies that limit foreign ownership or require Canadian-content in some cultural enterprises. Globerman is typical of the Fraser Institute in his promotion of a free-market economic norm against which every other economic arrangement is aberrant or irrational. His reasoning has persistently been skeptical that "market failure" exists in the Canadian cultural sector, even though this has been demonstrated time and again to be the case for many sectors of cultural production. It is absolutely the case that some cultural organizations in Canada would collapse without assistance. For film, television, and music, the meagre production prior to the mid-1960s federal support, and the emergence of a prolific media production industry following government programs to build one, is sound evidence that, left on its own, much of the Canadian culture market would not thrive. Still, Globerman writes, "even if a market failure problem exists, society might still be better off without any government intervention if the social costs of the intervention exceed the social benefits."[21] Here, the ideological undergirding of his claims is laid bare; for an analytical approach that requires evidence that benefits exceed costs, and requires finding these benefits in empirical economic metrics, he nonetheless tells us that even if the evidence points toward the benefits of government intervention, we might be nonetheless better off without it. With no support for this claim, and with a flexible sense of what would count as a social cost or benefit, we are soundly in the realm of belief, not evidence-based conclusions.

There are further contradictions. Where state interventions in culture produce market inefficiencies – almost by definition according to Globerman – he nonetheless recommends more government support for training. Why would this be the case? Would his ideological position not lead him to reject such distortions? On the contrary, state support used for shaping a labour force, aligned with market demands, allows an industrial sector to reap the benefits of a skilled workforce in which it did not invest.

Closer to our specific focus here, John Lester provides a comprehensive analysis of policy research that tries to measure the economic impact of the PSTC at both the federal and provincial levels.[22] He acknowledges the various limitations of doing so and notes possible consequences of the tax credit including lost revenue for the government, increased wages for workers, and increased tax revenue from foreign workers who would not pay such in Canada otherwise. His general conclusion is that tax break plans designed to attract foreign service productions do not meet their stated objective of making a positive contribution to the Canadian economy. In fact, they represent "a new economic loss to society that is almost 100 percent of the amount of the subsidy provided."[23] There are problems with this line of reasoning. First, tax incentives are not subsidies, a mistake often made by US critics of our "unfair" public supports for creative and cultural work. Second, in this statement Lester ignores that if what he says is accurate, then the cost to the economy is zero (economic loss exactly equals the amount of the support). With even one other additional benefit, however intangible or minor – let's say, the employment of a cultural worker who otherwise would be unemployed, perhaps drawing employment insurance benefits, and through that employment acquires training, experience, and job continuity – then the program ought to be pursued. Nonetheless, using a benefit-cost analysis that shows no economic cost, he concludes "that Canadians, on average, would be better off if the federal and provincial tax credits for foreign location shooting were eliminated."[24] Lester speculates that their elimination would reduce by one-third the volume of production, wages would fall, and some workers would need to retrain and leave the market. To ease the considerable pain involved, Lester recommends that the government provide transitional funds. These lines are offered in the spirit of cold realism. But consider what his reasoning recommends: the dismantling of a cultural sector.

As presented by Lester, there is no indication that the new resources available to government from the elimination of this program would be returned to the cultural sector beyond the transition funds to help cultural workers out of the cultural sector. One is left with the impression that the immiseration of cultural labour is worth the enrichment of the state. This, of course, is not directly Lester's endgame. The enrichment of the state provides standard conservative economic voices with evidence for easing of tax burdens elsewhere, so in the end, public coffers are not better off either.

A benefit-cost analysis is conventional for policy work, which aims to present in a clear and empirical fashion the most efficient allocation of resources to achieve agreed-upon objectives. The effective and ethical use of public funds is a major responsibility and duty, so any scrutiny that questions and verifies that trust is valuable. I take no issue with such scrutiny of public funds and programs. Globerman takes a comparable position, asking if private concerns could on their own achieve the same social and cultural goals without government assistance, with ruling measures of eligibility based on status in Canada of key creators, and "whether there are any identifiable benefits associated with government intervention in the entertainment sector and whether the benefits are likely to exceed any associated costs."[25] But problems arise with such an analytical orientation, in that there is a tendency to conceptualize all cultural matters as a question of economic value. Even public culture ends up reduced to in-flows and out-flows of funds. Priorities that are less economistic – say, democracy, equality, diversity, collectivity, justice, vibrancy, reconciliation – may be referenced, but they end up lumped together as "intangibles" and treated as immeasurable irritations. The fact is, for an argument that positions itself in favour of maximum free-market and minimum government intervention, the benefit-cost analysis used by Lester primarily examines the impact of the PSTC policy on government finances, asking what revenue it brings in and what costs extract funds. Lester identifies a "large economic loss" to Canada and Canadians, but he does not include any of the actual contributions that production spending makes to a provincial or national economy. Nor is there a meaningful assessment of the benefits to a sustained infrastructure for media production, whether to Canadian productions in the form of an active and trained skilled workforce or in terms of the economic multipliers that indicate additional economic activity for every dollar spent. Comparable measures exist in many jurisdictions across the world, including in the media production – and free-market – powerhouse of the United States. The idea that they shouldn't apply in Canada disregards the value of a cultural sector and its potential social, cultural, *and* economic benefits.

As Lester implies, though, it remains an oddity in Canadian policy that one would provide tax credits to non-nationals. Sure, many industries are structured to entice investment, especially from abroad. But there is something galling, on a basic level, about offering financial incentives to Hollywood producers when some Canadian cultural workers and artists do without. With Lester and Globerman, we see that unease with PSTCS exists among free-marketeers as well as cultural nationalists, who chafe at what they see as the promotion of the colonization of our media culture and infrastructure. The critiques of tax incentives for international productions confound what typically passes for right-wing and left-wing ideological positions. At different points in Canadian cultural policy history, economic arguments for government incentives have included "infant industry," roughly that new and promising sectors may require an initial level of investment that only government can provide, or "market failure," where, in the relatively small and geographically dispersed Canadian market, a particular good or service would not exist domestically without additional support. In actuality, the underlying rationale is not just about economic enrichment, but about the possibilities for a broad range of domestic cultural expression that would not be evident in the Canadian scene otherwise, and more opportunities for employment and work experience.

It is instructive to look at how comparable programs operate in other countries. In an important consultancy report, Maria de Rosa and Marilyn Burgess offer an extensive survey of how other countries establish criteria for defining national cultural content in order to enact cultural policy programs.[26] Using European countries and Australia as a basis of comparison, the authors outline the different ways countries support domestic film and television via tax credits, rebates, or funding envelopes. Though co-productions and incentives to foreign productions are not the focus of their study, the varying criteria for a qualifying national production are fascinating. Considering the criteria for access to different national versions of the CPTC, all responding countries have a cultural test that includes nationality of personnel involved in the production, the physical location of the production, and the specific nature of the content. Canada, in contrast, uses essentially one metric: nationality of key personnel.[27] Seven of the ten countries used a point system to measure the nationality of production personnel, but Canada restricts its measure to a ten-point system that recognizes major creative positions. The UK and the Netherlands expand consideration to a wider range of participants on scales of thirty-one points and

200 points, respectively. This, de Rosa and Burgess conclude, provides greater flexibility to those assembling a qualifying national production in those countries over the more restrictive, if more predictable, Canadian scale.[28] European countries count as "national" personnel anyone with EU or EEA status; in other words, to count a point as a "national" in France you could be Norwegian and reside in Spain. Not so in Canada, where only citizens and permanent residents count. And the other comparison countries all had lower spending demands. The UK required only 10 per cent of the budget be spent domestically while France and Spain required a minimum of 51 per cent. Canada was an outlier with 75 per cent of production and post-production spent locally.[29] De Rosa and Burgess indicate flexibilities in other countries, including the length of time copyright is held by a domestic entity, for access to domestic film and television tax credits. Direct funding via agencies like the Canada Media Fund and Telefilm were found to be comparable to what is available in other countries, though content played a more substantial role elsewhere.

In essence, the relative restrictiveness of the CPTC only works because of the existence of the PSTC. *Productions that end up benefitting from the PSTC as "service" productions in Canada might have qualified as "national" content in other countries.* The extent to which these two mechanisms work together to provide incentives to media production that match those of other countries needs more careful measurement and comparative study. But at the very least, the fact that what would be classified as a foreign service production in Canada might be a standard French, UK, or Australian production in their respective contexts tells us that our critical apparatus must work past the brute policy definitions of good cultural vs bad service productions.

New Ideological Horizons?

Service productions are a tough sell on a number of fronts. The use of Canadian skill and talent for productions that distance themselves from Canada, and may even deliberately work to hide their Canadian connections, seems to be an exercise in self-negation or self-abasement. Our considerable resources in media production orient themselves to the steady paying conditions provided by international projects. As a result, the stories and settings of service productions rarely spring from any Canadian specificity and can work against the efforts of organizations invested in expanding the representational frame in this country, like those of the Indigenous Screen Office.

Still, service productions, even those most stridently internationalized and location-drained examples, can betray the actuality of place, if only in the "Montreal Unit" or similar identifiable designations in the end credits. Additionally, there is the raw fact that with service projects work is to be had. The strengthening of a production scene provides spin-off benefits by developing an experienced and skilled workforce, which can be utilized by more particularly Canadian productions. To be sure, the regularity of work contexts, production crews, and networks means that some are more consistently employed on service productions and others on domestic projects. But this is not exclusively the case, and the flow in the career of below- and above-the-line personnel between these types of productions is considerable and ordinary. The regularity of a work environment also provides opportunities for labour to organize, to begin to standardize conditions and employment expectations, and to strengthen the unions, guilds, and associations that work on their behalf. Amanda Coles expands on related issues relevant to film and media labour in the next chapter. One illustration is actor Mia Kirshner's efforts to ignite a Canadian response to the #MeToo movement. Indeed, her initial public intervention was so immediate following the investigative news reports about Harvey Weinstein's criminal conduct, it preceded by two days the skyrocketing usage of #MeToo catalyzed by Alyssa Milano's tweet of the hashtag on 15 October 2017. As Kirshner outlined in a *Globe and Mail* op-ed, and as subsequently picked up and organized as #Aftermetoo, she understood that the target for improved security from harassment was going to be through the unions, where an institutionally backed set of labour standards and procedures could be enacted and enforced.[30] And her efforts, along with the many who supported them, resulted in concrete changes in policy and process at several key Canadian organizations. Kirshner's reference was not Canadian productions, point system approved as such or not, but work in Canada. Broadly speaking, the more uneven the work is, the less labour power can be coordinated and organized, and the more vulnerable talent is to contractual demands and work conditions that can range from unreasonable to exploitive. This is not to say that precarity has been or will be banished from the Canadian media production culture. On the contrary, it is a defining condition. But it is only through expanding numbers of participating skilled labour, and a consistently high demand for them, that standards can be requested, negotiated, and agreed upon, including matters of pay, hours, overtime, travel time, and reporting procedures for grievances. What purpose do we serve by rendering the actuality of media work in this country, regardless of the genre or funding provenance, inconsequential to Canadian life? We do not honour the skill, effort, and creativity of media production personnel by further alienating them from their contributions.

Elsewhere, I've written about the possibility of recognizing craft, that is, the specific set of material labour contributions to works.[31] The concept of craft works against the further dematerialization and erasure of contributions to service productions, and it stands in contrast to cultural criticism that acknowledges only the most official designations of nationality, those cultural-bureaucratic determinations of Canadian or hyphenate Canadian productions. Focusing on craft aligns our critical view with that of guilds and labour associations, whose Canadianness stems from federal and provincial labour codes rather than the nationality of the copyright holder of the final product, or the nationality of the director, screenwriter, or lead actors.

For lack of a better description, I am proposing a realpolitik approach to questions of national media culture that privileges the actuality of labour. My exploration here is by no means intended to be a resignation that, oh well, we don't have our own media culture so we might as well be happy working behind the scenes to make American movies look good. My claim is that we take seriously what happens when we have both cultural and service productions residing side by side in policy and production culture. Canadian scholars and cultural critics have spent pretty well all of our time thinking about those cultural works that we take for granted as Canadian and ignoring the considerable time and resources going into that parallel arena of the service production. Moreover, as discussed above, the shaky boundaries of nationality are not resolved by the categorical demarcations of policy definitions, despite their best efforts, making the difference between some Canadian and non-Canadian productions a moving and fuzzy line regardless. Our critical apparatus requires us to parse the variety of contributions, including parts of moving image works found in sequences, effects, soundscapes, and so on, that accrue. These contributions to media works, over time, constitute the totality of local media production output and continuity in career accomplishments.

This stance is not without risks. Jennifer VanderBurgh outlines some of the consequences of "tax credit thinking," reasoning that it funnels argumentation for "local" production into ranks according to market potential. Her study of the Nova Scotia scene finds minimal infrastructural support overall, as a result of this thinking.[32] Such a position resonates with that of Michael Dorland in his groundbreaking book *So Close to the State/s*, which remains a foundational study of the ascendancy of an economic discourse in Canadian film policy at the expense of other civic and democratic frameworks.[33] Undeniably, something is lost when the vitality of a cultural sector is supported and advanced primarily according to a logic of job creation, entrepreneurial assistance, and lucrative markets. And yet, two factors give me pause and suggest that additional contingencies have to enter our critique. First, much of cultural economics now centres on the "market distortion" of incentives to some cultural programs. Here, like attacks on public culture, tax credits are seen as not economically justified. The Fraser Institute is not alone in this ideological tendency. In many jurisdictions, particularly in the US, right-wing economists have been arguing forcefully, with some success, to eliminate tax credit and other forms of assistance to cultural workers. There are numerous limitations to their rationale, but generally speaking their economic models do not account for long-term benefits, which include training, tourism, quality of life, and the strengthening of public democratic engagement, nor the fullness of multiplier effects of spin-off economic activity resulting from media production work. Second, these models minimize how crucial continuous work, even when contract-driven, is for media production crews. The question should not only be whether we have the best, most lucrative, or most Canadian media production sector possible; the question should also be how might the labour conditions of the media production sector be made less precarious, less exploitive, more predictable, more equitable, more inclusive, regardless of the category of the production, cultural or service.

Notes

1 For a discussion of the drive to create "film-friendly" cities and regions, cf. Ben Goldsmith, Susan Ward, and Tom O'Regan's *Local Hollywood: Global Film Production and the Gold Coast* (Brisbane: University of Queensland Press, 2010). Carmody's comments originate from a question period during distinguished alumnus events honouring his career achievements at the Department of Communication Studies, Concordia University, Montreal, 4–6 April 2018. One of the few scholarly efforts to engage with Carmody's impact on the Canadian film production scene has been Charles Tepperman, "Of Golden Reels and Performance Envelopes: Reconsidering the Producer in Canadian Cinema," paper presented to the Film Studies Association of

Canada, Ottawa, June 2015. Thank you to Kathryn Armstrong for assistance with the final production of the chapter.

2   The films for which Carmody's productions won the Golden Screen Award (formerly the Golden Reel Award) were *Pompeii*, *The Mortal Instruments: City of Bones* (2013), *Resident Evil: Retribution* (2012), *Resident Evil: Afterlife* (2010), *Resident Evil: Apocalypse* (2004), *The Art of War* (2000), *Johnny Mnemonic* (1995), *Porky's* (1981), and *Meatballs* (1979).

3   For a detailed examination of the entwinement of local and international production, see Mike Gasher, *Hollywood North: The Feature Film Industry in British Columbia* (Vancouver: UBC Press, 2002). For a study of the place of the international market in Canadian television, see Serra Tinic, *On Location: Canada's Television Industry in a Global Market* (Toronto: University of Toronto Press, 2007). For a consideration of these issues internationally, see Greg Elmer and Mike Gasher, eds., *Contracting Out Hollywood: Runaway Productions and Foreign Location Shooting* (Lanham: Rowman and Littlefield, 2005).

4   UNESCO Institute for Statistics (UIS), "Culture: Feature Films (full dataset)," last modified June 2019, http://data.uis.unesco.org/. While differences in reporting from year to year affect UIS data, Canada shows some consistency in this comparative measure, however partial and imperfect it may be: eighteen countries produced more than Canada's 92 features in 2017; eighteen countries produced more than Canada's 105 in 2016; sixteen produced more than Canada's 103, 94, and 93 features produced in each of 2015, 2014, and 2013 respectively; and thirteen countries produced more feature films than Canada's 98 in 2012. For a critical discussion of cultural metrics, including those of UIS, see Jade Miller, "'Counting' Informal Media Industries," *Media Industries* 7, no. 2 (2020), https://doi.org/10.3998/mij.15031809.0007.202.

5   Statista, "Filmed Entertainment Revenue in Selected Countries Worldwide in 2019," September 2021, https://www.statista.com/statistics/296431/filmed-entertainment-revenue-worldwide-by-country/#statisticContainer.

6   Initially in *Canadian Forum* in 1985, "The Cinema We Need" essays later appeared in *Documents in Canadian Film*, ed. Douglas Fetherling (Peterborough: Broadview Press, 1988), 260–336.

7   Statistics Canada, "Labour Force Characteristics by Industry, Monthly, Seasonally Adjusted (x1000)," 5 October 2018, www150.statcan.gc.ca, table 14-10-0291-02.

8   Statistics Canada, "Culture and Sport Indicators by Domain and Sub-Domain, by Province and Territory, Product Perspective," 20 June 2018, www150.statcan.gc.ca, table 36-10-0452-01.

9   Canadian Media Producers Association, *Profile 2017: Economic Report on the Screen-Based Media Production Industry in Canada* (Ottawa: Nordicity Group, 2017), 4.
10 Justin Lewis and Toby Miller, "Introduction," in *Critical Cultural Policy Studies: A Reader*, eds. Justin Lewis and Toby Miller (Oxford: Blackwell Publishing, 2003), 2. For more on cultural citizenship, see Toby Miller, *The Well-Tempered Self: Citizenship, Culture, and the Postmodern Subject* (Baltimore: Johns Hopkins University Press, 1993).
11 Pierre Bourdieu, *Distinction: A Social Critique of the Judgement of Taste* (Cambridge, MA: Harvard University Press, [1979] 1984).
12 Jennifer VanderBurgh, "Ghostbusted! Popular Perceptions of English-Canadian Cinema," *Canadian Journal of Film Studies* 12, no. 2 (2003): 81–98.
13 Peter Urquhart, "You Should Know Something – *Anything* – about This Movie. You Paid For It," *Canadian Journal of Film Studies* 12, no. 2 (2003): 64–80.
14 One of the best renditions of this history remains Ted Magder, *Canada's Hollywood: The Canadian State and Feature Films* (Toronto: University of Toronto Press, 1993).
15 Canadian Heritage, "Economic Analysis of the Canadian Film or Video Production Tax Credit," Office of the Chief Audit and Evaluation Executive, Evaluation Services Directorate, September 2008, i. For a perceptive critique of the range of Canadian film policies introduced during this period, cf. Charles Tepperman, "Bureaucrats and Movie Czars: Canada's Feature Film Policy since 2000," *Media Industries* 4, no. 2 (2017): 62–80.
16 Canadian Heritage, "Economic Analysis."
17 It is worth keeping in mind that there are no co-production treaties with the United States. Though the term is sometimes applied, joint productions between Canada and the US are technically co-ventures, and they do not benefit from the relaxation of these rules as do actual treaty-derived co-productions, though exemptions can be requested of Telefilm Canada, and other incentives exist.
18 Canadian Heritage, "Economic Analysis of the Canadian Film or Video Production Tax Credit," September 2008, vi.
19 Canadian Media Producers Association, *Profile 2017: Economic Report on the Screen-Based Media Production Industry in Canada* (Ottawa: Nordicity Group, 2017), 77–82.
20 Steve Globerman, *The Entertainment Industries, Government Policies, and Canada's National Identity* (Vancouver: Fraser Institute, March 2014).
21 Ibid., 24.
22 John Lester, "Tax Credits for Foreign Location Shooting of Films: No Net Benefit for Canada," *Canadian Public Policy* 39, no. 3 (2013): 451–72.
23 Ibid., 452.

24 Ibid., 467.
25 Globerman, *The Entertainment Industries, Government Policies, and Canada's National Identity*, 16.
26 Maria de Rosa and Marilyn Burgess, "An International Comparative Study: How National Content Is Defined in Canada and Selected Countries for the Purpose of Providing Access to Public Support" (Ottawa: Communications MDR, December 2015).
27 Other programs encourage definitions that include distinctly Canadian story elements and locations, for instance the Telefilm Feature Film Fund.
28 Maria de Rosa and Marilyn Burgess, "An International Comparative Study," 4–5.
29 Ibid., 5.
30 Mia Kirshner, "I Was Not Protected from Harvey Weinstein. It's Time for Institutional Change," *Globe and Mail*, 13 October 2017.
31 Cf. Charles R. Acland, "An Empire of Pixels: Canadian Cultural Enterprise in the Digital Effects Industry," in *Reading between the Borderlines: Cultural Production and Consumption Across the 49th Parallel*, ed. Gillian Roberts (Montreal and Kingston: McGill-Queen's University Press, 2018), 143–70.
32 Jennifer VanderBurgh, "Screens Stop Here! Tax Credit Thinking and the Contemporary Meaning of 'Local' Filmmaking," *Canadian Journal of Film Studies* 25, no. 1 (2016): 135–48.
33 Michael Dorland, *So Close to the State/s: The Emergence of Canadian Feature Film Policy* (Toronto: University of Toronto Press, 1998).

16

Collective *Action!*
Unions in the Canadian Film and Television Industry

Amanda Coles

The past decade has produced a substantive body of scholarship in what is now an established field of cultural labour studies. The core debates in the field focus on a range of individual and organizational issues related to work and labour markets in the creative and cultural industries, of which screen industries are a key focus of inquiry. As a corpus of work, this international body of research sharply challenges narratives of "glamourous" work, providing concrete evidence of the ways in which work and labour markets in global screen industries display characteristics of less than top-quality work. This includes chronic employment and income insecurity; excessive hours; exclusionary networks; and status hierarchies and power differentials that (re)produce marked inequalities which operate vertically and horizontally within the labour market.[1] Most recently, scholars have focused attention on a deeply embedded industry culture in which sexual harassment is normalized and protected by powerful global media enterprises.[2]

This body of work makes two significant contributions to the broader literature related to creative industries and the creative economy. First, this literature has been instrumental in framing the productive activities of professionals working in the cultural and creative industries *as work*. Second, the focus on the *quality* of work in the creative and cultural industries has produced a theoretically and empirically sophisticated scholarship that challenges politically powerful "do what you love" narratives about work in the creative economy.[3] An interrogation of the "dark side of creative labour"[4] has brought conditions of informality, insecurity, and precarity as defining features of work and labour markets to the foreground of debates.[5] At the same time, a growing body of work examines the ways in which cultural workers exercise agency and resistance in negotiating the attending insecurity, informality, and precarity that is intrinsic to the project-based nature of work in the screen sector and CCIs more broadly speaking.[6]

Yet despite a sharpening focus on questions of collective agency and resistance, the literature on unions, the dominant form of collective organization for the workforce in the film and television industry, is generally underdeveloped. The existing literature on unions can be grouped into three main areas of intellectual inquiry: unions and workplace activism (most notably around strike-related action on Hollywood production),[7] unions and representing precarious workforces,[8] and a much smaller body of work that generally interrogates union strategies in navigating changing political-economic conditions of local labour markets.[9] As a whole, however, the body of scholarship on the role of unions as key industrial actors in the screen industries remains fragmented and partial. This, in turn, means that we fail to capture film and television production labour market dynamics in their full complexity.

My aim in this chapter is to advance our understanding of film and television labour markets through an analysis of unions as labour market institutions in the Canadian film and television production industry. The distinctive analytical focus for this chapter is on union activity *outside the workplace*, the traditional domain of union actions. Through an analysis of union workforce development and policy advocacy activities, I argue that unions are important industrial actors who shape the political economy of the Canadian film and television industry. The chapter opens with a brief organizational profile of the four national unions representing workers in the English-language independent film and television production sector, followed by a summary of the general workplace and professional protections the unions secure for their memberships through collective bargaining. As a step to understanding the role unions play as industrial development actors, the chapter provides a general overview of the main features of work and labour markets in the independent film and television industry in Canada. With this foundational knowledge established, the chapter then proceeds with my analysis of the ways in which unions are actively advancing the workforce and industrial development of the Canadian film and television production industry.

Prior to proceeding with the analysis, it is important to note two specific limitations of this chapter. First, the chapter does not meaningfully address the specific dynamics of French-language production labour markets and French film and television unions, such as l'Union des artistes; l'Association des réalisateurs et réalisatrices du Québec; le Syndicat des techniciennes et techniciens du cinéma et de la vidéo du Québec; and la Société des auteurs de radio télévision et cinéma. There are important elements of film and television production labour markets and unionization in Quebec that set them aside from English-language production labour markets in Canada. Most notably, the Quebec Status of the Artist Act operates as a distinctive form of labour market regulation in the Quebec film and television production industry. This act shapes worker rights, union jurisdiction, and the structure of collective bargaining for independent contractors specific to the Quebec film and TV production industry.[10] First introduced in 1987, Quebec's Status of the Artist legislation is widely considered the international gold standard for legislation designed specifically to improve the socio-economic standards for artists and cultural workers.[11] Space limitations in this chapter preclude an analysis of Quebec's specific institutional framework of labour market governance in relation to unions as workforce and industrial development actors more generally. A scholarly contribution in this field would greatly enrich and inform our understanding of political economy of cultural labour in Canada.

The second, and significant, limitation of this chapter is the absence of fine-grained occupational and demographic workforce participation and union membership data. Workforce datasets for the Canadian film and television industry are largely inaccessible for scholarly research purposes. What data exists is often highly fragmented, aggregated, and excludes important categories that are critical for labour market analyses. The consequence of this is that the research that examines white male colonial supremacy as a defining feature of work and labour markets in the Canadian screen-based industries is indicative rather than exhaustive.[12] High-quality workforce data would include comprehensive, open-access datasets from key industry and policy organizations, including funding bodies and unions, that enable analysis of labour market access and participation rates for equity-seeking groups across occupational categories in the production ecology. Numerous scholars and advocacy organizations are calling for a national industry data strategy. Data sovereignty for Indigenous production communities is of particular urgency, to complement the critically important Indigenous narrative sovereignty work currently being undertaken by the Indigenous Screen Office.[13]

Unions in the Film and Television Industry

The Alliance of Canadian Cinema Television and Radio Artists (ACTRA), the Directors Guild of Canada, the Writers Guild of Canada, and the International Alliance of Theatrical Stage Employees, Moving Picture Technicians, Artists and Allied Crafts of the United States, Its Territories and Canada (IATSE) are the four major national English-language labour organizations that represent creative, technical, logistical, and administrative workers involved in the development, production, and post-production stages of Canadian English-language independent film and television production. Other labour organizations have jurisdiction in localized regions. UNIFOR has two locals covering technicians in independent film and television production: ACFC West 2020 in BC, and NABET 700 in Ontario. The Teamsters represent transport workers in Alberta and British Columbia. The Canadian Media Guild also has jurisdiction in various public and private broadcasters across Canada, but does not represent workers in the independent production sector. The unions have a long history of organizing and representing film and television professionals in Canada. The following section provides a very brief overview of the membership profile and historical roots of the national unions who collectively represent over 50,000 workers in the Canadian English-language independent film and television production sector.

ACTRA

The Alliance of Canadian Cinema Television and Radio Artists (ACTRA) represents over 27,000 Canadian on- and off-screen performers in English-language recorded media. Worker categories specific to English-language independent film and television production include actors, animation performers, announcers, background performers, cartoonists, choreographers, chorus performers, dancers, singers, models, hosts, narrators, commentators, stunt performers, panellists, principal actors puppeteers, sportscasters, and vocal or dialogue coaches.[14] ACTRA's history dates back to the very beginnings of performer organizing in Canada with its roots in the Radio Artists of Toronto Society (RATS) in 1941. In 1943, RATS expanded into a national coalition of performer groups, becoming the Association of Canadian Radio Artists. ACTRA's history is a complex series of re-structures. The union first became known as ACTRA in 1963 as the Association of Canadian Television and Radio Artists.[15]

DGC

The Directors Guild of Canada (DGC) was founded in 1962 with a total membership of eighteen film directors. At present, the DGC represents over 5,500 key creative and logistical personnel in the Canadian film and television industry. Nationally, the DGC represents directors, assistant directors, location managers, production designers, production managers, and editors. The Directors Guild also represents other categories regionally, such as production coordinators in Nova Scotia and locations security in Ontario.[16]

IATSE

The International Alliance of Theatrical Stage Employees, Moving Picture Technicians, Artists and Allied Crafts of the United States, Its Territories and Canada (IATSE) represents approximately 16,000 members working in the Canadian independent film and television production sector, largely technicians. Formed in 1893 with a local in New York City, IATSE admitted its first two Canadian locals in 1898 – Local 56 in Montreal and Local 58 in Toronto – and in 1902 officially changed its name from the National Alliance to the International Alliance. IATSE represents over 150,000 entertainment industry professionals across Canada and the US working in "live theatre, motion picture and television production, trade shows and exhibitions, television broadcasting, and concerts as well as the equipment and construction shops that support all these areas of the entertainment industry."[17]

WGC

The Writers Guild of Canada is a national professional association representing more than 2,400 screenwriters working in film, television, radio, and interactive digital media in Canada. The WGC has been in existence in Canada for approximately forty years, via a variety of relationships and formal affiliations with ACTRA, beginning with the Association of Canadian Radio Artists in 1943. The Writers Guild became an independent labour organization in 1993.[18]

THE BASICS

Union jurisdiction is regionally specific. For example, the DGC represents production coordinators in the Atlantic region, but IATSE Local 411 represents this category in Ontario. Overall, the generally collegial relationships between unions is an extension of the highly collaborative nature of their members' workplaces; a fully unionized Canadian dramatic television series will regularly sign contracts with the WGC for writers, ACTRA for on- and off-screen performers, DGC for key creative and logistical personnel, and IATSE locals for technicians and camera persons.

ACTRA, DGC, IATSE, and the WGC, and indeed media and entertainment unions internationally, are informed by a strong craft tradition in the cultural industries that Banks argues offers "an organizational frame for the cultivation of collective consciousness and a corpus of skills, competences and job roles."[19] Under a craft union tradition, unions seek to "limit the supply of qualified labour, enforce training requirements, institute work practices and procedures, restrict the activities and numbers of apprentices, and provide relief to unemployed craftsmen (as) responses to the continual threat of a general over-supply of labour."[20] Collective agreements in the film and television sector cover basic issues such as wages, overtime, work weeks, rest periods, workplace safety, meal breaks, travel, per diem, benefits and vacation pay, and grievance and arbitration procedures generally. Craft-based collective agreement may also include industry- and job-specific items including terms of payment, copyright, credits, creative approvals, terms of use for creative output, work permits, minimum staffing requirements, protection of minors, limitations on nudity, cancellation or schedule change penalties, and health and risk management for stunt performers, for example. Overall, unionized work in the film and television industry is often relatively well paid, with unionized wages often (but not always, as in the case of some entry-level job categories) well above provincial minimum wages.[21]

Thus, unions in the film and television industry, like unions in other industries, play an important role in setting terms and conditions of work. However, I argue that the analytical value of understanding unions in the Canadian independent production sector comes from the role they play in shaping not just workplaces, but film and television production labour markets broadly speaking. Such an analysis first requires an understanding of general labour market dynamics themselves, to which we turn now.

Labour Market Organization: The Independent Production Model

Under the independent production model, the production of film and television content is developed, financed, and produced through small independent production companies. This stands in contrast to in-house content production by television broadcasters or motion picture studios. Canadian independent producers oversee the production of content for domestic or international content commissioners, generally broadcasters, foreign (largely US) studios, and, with increasing frequency, streaming platforms such as Netflix. The producers in the independent production sector take the form of "hundreds" of small to medium enterprises represented by the Canadian Media Producers Association.[22] In 2018–19, the total volume of film and television production expenditure in Canada reached an all-time high of $9.32 billion.[23] As figure 16.1 indicates, the majority of this activity was undertaken by the independent production sector, which includes three subsectors: Canadian television production (32 per cent), Canadian theatrical features (4 per cent), and foreign location and service productions (51 per cent).

A closer analysis of the total number of projects and the direct employment figures for each subsector reveals that each one has distinct internal labour market characteristics. Having a general understanding of the differences and relationships between the subsectors is key to developing a nuanced analysis of the role of unions as industrial development actors. The following section provides a brief outline of the production volume and employment profile of each of the three subsectors, followed by an overview of how the three subsectors share an interactive relationship in terms of the overall ecology of the film and television production industry in Canada.

CANADIAN THEATRICAL

The Canadian theatrical feature film subsector includes feature-length films made by independent production companies that are at least seventy-five minutes long and that are intended for first release in movie theatres.[24] Canadian theatrical features is the smallest subsector both in terms of overall production expenditure and in terms of projects and employment. In 2018/19, Canadian producers made 119 feature films in total, which the CMPA's 2019 *Profile* report calculates to have generated 3,100 FTE jobs.[25]

Unions in the Canadian Film and Television Industry 305

Broadcaster in-house
$1,234
13%

Canadian television
$2,888
32%

Canadian theatrical
feature film
$337
4%

Foreign location and service
$4,707
51%

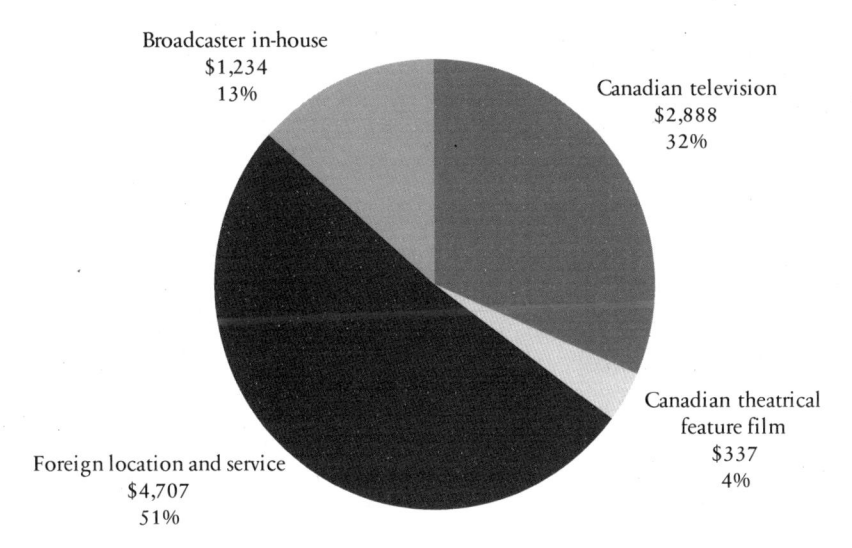

Figure 16.1 Film and television production in Canada by subsector, 2018/19, in millions of dollars. Data from CMPA, *Profile 2019*.

CANADIAN TELEVISION

Canadian independent television production is the second-largest segment in terms of production expenditure (figure 16.1), and the largest number of total projects. Canadian independent television production includes a variety of program formats (series, pilots, etc.) and genres, primarily fiction, that receive Canadian content certification through the Canadian content regulatory framework.[26] In 2018–19, this included 1,098 total projects: 739 television series, 118 television movies, and 241 types of "other" TV programming, including single-episode television programming and television pilots. For reasons I will discuss further below, while the subsector accounts for the largest number of discrete projects, it is the second-largest employment driver, generating 26,400 FTE jobs during this period (figure 16.2).

FOREIGN LOCATION AND SERVICE (FLS)

The foreign location and service subsector (FLS) is film and television content filmed in Canada, but in which the copyright is generally held by foreign producers.[27] In 2018/19, the FLS subsector was the largest of the three subsectors by total production expenditure (figure 16.1).

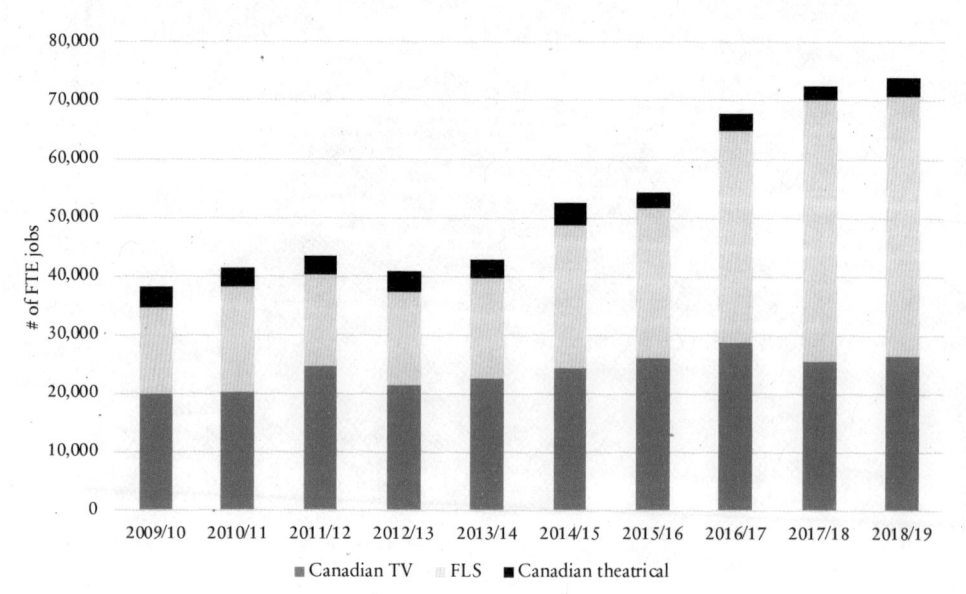

Figure 16.2 Direct FTE jobs in the Canadian independent film and television production industry, by subsector, 2009–19. Data from CMPA, *Profile 2019*.

FLS productions accounted for 465 projects in Canada including 164 feature films, 208 television series including miniseries, and 93 TV movies, pilots, and "other types of television programs."[28] The FLS sector is the largest employment driver, generating 44,400 direct FTE jobs (figure 16.2).

LABOUR MARKET CHARACTERISTICS

Generally speaking, the FLS sector reflects high volume production expenditures compared to a relatively small number of projects (figure 16.3). Figure 16.3 thus indicates that project budgets for the FLS sector are much larger on average than those for Canadian theatrical and television subsectors (figure 16.4). This is not surprising, as the FLS figures includes major US feature films, in addition to television projects. Larger budgets often offer casts and crews opportunities to stretch skill sets and develop new areas of expertise in relation to the creative demands of large-scale, complex shows. Yet, as I have written elsewhere, FLS projects often come pre-packaged with US key crew and creatives. It is thus important to understand that not all unionized

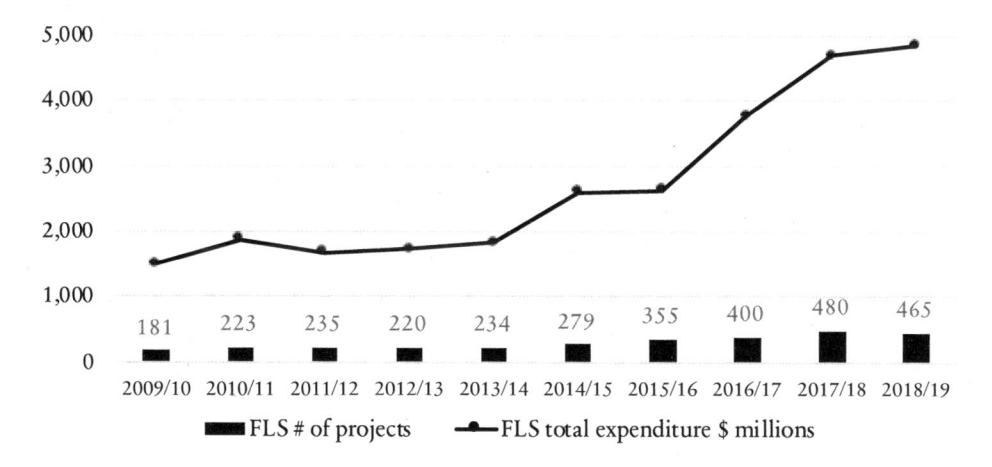

Figure 16.3 FLS total number of projects and expenditure in millions of dollars, 2009–19. Data from CMPA, *Profile 2019*.

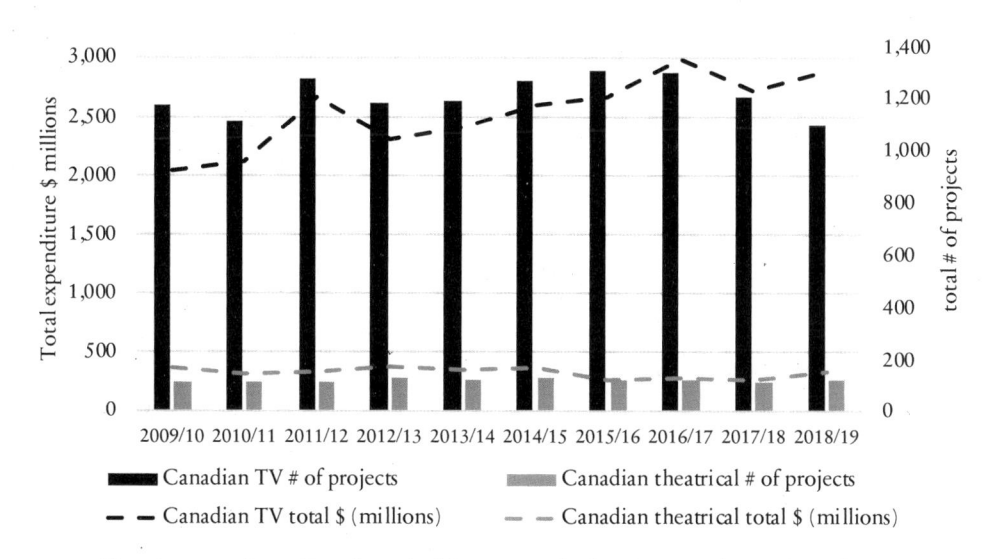

Figure 16.4 Canadian theatrical feature and television, total number of projects and expenditure, 2009–19. Data from CMPA, *Profile 2019*.

workers in the English-language film and television production industry in Canada share equal access to a major segment of the industry.[29]

For Canadian theatrical and television production, a comparatively large combined number of projects are undertaken with relatively small budgets (figure 16.4). Thus, while the foreign location and service subsector may provide higher wages and a high volume of work opportunities, those opportunities are concentrated in a comparatively small number of projects. The Canadian television and theatrical subsectors provide a wider range of projects from which film and television professionals have access to work. However, it is important to note that across all three subsectors, work opportunities are unevenly distributed in labour markets across the country.

Toronto, Vancouver, and Montreal are the three major production centres in which the majority of the film and television production activity in Canada takes place. Workers within these production centres have access to different types of work. For example, in 2018/19, 58 per cent of the foreign location and service production in Canada was filmed in British Columbia. Ontario and Quebec accounted for 45 per cent and 43 per cent of the production expenditures in the Canadian theatrical features subsector, and 47 per cent and 29 per cent respectively for the total production expenditures in the Canadian television subsector (figure 16.5). Thus, a director in BC seeking work on a Canadian television series is going to have far fewer opportunities to work locally than a Toronto-based director, for example.

All three subsectors share an interactive relationship in supporting the overall production ecology of the film and television industry in Canada. Union members frequently work across subsectors. The Canadian theatrical and television subsectors provide an important employment foundation for project-based work. As figure 16.2 shows, until 2016–17, the Canadian theatrical and television subsectors combined accounted for the majority of the FTE calculations. The Canadian theatrical and television subsectors also provide important opportunities for Canadian key creatives to exercise their craft telling scripted stories for domestic and international audiences. As foundational elements of the production industry, Canadian television and theatrical feature production also provides the ready-made, highly skilled labour pool required to attract and build foreign location and service production. FLS production provides opportunities for (some) professionals to work on large-budget, creatively challenging, high-profile projects, and to develop international networks. The FLS sector offers upskilling and

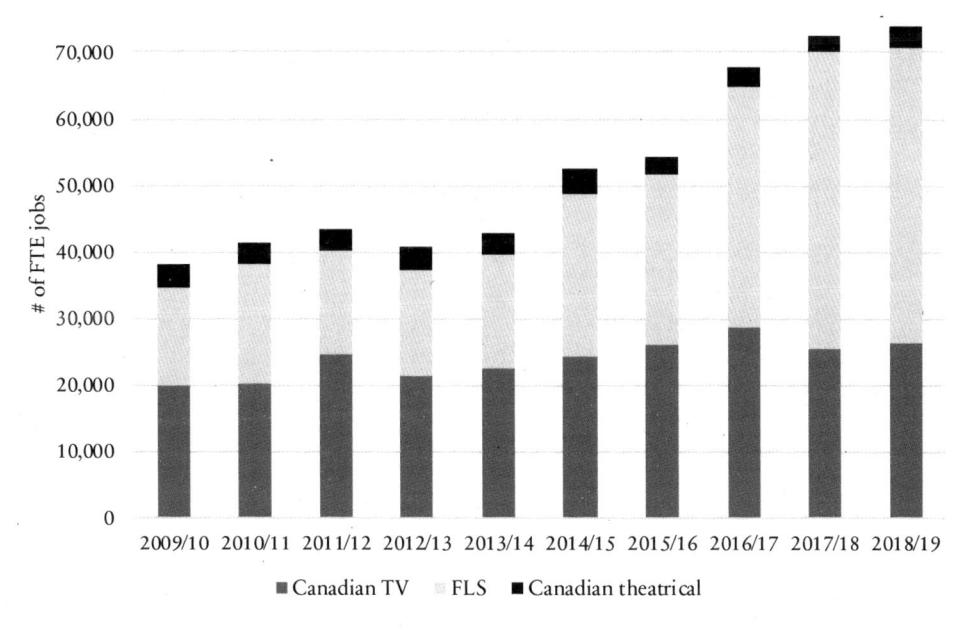

Figure 16.5 Production distribution by subsector, major production centres, 2018/19. Data from CMPA, *Profile 2019*.

professional development opportunities that spill over in their application in the development and production of Canadian content. It is thus essential to understand that Canadian theatrical, television, and FLS each have distinct, but interactive, relationships in supporting the overall production ecology in which film and television professionals earn their living.

The film and television production industry is thus a significant and growing economic and employment driver. It is also a complex and agile organization of highly mobile capital that relies on a highly skilled and flexible professional workforce as key ingredients for success in a non-routine labour-intensive production process. The organization of work under the independent production model means that labour markets in the independent film and television production sector are unstable and unpredictable. It is the instability and unpredictability of local labour markets that underpins the leadership roles that unions play as workforce and industrial development actors in the Canadian film and television production industry, to which we turn now.

Unions as Workforce Development Actors

Like workers in other sectors of the economy, those in the screen-based industries require support to adjust to rapidly emerging technological innovations and new job requirements. Unlike other workers, freelance and self-employed film and television workers do not have access to a consistent employer responsible for training and professional development of the workforce. Technological innovation produces routine and significant changes to job descriptions and workflows requiring new skills in advanced or emerging technologies and cross-platform creative, artistic, and business developments. By definition, professionals in the screen-based industries embark on a career of life-long skills upgrading and professional development. Additionally, the highly specialized nature of many jobs in the film industry, such as location manager, dolly grip, or production accountant, is not covered in post-secondary training programs and is generally underserved by industry training providers.[30] The gap between the supply of training options, and the ongoing demand for a highly skilled globally competitive workforce, leads unions and guilds to make development and delivery of training and professional development activities a core aspect of union business.

Training is built into the core function of the structure of the IATSE at the international level, whereby Education and Training is one of the eight departments that form the infrastructure of the international union.[31] IATSE 873 in Toronto has its own purpose-built training facility.[32] ACTRA Montreal offers seven-day video game workshops that cover video game theory, voice work, and performance capture skills.[33] The Directors Guild of Canada Ontario District Council offers professional development workshops that focus on specialized skill sets that are often not available elsewhere, such as production accounting and location management.[34] These internal union training programs are in addition to various partnerships and sponsorships the unions have with specialized training institutions and programs, such ACTRA's role as a founding sponsor of Women in the Director's Chair, and the long-standing partnership between International Cinematographers Guild IATSE Local 667 and Sheridan College in delivering motion picture camera assistant workshops.[35]

Inclusive conceptualizations of workforce development go beyond training and professional development programs to include a broad range of activities that various world-of-work actors undertake to support workers throughout various stages of their working lives and in relation to changes in their work environment.[36] An expanded understanding of workforce development is a useful framework for analyzing the form and function of various programs that the unions under analysis here offer to their members, and the ways in which these programs sustain workers' relationship to film and television industry labour markets over the long term.

Independent producers, taking the forms of single-cycle, project-based corporations in the independent production sector, offer no workforce support programs such as parental leave, sick leave, or retirement transition programs. Rather, it is the unions in the film and television production industry in Canada who administer health insurance, disability, parental leave, hardship funds, employee assistance plans, extended legal benefits, retirement benefits plans, and rights management for residuals. Examples include the DGC ReelLife Benefits Programs, the ACTRA Fraternal Benefits Society, IATSE Canadian National Health Plan, and the Canadian Entertainment Industry Retirement Plan. These programs are funded, in part, through contributions made by employers, and codified through the collective bargaining process. Yet they are designed and governed by unions, and without the unions the workforce would have very few workforce support structures at all.

Importantly, recent developments see unions turning their focus and resources to include mental health issues. In April 2018, the six BC-based film and television production unions[37] collectively developed and launched Calltime: Mental Health, the first industry-based program in Canada designed "to assist workers and employers grappling with mental health and addiction issues both in and out of the workplace."[38] Poor mental health and related issues such as addiction and family breakdown are long-standing issues for the workforce. Mental health and well-being are tightly linked to the conditions of chronic and simultaneous over/under work that define the film and television production work model, marked by employment and income insecurity on the one hand, and excessive and anti-social hours on the other.[39] This initiative is an excellent example of inter-union coordination and collaboration to address a systemic industrial issue that has a profound impact on the quality of work and life for their memberships.

Furthermore, many union programs, including Calltime: Mental Health, extend program support and services to entire households. Such an approach to workforce development plays a critical role in securing the relevance, importance, and value of the union as a community in its own right. Indeed, it is the relationship between the union, its members, their households, and the ways in which the experience of work is shaped by the broader political-economic context that leads the film and television unions to play a prominent leadership role as industrial development actors in policy networks.

Unions as Policy Actors

Unions have made a historical imprint on the shape of key Canadian cultural policy frameworks and continue to shape our cultural landscape. As Magder documents, the unions and guilds were vocal and influential advocates for federal support to develop the capacity of the Canadian independent theatrical and foreign location service production from the earliest stages of the development of the film industry in Canada:

> In 1963, the Quebec-based Association professionnelle des cinéastes joined forces with the recently formed Directors Guild of Canada to urge the federal government to provide support to the development of private-sector feature film production. Their plea was given added validity by Nat Taylor, one of the luminaries of Canada's private film industry. Taylor suggested that the Hollywood studios were more interested than ever in securing independent production for their distribution businesses. According to Taylor, Canadian producers had an advantage over their European counterparts because they could produce films that were "practically indistinguishable" from American ones.[40]

Union engagement in cultural policy is linked directly to the labour market interests of their members. Both the quantity of work and the quality of work in local, regional, and national labour markets is directly shaped by cultural policy choices and changes. Production volume across all three subsectors is subject to fluctuation as a consequence of a constellation of factors that shape where domestic and international producers decide to produce a project. Funding to federal institutions, including Telefilm Canada, the Canada Media Fund and the Canadian Broadcasting Corporation, Canadian content regulations, tax incentives and foreign worker immigration regulations, just for starters, all play a role in shaping what gets made in Canada and where. Because cultural policy operates as a form of labour market regulation for the film and television industry, unions have a strong track record as policy agents and allies.

ACTRA, the DGC, and the WGC have the highest profile and longest history as policy actors on a national scale. One of the constitutionally stated responsibilities of the ACTRA National Council is to develop and promote public policy objectives.[41] ACTRA (as RATS) was involved in the development of Canadian content regulations for radio, and throughout the 1960s was a strong proponent of increased, long-term, stable state funding for the Canadian film and television industry. ACTRA was a major supporter in the development of the Canadian Film Development Corporation (now Telefilm Canada), and in the early 1970s was consulted in the development of the system devised to determine eligibility for the feature film Capital Cost Allowance tax program. ACTRA has been involved in amendments to the Copyright Act, and ACTRA member and general secretary from 1965 to 1986 Paul Siren co-chaired Canada's delegations to UNESCO meetings that resulted in the Declaration on the Status of the Artist in 1980. Paul Siren subsequently went on to chair a federal task force whose recommendations resulted in Canada's Status of the Artist Act in 1992.[42] The past decade has seen ACTRA engage in policy advocacy on a number of issues related to digital content, copyright reform, foreign ownership, federal budget briefs, broadcasting and telecommunications regulation, international trade, and sustainable funding to support Canadian film and television production.

The DGC describes itself as "a visionary leader and partner in the development of the international Canadian screen-based industry at a policy and professional level."[43] Policy advocacy is written into the very fabric of the DGC's operations, whereby Article 4.13(d.iii) of the constitution lists one of the objectives of the organization as: "to propose policies on other issues affecting the interests of Directors, including ... (1) lobbying for national and international policy issues affecting Directors."[44] Early advocacy efforts in the sixties focused on the development of state financial support for the feature film industry. By the seventies, lobbying efforts had expanded to television broadcasting and engaged with Canadian content quotas. The economic impact of the recession of the nineties re-stimulated the DGC's participation as policy actors, and they have since been pressuring the federal government for improved fiscal and regulatory support for the Canadian film and television industry.[45] The past decade has seen the DGC actively engage in policy advocacy on submissions on copyright reform, international co-productions, the Canada Media Fund, federal budget briefs, digital content, foreign ownership, and numerous CRTC filings on specific license applications and ownership transfers.

The WGC's policy advocacy focuses solely on public policy that affects the Canadian theatrical and television subsectors, as WGC members are rarely engaged on foreign service productions. The WGC describes itself as "the vocal champion of Canadian drama, lobbying to ensure that Canadian writers have a place of primacy in the Canadian broadcasting system, and in film and digital media."[46] In the past decade, the WGC have been actively engaged in policy advocacy on copyright reform, international co-productions, vertical integration and ownership transfers in broadcasting, a national digital strategy, broadcasting and telecommunications regulatory reform, and CBC funding.

Despite its long history in organizing and representing artists and cultural workers in Canada, IATSE's engagement in federal policy advocacy is much more recent when compared to ACTRA, the DGC, or the WGC, with the majority of policy advocacy taking place after 2010. Policy interventions by the Canadian national office in the past decade include a submission to the Standing Committee on Canadian Heritage's Feature Film Policy Review; a brief submission to the consultative processes on the Canada Media Fund; an appearance before the Standing Senate Committee on Banking, Trade and Commerce with regard to the Conservatives' omnibus Bill C-10 that included proposed changes to the federal film and television tax credits for the film and television industry; changes to the Temporary Foreign Worker program on the film and television production sector; and a written submission on the development of a national digital content strategy. Specific IATSE locals are also more deeply involved in policy processes at the provincial level, and have played key roles in advocacy on provincial tax credits, for example.[47]

To summarize, film and television unions engage in a wide range of policy issues that travel horizontally across policy portfolios and vertically through layers of the state. The policy domains in which film and television unions are currently involved include international trade agreements, intellectual property rights, broadcasting and telecommunications regulation, media ownership, public broadcasting, intra-and international labour mobility and immigration, labour and employment relations, income tax averaging, and related issues for the cultural workforce.[48] In so doing, the unions actively shape not just the terms and conditions of work for their members, but the broader industrial context in which their members navigate their careers.

Conclusion

Unions are important labour market actors in the film and television production sector. Like organized labour more generally, they negotiate wages and working conditions through collective bargaining for their members. Yet the short-term, project-based nature of work in the independent production sector means that unions play an extended role as labour market actors. Unions offer a range of benefits and services to their freelance members who, in many cases, are not eligible for other social benefits, allowing many freelancers to maintain their ties to film and television production labour markets over the long term. Unions provide training and professional development, and are important institutions in reproducing the workforce in the absence of a standard employment relationship. The significance of the policy advocacy work unions undertake lies in their distinct interests as the leading voice of the workforce within policy networks. It is the unions who have the organizational capacity, time, resources, and expertise to clearly and consistently articulate the impact that various policy portfolios, choices, and changes have on the professional and personal lives of film and television production industry professionals.

The key point is thus: while the unions and guilds in the film and television production industry in Canada engage in collective bargaining and workplace representation for their members, their distinctive feature in the development, servicing, and promotion of the industry is the role they play outside of the workplace itself. A focus on the workforce and industrial development roles that unions play outside the workplace sharply highlights how the workforce, and the unions who represent them, both shape and are shaped by the political economy of the Canadian independent film and television production industry.

Notes

1 Susan Christopherson, "Working in the Creative Economy: Risk, Adaptation, and the Persistence of Exclusionary Networks," in *Creative Labour: Working in the Creative Industries*, eds. Alan McKinlay and Chris Smith (Basingstoke: Palgrave Macmillan, 2009), 72–90; Charles H. Davis, Jeremy Shtern, Michael Coutanche, and Elizabeth Godo, "Screenwriters in Toronto: Centre, Periphery, and Exclusionary Networks in Canadian Screen Storytelling," in *Seeking Talent for Creative Cities: The Social Dynamics of Innovation*, ed. Jill Grant (Toronto: University of Toronto Press, 2014), 77–98; Doris Ruth Eikhof and Chris Warhurst, "The Promised Land? Why Social Inequalities Are Systemic in the Creative Industries," *Employee Relations* 35, no. 5 (2013): 495–508; Irena Grugulis and Dimitrinka Stoyanova, "Social Capital and Networks in Film and TV: Jobs for the Boys?" *Organization Studies* 33, no. 10 (2012): 1311–31; David Hesmondhalgh and Sarah Baker, *Creative Labour: Media Work in Three Cultural Industries* (New York: Routledge, 2011); Deborah Jones and Judith

K. Pringle, "Unmanageable Inequalities: Sexism in the Film Industry," *The Sociological Review* 63, no. 1, suppl. (2015): 37–49; David Lee, "Networks, Cultural Capital and Creative Labour in the British Independent Television Industry," *Media, Culture and Society* 33, no. 4 (2011): 549–65; Keith Randle and Nigel Culkin, "Getting in and Getting on in Hollywood: Freelance Careers in an Uncertain Industry," in *Creative Labour*, eds. Alan McKinlay and Chris Smith, 93–115; Lorraine Rowlands and Jocelyn Handy, "An Addictive Environment: New Zealand Film Production Workers' Subjective Experiecc Wing-Fai, Rosalind Gill, and Keith Randle, "Getting In, Getting On, Getting Out? Women as Career Scramblers in the UK Film and Television Industries," *The Sociological Review* 63, no. 1, suppl. (2015): 50–65.

2. Shelley Cobb and Tanya Horeck, "Post Weinstein: Gendered Power and Harassment in the Media Industries," *Feminist Media Studies* 18, no. 3 (2018): 489–491; Sophie Hennekam and Dawn Bennett, "Sexual Harassment in the Creative Industries: Tolerance, Culture and the Need for Change," *Gender, Work and Organization* 24, no. 4 (2017): 417–34; Jinsook Kim, "After the Disclosures: A Year of #sexual_violence_in_the_film_industry in South Korea," *Feminist Media Studies* 18, no. 3 (2018): 505–8.

3. Miya Tokumitsu, *Do What You Love: And Other Lies about Success and Happiness* (New York: Simon and Schuster, 2015).

4. Mark Banks and David Hesmondhalgh, "Looking for Work in Creative Industries Policy," *International Journal of Cultural Policy* 15, no. 4 (2009): 415–30.

5. Ana Alacovska, "Informal Creative Labour Practices: A Relational Work Perspective," *Human Relations* 71, no. 12 (2018): 1563–89; Amanda Coles and Kate M. MacNeill, "Policy Ecologies, Gender, Work and Regulation Distance in Film and Television Production," in *Women, Labor Segmentation and Regulation: Varieties of Gender Gaps*, eds. David Peetz and Georgina Murray (New York: Palgrave MacMillan, 2017); Natalie Wreyford, "Birds of a Feather: Informal Recruitment Practices and Gendered Outcomes for Screenwriting Work in the UK Film Industry," *The Sociological Review* 63 (2015): 84–96.

6. Helen Blair, "Winning and Losing in Flexible Labour Markets: The Formation and Operation of Networks of Interdependence in the UK Film Industry," *Sociology* 37, no. 4 (2003): 677–94; Bridget Conor, "The Hobbit Law: Precarity and Market Citizenship in Cultural Production," *Asia Pacific Journal of Arts and Cultural Management* 12, no. 1 (2015): 25–36; Helen Kelly, "The Hobbit Dispute," *New Zealand Journal of Employment Relations* 36, no. 3 (2011): 31; Alice Mattoni, *Media Practices and Protest Politics: How Precarious Workers Mobilise* (New York: Routledge, 2016); Neil Percival and David Hesmondhalgh, "Unpaid Work in the UK Television and Film Industries: Resistance and Changing Attitudes," *European Journal of Communication* 29,

no. 2 (2014): 188–203; Ken Starkey, Christopher Barnatt, and Sue Tempest, "Beyond Networks and Hierarchies: Latent Organizations in the UK Television Industry," *Organization Science* 11, no. 3 (2000): 299–305.

7   Mark Banks, "Craft Labour and Creative Industries," *International Journal of Cultural Policy* 16, no. 3, (2010): 305–21; Conor, "The Hobbit Law," 2015.

8   Richard Saundary, Mark Stuart, and Valerie Antcliff, "'It's More Than Who You Know': Networks and Trade Unions in the Audio-Visual Industries," *Human Resource Management Journal* 16, no. 4 (2006): 376–92; John Amman, "Unions and the New Economy: Motion Picture and Television Unions Offer a Model for New Media Professionals," *WorkingUSA* 6, no. 2 (2002): 111–31; Lois S. Gray and Ronald L. Seeber, eds., *Under the Stars: Essays on Labor Relations in Arts and Entertainment* (Ithaca: Cornell University Press, 1996); Larry Haiven, "Expanding the Union Zone: Union Renewal through Alternative Forms of Worker Organization," *Labor Studies Journal* 31, no. 3 (2006): 85–116.

9   Christopherson, "Working in the Creative Economy"; Neil Martin Coe, "On Location: American Capital and the Local Labour Market in the Vancouver Film Industry," *International Journal of Urban and Regional Research* 24, no. 1 (2000): 79–94; Amanda Coles, "Unintended Consequences: Examining the Impact of Tax Credit Programmes on Work in the Canadian Independent Film and Television Production Sector," *Cultural Trends* 19, no. 1 (2010): 109–24; Amanda Coles, "Creative Class Politics: Unions and the Creative Economy," *International Journal of Cultural Policy* 22, no. 3 (2016): 456–72; David G. Murphy, "The Entrepreneurial Role of Organized Labour in the British Columbia Motion Picture Industry," *Relations Industrielles/Industrial Relations* 52, no. 3 (1997): 531–52.

10 Maude Choko and Bridget Conor, "From Wellington to Quebec: Attracting Hollywood and Regulating Cultural Workers," *Relations industrielles/Industrial Relations*, 73, no. 3 (2017): 457–78.

11 Garry Neil and Guillaume Sirois, "Status of the Artist in Canada: An Update on the 30th Anniversary of the UNESCO Recommendation concerning the Status of the Artist," *Canadian Conference of the Arts* (2010), https://www.ecthree.org/wp-content/uploads/2019/06/statusoftheartistreport1126101-copy.pdf.

12 For a discussion of the poor availability and quality of data on gender, racialization, and Indigenous production in the Canadian film and television production industry, see the following reports: Amanda Coles and Deb Verhoeven, "Deciding on Diversity: COVID-19, Risk and Intersectional Inequality in the Canadian Film and Television Industry," prepared for Women in Film and Television Canada Coalition (2021), https://wiftcanadacoalition.ca/wp-content/uploads/2021/10/DOD-Report_English_

September30-2021-1.pdf; Quebec English-Language Production Council and the Indigenous Screen Office, "The Canadian Indigenous Audiovisual Production Report 2010–11 to 2016–17" (2019), https://iso-bea.ca/wp-content/uploads/2021/09/IND.-Report-v.5-Mar15-19_to-email-EN.pdf; Nordicity, Inspirit Foundation, and Racial Equity Media Collective (REMC), "Racialized Funding Data in the Canadian Film and Television Industry" (2021), https://static1.squarespace.com/static/5da5e203aca5a576a25ef17f/t/619fe771ef4c07476c06d040/1637869451621/Racialized+Funding+Data+in+the+Canadian+Film+and+Television+Industry+-+Inspirit+Foundation%2C+REMC+and+Nordicity+%281%29.pdf.

13 For an excellent review of Indigenous data sovereignty in the Canadian context, see the First Nations Information Governance Centre, "First Nations Data Sovereignty in Canada," *Statistical Journal of the IAOS* 35 (2019): 47–69.

14 Alliance of Canadian Cinema, Television and Radio Artists (ACTRA), Canadian Media Producers Association, and Association Québécoise de la Production Médiatique, "Independent Production Agreement, January 1, 2019–December 31, 2021" (2019): Section A3, https://www.actra.ca/wp-content/uploads/2020/07/2019-2021-IPA-Online-version.pdf.

15 ACTRA, "InterACTRA: Celebrating 60 Years: The ACTRA Story" (2004), https://www.actramagazine.ca/wp-content/uploads/2021/01/ACTRAMagazine-2003-60thanniversary.pdf.

16 Directors Guild of Canada (DGC), "DGC National Constitution" (2020), https://www.dgc.ca/assets/Constitution/DGC-Constitution-June-27-2020-adopted-by-membership.pdf.

17 International Alliance of Theatrical and Stage Employees (IATSE), "About IATSE" (2021), accessed 3 December 2021, https://iatse.net/about/.

18 Amanda Coles, "Acting in the Name of Culture? Organized Labour Campaigns for Canadian Dramatic Programming," *Canadian Journal of Communication* 31, no. 3 (2006): 519–40.

19 Miranda J. Banks, "The Picket Line Online: Creative Labor, Digital Activism, and the 2007–2008 Writers Guild of America Strike," *Popular Communication* 8, no. 1 (2010): 20–33.

20 Tony Griffin, "Technological Change and Craft Control in the Newspaper Industry: An International Comparison," *Cambridge Journal of Economics* 8, no. 1 (1984): 44.

21 For an in-depth analysis of the history and fundamentals of collective bargaining in the motion picture television industry, see Alan Paul and Archie Kleingartner, "Flexible Production and the Transformation of Industrial Relations in the Motion Picture and Television Industry," *ILR Review* 47, no. 4 (1994): 663–78.

22 Canadian Media Producers Association (CMPA), *Profile 2019: Economic Report on the Screen-Based Media Production Industry in Canada* (Ottawa: CMPA, 2019): https://cmpa.ca/wp-content/uploads/2020/04/CMPA_2019_E_FINAL.pdf.
23 Ibid.
24 In order to qualify as Canadian, the film must be certified as Canadian content by the Canadian Audio-Visual Certification Office (CAVCO). The general CAVCO guidelines for the certification of a film or television program to qualify as "Canadian" are as follows: "the producer must be a Canadian and must act as the central decision-maker of the production from the development stage until the production is ready for commercial exploitation; the production must earn a minimum number of points based on the key creative functions that are performed by Canadians. Usually, a minimum of 6 out of 10; at least 75% of the production's services costs must be paid to Canadians and at least 75% of the production's post-production and laboratory costs must be paid for services provided in Canada by Canadians or Canadian companies; the production must qualify for certification under an eligible program category." Canadian Radio-television and Telecommunications Commission, "Canadian Program Certification Guide," last modified 7 January 2020, https://crtc.gc.ca/canrec/eng/guide1.htm.
25 CMPA, *Profile 2019*.
26 Ibid., 31.
27 As the CMPA notes, these figures include visual effects work done by Canadian visual effects studios for foreign film and television programs; CMPA, *Profile 2019*, 59.
28 Ibid., 59.
29 Coles, "Unintended Consequences."
30 Cultural Human Resources Council, *Training Gaps Analysis: Below the Line Film and Television Workers* (2008), https://www.culturalhrc.ca/sites/default/files/research/CHRC_Below_the_line_TGA-en.pdf.
31 IATSE, "About IATSE."
32 IATSE Local 873, "About Us: How to Apply" (2021), https://www.iatse873.com/how-apply-0.
33 The Abaton Calendar, "Audition for the 2020 ACTRA Montreal Videogame Workshop!" (2020), https://abaton.com/event/audition-for-the-2020-actra-montreal-videogame-workshop/2020-02-15/.
34 DGC Ontario, "Professional Development & Training" (2019), https://www.dgc.ca/en/ontario/becoming-a-member/training/.
35 Women in the Director's Chair, "About" (2017), accessed 3 December 2021, http://www.wdc.ca/about-2/; Sheridan College, "Motion Picture Camera Assistant Workshop," Faculty of Continuing and Professional Studies,

accessed 7 July 2022, https://caps.sheridancollege.ca/products/MEDA70011_MotionPictureCameraAssistantWorkshop1.aspx.

36. Ronald L. Jacobs and Joshua D. Hawley, "The Emergence of 'Workforce Development': Definition, Conceptual Boundaries and Implications," in *International Handbook of Education for the Changing World of Work: Bridging Academic and Vocational Learning*, eds. Rupert Malean and David Wilson (Dordrecht: Springer, 2009): 2537–52.

37. Teamsters Local 155, Directors Guild of Canada BC District Council, IATSE Local 891, International Cinematographers Guild IATSE Local 669, Union of British Columbia Perfomers/ACTRA, and ACFC West Local 2020 Unifor.

38. Calltime: Mental Health, "About" (2018–21), https://www.calltimementalhealth.com/about.

39. Wayne Lewchuk, "Precarious Jobs: Where Are They, and How Do They Affect Well-Being?" *The Economic and Labour Relations Review* 28, no. 3 (2017): 402–19.

40. Ted Magder, "Film and Video Production," in *The Cultural Industries in Canada*, ed. Michael Dorland (Toronto: James Lorimer and Company, 1996), 147.

41. ACTRA, "ACTRA Constitution" (2020): https://www.actra.ca/wp-content/uploads/2020/05/ACTRA-National-Constitution-24-April-2020.pdf, 14.

42. ACTRA, "InerACTRA," 40.

43. DGC, "ABOUT THE GUILD" (2021), https://www.dgc.ca/en/national/the-guild/about/.

44. DGC, "Constitution."

45. DGCOnline, "In Conversation with Tim Southam" (fall 2014), https://www.dgconline.ca/montage/in-conversation-with/in-conversation-with-tim-southam.

46. Writers Guild of Canada (WGC), "About the Guild" (2021), https://www.writersguildofcanada.com/about-the-guild.

47. Coles, "Creative Class Politics."

48. ACTRA, "ACTRA Report to the FIA North America (FIANA) & English-Speaking Group (ESG)" (Vancouver, Canada: 30 September 2019), https://www.actra.ca/wp-content/uploads/2020/03/2019-08-01-ACTRA-National-2019-FIANA-report-FINAL.pdf; DGC, "DGC Submissions" (2021), https://www.dgc.ca/en/national/advocacy/submissions/; IATSE, "About IATSE"; IATSE, "The IATSE Lobbies on Parliament Hill," accessed 7 July 2022, https://www.legacy.iatse.net/history/iatse-lobbies-parliament-hill; John Morgan Lewis, "Response to the Changing Workplaces Review Special Advisors' Interim Report" (14 October 2016), https://cirhr.library.utoronto.ca/sites/default/public/ontario_workplace_review_phase2/IATSE.pdf; WGC, "Policy" (2021), https://www.writersguildofcanada.com/policy.

17

Making *Room*
International Co-productions and Canadian National Cinema

Peter Lester

Assuming they had not yet changed the channel or gone to sleep, an estimated 34 million viewers were tuned into the 2016 Academy Awards when Brie Larson took home the Oscar for Actress in a Leading Role for her star-making performance in *Room* (Lenny Abrahamson, 2015). Buoyed by a strong publicity campaign, Larson's victory was the culmination of a series of triumphs throughout the end-of-year awards season. Considerably fewer viewers tuned in two weeks later to hear an absent Larson's name announced as a winner at the 2016 Canadian Screen Awards. Larson's "Candy Award" (dubbed as such by host Norm MacDonald in honour of the late John Candy) would be one of nine total awards won by *Room* that evening. Casual viewers of the Canadian Screen Awards might have understandably found themselves confused, not realizing that *Room* is, in fact, a Canadian movie. And truth be told, who could blame them? The film, after all, boasts a handful of recognizable American stars, is directed by an Irish filmmaker, and is set in an American city. Yet, few Canadian films throughout the nation's history have been so well-received by both audiences and critics as *Room*. Despite its traumatic subject matter – the film concerns the plight of a kidnapped young mother and her five-year-old son living in captivity in a tiny backyard shed, only to escape and encounter difficulties adapting to their newfound freedom – the film grossed $35 million, nearly triple its $13 million budget. It was the first Telefilm Canada–funded film (along with 2015 co-nominee *Brooklyn*) to be nominated for a Best Picture Academy Award since 1980's *Atlantic City*. In addition to her Oscar and Canadian Screen Award, Larson won a Golden Globe,

British Academy Award, and Screen Actors Guild Award. And according to unscientific, audience-driven metrics such as the Internet Movie Database user rankings, *Room* is the highest-rated Canadian film of all time, narrowly nudging out Denis Villeneuve's *Incendies*.[1]

However, because *Room* is a Canadian-Irish international co-production – even a majority Canadian-funded one – its status as a "truly" Canadian film, in the eyes of many, will consistently be called into question. Critics of the film's status as an authentic "Canadian" cultural product typically profess to like the film, but cite its clear lack of visibly Canadian markers. While the film is not obviously Canadian on the surface, its status as an international co-production marks it as representative of a prevalent trend in the Canadian film industry, perhaps even the definitive contemporary example. The tendency towards international financing and co-production, while by no means a recent phenomenon, has unquestionably become established as a dominant strategy for the production of films in Canada since the turn of the millennium. International co-productions are actively encouraged by prominent funding institutions across the country, such as Telefilm Canada, la Société de développement des entreprises culturelles (SODEC), and Ontario Creates.[2] Telefilm's 2018–20 Strategic Plan stresses the further encouragement of international co-production as a core component of its "Strategic Pillars."[3] Heritage Minister Mélanie Joly, in her 2017 unveiling of the new direction for Canadian cultural policy, singled out the importance co-productions have played in the Canadian film industry, and pledged to both "expand and modernize" co-production ventures.[4] And in the same year, Canada became the first non-European member of Eurimages, the international co-production fund managed by the Council of Europe.[5] On the prevalence of co-productions in the contemporary Canadian industry, veteran Canadian feature filmmaker Atom Egoyan notes quite simply: "these are how films get financed now."[6]

National cinema has long been a fraught concept in Canada, for a multitude of reasons, not least of which is its ongoing branch plant status for Hollywood production,[7] or the unresolved tensions stemming from the French-speaking vs English-speaking divide. While it is generally accepted that Canada is home to (at least) two national cinemas – an English-Canadian industry and a Québécois industry – international co-productions are nevertheless adjudicated and administered on a federal level, through Telefilm Canada, in conjunction with the Canadian Audio-Visual Certification Office (CAVCO). With this responsibility, implicitly, comes the burden (or privilege) of delineating the precise parameters of what constitutes a film's status as sufficiently "Canadian." In a contemporary moment when heightened globalization, transnationality, and the digital circulation of cultural products render understandings of an already contested notion of "nation" increasingly unstable, international co-productions cue us to consider just how we make sense of such a concept as national cinema.

As Paul W. Taylor has succinctly noted, international co-productions tend to exacerbate an already extant tension in the culture industries: "the cultural objectives require that the film or program reflect the cultural specificity of the originating country, while the industrial objectives necessitate that the finished product travel easily across borders. The fulfillment of one mitigates against the fulfillment of the other."[8] One of the defining characteristics of both English-Canadian and Québécois industries has been the unresolved conflict between industry and primarily economic concerns on one hand, and a more culturalist discourse of art, culture, and nation on the other. This tension is obvious from the early establishment of the Canadian Film Development Corporation (CFDC) in 1967, through the tumultuous tax shelter era of the 1970s, through to the policy shifts in the early 2000s.[9] Much of the contemporary discourse that surrounds international co-production in Canada hinges on this very axis, and as such, can be seen as yet another manifestation of this long-running crisis of industrial identity. In this chapter, I posit that international co-productions offer a fertile perspective into the critical study of Canadian cinema precisely because they prompt us to consider the evaluative criteria that we collectively understand as central to such a notion. While they may represent merely a particular funding and production structure at their core, international co-productions can fulfill a valuable function for grappling with the more amorphous, and contested, concept of "national cinema." The debates that ensue pertaining to co-productions' relative place within a national cinema reveals much about how a society understands and articulates its own conflicted sense of national culture. In the context of the English-Canadian industry, *Room* is both typical, in terms of the production model it represents, and exceptional, in terms of its national and international reception. As such, the film makes for an intriguing case study of the implications of international co-production within a specific national cinema. The example that the film provides, in terms of the mechanisms of its production and its ensuing reception by critics, audiences, and award-granting agencies, provides a telling distillation of many of the tendencies associated with international co-production more widely. The discourse that circulates as these films are produced, distributed, and exhibited comes from funding bodies and their required criteria, from festivals and award galas, from the box office, from reviews and critical opining, and from the feedback of audiences themselves. Taken together, these work to shape the conversation about what a society values in a national culture.

A Brief History of Co-production in Canada

In a historical, global context, international co-productions are a largely postwar phenomenon that involve producers from two or more nations partnering on the production of an individual film (or audiovisual production such as a television series). Generally speaking, producers are drawn to these arrangements because they allow for the pooling of resources, which often allows for higher budgets; they facilitate access to government production incentives in multiple countries; and they have the potential to expand the international market for the finished product. Typically, to qualify as official co-productions, and to benefit from the various tax and production incentives governments offer, film productions need to follow the guidelines and criteria established by co-production treaties. These are official agreements between nations that outline the various parameters that need to be met for official co-production status. To satisfy these criteria, producers from partnering countries have to carefully ensure that specific production requirements are met, such as the percentage of budget contributions and the nationality of key creative personnel. Accordingly, this can be a rather delicate balancing act, as producers are forced to compose the perfect alchemy to appease the administrative bodies in each respective country. Notably, issues of content or setting are not typically outlined by these treaties. Canada has fifty-eight co-production treaties with countries around the world, from obvious and major film-producing nations like the United Kingdom and France, to smaller nations like Malta and Uruguay.[10] The United States, it is worth pointing out, is not signatory to any international co-production treaty. Co-productions are, after all, in many respects a strategy by the other film-producing nations of the world to compete with Hollywood production. However, this is not to say that American producers do not partner with Canadian filmmakers, or those in other countries – this, of course, happens all the time. But these partnerships, often referred to as "co-ventures" rather than official co-productions, are not granted access to the special funding and tax incentives that official treaty co-productions enjoy.

Canada's history with official international co-production dates to the early 1960s, when it signed its first audiovisual treaty with France in 1963. Of course, narrative film production throughout the country dates much further back than this, and varying levels of international collaboration was not uncommon, particularly in Quebec. In fact, the history of collaborative relations between Quebec and France in particular made that country the obvious choice for Canada's first official co-production partner. While co-productions were especially popular in Europe throughout the 1960s, it wasn't until the late 1970s that producers began pursuing these arrangements in Canada to a significant degree. This was the era of the Capital Cost Allowance (commonly referred to as the "tax shelter" years), when economic concerns trumped culturalist ones, and "international appeal" became a governing motivation behind film production.[11] The number of Canadian co-productions increased significantly over the course of the 1990s, especially in terms of partnerships with European countries.[12] This tendency was punctuated by the end-of-the-millennium release of two relatively high-profile co-productions: François Girard's *The Red Violin* (Canada-Italy-UK, 1998) and István Szabó's *Sunshine* (Germany-Austria-Hungary-Canada, 1999).

Since the turn of the millennium, a consistent commitment to co-productions is evident, though the exact scale of that commitment has clearly been prone to fluctuation. Figure 17.1 indicates the total number of Canadian film co-productions from 2006 to 2020, as well as the total annual budget expenditures from all funding sources, and the percentage from Canadian sources. On one hand, there is clear fluctuation on a year-to-year basis, both in terms of the number of co-productions, and the budgetary commitments. Part of this can be explained by the typical ebbs and flows of an industry that is by its nature volatile, quick to respond to currency valuations, and changing tax environments. Likewise, the presence of the occasional blockbuster co-production such as *Resident Evil: Afterlife* (Paul W.S. Anderson; Canada-Germany, 2010) or *Pompeii* (Paul W.S. Anderson; Canada-Germany, 2014), with budgets in the $60–$100 million range, can easily skew the numbers on a year-to-year basis. Despite these discrepancies, a certain stability over this fourteen-year period can be seen, with overall budgets hitting an average of roughly $200 million, and Canadian contributions comprising roughly half of this, around $100 million annually. There is no necessary correlation between a film receiving funding from Telefilm Canada and its status as an international co-production. As mentioned previously, Telefilm, in conjunction with

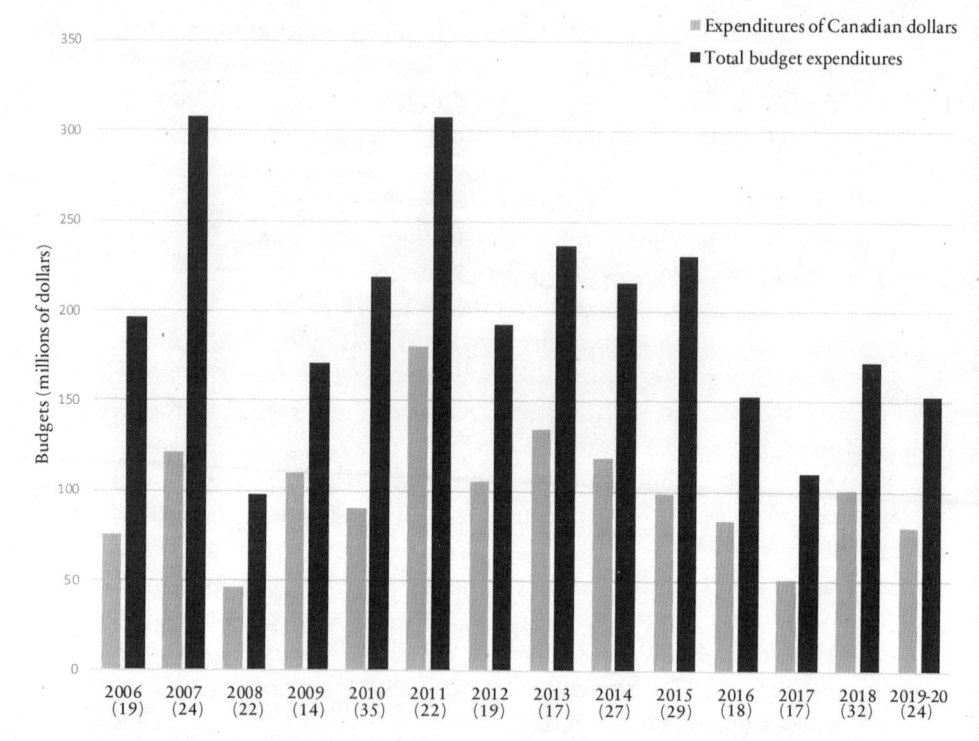

Figure 17.1 International co-productions (film) in Canada, 2006–20. Compiled from Telefilm Canada annual statistics on co-production, 2006–20. Statistics from 2006 to 2018 represent totals from the calendar years, whereas the statistics from 2019–20 represent the fiscal year (1 April 2019 to 30 March 2020).

CAVCO, is responsible for oversight of all treaty co-productions, regardless of a film receiving Telefilm funding or not. Likewise, Telefilm oversees the coordination of televisual co-productions, even though the direct funding of Canadian televisual programming is typically the domain of the Canada Media Fund.

The co-production model in Canada tends to be more prominent in English-language productions but is nevertheless common throughout French-language production as well. Table 17.1 indicates the breakdown of international co-productions by year, according to the language of the project. French-language projects are consistently fewer in number per year but range from as high as roughly one-third of all productions (2006, 2015) to as low as 13 per cent of the total (2013.)[13] Overall budget expenditures, accordingly, are consistently higher for English-language productions. Perhaps unsurprisingly, the United

Table 17.1 International co-productions in Canada by language of project (film, television, digital media)

Year	English	French
2019–2020	36	10
2018	43	15
2017	35	20
2016	37	11
2015	44	22
2014	52	12
2013	54	8
2012	43	17
2011	41	14
2010	45	16
2009	43	13
2008	61	26
2007	52	17
2006	42	22

Kingdom and France are the international partners with the most shared projects in any given year.

Recent developments would indicate an emerging embrace of the co-production model by Indigenous filmmakers and production companies. While Indigenous film production in Canada has historically been more pronounced in the documentary sector, there has been a notable rise in feature-length narrative cinema since roughly the turn of the millennium, with two films in particular paving the way: Shirley Cheechoo's *Bearwalker* (originally *Backroads*, 2000) and Zacharias Kunuk's *Atanarjuat: The Fast Runner* (2001). Isuma, the Inuit video collective and production company responsible for *Atanarjuat*, opted for a co-production arrangement for its follow-up film, partnering with Denmark for the production of *The Journals of Knud Rasmussen* (Norman Cohn and Zacharias Kunuk, 2006). Denmark was a logical partner for the film, as it centres on the historical encounter between the titular Danish/Greenlandic explorer and his team of anthropologists, and a group of Inuit from the Igloolik region, in the early 1920s. A more recent example, Elle-Máijá Tailfeathers and Kathleen Hepburn's 2019 co-written and co-directed film *The Body Remembers When the World Broke Open*, is a treaty co-production with Norway. The film, based on an actual event from Tailfeathers's life, documents a chance encounter between two Indigenous women in downtown Vancouver. On the surface, the film would initially appear to have little to do with Norway. Yet the most direct connection is through Tailfeathers herself, who is Blackfoot on her mother's side, and Sámi on her father's side (as is the character she plays onscreen, Áila). The International Sámi Film Institute is in fact one of the various partners in the film's production, in addition to the Norwegian Film Institute. The film was acquired for global distribution by Ava DuVernay's ARRAY Releasing and was picked up for streaming by Netflix in the United States.[14] Tailfeathers, incidentally, also stars in another recent Indigenous international co-production: Cree-Métis filmmaker Danis Goulet's *Night Raiders* (2021). Goulet's dystopian debut feature was produced through the partnership of Canadian production companies Alcina Pictures and Eagle Vision, and the New Zealand company Miss Conception Films. Maori filmmaker Taika Waititi, whom Goulet met and befriended in 2004 at a filmmaking workshop in New York, serves as the film's executive producer.[15] The film received the widest theatrical release of an Indigenous film in Canadian history, opening in eighty separate locations.[16] Both *Night Raiders* and *The Body Remembers When the World Broke Open* have benefitted from the increased global exposure that co-productions can provide, not to mention the increased attention that comes with the involvement of such international figures as Waititi and DuVernay. Furthermore, both films' considerable reach in terms of distribution is, in part, indicative of a growing, wider interest in global Indigenous-led narrative filmmaking.

Making *Room*: Canadian-Irish Co-productions

From a production standpoint, *Room* is rather typical for an international co-production. The film's producers have openly discussed how a more traditional single-nation funding structure would not have permitted the budget they enjoyed. Budgetary concerns are likely the driving reason producers pursue these initiatives in the first place. David Gross, one of *Room*'s Canadian co-producers, claims that if the film was not made as a co-production, its budget would have been as much as 30–40 per cent lower, and the tax subsidies from both Canada and Ireland allowed them to make the film in a way that simply would not have been possible otherwise.[17] As a Canadian-Irish co-production, and in keeping with the treaty signed between those two countries, key production details and personnel were spread out between the two nations.[18] The screenplay (as well as its source material, the novel of the same name) was written by Emma Donoghue, an Irish-born Canadian citizen, while the film's director is Irish filmmaker Lenny Abrahamson. *Room* was shot in and around Toronto, with editing and post-production largely completed in Ireland. Though the film boasts the presence of major international performers Brie Larson, Joan Allen, and William H. Macy, the cast is rounded out by a largely Canadian ensemble, including the star-making performance of ten-year-old Jacob Tremblay. For many Canadians, the presence of supporting performers such as Wendy Crewson or Tom McCamus (or for a particularly well-trained eye, Joe Pingue) can betray a production's Canadian origins. Typically, audiences familiar with these performers are not only able to merely identify them, but rather semiotically understand them as markers of a Canadian production (or at least, as a production that is filmed in Canada).

Canadian-Irish co-productions are not the most numerous of Canadian collaborations – as previously mentioned, those tend to be with France and the United Kingdom – but those that are produced between these two nations tend to be disproportionately successful. This is a noticeable tendency that encompasses both film and television production. In the past decade, Irish-Canadian co-productions have yielded, among others: *Brooklyn* (with the UK as a third partner), a film that out-grossed *Room* and nearly matched its awards success; *The F Word* (Michael Dowse, 2013), which features a high-profile international cast including Daniel Radcliffe, Zoe Kazan, and Adam Driver; the breakout success *Maudie* (Aisling Walsh, 2017), based on the life of Canadian folk artist Maud Lewis; and the Oscar-nominated, Angelina Jolie–produced animated film *The Breadwinner* (Nora Twomey, 2017, co-produced with Luxembourg). In television, similar international success has been found with *The Borgias* (Showtime, 2011–13, co-produced with Hungary) and *Vikings* (History, 2013–present). Significantly, and no doubt largely in response to this stream of critical and financial success, the Canada-Ireland Co-production Treaty was renewed and revised in 2016, and the assumption is that further resources will surely be directed towards future collaborations, particularly given Canada's recent entry into Eurimages.[19]

Thematic Renderings

An ongoing concern regarding international co-productions is the perceived threat that they pose to distinctive national culture and character. These fears are notably manifested in the so-called Europudding films: co-productions between various European nations that "unconvincingly blend together different cultural and linguistic elements or which downplay those differences, only to appear bland and indistinct."[20] By the very nature of their financial makeup, co-productions are frequently saddled with an accompanying fear of "cultural homogeneity," where the distinctiveness of local, domestic production is at risk of disappearing within the bland, generic and universalizing process of international cultural production. Accordingly, a fear of such a tendency accompanies the discussion of co-production in the context of the Canadian film industries.

As a field of study, film and media studies in Canada took a decidedly political economic turn in the 1990s, when a rather substantial body of work was published that considered the Canadian film and media industries in relation to the federal government, the United States, and the rest of the world more generally.[21] An outgrowth of this tendency was the first scholarly push to understand co-production within the context of the oft-opposed culturalist/economist imperatives that accompany discussions of Canadian film. In a detailed study of film production in Canada covering the span of 1970–91, Finn, Hoskins, and McFadyen noted the "accepted industry knowledge" that in the case of co-productions, "pooling of financial and creative resources is good economically but inevitably involves compromises that undermine Canadian distinctiveness and artistic integrity."[22] Yet, they made clear in their conclusions that this "knowledge" had no sound basis, and they found "no support for the assumption that there is a trade-off between Canadian orientation and commercial success, that international co-productions are less likely to have a Canadian orientation or enjoy critical acclaim than purely domestic productions."[23] In a more recent study of the rising body of international co-productions produced in Canada during the 1990s (and including television production), Doris Baltruschat found evidence to the contrary. Baltruschat's study found co-productions from that decade to be less rooted in specific national circumstances, and as a result they bore far less engagement with local political or cultural content. She writes, "the market-driven orientation and appeals of international co-productions contribute to the undermining of that public space deemed central for critical reflection, cultural representation and public deliberation. This erosion of the public sphere is injurious for democracy and public well-being."[24] For Baltruschat, co-productions' inclination towards the universal and the generic carried serious ramifications for the health of a national (i.e., Canadian or Québécois) culture. Likewise, in a study specific to the Canadian television industry, Serra Tinic has noted the potential harm that these tendencies might exert on domestic, nationally focused production.[25]

While a comprehensive survey of international co-productions is beyond the scope of this chapter, there are nevertheless some general observations that can be made. For instance, keeping with the case study of Canadian-Irish co-productions released in recent years, no consistent model or tendency is immediately apparent. In other words, there appears to be no direct correlation between a film's status as a co-production, and that film's respective engagement with traditional markers of national cultural content. Co-productions have often led to vague transnational tendencies within their narratives or delivered narrative trajectories that deliberately seek to reflect the specific international quality of their funding structure (and of their partner nations in particular). But just as often, this is not the case at all. On one hand, the enormously successful (and forever historically paired) *Room* and *Brooklyn* display little interest in "Canadian culture." The former, though shot in Toronto, is set in a deliberately generic American city (briefly identified as Akron, Ohio). The latter is likewise set in the United States (as well as Ireland) but was shot in Quebec (its producers argued that Montreal, more than contemporary Brooklyn, resembles the Brooklyn of the film's era).[26] While *Brooklyn* features a narrative that no doubt resonates with many immigrants to Canada, its transnational axis focuses squarely on Ireland and the United States. Other Canadian-Irish co-productions, however, offer something quite different. *The F Word*, for instance, is both shot and unambiguously set in Toronto (though tellingly, the characters embark on a seemingly arbitrary Irish sojourn late in the film's narrative). The city of Toronto is likewise front and centre in *Unless* (2016), directed by Irish filmmaker Alan Gilsenan. Based on a novel by Carol Shields, the film stars American Catherine Keener as a mother dealing with her daughter's seemingly inexplicable decision to live on the streets. Toronto's famous Honest Ed's discount store is featured prominently in the film, which was shot shortly before the Bloor Street landmark's closing in 2016. A Canadian-Irish transnational experience is found in *Stay* (Wiebke von Carolsfeld, 2013), a film about the complicated relationship between an Irish man (Aidan Quinn) and a Canadian woman (Taylor Schilling). The film has a thoroughly transnational narrative with equal amounts of time spent in both Ireland and Canada. Likewise, a similar Canadian-Irish transnational narrative is found in *Death of a Ladies' Man* (Matthew Bissonnette, 2021), which follows the exploits of a charming, alcoholic university professor, played by Irish actor Gabriel Byrne, plagued by hallucinations caused by an inoperable brain tumor. Set to the music of Leonard Cohen, the film is thoroughly "Montreal" in its orientation, yet the entire second part of its tripartite structure is set (and shot) in Ireland, as Byrne's character retreats to his childhood home to write a novel and reconnect with his long-dead father (Brian Gleeson), who appears to him frequently. Of this limited sample group, *Stay* and *Death of a Ladies' Man*, with their storylines and characters largely hinging on Irish/Canadian/Québécois axes, are perhaps the most fully realized examples of narratives that reflect their international production structures.

Maudie, though directed by an Irish filmmaker and with international stars Sally Hawkins and Ethan Hawke as its lead performers, is unequivocally "Canadian" in its orientation, as a biopic of the famed Nova Scotia folk artist Maud Lewis.[27] Significantly, the film was a considerable critical and box office success, and serves to echo Finn, Hoskins, and McFadyen's findings from earlier decades, which ran counter to the accepted knowledge of Canadian co-productions. The Irish equivalent to a film like *Maudie* might be Pat Collins's *Song of Granite* (2017): a biopic of Irish *sean-nós* singer Joe Heaney. Though the two films share little in terms of film form and differ radically in their respective takes on the biopic genre, their subjects, Lewis and Heaney, are beloved national folk artists. Just as *Maudie* is thoroughly "Canadian" on the level of content, *Song of Granite*, though a Canadian-Irish co-production produced with the participation of Telefilm and SODEC, is resolutely an "Irish" film, in the same sense.[28] Conversely, however, Québécois director Philippe Falardeau's co-production *My Salinger Year* (2020) demonstrates little diegetic concern either for Canada or for Ireland. The film, an adaptation of American novelist Joanna Rakoff's memoir of her time working at a famous literary agency, was shot in Montreal, but takes place almost entirely in Manhattan. For Irish-Canadian co-productions, it is clearly within the domain of television that the most "generic" production is found (a tendency that perhaps, in part, explains Baltruschat's divergent findings from those of Finn, Hoskins, and McFadyen), with the recent notable examples of *Vikings* and *The Borgias*, which would appear more in line with the "immortal cosmopolitanism" that Shawn Shimpach has identified in his study of the earlier Canada-France co-produced television program *Highlander: The Series* (1992–98).[29]

The narrative setting and content of these productions is relevant to this discussion because much of the controversy surrounding *Room* and its subsequent reception by the critical community in Canada stemmed from this issue in particular: the film's apparent failure to be "visibly Canadian." The day following the film's massive victories at the Canadian Screen Awards, the senior film writer for Toronto's NOW Magazine, Norman Wilner, wrote an angry reaction piece. He remarks, "*Room* is a good movie. I liked it a lot. But is it Canadian enough to compete with movies like Egoyan's *Remember*, Anne Émond's *Our Loved Ones* or Philippe Falardeau's *My Internship in Canada*? How about Paul Gross's *Hyena Road*, which wore its Canadianness on its sleeve?"[30] Implicit in Wilner's comments is the notion that a film's cinematic "quality" is effectively a less relevant factor for the Canadian Screen Awards than its ability to be demonstrably Canadian. He appears to be advocating a "Most Canadian Motion Picture" award, as opposed to a "Best Canadian Motion Picture" award. Wilner furthers this argument by citing an anonymous filmmaker acquaintance: "Don't pretend you're celebrating Canadian talent and then give Brie Larson an award because her producers took advantage of some tax credits."[31] In a similar vein later in the year, the Canadian producer, occasional director, and contributing columnist to the *Montreal Gazette* Kevin Tierney wrote an article titled "Why Canadian Films Are Pretending to Be American Again." After dismissing *Brooklyn* as an example of mere tax incentive opportunism, Tierney asserts: "Sadly, the wonderful film *Room*, another Ireland-Canada co-production, lowers the bar a little further. A Canadian novel, adapted by Canadian author Emma Donahue [sic], the film is directed by an Irish filmmaker and completely shot in Toronto."[32] Curiously, Tierney singles out many of the film's Canadian components in his attempt to dismiss its actual Canadian character. The gist of his argument is succinctly summarized as such: "Visibly Canadian is certainly no longer the rallying cry at Telefilm."[33] This metric of "visibly Canadian" is one that has been consistently invoked, whether explicitly or implicitly, throughout discursive formations regarding Canadian audiovisual culture. Tierney's appeal to this notion nostalgically harkens to the era of Canadian Heritage's "From Script to Screen" policy introduced in the early 2000s, and to Telefilm's ensuing Canadian Feature Film Fund, which did in fact contain a requirement that funded films not "disguise" their Canadian location.[34] As a producer (*Bon Cop, Bad Cop*, 2006) and a director (*French Immersion*, 2011), "visibly Canadian" was clearly a governing framework for the projects Tierney undertook, and a topic about which he felt passionate.

While there is no doubt a certain cultural appeal in the notion of undisguised national representation, particularly in a country such as Canada which has long wrestled with notions of cultural and national identity, the premise that Canadian filmmakers can only make films that are set in Canada is nevertheless prescriptive, parochial, and creatively limiting. Insisting upon it, at the level of cultural policy, is arguably quaint and anachronistic in today's transnational media environment. Furthermore, to dismiss *Room* on these grounds fundamentally misses the point of the film. The film is not simply arbitrarily set in the United States to appease an assumed North American audience. Rather, its middle American setting is intentional. While Emma Donoghue's novel and subsequent screenplay were loosely inspired by the headline-making Josef Fritzl case in Austria, the occurrence of such captivity cases has been far more numerous in the United States in recent decades than anywhere else. While the horrific and traumatic events at the film's core are unquestionably conceivable in a Canadian context, the film is primarily concerned with a predominantly American phenomenon. Coincidentally, in fact, after both the novel and screenplay had been written, a remarkably similar case came to light in 2013, when three women abducted between 2002 and 2004, Michelle Knight, Georgina DeJesus, and Amanda Berry, managed to escape their captor Ariel Castro. Eerily, those events occurred in Cleveland, Ohio (a short distance from *Room*'s Akron), and one of the women, Amanda Berry, gave birth to a child in captivity, who was six at the time of their escape (*Room*'s Jack is five, and also born in captivity).

The film's setting was not a product of the universalizing, marketing tendencies often associated with international co-production. Donoghue deliberately set the film in the United States – a decision, she explains, that is crucial to the intents of the film.[35] She states: "I wanted Ma to be under pressure to pay her medical bills. America has a sense of itself as the country where everybody wants to end up. I thought it would be wonderfully ironic if Ma and Jack found life on the outside extremely non-idyllic."[36] *Room*, in other words, is a "Canadian story," in that it's a story written by a Canadian living in Canada (Donoghue became a citizen in 2004), that happens to be about characters in the United States.[37] A recent study found that many Canadian screenwriters, of television and film, find the Canadianness in their work in terms of a matter of perspective, or orientation, rather than the more overt national qualities of the writing itself.[38] Canadian stories, in other words, do not necessarily have to be stories about Canada. The ado over the film's status as not visibly Canadian takes on additional significance when compared to other award-winning, but not visibly Canadian, films released in recent years. Consider for example Kim Nguyen's *Rebelle* (*War Witch*, 2012), a solely Canadian-funded film, shot throughout the Democratic Republic of the Congo, and set in an unnamed sub-Saharan

African nation. Like *Room*, *Rebelle* was a big winner at the Canadian Screen Awards, winning ten awards in all, including Best Picture, and was also nominated for the Academy Award for Best Foreign Language Film. Though the film was certainly met with accusations of cultural appropriation, criticism of the film did not typically hinge on its inability to be "visibly Canadian."[39] Likewise, another recipient of a number of Canadian Screen Awards, the recent Canada-Ireland-Luxembourg co-production *The Breadwinner* is an animated film set in Afghanistan, with nothing remotely Canadian about its setting or narrative preoccupations. Yet, similarly, the film does not appear to have suffered the same accusations that *Room*, or *Brooklyn*, endured. This would seem to suggest that the concern over a Canadian film's status as visibly Canadian is not so much the issue, as is its relative status as visibly "not American," a tendency no doubt reflective of the nation's ongoing anxiety over the threat of American cultural colonialism.

Furthermore, to simply dismiss *Room* as a "tax grab," as Tierney, Wilner, and his filmmaking associate clearly do, is both inaccurate and unfairly reductionist. In reality, the vast majority of films produced in Canada benefit from tax incentives, typically the Canadian Film or Video Production Tax Credit for domestic productions, or the Film or Video Production Services Tax Credit accessible to foreign-owned productions, in addition to various provincially based incentives. The charge of being merely a tax grab is a deliberate attempt to invoke the spectre of the Capital Cost Allowance of the 1970s and 1980s, a notorious low point for many Canadian cultural nationalists. This is another irony of the Canadian film industry: that an industry that has historically been highly dependent on tax incentives, for both domestic production as well as runaway foreign investment, consistently invokes the label of "tax grab" as a dismissive and derisive term.

The sentiments found in these opinion pieces articulate some of the prevailing institutional critiques in Canada, directed at bodies such as Telefilm Canada, or the Canadian Academy of Cinema of Television (which administers the Canadian Screen Awards). And through these critiques, we see one particular version of an idealized Canadian cinema taking shape, for better or for worse. Discussions of co-productions typically fall into simplistic good or bad arguments. Producers who have been successful with them tend to sing their praises, while critics and other filmmakers with strong local sensibilities complain when they win awards, or run counter to a sense of national cohesion. Yet generalizing arguments about co-productions and their respective positive or negative presence in the Canadian film industry largely miss the point. They assume that their ontological status can be neatly summarized as either fundamentally market-driven products or artistic or cultural contributors, when the diversity of actual production is far more complex and complicated. A healthy national cinema is one that flourishes both economically and culturally, tendencies that recent successful Canadian co-productions have in varying capacities demonstrated. Rather than merely assuming and taking for granted the notion that international co-productions are inherently detrimental to a coherent national cinema, it might instead be constructive to consider the ways in which they prompt us to pause and envision just precisely of what a national cinema might consist.

Notes

1 Arik Motskin, Zack Gallinger, and Daniel Frank, "Forget the Critics: The Best Canadian Films of All Time," *The 10and3*, 10 February 2016, http://www.the10and3.com/the-best-canadian-movies-of-all-time-by-the-numbers.
2 The Ontario Media Development Corporation was rebranded as Ontario Creates in 2018.
3 Telefilm Canada, "See Bigger: 2018–2020 Strategic Report," 2018, https://telefilm.ca/wp-content/uploads/strategic-plan-telefilm-2018-2020.pdf. Telefilm's commitment to co-production can be symbolically assumed from the prominence it is given on its website, as it appears immediately after "Funding" on the menu on the main page.
4 Canadian Heritage, "Creative Canada Policy Framework," October 2017, https://www.canada.ca/en/canadian-heritage/campaigns/creative-canada/framework.html.
5 Canadian Heritage, "Canada Strengthens Its Cultural and Economic Ties with Europe," Press Release, 15 March 2017, https://www.canada.ca/en/canadian-heritage/news/2017/03/canada_strengthensitsculturalandeconomictieswitheurope.html.
6 Atom Egoyan cited in Michael D. Reid, "Oh, Canada! Our Home and Native On-Screen Land," *Movie Entertainment Magazine*, July 2016, http://www.themovienetwork.ca/movie-entertainment/article/Canada-Film-Industry. Incidentally, although Egoyan is often considered one of the most prominent English-Canadian filmmakers of the past thirty years, only about half of his films have been uniformly Canadian-funded films. The rest have been international co-productions, co-ventures, and even a full-blown American film (*The Devil's Knot*, 2013). Likewise, David Cronenberg, another titan

of English-Canadian film, has not made a uniformly Canadian film since 1983's *Videodrome*.

7 Manjunath Pendakur, *Canadian Dreams and American Control: The Political Economy of the Canadian Film Industry* (Detroit: Wayne State University Press, 1990).

8 Paul W. Taylor, "Co-productions – Content and Change: International Television in the Americas," *Canadian Journal of Communication* 20, no. 3 (1995), https://cjc-online.ca/index.php/journal/article/view/888/794.

9 Charles Tepperman, "Bureaucrats and Movie Czars: Canada's Feature Film Policy since 2000," *Media Industries* 4, no. 2 (2017): 63.

10 This total includes two treaties with France that address film and television separately. All co-production treaties are publicly available on Telefilm's website: https://telefilm.ca/en/co-production/international-treaties.

11 Ted Magder, *Canada's Hollywood: The Canadian State and Feature Films* (Toronto: University of Toronto Press, 1993), 169.

12 Doris Baltruschat, "International TV and Film Co-production: A Canadian Case Study," *Media Organization and Production*, ed. Simon Cottle (London: Sage Publications, 2003), 151.

13 In its annual statistics on co-production numbers according to the language of each project, Telefilm unfortunately does not distinguish between film, television, and digital media productions.

14 Jordan Pinto, "Netflix Acquires 'The Body Remembers' for the U.S.," *Playback*, 10 October 2019, https://playbackonline.ca/2019/10/10/netflix-acquires-the-body-remembers-for-the-u-s/.

15 Christ Knight, "Danis Goulet's Film a First for New Zealand-Canada Indigenous Co-operation," *National Post*, 26 June 2020, https://nationalpost.com/entertainment/movies/danis-goulets-film-a-first-for-new-zealand-canada-indigenous-co-operation.

16 Canada Media Fund, "Night Raiders Comes Home," 20 December 2021, https://cmf-fmc.ca/now-next/articles/night-raiders-comes-home/.

17 David Gross cited in Etan Vlessing, "Why Canadian Co-productions Thrive in Ontario," *The Hollywood Reporter*, 12 September 2015, https://www.hollywoodreporter.com/news/tiff-2015-why-canadian-productions-822452.

18 *Room* was produced in accordance with the 1989 Canadian-Irish co-production treaty, which stipulates that the contributions of participating member states in terms of creative and technical personnel should be in proportion to the investment – though specific positions are not spelled out specifically. The Canadian-Irish treaty was revised and re-signed in 2016, and stipulates in greater detail the specific roles that need to be filled by citizens of the partner states.

19 Katie McNeice, "Irish-Canadian Co-production Activity Likely to Increase as Canada Joins Eurimages," *Irish Film and Television Network*, 16 March 2017, http://www.iftn.ie/news/?act1=record&only=1&aid=73&rid=4290391&tpl=archnews&force=1. The 2016 Audiovisual Co-production Treaty between the Government of Canada and the Government of Ireland contains a few notable differences from the 1989 treaty that it replaced. Significantly, the minimum budgetary contribution for both states was lowered from 20 per cent in the 1989 treaty to 15 per cent in the revised treaty. Furthermore, the language detailing the contributions of key personnel from the partnering nations is more concrete in the 2016 version, specifying, in the case of live action fiction, that at least seven of eight key positions in the production be filled by Canadian or Irish nationals – in other words, only one key position may be occupied by a citizen of a third non-partnered nation (though language exists for some flexibility on this issue).

20 Huw David Jones, "The Cultural and Economic Implications of UK/European Co-production," *Transnational Cinemas* 7, no. 1 (2016): 5; Mariana Liz, "From Co-production to the Euro-pudding," in *The Europeanness of European Cinema: Identity, Meaning, Globalization*, ed. Mary Harrod, Mariana Liz, and Alissa Timoshkina, (London: I.B. Tauris, 2015): 73–86.

21 See, for example: Magder, *Canada's Hollywood*; Pendakur, *Canadian Dreams and American Control*; and Michael Dorland, *So Close to the State/s: The Emergence of Canadian Feature Film Policy* (Toronto: University of Toronto Press: 1998).

22 Adam Finn, Colin Hoskins, and Stuart McFadyen, "Telefilm Canada Investment in Feature Films: Empirical Foundations for Public Policy," *Canadian Public Policy* 22, no. 2 (1996): 154–5.

23 Ibid., 158.

24 Baltruschat, "International TV and Film Co-production," 167.

25 Serra Tinic, *On Location: Canada's Television Industry in a Global Market* (Toronto: University of Toronto Press, 2005), 105.

26 Simon Houpt, "Oscar Nods Give Canadian films Room, Brooklyn a Second Life," *Globe and Mail*, 14 January 2016, https://www.theglobeandmail.com/arts/film/canadian-dramas-room-brooklyn-garner-best-picture-oscar-nods/article28181024/.

27 The biggest controversy surrounding *Maudie* had little to do with its co-production status, and everything to do with the decision to shoot the film in Newfoundland rather than on location in Nova Scotia. Tara Thorne, "Maudie: Wrongly Located, but Beautifully Shot," *The Coast*, 12 April 2017, https://www.thecoast.ca/halifax/maudie-wrongly-located-but-beautifully-shot/Content?oid=6900367.

28 Joe Heaney grew up in the small area of Carna, in County Galway, Ireland, which coincidentally happens to be the precise region in Connemara where certain scenes in *Death of a Ladies' Man* were shot.
29 Shawn Shimpach, "The Immortal Cosmopolitan: The International Co-production and Global Circulation of *Highlander: The Series*," *Cultural Studies* 19, no. 3 (2005): 338–71.
30 Norman Wilner, "The Canadian Screen Awards Went Seriously Off-Mission Last Night," *NOW Magazine*, 14 March 2016, https://nowtoronto.com/movies/the-canadian-screen-awards-went-seriously-off-mission-last-n/.
31 Ibid.
32 Kevin Tierney, "Why Canadian Films Are Pretending to Be American Again," *Montreal Gazette*, 9 December 2016, http://montrealgazette.com/entertainment/movies/kevin-tierney-why-canadian-films-are-pretending-to-be-american-again.
33 Ibid.
34 Tepperman, "Bureaucrats," 67.
35 Tom Ue, "An Extraordinary Act of Motherhood: A Conversation with Emma Donoghue," *Journal of Gender Studies* 21, no. 1 (2012): 102.
36 Jake Kerridge. "How *Room*'s Emma Donoghue Turned Her Dark Bestseller into an Oscar Contender," *The Telegraph*, 16 January 2016, https://www.telegraph.co.uk/film/room/emma-donoghue-interview/.
37 While the novel is more ambiguous about the setting of the story, the film makes it clear that it occurs in Akron, Ohio.
38 Michael Coutanche, Charles H. Davis, and Emilia Zboralska, "Telling Our Stories: Screenwriters and the Production of Screen-Based Culture in English-Speaking Canada," *Canadian Journal of Communication* 40 (2015): 261–80.
39 Rachel Mutombo, "The African Experience on Film: Whose Story Is It to Tell – and What Aren't We Seeing?" *The Filmmakers*, CBC, 29 August 2017, http://www.cbc.ca/arts/the-filmmakers/the-african-experience-on-film-whose-story-is-it-to-tell-and-what-aren-t-we-seeing-1.4266952.

18

Troubling Toronto Queer Festivals
Transgressions in and of Queer Counterpublics

Aimée Mitchell

Introduction

In this chapter I revisit the emergence of the Inside Out LGBT Film Festival in the early 1990s in order to understand its development from a grassroots festival into a commercially driven, homonormative cultural event by the early to mid-2000s.[1] I do so in order to situate the emergence of the Toronto Queer Film Festival (TQFF) in 2016 as one site of resistance against the contemporary commercialization of queer spaces, in an effort to return to and reimagine what queer- and trans-focused grassroots film festivals can/could be. I specifically take up the trajectory of the Inside Out LGBT Film Festival in Toronto to explore the common factors that have led formerly grassroots festivals on the margins to slowly gravitate towards the centre of mainstream culture, and in turn, come under the influence of normative structures and rhetoric they once stood in opposition to. By reflecting on queer and trans festivals as relational spaces that emerge from queer and trans arts, culture, and activism in Toronto, I trace the tensions between these counterpublics and their relationships with mass public culture.

One of the primary reasons why grassroots LGBT and queer festivals in Canada have turned to corporate support and mainstream programming is to secure long-term stable funding and audiences for their festivals. Canadian cinema and especially queer Canadian cinema and festivals have perpetually experienced financial scarcity in arts funding, in addition to the lack of a robust commercial film market. Yet as Thomas Waugh argues in the introduction to his seminal book *The Romance of Transgression in Canada,* while Canadian cinemas commercially struggle, it is under these conditions that Canadian cinemas can be transgressive and operate under a queer sensibility. He writes: "Our subsidized and perennially crisis-ridden film efforts are virtually defined by the absence of a commercially grounded and interactive audience ... but that commerciality and popularity paradoxically could both foster and brake their transgressiveness ... Our Canadian cinemas (and videos) are defined, rather, by their artists, audiences, and stakeholders, by their longing *search* for some kind of impact and pop persistence."[2] Waugh situates the early Canadian queer film and video festivals within this context of transgressiveness, describing the network of regional micro-cinemas, and I would add here artist-run centres, to be "inflected, as it will be repeatedly stressed, not only by cultural, creative, and textual realities, but also everything from funding protocols to local education resources ... from local censorship practices to exhibition and broadcast patterns, even to climate."[3] The network and its respective communities helped to create queer spaces and the canon of Canadian queer cinema within a climate of precarity on a series of levels. For the scope of this essay, I will focus on but a few of these stressors to understand the intersections Inside Out's histories hinge upon.

Led by artists and activists, Canada's early queer festivals used film and video to confront queer representation in popular media and to speak out about the policing, safety, and rights of the queer community engaged in ongoing HIV/AIDS advocacy, while also offering up alternative representations of queer experiences.[4] But what happens to these festivals when they become mainstream, corporatized, and apolitical? What happens when they are no longer transgressive? Who do large, capitalist-driven LGBT festivals serve? How does the corporatized LGBT festival circuit shift or displace the histories of these spaces, their communities, and the media art that emerged out of their discreet sociopolitical histories?

Reclaiming Spaces and Screens

The Toronto Queer Film Festival first emerged in June of 2016 during Toronto Pride as a response to the city's lack of screens showing radical queer and trans media art. At the time, I was working as the distribution manager at the Canadian Filmmakers Distribution Centre (CFMDC), which holds one of the largest collections of artisanal queer and trans film in Canada, and was witnessing firsthand the trend towards normative, commercially viable, mainstream LGBT programming. The shift towards commercial, mainstream, or neutered representations of queer and trans life was resulting in experimental, radical, and political media art being overlooked by prestige domestic and international LGBT film festivals.

I had been having conversations with artists and peers about the barriers facing experimental and radical queer and trans media artists, expressing frustrations regarding the lack of diversity in large mainstream LGBT festival programming in terms of representations of race, class, politics, gender, sexual expressions, and artistic practices. Through my role as a distributor, I witnessed the financial barriers facing queer and trans artists trying to access prestige festivals. Costly festival submission fees force many artists living close to or below the poverty line to be selective about which festivals they choose to submit their work, creating gatekeeping.[5] Limited access to travel grants further constrains artists struggling to budget how to attend their own out-of-town film screenings. These costs cut particularly deep when programmers have the audacity to ask artists, specifically those who have only had the capacity and means to create short works, to screen their films for free in exchange for "exposure." This unspoken practice has been rampant in general film festival culture (not just LGBT festivals), and continues to be a major disservice to artists who struggle to make ends meet and make art. Festival distribution strategies become even more delicate for queer and trans artists. Our current festival economy serves festivals rather than the artists who populate the screens. Thus, commercial filmmaking with secure distribution and promotional budgets becomes the targeted festival market with commercial distributors vying for rights, while the work of independent and non-commercial artists and their conditions of artistic labour are overlooked.

Through my position at CFMDC I came to understand the economies of the global and national LGBT film festival network, its programmers and their specific set of tastes. I began to see patterns in programming and could anticipate what films were going to be successful within the festival circuit. Films that were often being selected were narratives and predominantly featured normative, upper-middle-class, white, lesbian and gay love stories. When the narrative happened to be trans, it was usually a very prescriptive and reductive story about someone's legible transition experience rather than nuanced work engaged with trans lived experiences. While there are always exceptions to this trend, apolitical and normalizing feel-good narratives dominate programming selections both domestically and internationally.

Assimilationist homonormativity has been all too present in the mainstream corporately funded LGBT festival circuit. This trend in the 2000s is nothing new – the corporate pinkwashing of LGBT festivals has been but one avenue wherein the rise of homonationalism and homonormativity has taken root, fostering "a privatized, depoliticized gay culture anchored in domesticity and consumption."[6] While many lesbian and gay festivals have rebranded themselves under the catch-all umbrellas of LGBT, LGBTQ, queer, or otherwise, the gesture towards progressive inclusivity can feel vacant when the programming does not follow suit. As a distributor of Canadian cinema, I had been adamant in finding screens and audiences for all the queer and trans work coming into the CFMDC collection – specifically the experimental and politically charged work that was being overlooked in programming. This seemed to be a hard sell to programmers who were looking for something palatable for a mainstream gay and lesbian audience.

Homonormative trends in LGBT film festivals in the past several decades have led programmers to play it safe, rather than take programming chances that could possibly fly in the face of wealthy white gay membership donations, corporate sponsorship, and festival branding. Programmers instead request screeners for popular films they find in festival catalogues and dial their selections in from the "safe list" created by the mainstream North American and European festival circuits. As Jonathan Petrychyn explains: "Combined with the global trend toward a more institutionalized queer film market, the possibilities for queer festivals to be sites of radical left politics, and to become anything more than sites of homonormative consumption, diminishes."[7]

The Toronto Queer Film Festival emerged in response to this lack of a community screen to present radical queer and trans art being made on the margins. TQFF was created with the aim of making an accessible and barrier-free festival for artists and audiences outside of the commercial, neoliberal, and mainstream festival circuit. TQFF emerged in the spirit of a grassroots, activist-driven, community festival that operates collectively and is predominantly run by artists for artists without the support of corporate sponsorship.

A Queer Festival in the Act of Always Becoming

Each year, TQFF explores what a queer and trans festival is and could become through its festival mandate and programming. To follow a line of thought offered by festival scholar Skadi Loist, the artist-centred mandate of the festival asks: who gains from the festival circuit and its workers?[8] TQFF, like most collectives, emerged as a site of response to the contemporary moment, to critique and create conversation regarding the status of current film festival culture – LGBT, queer, and otherwise.

Figure 18.1 Toronto Queer Film Festival 2017 poster, designed by Gardenia Flores.

In the context of queer spaces and counterpublics, it is a reworking and interrogation of the reclaimed definition of "queer," specifically in opposition to how it is being mobilized as a brand by LGBT festivals that are adopting the term as a catch-all to sweep over shifting sex and gender identity politics, rather than evoking its radical activist roots. It is also a place to question the popularity and usefulness of queer as theoretical framework.

TQFF mobilizes the term "queer" in ways that reach beyond a reductive categorical use of the word. Queer, for the collective's purpose, is an evolving, pliable, and slippery term. A singular term must remain this way – as it cannot speak to or encompass the complex spectrum or intersections of lived experiences of queer- and trans-identified lives. The collective engages with it as both a radical aesthetic and political mode of resistance, which is playful, experimental, and transgressive. Queer, as a political mode of resistance, is activated in TQFF's festival programming, which attempts to create space for issues including migration and border imperialism, racial oppression and white supremacy, the commodification of queer and trans culture, settler colonialism, and pinkwashing. Festival programming prioritizes films made by 2Spirit, trans, and queer IBPOC (Indigenous, Black, and people of colour), Deaf, Mad, and disability-identified media artists, sex workers, porn makers, and other communities often marginalized in mainstream LGBT cultural programming and spaces. It has been crucial that the collective, the programming team, and festival staff also reflect the communities the festival serves.

In what initially began as a small ad hoc collective, TQFF is continually trying to imagine something more beyond the present festival climate.[9] Evoking José Esteban Muñoz and his book *Cruising Utopia*, I would argue that small grassroots festivals like TQFF, in addition to the continued resilience of small community-centred Canadian festivals, are operating as queer utopias, dreaming beyond the "here and now," in an effort to imagine into reality the types of communities (and festivals) we desire beyond the reach of late capitalism – however naïve this may seem. For Muñoz, queerness never quite exists yet, but can be seen on the horizon; it is never quite in reach as it unfolds out into a future. The future, and the possibilities queerness holds, are where we can collectively dream. Muñoz writes: "Queerness is essentially about the rejection of a here and now and an insistence on potentiality or concrete possibility of another world."[10] He conceptualizes queerness as a "grid in which we do not claim to always already know queerness in the world," and in doing so, this "potentially staves off the ossifying effects of neoliberal ideology and the degradation of politics brought about by representations of queerness in contemporary popular culture."[11]

The nature of a community-centred queer and trans film festival, and its cycle that begins anew each year, lends itself to Muñoz's notion of queerness and its futurity. The "then and there" of queer time looks towards a horizon of possibilities, rather than the "here and now," which he argues belongs to "straight time," or a neoliberal notion of time that claims, "there is no future but the here and now of our everyday life."[12] Thus queer futurity dares to look to the horizon and rejects the reality of things as they are, and dares to propose another option – a dream or utopia.

Each year TQFF extends itself a little more in terms of what the collective wishes and wants a queer and trans festival to be. At its core, it is a festival that prioritizes folks who are marginalized within mainstream LGBT festivals; one where artists are put first, and paid for screening their work; where there are no submission fees; where programmers do not gatekeep and open calls for submissions are thoughtfully considered; where programmers debate and continuously interrogate value systems of taste and aesthetics that are not rooted in production values or social norms; where artists are supported, not only through exhibition, but also in the creation of new work. TQFF is committed to a festival that will turn no one away at the door; will accommodate artists and audiences through care attendants, closed captioning, ASL interpreters, and accessible venues; will facilitate thoughtful and difficult discussions beyond a Q&A through artist roundtables and workshops; and more. More exists just beyond the horizon as the festival repositions itself year after year in hopes of unfolding in ways that do not accept the "here and now," and continues to respond to the evolving of the "then and there."[13]

Precarity and Collectivity

TQFF's longevity, like so many other arts festivals, remains bound to the precarious cycle of government arts council funding in Canada. This is one expression of the underfunded perennial crisis that Waugh is referring to – the competitive, peer-assessed, mandate-driven competition that artist-run centres, festivals, and artists alike must adhere to. It is the catch-22 of remaining a small community-driven festival: while TQFF is a festival that resists concepts of nationhood and borders, it relies on federal, provincial, and municipal government arts funding for primary financial support. The success of these grants dictates the scope of the festival, and to some degree, the programming due to funding criteria.

The Canadian granting system does not allow for robust financial stability, especially in the early development of ad hoc groups and collectives, which is one of the reasons why queer and trans festivals that are unable to secure stable arts funding in their early years tend to be short-lived – volunteer organizers burn out in these labours of love, but the systemic reality is that organizers were never set up to succeed.

Artist and scholar Christina Battle has highlighted the ways in which the structure of arts council funding in Canada impedes the important radical work of collectives, arguing for more support in how they do outreach, organize, and operate. Battle notes there is pressure embedded within the funding system for collectives to swiftly adapt and follow "the path of institutionalization," encouraging collectives to restructure in order to establish themselves within the landscape of arts organizations and become eligible for operational funding.[14] In doing so, collectives shift to a hierarchical structure, which fundamentally sits in opposition to the spirit and aims of collective organizing: "This inevitable path towards institutionalization not only discourages those who want to work with communities that might not embrace the formal institutional structures that are required by the state, but also squelches the very energy and activity that makes collectives so fertile in the first place."[15] Noting this pressure towards bureaucracy and hierarchy, Battle highlights that as organizations mature they come under the danger of aligning too closely with government funding bodies, seen through the jargon of strategic planning, project initiatives, and a focus on outcomes or concrete deliverables.[16] In doing so, homogenization sets in, and with it, a loss of diversity, new ideas, and experimentation – qualities which many artist-run organizations wish to centre, but can drift away from over time. Battle reframes the assumption that artistic spaces "are radical and progressive merely because they are artist-run."[17] I will come back to this point later in regards to the history of Inside Out LGBT Film Festival, but here I would like to echo Battle's insistence on making room for different approaches to radicality and diversity in contemporary art organizations. By shifting more funding towards ad hoc groups and collectives, thereby allowing them to operate within their own models of organizing, the landscape of arts organizations in Canada could diversify and learn more about on-the-ground and responsive ways of making, distributing, and exhibiting art in the contemporary moment. Battle exclaims, "What if more funding was made available to ad hoc groups and collectives, those who come together in response to the contemporary moment, at a more frequent rate, allowing them to better enact new strategies and new ways forward? This could foster a rapid and ever changing cycle of new ideas from a wide range of voices and perspectives, those that are new to the sector and perhaps even unexpected."[18] But the current inability for many ad hoc groups and collectives to forecast their financial future means fundraising within communities and working with like-minded organizations to create partnerships and sponsorship opportunities that are mutually beneficial. The popular alternative is to turn to corporate and private sponsorship to offset government arts and cultural funding, like so many other (queer) festivals across Canada, but this is precisely what TQFF stands in strict opposition to, informed by the current commercialization of queer culture and influencing of the "good" queer consumer. The choice to accept corporate and private funding, however, is not without nuance, as the case of Inside Out will demonstrate. But Inside Out's compromise loosened, and in some ways, required the organization to forget their political and radical roots in order to become financially secure and sustainable.

Facing the reality of burnout while also wanting to pursue growth, TQFF had to accept the path towards institutionalization in order to grant the collective members some financial security. In early 2019, the Toronto Queer Media Arts Centre, better known publicly as TQFF, incorporated and became a registered charity in steps towards year-round operational funding by the Canada Council. In doing so, the collective had to legally establish a board of directors, separating those in the collective into staff and board roles. It remains to be seen how the collective members will navigate this transition in the long term, and how (if the spirit of collectivity can be maintained) they could possibly help to create new models for staff-board relationships and responsibilities within the media arts sector and speak to the power of the arts councils. Perhaps this is where Inside Out's historical trajectory can inform steps ahead, rather than be a history set up in opposition to the emergence of TQFF. But to evoke Battle, under this new hierarchical, institutionalized structure, how will TQFF remain "dedicated to social justice and challenging the status quo?"[19] Or do the emergent properties of radicality wither once pinned down within the structures of bureaucracy? Is there really a way to shift the system from within? Here is where Battle's call for new models of collectivity could be useful, if TQFF can continue to be the responsive, critical, and queer experiment it is, evoking Muñoz's sense of futurity. It could be an exciting possibility for the "then and there" to punch holes in the restrictive neoliberal late capitalist ways of the "here and now."

Histories and Cycles of Collectivity

When TQFF initially began, Toronto media and some individuals within queer communities were quick to place the festival in opposition to Inside Out. Some responded by asking, "Why do we need another queer festival?" To reiterate, TQFF emerged in response to a need for a community screen to showcase radical queer and trans art made by artists on the margins of the mainstream – the mainstream being Inside Out. Many of the films TQFF screens have never been shown in Toronto, or even in Canada. Initially, the festival was also created as an alternative space for folks to gather during Toronto Pride, which has become an aggressively corporate month-long party, and overlooks the ways Pride is not always celebratory for everyone. In an interview with *Xtra*, one of TQFF's co-founders Kami Chisholm explained, "Part of the reason for putting the event in the middle of Pride is to organize an alternative space ... Its focus is on talking about and showing work by and for the communities that are the most marginalized, people who feel they don't have a place at Pride. It's also important to show that we can do things without corporate sponsors. All we need is our talents and the will to come together."[20] This desire to create a counterpublic is not all that different from the reasons why Inside Out emerged over thirty years ago.

Being involved in the emergence of TQFF, I approached the goals of the festival, especially in its first iteration, as an answer to a need that was emerging within the landscape of queer and trans media makers in Toronto in situ. The first festival was predominantly trans activist video art, provocations into queer and trans body politics, sex-play, and works that directly addressed the homogenization and co-opting of queer life into mainstream culture. It felt timely in the wake of Toronto hosting World Pride. But what I did not yet understand was why there was some bristling within queer communities at the mention of a queer- and trans-focused festival reclaiming a community screen. TQFF touched upon a history within the Toronto queer and trans arts landscape that the collective did not know intimately. In turn, it revealed TQFF's generational blind spot. A generational gap allowed TQFF to emerge and do the work of organizing without the shadow of the past impeding it, yet at the same time, the festival's vision was based on a grassroots blueprint embedded with histories that the collective was not personally acquainted with.

There is a swampy, murky, complicated tangle of queer and trans metahistories that have been fought for and laid out here in Toronto's queer and trans art landscape – and not just by the fictitious singular idea of "the community" against the homophobic straight world, but within, traced out across artistic disciplines surrounding race, class, and transphobia. The ArQuives are full of these histories and personal relationships.[21] There is certainly not space here to do the intersections of these histories justice, although I am interested in pursuing these winding paths elsewhere in order to better understand the deeply nuanced histories and relationships that inform this queer and trans media art landscape. But for the purposes of this chapter, I am interested in teasing out some undercurrents of Inside Out's institutional history to understand its cultural footprint and its position in relation to the queer and trans community, while knowing this merely scratches the surface of a rich and complicated history.

To return to the emergence of TQFF as a "competitor" of Inside Out: it seemed strange and somewhat myopic to me that there was an air of competitiveness and confusion over the need for another festival within splintered queer and trans communities. To ask Inside Out to be all things for queer and trans cinema and communities seemed like an unsustainable and dangerously homogenizing platform for what queer and trans media art encompasses. Yes, Inside Out is the largest and longest-running LGBT film festival in Toronto, but there have been, and currently are, numerous other festivals and collectives that have emerged over the years in response to community gaps and needs.

Trans Lives and Art Matter: Counting Past 2

Most notable was the emergence of Counting Past 2: Performance-Film-Video-Spoken Word with Transsexual Nerve! (1997–99, 2002), run by Mirha-Soleil Ross and the first festival of its kind in North America.[22] Ross, a trans artist, performer, sex worker, and activist, sought to carve out a festival that exclusively showcased the voices and experiences of the transgender community – something that gay and lesbian festivals like Inside Out were failing to hold space for in a meaningful way. It points to the fractured sensibility of gay and lesbian communities in relationship to other queer and trans identities. The most significant example of this can be found in the 1993 Inside Out program called "Gender Blender," which labelled trans identities and other gender expressions as "sexual anomalies," thus diminishing representations of trans issues and lifestyle to a sideshow spectacle: "Bearded ladies, chicks with dicks, and drag queens are among the queer sightings in Gender Blender, an evening of gender-bending film and video. Throwing open the question of sex and its relation to gender identification and sexual orientation, this programme explores cross-dressing, transsexualism, transvestism, androgyny, and other sexual anomalies."[23] This classification and othering of the trans community outraged Toronto trans activists into forming the Transsexual Activist Collective (TAC), who retaliated by circulating a flyer that reproduced the program description and responding, "NO TO THE GERALDO APPROACH! TRANSSEXUALS ARE NOT YOUR ENTERTAINMENT!!"[24] Viviane Namaste in her book *Invisible Lives: The Erasure of Transsexual and Transgendered People* notes that "this strategy interrogates the staging of transgendered subjects within a lesbian and gay setting,"[25] adding that Inside Out's "description represents one of the many ways in which lesbian and gay identities position others as 'anomalies' in order to portray themselves as 'natural.'"[26] While Inside Out was creating a queer counterpublic, who was welcomed, represented, and validated was in question. In 1999, letters from trans activists and organizers of Counting Past 2 to Inside Out's executive director and programming team addressed continued problems between Inside Out, representative of gay and lesbian community, and the trans community. The letters list in detail a series of current and historical concerns with the festival including an overall lack of consultation with community, concerns with the content of trans programming (often including work made by lesbian and gay filmmakers rather than by those within the trans community), the use of the word "tranny" in previous program guides, and the misuse of pronouns by Inside Out program presenters, who simply laughed off their misgendering.[27] These letters of complaint called for volunteer and organizer educational training, insisting on involving the trans community on programming committees, correcting the misuse of pronouns and shutting down derogatory comments during Q&As, and including the trans community in the management structure of the festival.[28] One letter explicitly addressed the absence of Inside Out members in attendance at Counting Past 2, demonstrating a lack of a real interest in trans art and culture, or a genuine interest in the trans community itself:

> The Inside Out members have never come to Counting Past 2 in Toronto every September. Yet they travel all over the world to check out lesbian & gay film & video festivals. So why can't they come to an event that is important to us & in the same town? This shows me that the Inside Out is not really interested in TS culture & work. In short the Inside Out members have never made any real attempt to meet with members of the TS communities to find out about our concerns or issues; instead they have acted unilaterally. It seems to me that the only

reason they are doing so now is that they are aware that we can & will publicly embarrass them otherwise. Thus I feel that it is necessary to remind that that is exactly what we will do if we are not consulted as equals & treated with the same respect due any other minority.[29]

Counting Past 2 emerged in response to having trans identities framed, dismissed, or only made permissible for festival screenings through the gatekeeping of gay and lesbian programmers. Ross created the festival "after almost a decade of struggling with *the* big wigs at queer film festivals either not showing any interest in my work (which is concerned mainly with transsexual sexual representation) or telling me that my films were not 'transgender' enough to fit in their queer programs."[30] Trish Salah, an Arab poet, scholar, activist, and participant in Counting Past 2, situates a discussion regarding queer festival gatekeeping and artistic "taste" by utilizing Pierre Bourdieu's concept of habitus. Salah explains that "Bourdieu argues not only the class-based (and thus constructed) character of taste, but its animation through 'unconscious' belief and subjectively inhabited 'dispositions.'"[31] Through the habitual attributes of social class and its particular perceptual and affective influence, normative value systems emerge.[32] Salah argues:

> Recalling Bourdieu's model of habitus brings together the inherited attributes of social class with experiential history, allowing us to think about the ways in which "low class," earnest, or identity political transsexual art might suffer not only in the judgment of art world snobbery, but how the production and content norms of lesbian and gay film festivals might become naturalized as "standard criteria" for interesting cultural work by members of sexual minorities, and finally how personal histories in feminist and queer debate might translate into demographic or generational postures of exhaustion or boredom in response to identity political work. Indeed, the work of affective distinction might also manifest as middle-class discomfort at the felt presence of poor, sex-working, substance-using, or otherwise marginal others.[33]

The refusal of mainstream LGBT programmers to show interest in Counting Past 2's programming due to the DIY production values of works screened, combined with what Salah argues to be the uninterest in engaging with the lived experience of trans artists and their political work, pointed towards a gay and lesbian middle-class discomfort felt in the presence of the marginalized other. Counting Past 2 prioritized a space created for the trans community to come together "rather than playing to the expectations that privilege 'insider' queer viewing pleasure over the production of knowledges, narratives, and image repertoires that open the space for transsexual lives and politics."[34] Thus Counting Past 2 refused to appeal to the notion of "good taste" of mainstream cinema that larger LGBT film festivals were striving towards in order to gain cultural cache.

Counting Past 2 was staged four times before it went dark, and over the course of its existence, resistance, and intervention, it gained audiences and support from trans and queer communities and allies in Toronto.[35] The festival itself was primarily funded by Ross and her partner Mark Karbusicky, without the support of any council funding, which made the festival difficult to sustain – both financially and in the face of personal burnout. Sustaining the festival was difficult on a series of levels highlighted by Ross, including the lack of trans work circulating within festival circuits, but also the inability for the trans community to be able to make work while living below the poverty line – though this was also the impetus for Counting Past 2 to exist in the first place.[36]

Commenting on the difficulty of sustaining trans-centred counterpublic spaces, Trish Salah writes, "This difficulty returns us again to the question of the value of transgendered, transsexual, and sex worker labour, and of how 'the other of the other' might sustain herself without being subsumed in, or perhaps precisely negated by, the more successful counter-hegemonic productions of queer and feminist cultures. This question becomes more acute still if we mark the ways in which queer and feminist liberalism have entered post-feminist and homo-normative accommodation with neo-liberal economics and cultural governance."[37] Both Salah and Namaste articulate the impact of othering trans bodies, lives, and art by queer culture – negotiating or negating value based on legibility and consumability by mainstream gay and lesbian culture.

Inside Out: Collective to Commercial

Inside Out emerged in a time when the politics of representation was at the forefront of cultural life, and although it aimed to represent the voices of marginalized queer communities, its scope of inclusivity and who it attempted to represent and speak for was being brought into question by the trans community. Joceline Andersen notes that Inside Out was created at a moment when "the solidarity within gay civil rights was being fractured into the oppositional perspectives of diverse queer communities ... moving away from a period where queer identity had let itself become defined and united by disease and discrimination, and was returning as a civil rights movement that separated political from medical concerns."[38] On the one hand, the Inside Out collective of the early 1990s seemed dedicated to recognizing diversity across race and gender lines, addressing "marginalization within a marginal community," while also "embracing cultural production outside of activism ... featuring 'normal' people with jobs and families that contrasted narratives of tragedy" to resist mainstream media's narrativization of the AIDS crisis.[39] From its inception, Inside Out collective found itself walking the line between a festival founded in liberationist politics invested in "celebrating sexuality, eroticism, and pornography, resisting state regulation and police repression ... challenging the notions of community standards, of public and private, and of consent regarding sexuality and sexual behaviour,"[40] while also being implicated in the creation of a value system or a "standard criteria" of queer representation that helped to shape what forms of transgression would become legible and accredited on the festival circuit. Inside Out's commitment to community while also wanting to become a cultural influencer on the international festival circuit became a difficult balance to maintain. Thinking back to Battle's point about what happens to the radicality of collectivity when it comes too closely in contact with the rules of the neoliberal game, it seemed inevitable that Inside Out would need to leave its transgressive edge behind over time in order to grow within the festival industry.

Ironically or aptly, Inside Out emerged out of another event that had also created exclusion within communities. Inverted Image, put on by *Xtra!* at the Harbourfront Centre in November of 1986, showcased thirty-one feature-length gay films over the course of ten days.[41] The festival had a strong turnout, but "it excluded much existing lesbian and gay production in film and video."[42] Motivated to address the gap in programming, and with the encouragement of local queer artists including Michelle Mohabeer, Colin Campbell, John Greyson, and Lynne Fernie, Inside Out finally emerged after over a decade of gestation.[43] The collective incorporated in December of 1990 with the help of Gillian Morton, Paul Lee, and Christopher Eamon. The first festival was staged in March of 1991, programmed by Marie Dennis and Jeremy Podeswa. Similar to TQFF, the initial collective sought to showcase short queer experimental and transgressive works, with "DIY production values [that] could not find a venue in the art house circuit or the burgeoning film festival phenomenon of the largely narrative New Queer Cinema."[44] Early programming featured film and video programs focusing on AIDS activism, gay porn, queer erotic fantasies, and the playful BDSM "sexercises" of Maria Beatty and Annie Sprinkle.

But as Andersen points out, "There were inherent contradictions in Inside Out's commitment to promoting a positive image that would combat homophobia while celebrating the raw sexuality that characterized many queer works and which cultural conservatives found offensive."[45] In the eyes of cultural conservatives in the late 1980s and early 1990s, Inside Out's programming could be scrutinized under Canadian obscenity legislation governing what can be deemed sexually explicit and censored through the vague enforcement of "community standards" by police.[46] Queer film festivals were directly affected by the Butler decision by way of Canada Customs choosing to turn away films and videos at the border due to their "obscene" sexually explicit content.[47] A call for censorship by conservative taxpayers also challenged the validity of funding queer festivals that exhibited queer pornography, erotica, and films or videos that celebrated alternative sexual expressions and experiences. As counterpublics, film festivals became forums to organize in opposition not only to film censorship, but the overall policing of queer sexuality and sexual expression. Exacerbated by the Butler decision, queer liberationists sought to carve out "queer community standards" and spaces that offered alternative social mores in order to challenge the policing of sexuality and sexual expression by the state.[48] In tandem, liberationists were also challenging anti-pornography feminists and LGBT equal-rights activists who were adopting assimilationist politics in an effort to normalize gay culture into mainstream society by abiding to the Supreme Court's "national (heterosexual) standards" regarding sexual censorship.[49]

Inside Out's early program guides almost read like a community forum, reflecting politicized community engagement and mobilized as a platform to speak out against the ongoing censorship. An advertisement included in the 1992 program for the Feminist Caucus of the Ontario Coalition against Film and Video Censorship addressed how under Section 163 (8) police could determine what was obscene under the guise of protecting women's bodies from exploitation. These street-level value judgments were policing queer bodies, which included the content of film and video art, specifically targeting queer art, safe sex videos, erotica, and pornography.

The Inside Out collective used the opening remarks to its 1993 festival program to address the censorship happening within the community, addressing the police seizure of issues of *Bad Attitude*, a lesbian erotica magazine, from Glad Day Bookshop the previous year: "Recent judiciary decisions, continued police action, and the current climate at Canada Customs threatens to endanger festivals such as ours, and individual civil liberties as well – reminding us of the fragility of our assumed rights. The importance of our community's resistance to such oppression cannot be underestimated. This year's festival is packed with titles which express the sensibility of this resistance by revealing the more often than not forbidden images of lesbian and gay sexualities and identities."[50] Resistance against the policing of gay and lesbian sexualities and identity expressions became a pivotal theme for festival programming that year. However, the 1993 program guide was the site of multiple tensions: this was the same program in which trans sexualities and gender expressions were not treated with care in a climate of policing identities, which points to the fraught lines regarding censorship, value, and taste – not just from external political conservatives, but within queer and trans communities.

But what gained the most public attention in the 1993 guide was the "obscene" language used to describe the programming, including the synopsis for Jon Lindell's video, *Put Your Lips Around Yes* (1991), that read: "sex/rock/rhythm ... erotic/verbal/rollercoaster ... eyeball/tonguetwister. Fuckin' Hot Video."[51] This and other "obscene" and explicit language in the guide led to backlash from homophobic right-wing taxpayers when the programs were discovered on display at the Scarborough Public Library Morningside Branch and the Scarborough Civic Centre. The content of the guide was used to challenge the legitimacy of Inside Out receiving Toronto Metro Council cultural funding and called into question the validity of funding queer cultural events or arts organizations in general. Twelve "anti-grant" delegates took their complaints to Metro chairman Alan Tonks demanding that Inside Out's funding be revoked, along with Buddies in Bad Times Theatre who also came under scrutiny for hosting and advertising queer S&M seminars. Statements read to the Metro Council's management committee did not bother to hide their hate speech and contempt, calling gay and lesbian arts programming "trash," blaming both cultural events in promoting "perverts and exhibitionists" to come out of the closet, and to do so in public space using taxpayer dollars.[52] Some anti-grant supporters wanted to see all arts and culture funding cut completely and put into the police budget, insisting that cultural and "homosexual special interest groups" should not be able to hold events if they cannot raise their own funds and maintain operations through their own revenue.[53] Diane Malott, one of the loudest voices in the anti-grant twelve, exclaimed, "In a nutshell, if it's culture, it sells. If so few people buy it that you can't make a go of your artistic endeavour, it isn't culture. It's a flop."[54] The contempt of conservatives in the midst of the 1990s recession was palpable, but the homophobic attacks even more so. Over 200 arts and cultural organizations received funding that year from the Metro Cultural Grant, and yet only two organizations came under scrutiny, and both were queer. The grant committee recommended both organizations to receive funding that year, but the decisions were overturned in late June by the Metro Council Management Committee, recommending to withhold Buddies in Bad Times Theatre's $26,000 in funding, while cancelling Inside Out's $4,000 altogether.

It did not take long for the greater Toronto arts community to rally behind both organizations through a public action called "Hands around Metro," holding a press conference, and filling City Hall in early July as the votes came down.[55] Council voted to continue funding for Buddies in Bad Times Theatre, while a last-minute change in vote by Councillor Marie Labatte resulted in Inside Out losing its funding.[56] The loss of $4,000 equated to 1 per cent of city arts funding, and was received as a warning call from council to arts organizations that if they are being publicly funded, they "had to exercise some degree of taste and value judgement" in their programming.[57] The ruling demonstrated Metro Council's ability "to scapegoat any kind of group that's not doing art as they define it."[58]

The larger Toronto arts community sought ways to support Inside Out in having its funding restored, as this political intervention into the arm's length, peer-reviewed adjudication system was a harbinger for future council interventions resulting in funding cuts and censorship. While this was happening in the climate of the Butler decision, it also echoed and was affected by the censorship wars of the 1980s, resulting in the Film Classification Act in 1988. Throughout the 1970s and 1980s media artists and exhibitors pushed back against the Ontario Film Review Board's (OFRB) requirement to submit film and video art for approval before public screenings, ensuring that the content is suitable for public consumption and stamped with a classified rating.[59] Arts organizations were being asked to comply with a system set up for the commercial film industry, a system that overlooked artistic expression, rights, and freedoms. Similar to the arbitrary use of council power in the decision to revoke Inside Out's funding, the OFRB wielded their power to censor and ban works of art on an ad hoc basis. In April of 1985 arts organizations from across Ontario participated in the *Six Days of Resistance against the Censor Board: Ontario Open Screenings* that featured works that had not been submitted to the board before screening, calling for the dismantling of the OFRB and its system of cutting or banning works.[60] The eventual result of continued resistance was the 1988 Film Classification Act that allowed art galleries with a permanent space and film festivals running under two weeks to either submit written documentation describing all films and videos for approval, or restrict their audiences to 18 years or older and post signage, thus bypassing the reviewing process. Taryn Sirove questions whether the change to the Ontario Film Classification Act was a truce or compromise between the provincial body and the Ontario arts community – arts organizations either had to abide by the bureaucratic process by submitting documentation, which is a time-consuming burden on small organizations and collectives, or opt to self-censor with the R rating, restricting their audiences.[61] Either option still led to some mode of censorship, although as Sirove notes, in the 2000s the OFRB seems to be turning a blind eye to arts organizations who operate illegally and rarely enforce the law.[62] But in 1993, "the anti-granters" against Inside Out highlighted that the 1988 changes to the act was one way "special interest groups" were gaining access to taxpayer funding. In her statement to city council,[63] Diane Malott argued, "Is this grant fiasco, in fact, due to Metro staff? The director of the Cultural Affairs department, Kathleen Sharpe said that the Film Review Board reviewed all films shown at this homosexual movie festival. Everyone knows if you call anything a 'festival' you can bypass the censors. As a matter of fact, Asst. Director Allan Coleclough says they've never heard of this festival or any of the movies except one that was banned [*The Boys of St Vincent*]."[64]

Inside Out pushed back on council's decision to cancel funding with the help of a community that was all too familiar with fighting censorship. Spearheaded by Vtape's Colin Campbell, Lisa Steele, and Kim Tomczak, a letter also endorsed by Sky Gilbert, artistic director of Buddies in Bad Times Theatre, Steven Pozel, director of the Power Plant, and Helga Stephenson, executive director of the Festival of Festivals, was circulated to the 200 Toronto arts and culture organizations that received funding from the city. The letter appealed to funded organizations for a $20 donation from their own city-awarded grant monies to help restore Inside Out's $4,000. The gesture sought to support Inside Out while also sending a clear message to Metro Council that "the

Arts community is united in its opposition to any interference in the armlength evaluation and funding process for artists and art organization."[65] Along with the letter was a thorough information package, outlining the issues and the call to action not only to donate, but to do so publicly by signing and returning a tear-off note that would be delivered to Metro chairman Alan Tonks explaining the source of the donation and its support being not only for Inside Out, but the arm's length granting process itself.[66]

Despite the outpouring of support throughout the appeal process, including a supportive deputation by the ex-chairman of the Ontario Film Review Board, Inside Out did not have their funding reinstated for the 1994 festival.[67] They were, however, able to recoup the loss of the $4,000 through donations from Toronto arts organizations and community members. The collective took to the opening remarks of the 1994 festival program to publicly speak out against the ongoing homophobia, censorship, and attacks on freedom of expression:

> For some, the phrase "the public" denotes something belonging to others, something upon which lesbian and gay communities have no claim. By conceding the idea that the bounds of "good taste" are synonymous with what properly belongs to the public realm, we make it easy for those who view our communities and our sexualities as undeserving of public life to (re)assert such views. We must ask ourselves if we really want to support such a fragile notion of the public; whether the most repugnant acts are in fact those connected to sexuality or sexual self-expression at all; and, whether the public is something that can be owned by one group, to the exclusion of others. We might also ask ourselves whether we can afford to let our desire to be dignified, tasteful or respectable lead us to an acceptance of standards of obscenity and good taste that are currently fashioned by people who give themselves license to promote hate and use public forums such as Metro Council Chambers to refer to other citizens as "sodomizing pigs," and who have publicly called for "death to homosexuals."[68]

Inside Out continued to call on the community to write in support to reinstate the festival's funding for the 1995 iteration of the festival, and with the help of city councillor Olivia Chow, Inside Out's funding was eventually restored. But it was the last time an Inside Out Festival programme introduction opened with political venom.

In the years following the funding scare, there were major shifts made in the infrastructure of the festival. In 1996, Inside Out ceased to operate as a collective and a board of directors was introduced.[69] In the years following, the board included CEOs of Famous Players and the Ontario Film Development Corporation, both key players in the production and distribution of cinema in Ontario.[70] The transformation of Inside Out from a collective into an institutionalized organization is a well-beaten "path laid out by queer arts organizations in the U.S., which in the 1980s had begun to mimic government structures in order to clearly define accountability and thus reassure funding bodies that there was appropriate bureaucratic process in place to receive and responsibly allocate their monies."[71] It felt like a timely and safe move in the wake of Metro Council's funding ruling: Inside Out's professionalization would help to secure allies in high places and take on a neoliberal institutionalized structure in order to play by the rules of funders.

In 1997, the organization changed hands with festival coordinator (later festival director) Joanne Cormack leaving, and curator and artist Elle Flanders leading the organization under the new title of executive director. Program introductions shifted from a platform to speak out about issues facing the local queer community, to a focus on the festival itself, citing its accomplishments and building its capacity. The shift in focus was clearly geared towards the festival's longevity and ensuring it would never again face financial scarcity. The priorities became the festival's strategic planning, fundraising, and financial future. Flanders ushered in a new business model that leveraged corporate sponsorship to foster the growth of the festival into the mainstream in an effort to protect the queer space and community Inside Out had collectively created and publicly fought for. Smirnoff, Air Canada, AOL Canada, and Rogers Communications all came on board to help bolster the festival's visibility and boost box office earnings. By 1999 there were established tiers of sponsorship, including support by Holiday Inn, Show Case Television, Mastercard, Starbucks, and Volkswagen came on board in exchange for Inside Out helping these and other companies reach the "loyal gay consumer," as described in a sponsorship letter.[72] In the words of filmmaker and former Inside Out program coordinator and committee member Richard Fung, "In the neoliberal context festivals become increasingly like commercial television in the terms Raymond Williams described, delivering audiences to advertisers."[73]

These efforts to increase the growth and credibility of the festival through corporate sponsorship happened in tandem with the festival moving out of smaller exhibition spaces in the city. Inside Out occupied the Euclid Theatre (at both the Euclid and College locations), CineCycle, Buddies in Bad Times Theatre, the Metro Central YMCA, the John Spotton Cinema at the NFB, and the Art Gallery of Ontario's Jackman Hall. But under Flanders's direction the festival migrated into commercial venues including the Cumberland theatre in Yorkville in 1998 and in 1999, then the multi-screen Famous Players venue downtown at Richmond and John St, taking the festival further and further away from counterpublic safe spaces for queer and trans communities. According to Andersen's interview with Flanders, she argued that these advancements into the mainstream were still informed by a "radical political stance" in the way that the festival was confronting and queering commercial spaces and corporate brands.[74] Yet these sentiments and commitments to growth aided in the corporatization of queer culture.

On screens, the ratio of political and radical films being programmed gradually dissipated compared to its early years, as the festival grew in capacity and budget, making way for feature-length films with slick production values. Inside Out sought to become part of the larger queer festival circuit and began to speak the language of mainstream commercial film festivals vying for premiere status for feature-length queer films that were crossing over into the mainstream theatrical market. As Flanders's successor Scott Ferguson noted in his introduction to the 2006 festival, Hollywood by the mid-2000s had "embraced queer stories," and while these depictions were often normative and problematic in terms of representation, the depiction of queer life by mainstream culture had nonetheless arrived.[75] While Inside Out continued to make space in their programming for emerging queer filmmakers, the arrival of mainstream commercial LGBT cinema with its Hollywood production values became the centrepieces of the festival garnering large box office draws. Programming high-profile films bolstered the cachet of a mainstream festival experience, complete with premieres, pink carpets, galas, and afterparties catering to the international distribution market. Inside Out became a big gay corporate party – overshadowing the political site of resistance it had been for diverse communities of queers.

Inside Out's more recent branding has adopted a much softer political edge than the aspirations of the Inside Out Collective of the early 1990s. Under the leadership of Scott Ferguson (2001–15) and Andria Wilson (2016–20), Inside Out has attempted to balance out the festival's interest in being both a community screen and a major player in the mainstream festival circuit by reframing commercial and corporate industry involvement, centring their support for filmmakers and audience accessibility. In doing so the festival continues its interests in industry development through pitch competitions, film financing opportunities, and partnerships with OUTtv, Telefilm, and most recently, Netflix and Crave, for production and distribution support. Yet these access points of support and dissemination of queer content involve production and distribution models focused on higher production values to pull queer art out of its special interest market and into the mainstream. It is a double-edged sword that creates hierarchies of value tethered to a specific kind of legible commercial aesthetic, thereby opening the door for commercial interests on queer life and artmaking. It tames the rawness and messiness of queer life on the margins – if these modes of support manage to reach out that far.

Attending mainstream LGBT festivals like Inside Out has become a pleasurable lighthearted cinematic event where the simple act of viewing a queer film is about as politically charged as it gets. As Alexandra Chasin has argued, "consumption becomes a form of political participation, perhaps supplanting other, more direct, models of participation."[76] Thus the kind of spectatorship that is evoked by the consumption of mainstream and normative representations of queer experiences can create an environment of political complacency. By primarily programming mainstream films that mobilize normative storylines and modes of address, audiences are cheated out of access to cinema that challenges aesthetic forms and raises political awareness. Patricia White writes, "Dismissals of the vapid assimilationist values of the romantic comedies and coming-out stories that festivals are often obliged, [by economic and publicity demands], to highlight need to take into account viewers' varying cultural competences, their access to innovative forms."[77] Thus, there need to be alternative screens for alternative stories in order to regain politically active spectators. As Richard Fung notes, when one "programs a festival, one also programs the audience and the community."[78]

Conclusion

Fung also acknowledges the push towards commercial professionalization in a corporatized festival climate is a part of festivals responding to a shifting climate of media consumption, audience interests, and ambitious artistic development. "But it's important to stand back and take stock of the broader forces at work in these shifts. And to resist."[79] TQFF is one example of a grassroots counterbalance to this shift towards commercialization. Inside Out emerged amidst a boom of Toronto festivals in the early 1990s, many of which addressed the politics of representation in the city's cultural community. Its politics of representation were fraught not only on the greater cultural community stage facing censorship and funding precarity, but within fractured queer and trans communities. While its early mandate was to create a screen for transgressive "queer" experimental work, the parameters of representation, of which subjects would be valued, legitimized, and viewed, was and continues to be a charged debate that stretches beyond the realm of art and into lived experiences. Inside Out's early growth faced censorship and funding precarity that informed its formal institutionalization and commercialization, although there is a larger and more complex web of contexts and metahistories at play. While Inside Out's institutionalization led it to become a mainstream LGBT film festival in Canada that inevitably is implicated in propping up queer assimilationist politics and homonormativity, its contribution to the landscape of Toronto queer and trans art and culture is nonetheless significant. In its emergence Inside Out claimed a counterpublic and screen that was long overdue. In fighting censorship with the solidarity of the Toronto arts community, it helped to defend the boundaries of rights and freedoms of artistic expression – something TQFF and its programming still benefits from. In its emergence, conversations around the segregation of gay, lesbian, 2Spirit, bi, trans, and other queer identities, lives, and experiences could be explored and confronted. However fraught, this counterpublic opened up a space to have conversations and to push the boundaries of art, politics, and representation. Yet, Inside Out admittedly also wanted to grow into a "reputable" mainstream festival, modelling itself on the Festival of Festivals (TIFF), which was gaining momentum during the early 1990s. Aligning itself with a mainstream model early on to legitimize and also survive has resulted in the growth the festival has wanted to see. But as Christina Battle notes, "Time is essential in paving the way toward institutionalization, and with longevity can come a squelching of new ideas, risk taking, and experimentation, all of which are critical for remaining radical and progressive."[80] As Inside Out invests its screens in the mainstream, there is inevitably space on the margins for new voices to emerge, counteract, and occupy a position of radicality, continuing a healthy and responsive cycle of artmaking on the margins. The ecology of the artist-run communities relies on cycles of resurgence in order to thrive. But how does TQFF remain close to its initial mandate of radicality through an institutional restructuring that is at odds with the nature of bureaucracy? Can models of collectivity be integrated, as Battle suggests?

The counterpublic that emerges each year through TQFF is an example of what Svetla Turnin and Ezra Winton have called the "affective architecture" of an activist film festival. Affective architecture describes how a community gathers and is shaped by a shared experience that takes into consideration "a felt reality" through which the social structures that influence our cultural and ideological differences can emerge.[81] It is within this self-reflexive space that grassroots queer film festivals like TQFF can not only bring a criticality to on- and off-screen programming, but also consider the festival's own implication in the reproduction of power, which in turn determines who feels seen and welcomed to participate in the makeup of its affective architecture. The framework of affective architecture allows queer counterpublics to remain mindful of their own constructs, while also evoking Muñoz's notion of queer futurity. Working in a mode of self-reflexivity allows a community to situate its present to both the past and the future, or rather, the horizon where queerness exists, because "queerness is not yet here."[82] Looking beyond the "here and now" of normative time is an active and ongoing practice that counterpublics, including queer film festivals, must engage with in order to examine their effect and role within a community. It is a practice that considers the experiences of the past, in accord with aspirations for the future.

Active self-reflexivity might be one way in which TQFF can hold on to its roots in radicality over the course of its development. Time will tell. In some ways this chapter simply traces collective histories that echo some very familiar cycles that artist-run arts organizations in Canada struggle through. What I am interested in is how TQFF's trajectory will come to pass, and whether or not it will find a way to sustain radicality – remaining tuned in to what is happening on the margins while also balancing its relationship to funders and the structures of institutionalization, keeping its transgressive and experimental roots alive.

Notes

1 Inside Out LGBT Film Festival is the current name of the festival, though it has gone through a series of iterations that speak to its historical politics of representation and the evolution of media formats: Inside Out Lesbian and Gay Film and Video Festival of Toronto (1991); Inside Out Toronto Lesbian and Gay Film and Video Festival (1999); Inside Out Toronto LGBT Film and Video Festival (2009); Inside Out Toronto LGBT Film Festival (2011).

2 Thomas Waugh, *The Romance of Transgression in Canada: Queer Sexualities, Nations, Cinemas* (Montreal and Kingston: McGill-Queen's University Press, 2006), 5.
3 Ibid., 14.
4 Janelle MacDonald, "'Who Designed These Boxes Anyway?': Queer Film Festivals in Canada: The Economics and Politics of Queer Space" (master's thesis, Carleton University 2006), 15–16.
5 Canada Council for the Arts, "A Statistical Profile of Artists in Canada in 2016," 27 November 2019, https://canadacouncil.ca/research/research-library/2019/03/a-statistical-profile-of-artists-in-canada-in-2016.
6 [6] Lisa Duggan, "The New Homonormativity: The Sexual Politics of Neoliberalism," in *Materializing Democracy: Toward a Revitalized Cultural Politics*, eds. Russ Castronovo and Dana D. Nelson (Durham: Duke University Press 2002), 179.
7 Jonathan Petrychyn, "The Queer Film Festival Quandary," *the briarpatch*, 1 April 2017, https://briarpatchmagazine.com/articles/view/the-queer-film-festival-quandary.
8 Skadi Loist, "Precarious Cultural Work: About the Organization of (Queer) Film Festivals," *Screen* 52, no. 2 (2011): 273.
9 TQFF is made up of IBPOC, trans, 2Spirit, and cis-white queer folks. I was a co-founding member but left the organization in March of 2019. This chapter is written from my personal perspective, and is from the position of a white bi/queer cis woman without a visible disability, and consciously navigating the inherent privilege this position holds. This chapter does not stand in for or represent the work that TQFF does as a whole. The opinions here are my own, and not those of TQFF. While this may seem like an odd or somewhat formal way forward, this preface comes from a place of deep sincerity and respect for an organization that I am proud I could be a part of, and admiration for the work TQFF continues to do.
10 José Esteban Muñoz, *Cruising Utopia: The Then and There of Queer Futurity* (New York: New York University Press, 2009), 1.
11 Ibid., 22.
12 Ibid.
13 Ibid., 1.
14 Christina Battle, "Distributed Systems and the Collective Model for the Media Arts Network of Ontario," in *Other Places: Reflections on Media Arts in Canada*, ed. Deanna Bowen (Toronto: Media Arts Network of Ontario, 2019), 297.
15 Ibid.
16 Ibid., 290.
17 Ibid., 291.
18 Ibid., 295.

19　Ibid., 291.
20　Chris Dupuis, "How One Local Festival Wants to Bring Queer Back to Toronto," *Xtra*, 21 June 2016, https://www.dailyxtra.com/how-one-local-festival-wants-to-bring-queer-back-to-toronto-71318.
21　The ArQuives (formerly the Canadian Lesbian and Gay Archives) are Canada's LGBTQ2+ archive. Founded in Toronto in 1973, the ArQuives are currently the largest independent LGBTQ2+ archive in the world. See https://arquives.ca.
22　Trish Salah, "Notes towards Thinking Transsexual Institutional Poetics," in *Trans/acting Culture, Writing, and Memory Essays in Honour of Barbara Godard*, ed. Eva C. Karpinski, Jennifer Henderson, Ian Sowton, and Ray Ellenwood (Canada: Wilfrid Laurier Press, 2012), 172.
23　Inside Out program guide from 1993 quoted in Viviane Namaste, *Invisible Lives: The Erasure of Transsexual and Transgendered People* (Chicago: University of Chicago Press, 2000), 12.
24　Namaste, *Invisible Lives*, 12–13.
25　Ibid., 13.
26　Ibid., 12–13.
27　Correspondence to Inside Out, "TS/TG Issues with Inside Out," February 1999, Box 5, Folder F0096-03-51, Inside/OUT Collective fonds, The ArQuives, Toronto, Ontario, Canada.
28　Ibid.
29　Ibid., Box 5, Folder F0096-03-5.
30　Mirha-Soleil Ross, "Counting Past 2, Background and Objectives" (Counting Past 2 website, 2000), quoted in Salah, "Notes towards Thinking," 173.
31　Salah, "Notes towards Thinking," 174.
32　Ibid., 174.
33　Ibid., 174–5.
34　Ibid., 177.
35　As Trish Salah mentions in her essay, "Notes towards Thinking Transsexual Institutional Poetics," while the website of Counting Past 2 is no longer online, one can still access it through the Internet Archive's (archive.org) Wayback Machine. Search http://www.countingpast2.com for more details on the festival's mandate, organizers, programming, and sponsorship.
36　Mirha-Soleil Ross, "Counting Past 2, Background and Objectives," http://www.countingpast2.com.
37　Salah, "Notes towards Thinking," 181.
38　Joceline Andersen, "From the Ground Up: Transforming the Inside Out LGBT Film and Video Festival of Toronto," *Revue Canadienne d'Études cinématographiques/Canadian Journal of Film Studies* 21, no. 1 (2012): 40.
39　Ibid., 40.

40　Tom Warner, "Queer Community Standards and Queer Spaces," in *Never Going Back: A History of Queer Activism in Canada* (Toronto: University of Toronto Press 2002), 266.
41　Tom Warner, "Between Queer and the Mainstream," in *Never Going Back*, 334.
42　"The Inside Out Collective History," 1993, Box 1, Folder F0096-01-01, Inside/OUT Collective fonds, the ArQuives, Toronto, Ontario, Canada.
43　Ibid.
44　Andersen, "From the Ground Up," 40.
45　Ibid., 43.
46　Tom Warner, "Queer Community Standards," 266.
47　In 1987, Donald Butler of Winnipeg, MB, was arrested twice for illegally selling pornographic videos, magazines, and toys in violation of the Criminal Code. He was initially charged with 250 counts of selling obscene material, but the judge lowered the charges to eight counts, arguing that some of the content was protected as freedom of expression under the Canadian Charter of Rights and Freedoms. Anti-pornography feminists protested the ruling, demanding a retrial, which was reviewed by the Supreme Court of Canada. Women's groups presented testimony to demonstrate how socially harmful pornography can be, regardless of freedom of expression. In 1992 the Supreme Court ruled in favour of banning pornography, complicating censorship law and freedom of expression in Canada. It was an anti-pornography victory, but compromised freedom of sexual expression, which directly affected the queer community. For a more in-depth look into how the Butler decision affected the queer community, see Tom Warner's *Never Going Back* (2002) and *Bad Attitude/s on Trial: Pornography, Feminism, and the Butler Decision*, eds. Brenda Cossman, Shannon Bell, Lise Gotell, and Becki L. Ross (Toronto: University of Toronto Press, 1997).
48　Warner, "Queer Community Standards," 270.
49　Ibid.
50　Inside Out 1993 Program Guide, page 1, https://www.insideout.ca/uploads/HISTORY/guide%201993.pdf.
51　Ibid, 3.
52　"Cultural Grants Debate, Metro Council 29/03/93," 1993, Box 25, Folder F0096-06-01, Inside/OUT Collective fonds, the ArQuives, Toronto, Ontario, Canada.
53　Ibid.
54　Ibid.
55　"Hands around Metro," 1993, Box 25, Folder F0096-06-04, Inside/OUT Collective fonds, the ArQuives, Toronto, Ontario, Canada.
56　"News Coverage and Transcripts," July 1993, Box 25, Folder F0096-06-03, Inside/OUT Collective fonds, the ArQuives, Toronto, Ontario, Canada.
57　Ibid.

58 Ibid.
59 Taryn Sirove, "Truce or Compromise? Censorship, Media Regulation, and Exhibiting Policies in Ontario," in *Explosion in the Movie Machine: Essays and Documents on Toronto Artists' Film and Video*, ed. Chris Gehman (Toronto: Images Festival, Liaison of Independent Filmmakers of Toronto, and YYZ, 2013), 153–4.
60 "Statement of Unity," in Gehman, *Explosion in the Movie Machine*, 171.
61 Taryn Sirove, "Truce or Compromise?," 153–4.
62 See Sirove's example of Pleasure Dome, who openly operated illegally, in "Truce or Compromise," 155.
63 "Cultural Grants Debate, Metro Council 29/03/93," 1993, Box 25, Folder F0096-06-01, Inside/OUT Collective fonds, the ArQuives, Toronto, Ontario, Canada.
64 *The Boys of St Vincent*, a CBC and NFB co-production, was shown at Inside Out in 1993. The film was restricted from television broadcast due to a pending court case, but was made available to festivals for screening. "Appeal from the Inside Out Collective," 18 November 1993, Box 26, Folder F0096-06-10, Inside/OUT Collective fonds, the ArQuives, Toronto, Ontario, Canada.
65 "IOC Emergency: Funding Cut Information," 1993, Box 25, Folder F0096-06-05, Inside/OUT Collective fonds, the ArQuives, Toronto, Ontario, Canada.
66 Ibid.
67 "Metro Management Committee," Box 26, Folder F0096-06-10, Inside/OUT Collective fonds, the ArQuives, Toronto, Ontario, Canada.
68 Inside Out 1994 Program Guide, page 3, https://www.insideout.ca/uploads/HISTORY/guide%201994.pdf.
69 Inside Out 1996 Program Guide, page 2, https://www.insideout.ca/uploads/HISTORY/guide%201996.pdf.
70 Andersen, "From the Ground Up," 44.
71 Ibid.
72 Ibid., 46, 48.
73 Richard Fung, "We Like to Watch: Toronto's Passion for Film Festivals," in Gehman, *Explosion in the Movie Machine*, 148.
74 Andersen, "From the Ground Up," 47.
75 Inside Out 2006 Program Guide, page 5, https://www.insideout.ca/uploads/HISTORY/guide%202006.pdf.
76 Alexandra Chasin, *Selling Out: The Gay and Lesbian Movement Goes to Market* (New York: St Martin's Press, 2000), 24.
77 Patricia White, "Introduction: On Exhibitionism," in "Queer Publicity: A Dossier on Lesbian and Gay Film Festivals," *GLQ: A Journal of Lesbian and Gay Studies* 5, no. 1 (1999): 75–6.

78 Richard Fung, "Programming the Public," in "Queer Publicity: A Dossier on Lesbian and Gay Film Festivals," GLQ: A Journal of Lesbian and Gay Studies 5, no. 1 (1999): 89–93.
79 Fung, "We Like to Watch," 149.
80 Battle, "Distributed Systems," 291.
81 Ezra Winton and Svetla Turnin, "The Revolution Will Not Be Festivalized: Documentary Film Festivals and Activism," in *Activist Film Festivals: Towards a Political Subject*, eds. Sonia Tascón and Tyson Wils (Chicago: University of Chicago Press, 2017), 88.
82 Muñoz, *Cruising Utopia*, 1.

From Showcase to Lightbox
Programming the National on the Festival Circuit

Diane Burgess

The rise of Canadian art cinema in the decade and a half leading up to 2000 has been attributed, at least in part, to the concurrent growth of a vibrant film festival sector, from Geoff Pevere's assertion of the integral role of Perspective Canada at the Festival of Festivals (later TIFF) in the coalescence of the Toronto New Wave[1] to my discussion of the Vancouver International Film Festival's showcasing of the Pacific New Wave.[2] Brenda Longfellow also has argued for the "instrumental role" of Cannes in focusing international attention on English-Canadian auteurs like Patricia Rozema, Atom Egoyan, and Don McKellar.[3] From a federal policy perspective, Telefilm Canada supported access to international events and markets, as well as institutional development in the domestic sphere. In the domestic context, a confluence of festival programming, cultural policy initiatives, and a burgeoning domestic circuit contributed to the circulation of critical capital associated with ideas of Canadian national cinema.[4]

However, by the early 2000s, domestic festival proliferation was reaching an apex that would raise questions about sustainability. At the same time, major Canadian festivals had established year-round organizational footprints and achieved institutional maturity as they began to venture further into non-festival-season exhibition. In this chapter, I will explore the changing role of film festivals in English-Canadian cinema post-2000, with a particular focus on their institutional presence both as nodes in national and international circuits, and as gatekeepers in critical debates about cinematic value.[5] A necessary first step in understanding the Canadian film festival landscape involves unpacking some slippery terminology related to how festivals are defined in the context of their connections to the global film industry, local film communities, and the circulation of national film culture.

Defining the Industry Festival

The showcasing of Canadian films at international and domestic festivals has played a key role in both the marketing of cultural products and in the branding of national cinema at home and abroad. Although cultural capital (and the variant, critical capital) points to the shared recognition (by critics, scholars, and audiences) of a film's aesthetic value, festival circulation also impacts a film's potential economic value through the accumulation of symbolic capital. A useful distinction can be made between a broad class of festivals that survey the annual cinematic output of the world's film industries (industry festivals)[6] and themed or special interest film festivals that present niche programming (specialized festivals). In the Canadian context, the industry festivals play an intermediary role in the film industry value chain as sites for product exposure and marketing prior to commercial release. Even though TIFF is the only Canadian film festival with a market presence comparable to a major international event like Cannes, other international survey festivals, such as the Atlantic Film Festival or the Vancouver International Film Festival, serve as significant regional hubs for industry stakeholders, providing opportunities for networking and professional development, while also giving awards to local films and filmmakers. Specialized festivals tend to focus more on community building and audience access than on competing against major industry festivals to secure premiere screenings. In Vancouver alone, examples of specialized festivals include the Vancouver Queer Film Festival (Out on Screen), Vancouver Asian Film Festival (VAFF), Rendez-vous de cinéma québécois et francophone de Vancouver, European Union Film Festival, Vancouver International Mountain Film Festival, and the Vancouver International Women in Film Festival.

In her hierarchical typology of the film festival world, Skadi Loist explains that "after a top-tier festival premiere, a film will further trickle down second- and third-tier events and simultaneously move along the multiplicity of rhizomatic channels of parallel thematic circuits."[7] Loist's model draws attention to the significance of premieres in setting a film's initial value, which is to a certain extent inextricably linked to the festival's perceived value as a "symbolic banker."[8] But her typology also highlights the role of the circuits and networks that are formed.

Arguably, as evidenced in the examples from the beginning of this chapter, it is the initial articulation with top-tier festival circulation that influences canon formation for national cinema. Whether on an international stage at Cannes or a national one at TIFF, it is the context of the showcase – especially the proximity to a major industry festival – that informs the relative symbolic and cultural value of films on festival circuits. In addition to positioning national cinema in a cosmopolitan context of other cinema classifications, circuit connection to a top-tier festival draws significant attention from buyers, critics, and audiences. At specialized festivals, the context of the showcase narrows, but shared attention remains significant.

An additional useful distinction can be made based on the balancing of an industry trade forum with public screenings. For example, the current iteration of the Banff World Media Festival (formerly the Banff Television Festival) lacks a showcase or screening event for their Rockie Awards competition, but instead provides industry delegates with conference-style sessions, networking events, and an awards gala. The expectation that festivals contribute to developing industry capacity has long been rooted in federal funding guidelines that stressed their role as a "springboard" and later specifically added "professional impact" to the evaluation framework.[9] Access also comprised a fundamental goal of federal support – one that the Canada Showcase guidelines assessed in terms of presentation and public engagement, but that would later become increasingly attached to cinema audiences. The genesis of the Banff Television Festival was an International Feature Film Festival organized in conjunction with Edmonton's 1978 hosting of the Commonwealth Games and intended as a one-off event.[10] The following year, with support from the Festival Office of the Canadian Film Development Corporation (later Telefilm Canada) and the Banff Centre, the organizers launched a festival focused on made-for-TV movies (by 1981, their focus had shifted fully to television programming).[11] In Telefilm's annual reports, Canada Showcase lauded the Banff Television Festival as one of the country's "major national events" (along with the Montreal World Film Festival, Toronto International Film Festival, and Vancouver International Film Festival). However, by the 2004 Secor Report, Banff was no longer listed with the major film festivals.

The early 2000s saw a series of changes to federal festival support that were connected both to Secor Consulting's study of Canada's four major film festivals, as well as to corporate restructuring at Telefilm, which included a separate policy review of investment in the domestic festival sector. One of the review documents prepared for Telefilm includes the clarification that support for television festivals involved an internal "transfer of funds" to Canada Showcase since the program was technically financed as part of the Canada Feature Film Fund (CFFF).[12] This distinction between television and film festivals appears to focus predominantly on the public audience (specifically, the cinema audience targeted in the CFFF's box office objective), given that the Secor Report repeatedly mentions that VIFF's trade forum serves both film and television professionals. The model of a film festival as springboard plus access is reinforced in the summative policy review document, which included the recommendation that festivals with audiences "comprised wholly of trade professionals" be excluded from Canada Showcase.[13] While the policy review of the early 2000s sought to streamline support for a sector that had grown rapidly through the late 1980s and 1990s, it also marked the final stage of an industrial turn in Telefilm's domestic festival support. As part of the CFFF, Canada Showcase briefly mirrored the performance measurement focus of Telefilm's production investments before shifting to a perspective on access that would increasingly associate domestic festival audiences with the spread of cultural capital.

A Changing Policy Field

Before these changes, the potential connections between film production and a growing festival circuit, expressed in earlier iterations of the script-to-screen policy framework, invite an Innis-esque analogy to the birth of the railroad. A domestic film festival circuit could forge connections across Canada's vast geography, while simultaneously fending off the threat of American cultural annexation. This analogy fits with the widely held view of festivals as an "alternative distribution network" that serves to counteract Hollywood's stranglehold on mainstream theatrical screens.[14] It also brings to mind Thomas Elsaesser's description of the festival circuit as a "motor" that both drives and sustains European cinema.[15] However, these analogies place the focus on how festival circuits impact the circulation of films, rather than on the mechanisms by which individual organizations interconnect. As Dina Iordanova has argued, festivals must be seen as discrete exhibition sites that collaborate, often reluctantly, in order to manage rather complicated supply chain needs.[16] Thus, proliferation on the fall circuit can be understood in terms of new events stepping into the flows of films, guests, and even buzz in order to bring the festival experience to their local audiences. For example, when the Calgary International Film Festival launched in 2000, their scheduling overlap with the beginning of VIFF created the potential for westward itineraries on the fall domestic circuit to add a brief stopover.

The bulk of Telefilm's support for domestic festivals was allocated through the Canada Showcase program and was aligned with the Crown corporation's overarching objectives of building both audiences and industry capacity in Canada. In 1999, the program was transferred from Communications and Public Affairs to the Operations department in recognition of an "increasingly pivotal" role for Canadian festivals in "the business plans of Telefilm's regional offices."[17] Between 2002 and 2005, Canada Showcase provided approximately $7.4 million in grants (ranging from $3,000 to $550,000) to fifty-two festivals.[18] Increased pressure on public funding resources, particularly from the growing number of smaller festivals, led Telefilm to consider a two-tiered approach that would distinguish between events of "national or regional relevance" and "local, culturally specific and emerging events."[19] Contemporaneous with these developments was a failed effort by federal and provincial public funding agencies to intervene in the Montreal festival sector by diverting their support away from the World Film Festival.

As I have argued elsewhere, "the untenable festival traffic jam and the failure of the new [Montreal] event selected for funding provide little positive support for Telefilm's initial efforts to take a proactive role with the domestic festival circuit."[20] It was evidently too late for public partners to step in as arbiters for the domestic festival sector, as the established festivals had already developed sufficient institutional autonomy to withstand pressure from a single stakeholder group. In *Take One*'s coverage of Montreal's 2005 trio of major festivals, Maurie Alioff captured some of the stakeholder infighting that ultimately led to the demise of the New Montreal FilmFest (Festival International de Films de Monréal), the event that had been "intended to wipe Losique off the map."[21] Despite the loss of funding support, Serge Losique's Montreal World Film Festival persisted, while the New FilmFest's program director Moritz de Hadeln (former festival director at Berlin and Venice) publicly squabbled with his event's organizers (L'Équipe Spectra).[22] Prior to imploding in a series of staff dismissals and board resignations, the New FilmFest courted a merger with the Festival du nouveau cinéma, and as 2005 drew to a close, Alioff noted that many were calling for either a government inquiry or another government-funded festival study.[23]

In 2008, Telefilm shifted film festival funding away from the production stream of the Canada Feature Film Fund with the creation of the Festivals Performance Program, which provided stable funding for established Canadian festivals with feature film audiences in excess of 100,000, and the competitive Skills and Screens Program. A few years later in 2012, Skills and Screens was replaced by the Promotions Program. The gist of the revised guidelines for smaller festivals was a narrowed definition of access that shifted from building industry capacity to serving diverse communities. Within this framework, the smaller, specialized, or emerging film festivals were seen less as networking hubs for industry professionals, and more as conduits for reaching public audiences. By 2015, domestic festival support was consolidated into one overarching Promotions Program, alongside national awards ceremonies, alternative distribution networks, conferences, and other promotional activities. In the program's objectives, promotion is discussed in terms of "public awareness" and "regional access."[24] Although the idea of complementary distribution networks (as a potential alternative to the traditional theatrical distributor-exhibitor model) has had a long history in Canadian feature film policy, by 2015, it would be fully cleft from modes of exhibition that comprise production revenue streams. In 2018, Telefilm introduced a Theatrical Exhibition Program to support the release of Canadian films in Canadian theatres.

Telefilm's newly rationalized program structure clearly distinguishes between the promotional role of a festival screening and the commercial revenue stream of theatrical exhibition. This clear separation, along with the addition of exhibition support, points to the potential for strengthening domestic box office share while removing the implication that film festivals could boost market presence as an alternative distribution circuit. However, this clarification also imposes a rigid view of the value chain that avoids the question of whether the pre-release accumulation of symbolic capital on the international festival circuit differs from the promotion of public awareness. In other words, if the acquisitions-related activities on the international festival circuit impact symbolic value, how do the industry festivals on the domestic circuit influence the gatekeeping decisions of distributors? If festival development is encouraged at a lower tier of specialized festivals, then what does this mean for the industry showcasing of national cinemas? The movement of Canadian cinema into specialized festival spaces – exemplified in the rise of National Canadian Film Day – has perhaps most significantly occurred with TIFF's Canada's Top Ten touring festival.

TIFF as Gatekeeper: Canada's Top Ten Film Festival

For almost two decades – from 2001 to 2018 – Canada's Top Ten Film Festival would begin its run in January, initially at Cinematheque Ontario (in Jackman Hall at the Art Gallery of Ontario) until the 2010 opening of TIFF Bell Lightbox. Based on an annual top-ten list (released each December by the Toronto Film Festival Group), this touring festival featured Canadian films that either had a commercial release or screened at a major film festival in Canada the previous year. At their fall festival, TIFF retired their national cinema program Perspective Canada in 2004, and its replacements, which showcased first features and short films, were folded into international programming in 2011 and 2015 respectively. In each instance, TIFF cited pressure from filmmakers who characterized the national sidebars as "ghettoized" when "Canadian cinema is strong enough to swim in international waters."[25] Indeed, in her 2004 article about "Film Festivals, Programming, and the Building of a National Cinema," former Perspective Canada programmer Liz Czach asked whether "a dissolution of a national cinema series [is] the ultimate sign of success."[26] But this prompts the question: whose success? Was shutting off the festival's national spotlight a signal of the strength of the filmmakers, or did it perhaps say more about the shifting values of TIFF as an A-list event that had attained global status?

In the lead-up to the construction of Bell Lightbox, the Toronto International Film Festival Group increasingly positioned their organization in global (rather than national) terms – from a programming vision statement about "lead[ing] the world in creative and cultural discovery through the moving image" to the designation of the planned film centre as a "global landmark."[27] Of course, all of this was happening in the broader context of rising neoliberalism, Toronto's growth as a global city, and TIFF's efforts to leverage funding for their new facilities. And I'm not trying to suggest that Canadian filmmakers were not strong enough to "swim in international waters;"[28] indeed, Canadian cinema at the turn of the millennium had a robust international profile thanks to the rise of auteurs who gained recognition on the A-list international festival circuit. Instead, it is important to acknowledge the tendency to downplay (or even elide) the politics of festival programming in favour of a focus on some inherent qualities of the films themselves.

In her discussion of film festival programming, Roya Rastegar nods indirectly to ongoing debates about the absence of women directors at Cannes when she asserts that the program homogeneity of industry-based film festivals is "a limitation imposed by notions of taste and aesthetics operating within the curatorial process."[29] In her assessment, it is misleading for festivals to disavow their curatorial role by placing the focus on "universal problems [in the industry] that their festival is not responsible for."[30] Similarly, in the Canadian context, the retirement of Perspective Canada needs to be seen as a curatorial problem that TIFF was solving. Elsewhere in her article, Czach cites Ruby Rich's observation that "the suspicion of any agenda – political or national – is seen to interfere with the magical and utterly unsubstantiated notion of quality."[31] Consequently, for a national showcase like Perspective Canada, the criteria for selection can appear to prioritize diversity and representation over quality, thus potentially undermining the critical value associated with being programmed at a prestigious industry festival.

Rather than dispersing in the afterglow of Perspective Canada's successful retirement, the canonical impulses associated with programming Canadian cinema, along with the spotlight's celebratory energy, shifted to the Top Ten Film Festival. According to the website, TIFF established Canada's Top Ten Film Festival to "[celebrate] and [promote] contemporary Canadian cinema and [to raise] awareness of Canadian achievements in film."[32] It is not to be confused with the Top Ten Canadian Films of All Time – the rankings compiled by TIFF approximately every ten years since 1984 when the festival's first Ten Best list accompanied the Northern Lights retrospective and the launch of Perspective Canada.[33] The Top Ten List emerges from TIFF's polling of critics, academics, and industry professionals (about 100 for the 1984 list, and 200 for the 2015 ranking) whereas the Top Ten Festival program (an alphabetized, unranked list) was finalized by a jury. There is some additional murkiness in that "See the North" was part of the Top Ten Festival's promotional logline and also refers to a program of new Canadian films that tours the US (organized by Telefilm in partnership with TIFF). And, Perspective Canada is the name of the curated program of market screenings that Telefilm organizes on the international film festival circuit. This tangle of repeated names either points to serendipitously sloppy brand management (that amplifies more than it confuses) or perhaps highlights the tenacious presence of TIFF as a thought leader when it comes to Canadian cinema. Interestingly, TIFF trademarked the name Canada's Top Ten Film Festival.

Speaking of names, Canada's Top Ten became more of a programming gimmick than a description of the actual festival. The 2018 edition included ten features, ten shorts, and ten student shorts, along with a special screening of *Bethune*, and an Open Vault free screening.[34] In fact, Canada's Top Ten Film Festival eventually resembled a mini-TIFF, with an industry forum, a couple of "In Conversation With ..." one-on-one interviews, and a People's Choice Award. It even ran for ten days. After the ten-day event in January at Bell Lightbox, some of the films embarked on a Canadian tour to seven major cities over the course of the spring. Despite the website's promotional reference to a "nationwide tour," the festival did not travel any farther east than Montreal or any farther north than Edmonton. In addition, the Montreal screenings at the Phi Centre clearly targeted English-speaking audiences, as French-language films were shown with English subtitles and English language films were shown without subtitles.[35] Thus, it is important to note that the invocation of the national in Canada's Top Ten focused on an English-Canadian construction of a "national" cinema canon.

There was certainly a benefit to the timing and attention afforded by having the Top Ten Festival scheduled during the winter. These films could gain renewed attention once they were separated from the frenzy of the fall festival (with its heightened focus on award season launches), and the timing could help to bridge attention momentum to a commercial launch (as Canadian films tended to be released in mainstream theatres in the spring). In this way, Canada's Top Ten Festival promoted access to national cinema in a form of TIFF outreach that is reminiscent of the Film Circuit. Founded in 1989, the Film Circuit comprises a grassroots network that facilitates access to both international and Canadian films in communities across Canada.[36] In their research on the Film Circuit, Claudia Sicondolfo and Wendy Donnan refer to TIFF's role as an intermediary between the regions, the distributors, and the exhibitors – a role for which they receive federal funding support.[37] There are a couple of key insights that emerge from considering the Top Ten Festival in the context of TIFF's outreach programs. First, Sicondolfo and Donnan note that there has been little outreach from TIFF in recent years to attract new Film Circuit partners; based on their interviews, they argue that one reason for the Film Circuit's stalled growth is that the arrival of Bell Lightbox necessitated funding cuts to "accommodate for the expenses of the new infrastructure."[38]

Sicondolfo and Donnan further assert that TIFF emerges as a powerful cultural and economic gatekeeper, a position that is solidified by the extent to which "the need for access sustains [exhibitors and distributors] within a circuit that upholds TIFF's dominance."[39] This pattern can also be seen with the Top Ten Film Festival, as local art house cinemas present event-driven content while piggybacking on TIFF's marketing campaign and brand recognition. From a programming perspective, TIFF's re-curation of national cinema highlights was a double-edged sword for Canadian film. Of course, films stood to benefit from the program's timing and the potential to generate interest and accessibility – two qualities that are often mentioned in association with Top Ten lists (both in terms of reaching audiences, but also as a precondition for getting on that list in the first place). Since eligibility for the Top Ten Festival required that the film had already had a commercial or major festival screening, the result was the creation of a second gate, or perhaps more accurately a funnel, as the number of films chosen for the spotlight series was a narrow subset of those that cleared a first hurdle. An unfortunate by-product of this model is that it even further disadvantages films that did not screen at a major Canadian festival: How does an individual indie film reach audiences when local art houses rely on event-driven programs that are, in effect, touring festivals organized by TIFF?

In addition to considering TIFF's increasing presence as a gatekeeper for national cinema, it is necessary to explore the implications for canon formation. Rastegar draws a useful distinction within the work of film festival programming, between editorial and curatorial processes.[40] The editorial aspect of programming involves culling a small number of festival selections from hundreds (or, in the case of A-list festivals, thousands) of submissions. Czach also has mentioned the "sheer volume" of vetting in her discussion of the affective labour of festival programming, noting the exhausting reality of "[wading] through many hours of mostly mediocre work to stumble upon the rare outstanding film."[41] She even crunched the TIFF Fact Sheet numbers to point out that, in 2013, "filmmakers had an approximately 7 percent chance of getting a film into TIFF."[42] For the second aspect of programming, Rastegar refers to the origins of "curate," from the Latin "to care," and its eighteenth-century use to describe a "spiritual guide" or cleric.[43] She explains that, in today's context, curators "build the framework in which audiences see and engage with artwork in such a way that can resonate within broader cultural, political, and social contexts."[44] Programmers, in their role as curators, are able to spot trends, and potentially to challenge norms, as they mediate between filmmakers and festival stakeholders, "each with their own approach to valuing films."[45]

For Canada's Top Ten Film Festival, the selection framework suggests a focus on editing over curation, as the programmers appear to avoid having to confront the unforgiving terrain of Canadian cinema. In addition, the final selection was made by a jury. What this means is that the programmers seemed to eschew their curatorial role in favour of allowing the annual highlights to be determined by a panel of experts. Of course, it is important to remember that the pool of potential entries comprised films that were already programmed at major festivals; but despite TIFF's annual press release about their Canadian slate, the absence of a cohesive Perspective Canada program seems to shut down meaningful dialogue about the politics of selection. In the CBC's coverage of Canadian highlights at TIFF 2017, Leah Collins noted that "you'd have better luck winning Roll Up the Rim than you would weeding out the Canadian features from this year's TIFF schedule."[46] In his 2010 *Globe and Mail* coverage of TIFF's CanCon contingent, Liam Lacey observed that retiring Perspective Canada had "[discouraged] ... viewing Canadian cinema as a genre with certain themes ... [in favour of] seeing it as a fairly arbitrary category."[47] After that comment, Lacey proceeded to divide the features between "French Quebec and the rest of Canada," to poke fun at the "hopeful exclamation mark" of the Canada First! program, and then to divvy up the shorts quantitatively by region.[48] The persistence of old categories and the ongoing presence of insider references to taste suggest that it is not necessarily easy to navigate the shift in understanding canon formation when the idea of nation is banished from national cinema.

The 2018 trailer for the Top Ten Festival entices viewers to "See the North in a new light," after presenting a montage of film clips that offers a vision of Canadian cinema as a genre – diversity, animation, landscape, darker themes.[49] The 2017 trailer presents a similar montage, accompanied by Canadian artist Charlotte Cardin's bluesy "Dirty Dirty."[50] With the chorus riff, "And I will wash off all the dirty, dirty thoughts I had about you," the resulting double entendres bring to mind Katherine Monk's *Weird Sex and Snowshoes*; this 2002 book was adapted into a documentary, directed by Jill Sharpe, which plumbed the question of how to define Canadian cinema. Since none of the individual films in the festival trailers are explicitly identified, the invitation to #SeetheNorth marks the culmination of a shift from building a national cinema to branding. It is less about what constitutes Canadian cinema than it is about the surface idea of national cinema. The use of lumberjack plaid as a backdrop (similar to the antlered mascot of National Canadian Film Day) evokes a nostalgic idea of Canada (but also one that is evacuated of any troubling political complexity). In 2004, Czach noted that "programming decisions amount to an argument about what defines that field, genre, or national cinema."[51] Citing the decision to open Perspective Canada in 1996 with Deepa Mehta's *Fire*, Czach further explained that film festival programming could contest paradigms and "work to define and redefine the concept of nation itself."[52] Aside

Figure 19.1 The red and black checks of lumberjack plaid provide the backdrop for the Canada's Top Ten Film Festival trailer in a promotional tweet from TIFF that invites audiences to #SeeTheNorth.

from the narrow scope of Canada's Top Ten and the elision of critical dialogue about canon formation, another concern about the touring festival is the silencing of local art house curation, with TIFF positioned as a powerful gatekeeper for Canadian cinema culture.

In 2018, the Top Ten Festival ditched jury selection and was instead curated in-house by TIFF's programming staff. Interestingly, this was not mentioned in the press release nor in the review essay posted on TIFF's website.[53] Penned by "Staff," the review is a hybrid blending of a programmer's essay that shifts partway through into the promotional voice of a press release. The essay sets the context for the top Canadian films of 2017 in relation to Telefilm's increased support of first- and second-time filmmakers through a newly revamped Talent to Watch program and Cameron Bailey's January editorial in the *Globe and Mail* calling on filmmakers to tell Canadian stories. This background is followed by senior programmer Steve Gravestock's assessment that this year's selection "champions talent from across Canada ... [and] perfectly showcases the range of genres that Canadian filmmakers are exploring."[54] Half of the ten features in the program "are from first- or second-time filmmakers with a strong presence from female and Indigenous artists."[55] Coverage of the announcement pointed out notable exclusions, like

Long Time Running and *The Breadwinner*. Peter Howell of the *Toronto Star* noted that Denis Villeneuve's *Blade Runner 2049* was American, and that Sarah Polley and Jean-Marc Vallée had been working in television (on *Alias Grace* and *Big Little Lies*), leading him to conclude that "it may just be that they've graduated beyond the admittedly narrow confines of Canada's Top Ten Film Festival"[56] – an assessment that echoes the arguments that were made against Perspective Canada almost a decade before.

By 2019, the January festival had been dropped as the showcase of the previous year's "essential Canadian films" in favour of a new Canada's Top Ten Theatrical Series.[57] The 2018 list was still announced in early December, but the ten feature films now would be given the opportunity for a theatrical run at TIFF's Bell Lightbox over the course of the year. This modified approach points to a trade-off between festival buzz and increased theatrical screen time, or as film critic Peter Howell explained it, "losing a little champagne ... and other hoopla"[58] – a concession that raises age-old questions about what drives audience access to national cinema.[59] Howell described the retirement of the Top Ten Festival as "an advance disguised as a retreat," noting that the features would get "roughly three times more viewings" in a week-long Lightbox release as well as the "significantly increase[d] ... likelihood" of a full review.[60] In contrast, films screened at festivals tend to receive only capsule-sized reviews with full coverage held for the theatrical launch. The week-long theatrical run in Toronto also would contribute to eligibility for the Canadian Screen Awards, whose 2020 regulations required a minimum seven-day commercial theatrical run in two different major cities.[61] In an interview about the changes, TIFF co-head Cameron Bailey mentioned both award eligibility and the expectation "from funding agencies that want to see that you had a release for your feature film."[62] As a result, the new Theatrical Series could alleviate pressure points in feature film distribution, while still generating much-needed symbolic capital. For Howell, the "retreat" presented by the retirement of the showcase appears to be connected to the Top Ten Film Festival's recent struggles with "plateaued" attendance.[63] But, when it comes to attracting viewers, it is not clear whether the changes will offset the attention that a festival can generate. Filmmaker Andrew Cividino (*Sleeping Giant*) deems the exhibition access a "net positive," but notes that he "will miss the festival atmosphere" and wonders whether the collective attention "can sustain itself while being so diffusely spread across the calendar year."[64]

Beyond the impact of Canada's Top Ten on the gatekeeping of canon formation in the national context, the rise and fall of the Top Ten Festival needs to be considered as a manifestation of TIFF's evolving year-round presence. As a cultural organization, TIFF has transformed from a major international film festival (that is a global player in the film industry) to a permanent institutional fixture in the exhibition landscape. Over the course of the 2000s, the Toronto International Film Festival Group morphed from an umbrella organization that oversaw a cluster of festivals, outreach programs, and cultural initiatives into a singular global brand captured by an acronym. TIFF (or the lowercase variant used for the logo) now refers both to the charitable cultural organization and to its flagship fall festival. With the construction of Bell Lightbox, which opened in 2010, operational activities have been consolidated at TIFF's headquarters and programming activities have been progressively rationalized as components of a cohesive cultural centre. The retirement of the Top Ten Festival fits within broader program restructuring that included changes to kids programming with the cessation of the Kids International Film Festival (formerly part of the Sprockets International Film Festival for Children, which started in 1997).[65] These programming changes occurred in conjunction with a new strategic plan (Audience First), which also coincided with leadership changes as long-time CEO Piers Handling departed and Joana Vicente was later hired as the new executive director and co-head (alongside Cameron Bailey). The Audience First plan stresses "transformative experiences"[66] and has tended to be mentioned in relation to staying nimble in the streaming era or revitalizing an organization at a crossroads (with layoffs[67] and hints of attendance woes at Lightbox). Thus, the changes to TIFF's support for Canada's Top Ten can be attributed to organizational restructuring and sectoral shifts in exhibition, in addition to the fading ethos of the national cinema showcase.

Shared Attention, Community Building: NCFD

The erosion of the critical value of national programming is exemplified in the *Variety* review for the US theatrical launch of 2018 Canada's Top Ten list-maker *Firecrackers*. As a festival circuit regular, Debruge explained that he overlooked the film at TIFF due to the conventional belief that local content at major events reflects supportive rather than critically driven programming, noting: "when it comes to Toronto, don't waste your time on Canadian fare."[68] As TIFF's role in national cinema programming has dispersed to a year-round theatrical series, the shared attention fostered by the showcase format has largely been displaced to specialized events. For example, a festival like National

Canadian Film Day (NCFD) is not implicated in the negotiation of symbolic value on the industry circuit, except perhaps to extend the long tail for certain films or in the creation of future consumers of Canadian cinema. As a bundle of events, rather than a stop on a circuit, NCFD challenges conventional spatially focused definitions of the film festival, but also highlights the importance of temporal attributes. In her theorization of the temporal features of the film festival, Janet Harbord asserts the significance of liveness that emerges from how the festival "re-institutionalizes the collective attention of film viewing"[69]: "The film festival provides for a time that is not later, not whenever, not at home nor watching on a train on a mobile, but now."[70] She differentiates the festival experience from the "deregulated" (or loosely unstructured) temporal environment of contemporary daily life, and explains that the collective assembly "at one place and at one time" establishes a shared context for the contingent happenings that distinguish the festival as a singular event.[71] It is interesting to note that Harbord's examples of contingent occurrences (or "accidents") that help to distinguish the festival's screening schedule from everyday urban film programming tend to comprise para-screening controversies like heelgate at Cannes in 2015.[72] Whether it is about shared attention or communal viewing, this notion of liveness asserts the temporal dimension of the film festival as a necessary complement to spatial frameworks that root festivals within particular locations (as industry hubs, alternative exhibitors, or local sites for cinemagoing culture).

Dubbed "the world's largest film festival,"[73] NCFD encompasses a nation-wide range of screening, streaming, broadcast, and public events that take place on a set day in late April. The fifth annual NCFD, which took place on 18 April 2018, featured more than 700 screenings of Canadian films. In calling itself a film festival, NCFD foregrounds shared attention on national cinema, but the audiences are dispersed, both temporally and geographically. Thus, NCFD fragments the notion of communal viewing to consider space as national, such that the festival unfurls like a wave passing across Canada's six time zones. Organized by the non-profit charitable organization Reel Canada, the festival includes local public screening partners, streaming and broadcast partners, and an interactive webcast for high school students (RCtv) co-produced by CBC. Reel Canada curates a "sampler" of Spotlight Films and provides screening partner resources (e.g., a pre-show video, introduction script),[74] but otherwise serves more as an outreach coordinator that facilitates access to films than as a programmer who selects them.

As a set of individual local events, the NCFD festival as a whole is technically no longer about what happens "at one place and at one

Figure 19.2 A promotional banner for National Canadian Film Day on 19 April 2017, featuring the moose as mascot, as well as the Reel Canada logo and Canada 150 sesquicentennial logo.

time,"[75] but rather involves the culmination of similar activities occurring in many places at many times. With the inclusion of a curated NCFD playlist on Encore+, the Canada Media Fund's YouTube channel, festival participation could happen alone (potentially on a different day). And, with screenings at international embassies and consulates, participation could happen abroad, potentially even within the context of another film festival; as part of NCFD 150 in 2017 (an expanded celebration that incorporated the sesquicentennial, Canada 150), Zacharias Kunuk's *Maliglutit (Searchers)* screened during the Beijing International Film Festival.[76] This spatial and temporal fragmentation of the festival's liveness evokes the deregulated temporality that Harbord attributed to contemporary film culture, potentially undoing her conceptualization of a "specific temporality" that "gathers together the time of the film and the time of viewing."[77] Instead, the technological innovations of digital culture reconfigure (or perhaps deregulate) festival temporality, in order to (re)assemble a collective experience of national cinema – in part through the use of social media to stitch the disparate moments together, but also via a nostalgic branding of national culture (in this case represented by a moose as festival mascot, whose antlers are festooned with unspooling celluloid).

In other words, NCFD reimagines communal viewing in national terms – centring the "projection" of Canadian cinema for one day – and thus seems to expand, rather than disrupt, the definition of a film festival.

The budget boost provided by a 2017 sesquicentennial grant helped the event gain traction, prompting queries from community partners who now assumed the festival would be a calendar fixture.[78] Reimagined as a fully online event due to COVID-19 restrictions, the 2020 edition (with the tagline "Our stories keep us company") included a four-and-a-half-hour CanFilmDay livestream, featuring guests like Sandra Oh, Jay Baruchel, and Atom Egoyan, and reportedly generating over 1.6 million impressions.[79] Despite the popularity of National Canadian Film Day, and its apparent success as a festival that celebrates national cinema, it is important to note that the programming focuses on films that have already been released. Founded in 2005, Reel Canada's mandate focuses on cultural nationalism – "uniting our nation through film" as a "way to celebrate our cultures and shared values" – and the organization's main programs provide educational resources to high schools and English language classes for new Canadians, with NCFD as a relatively recent initiative.[80] Unlike industry film festivals, NCFD is not targeting premieres, but instead presents films that have already established their critical and cultural value (often on the international festival circuit). This shift to celebrating national cinema at specialized festivals also coincides with changes to federal film policies that increasingly associate domestic festival audiences with the spread of cultural capital.

Conclusion: The Festival as Lightbox

Almost fifteen years after the disbanding of Perspective Canada, the answer to Czach's question about "the long-term necessity of a national cinema series"[81] is complicated. Canada's Top Ten Film Festival, with its outreach tour, recreated the national cinema ghetto as a secondary circuit and the festival ultimately succumbed to the same fate as Perspective Canada. Recently, TIFF has increased their curatorial involvement with Canada's Top Ten, using the list to take a stand on hot-button issues related to access and diversity in the film industry. Bailey's newspaper editorial (calling for filmmakers to tell Canadian stories) prompted an emailed response from filmmaker Kevan Funk, who challenged the "scapegoating [of] filmmakers" in light of "systemic issues" such as "institutional and corporate conditions that exist in this country [that] very much shape the films that get made."[82] The subsequent publication of Funk's email on TIFF's website, and the conversation it provoked, serve as a reminder of the festival's powerful potential as a catalyst in discourses about national cinema. Yet, it is also important to consider the entirety of TIFF's curatorial agenda as a global industry festival in a national context. With the shift to a Theatrical Series for Canada's

Top Ten, TIFF has repositioned its effort to provide a springboard for Canadian films in conjunction with an effort to reimagine their institutional presence in a transformed marketplace. As the celebration of national cinema has shifted from a premiere showcase to secondary circuits and specialized festivals (like NCFD), there is a growing split between the spread of cultural capital (associated with access) and the accumulation of symbolic capital (as an estimation of convertible value).

At the same time, the increasing association of national cinema showcases with Canadiana – from lumberjack plaid to a beaver with a movie camera (see figure 19.2) – invites a critique of knowledge production and cultural capital. With their cozy and lightly humorous allusions, these approaches to festival branding seem to encourage a more nostalgic than ironic perspective on the unifying cultural potential of national cinema. The folkloric invocation of the lumberjack (or bûcheron) suggests a subtle nod to Quebec while also providing the literal backdrop for the invitation to #SeeTheNorth (see figure 19.1). Within film festival studies, there have been calls to examine circulation and gatekeeping in ways that reconsider "the dominant industry's film and nation-making conventions"[83] and allow for "rethinking the film canon beyond the limits of the centres of cultural power."[84] Earlier in this chapter, I explored the federal policy shifts that rationalized funding support for a growing domestic film festival sector. These changes provided an institutional foundation for a hierarchical typology of film festivals that foregrounded industrial development as well as articulation within global festival networks. Within this policy framework, TIFF stood out as the benchmark that positioned Canada on the global stage amongst top-tier international events. The increasing refinements to Telefilm's categorization of major national film festivals, which eventually excluded the Banff Television Festival, bring to mind Antoine Damiens's discussion of the tendencies within film festival research to highlight certain "festivals that matter."[85]

Damiens offers an epistemological critique of assumptions that are baked into film festival studies, guided both by the field's "quest for academic legitimacy"[86] and by the divergent disciplinary traditions that further cleave festival analyses rooted in industry studies from those grounded in identity politics. This "critique (or queering) of festival studies"[87] sits alongside efforts to decolonize media scholarship, the latter exemplified in a special issue of *Canadian Journal of Film Studies / Revue Canadienne d'études cinématographiques* focused on "Indigenous cinema and media in the Americas." In their introductory essay, guest editors André Dudemaine, Gabrielle Marcoux, and Isabelle St-Amand note that systemic change needs to "[go] beyond a simple integration of Indigenous voices into a neocolonial system."[88] Their essay includes a brief history of the role of the Montreal First Peoples Festival in convening transnational networks. Another significant festival, imagineNATIVE, is examined by Caroline Klimek for its role in new media as an expanded cinema venue. Klimek's study also notes the involvement of the imagineNATIVE Film and Media Arts Festival in a federal cultural policy shift towards support of the Indigenous screen-based media industry in Canada.[89] The long process of writing this chapter was shaped by myriad changes, from the cancellation of TIFF's Canada's Top Ten Festival to a global pandemic to systemic shifts towards inclusion in Canadian cultural policy. Accordingly, I call on festival studies scholars to renegotiate the terrain I have mapped in this chapter as a necessary next step in developing festival research in the context of a geo-located historiography of "Canadian national cinema."

The vision statement for Bell Lightbox asserted that "the art of the moving image needs a light box and our Canadian films need a catalyst from which they can exert their influence on North American and international markets."[90] Indeed, as the domestic film festival sector continues to evolve post-2000, it is evident that the film festival has become the dominant institutional presence that shapes Canadian national cinema. Elsewhere on the fall domestic circuit, VIFF embarked on a corporate rebranding under the leadership of new executive director Jacqueline Dupuis. In 2016, the festival debuted a new logo and set out a new model of FILM+ that aimed to unite cineastes, TV fans, and gamers under the umbrella of "screen-based entertainment."[91] Admittedly, it is difficult not to see VIFF's "expanded cinema" ethos as a response to TIFF's repositioning as a global organization. Similar to how VIFF's previous tagline of "Same Planet. Different Worlds." used to invite comparisons to TIFF's star-studded glamour,[92] the chunky block capitals of VIFF's new logo stand in contra-distinction to TIFF's svelte lowercase. VIFF's focus remains decidedly regional, with the idea of expanded cinema clearly grounded in the dominant creative industry activities of the Pacific Northwest. Its national showcase was re-named True North (which fits the current idea of national cinema espoused by NCFD and the Top Ten Festival), and in 2016 included a Future // Present sidebar comprised of projects "made well outside the conventional industry framework."[93] But, even as VIFF engages with national programming, there is the issue of garnering national attention and the question of how symbolic capital accumulates for Canadian cinema. In other words, the question remains of how changes in the festival sector will ultimately influence the curatorial debates and barriers to entry that shape canon formation.

Notes

1 Geoff Pevere, "Middle of Nowhere: Ontario Movies after 1980," *Post Script* 15, no. 1 (1995): 9–22. See also Cameron Bailey, "Standing in the Kitchen All Night: A Secret History of the Toronto New Wave," *Take One* 9, no. 28 (summer 2000): 6–11.

2 Diane Burgess, "Charting the Course of the Pacific New Wave," *CineAction* 61 (2003): 29–33.

3 Brenda Longfellow, "Surfing the Toronto New Wave: Policy, Paradigm Shifts and Post-Nationalism," in *Self Portraits: The Cinemas of Canada since Telefilm*, eds. André Loiselle and Tom McSorley (Ottawa: The Canadian Film Institute, 2006).

4 Liz Czach, "Film Festivals, Programming, and the Building of a National Cinema," *The Moving Image* 4, no. 1 (spring 2004): 82; Diane Burgess, "Why Whistler Will Never Be Sundance, and What This Tells Us about the Field of Cultural Production," *Canadian Journal of Film Studies / Revue Cannadienne d'études cinématographiques* 23, no. 1 (spring 2014): 94. See also Marijke De Valck, "Film Festivals, Bourdieu, and the Economization of Culture," *Canadian Journal of Film Studies / Revue Cannadienne d'études cinématographiques* 23, no. 1 (spring 2014): 74–89.

5 Although much of the content of this chapter could be applied generally to the Canadian film festival sector, my focus is on English-Canadian examples – including industry festivals that articulate into national or international circuits. The Montreal World Film Festival has a significant presence in the development of federal film festival policy. However, a detailed consideration of Quebec festivals and French-language cinema (which articulates unevenly into national content flows) is beyond the scope of this chapter.

6 With the term "industry festival," I am combining Mark Peranson's "two ideal models" – business and audience festivals – which differ in their organizational characteristics and political clout but share similar programming interests (i.e., broad survey-style categorizations based on geographical region or auteur designations). Even though the bulk of market activity (i.e., sales and acquisitions) occurs at business festivals, both types of festivals arguably aspire to positioning on international festival circuits; Mark Peranson, "First You Get the Power, Then You Get the Money: Two Models of Film Festivals," in *dekalog3: On Film Festivals*, ed. Richard Porton (London: Wallflower, 2009).

7 Skadi Loist, "The Film Festival Circuit: Networks, Hierarchies, and Circulation," in *Film Festivals: History, Theory, Method, Practice*, eds. Marijke de Valck, Brenden Kredell, and Skadi Loist (London: Routledge, 2016), 52.

8 Burgess, "Why Whistler," 94.
9 In Telefilm Canada's *Annual Report 1998–1999*, Canadian festivals were referred to as "springboards for Canadian productions." The 2002–03 Canada Showcase assessment criterion for "performance reporting" included industry attendance as well as media coverage and public attendance (7). In the revised 2006–07 Canada Showcase evaluation grid, one-quarter of the event impact score addresses "professional impact" as a more qualitative measure of quality, relevance, and professional involvement (6). Telefilm Canada, *Annual Report 1998–1999*, September 1999, https://telefilm.ca/en/transparency/annual-reports; Telefilm Canada, "Canada Showcase Guidelines for 2002–2003," www.telefilm.gc.ca; Telefilm Canada, "Canada Showcase | Guidelines for 2006–2007," www.telefilm.gc.ca.
10 Keith Acheson, Christopher J. Maule, and Elizabet Filleul, "Cultural Entrepreneurship and the Banff Television Festival," *Journal of Cultural Economics* 20 (1996): 321–39.
11 Ibid., 322, 325.
12 Secor Consulting, *Analysis of Canada's Major Film Festivals* (report prepared for Telefilm Canada and the Société de développement des entreprises culturelles [SODEC], 2004), www.telefilm.gc.ca; Kelly Sears Consulting Group, "Evaluation of Canada Showcase Program: Summary of Stakeholder Interviews" (prepared for Telefilm Canada), 2007, 8n5, www.telefilm.gc.ca.
13 Kelly Sears Consulting Group, "Evaluation of Telefilm's Support to Canadian Audiovisual Festivals: Findings and Recommendations" (prepared for Telefilm Canada), 2007, 13, www.telefilm.gc.ca.
14 Dina Iordanova, "The Film Festival Circuit," in *Film Festival Yearbook 1: The Festival Circuit*, eds. Dina Iordanova and Regan Rhyne (St Andrews: St Andrews Film Studies, 2009), 23.
15 Thomas Elsaesser, "Film Festival Networks: The New Topographies of Cinema in Europe," in *European Cinema: Face to Face with Hollywood* (Amsterdam: Amsterdam University Press, 2005), 84.
16 Iordanova, "The Film Festival Circuit."
17 Telefilm Canada, *Annual Report 1998–1999*, 30.
18 Kelly Sears Consulting Group, "Evaluation of Canada Showcase," 9.
19 Drisdell Consulting, as cited in Diane Burgess, "Bridging the Gap: Film Festival Governance, Public Partners and the 'Vexing' Problem of Film Distribution," *Canadian Journal of Film Studies / Revue Cannadienne d'études cinématographiques* 21, no. 1 (spring 2012): 10.
20 Burgess, "Bridging the Gap," 14.
21 Maurie Alioff, "Montréal: The Montreal World Film Festival (8/24–9/4/05), Le Festival International de Films de Montréal (The New Montreal FilmFest) (9/18–25/25), Le Festival de Nouveau Cinéma (10/13–23/05)," *Take One 14*, no. 52 (December–March 2006): 40.

22 Ibid.
23 Ibid., 41. See also Matthew Hays, "New Montreal FilmFest Admits Defeat," *Playback: Canada's Broadcast and Production Journal*, 7 November 2005, 1. The New Montreal FilmFest folded in 2006.
24 Telefilm Canada, *Promotions Program Guidelines*, 28 May 2015, 2, https://telefilm.ca/wp-content/uploads/guidelines-promotion-2015.pdf. These guidelines were updated as of 15 December 2017, and the objectives and eligibility criteria that I have cited remained the same.
25 Canadian Press, "TIFF 2015: Why There's No Canadian-Themed Program," CBC News, 7 September 2015, http://www.cbc.ca/news/entertainment/tiff-2015-why-there-s-no-canadian-themed-program-1.3218340. It is interesting to note that TIFF's disbanding of Perspective Canada occurred contemporaneously with policy changes at Telefilm. By 2006, the Canada Showcase guidelines had removed quantitative Canadian content thresholds in favour of a qualitative assessment of how films were presented – "perhaps signalling an acknowledgement of the changing contours of national cinema programming – such that prestigious slots matter more than a carefully-bounded national showcase" (Diane Burgess, "Negotiating Value: A Canadian Perspective on the International Film Festival" [PhD diss., Simon Fraser University, 2008], 224).
26 Czach, "Film Festivals," 83.
27 Toronto International Film Festival Group, as cited in Burgess, "Negotiating Value," 187, 150.
28 Canadian Press, "TIFF 2015."
29 Roya Rastegar, "Seeing Differently: The Curatorial Potential of Film Festival Programming," in de Valck, Kredell, and Loist, *Film Festivals*, 183.
30 Ibid.
31 Czach, "Film Festivals," 83–4.
32 https://www.tiff.net/canadas-top-ten/?tab=about.
33 Blaine Allan, "Top-Ten Film History," *Canadian Journal of Film Studies / Revue Cannadienne d'études cinématographiques* 23, no. 2 (fall 2014): 115–29.
34 TIFF, "TIFF Unveils Top Ten Canadian Films of 2017," Press Release, 6 December 2017, https://assets.ctfassets.net/22n7d68fswlw/2Xhdf3VLluOi2ycwo4Q4y8/ea9bfb27b1e5d5b37c648657120a439d/17th_Annual_Canada_s_Top_Ten_Film_Festival.pdf.
35 https://phi-centre.com/en/event/canadas-top-ten-2018-en/.
36 TIFF, "About Film Circuit," http://v1.tiff.net/filmcircuit-about. The Film Circuit began as an initiative of the Cinéfest Sudbury International Film Festival and became a TIFF property in 1995. There is some uncertainty about the precise timeline as the Northern Film Circuit started in 1992 (https://cinefest.com/about-us) and 1989 marked the inaugural Cinéfest.

37 Claudia Sicondolfo and Wendy Donnan, "When Circuits Go Local: Examining TIFF's National Outreach Program Film Circuit," conference presentation at Circuits of Cinema | Histories of Movie and Media Distribution (HOMER Network), 24 June 2017, Ryerson University, Toronto.
38 Ibid.
39 Ibid.
40 Rastegar, "Seeing Differently," 182.
41 Liz Czach, "Affective Labor and the Work of Film Festival Programming," in de Valck, Kredell, and Loist, *Film Festivals*, 202.
42 Ibid., 203.
43 Rastegar, "Seeing Differently," 182.
44 Ibid.
45 Ibid., 183.
46 Leah Collins, "10 TIFF '17 Films That Are 'Secretly Canadian,'" CBC *Arts*, 31 August 2017: https://www.cbc.ca/arts/10-tiff-17-movies-that-are-secretly-canadian-1.4270755.
47 Liam Lacey, "TIFF Slate Reflects New Indie Spirit," *Globe and Mail*, 11 August 2010, R1-2.
48 Ibid.
49 TIFF Trailers, *Canada's Top Ten Film Festival Trailer* | TIFF, 6 December 2017, https://www.youtube.com/watch?v=6wTJ879dnZk.
50 TIFF Trailers, *Canada's Top Ten Trailer* | TIFF 2017, 7 December 2016, https://www.youtube.com/watch?v=VXest6RJUFw.
51 Czach, "Film Festivals," 85.
52 Ibid.
53 TIFF, "These Are the Best Canadian Films of 2017," 6 December 2017, https://www.tiff.net/the-review/best-canadian-films-of-2017/.
54 Ibid.
55 Ibid.
56 Peter Howell, "Why You Probably Haven't Heard of Canada's Top Ten Films of 2017," *Toronto Star*, 7 December 2017, https://www.thestar.com/entertainment/movies/2017/12/07/why-you-probably-havent-heard-of-canadas-top-ten-films-of-2017.html.
57 Regan Reid, "TIFF Drops Top 10 Fest, Adds Year-Round Canadian Film Series," *Playback*, 7 November 2018, https://playbackonline.ca/2018/11/07/tiff-drops-top-10-fest-adds-year-round-canadian-film-series/.
58 Peter Howell, "TIFF Strategically Trades Champagne for Screen Time for Canada's Top Ten Movies," *Toronto Star*, 6 December 2018, online edition, ProQuest (2150628046).
59 Trading buzz for additional screenings also brings to mind Charles Acland's critique of screen time as a measure of value because "it does not tell us if

anyone is actually in the seats." Charles Acland, "Screen Space, Screen Time, and Canadian Film Exhibition," in *North of Everything: English-Canadian Cinema since 1980*, ed. William Beard and Jerry White (Edmonton: University of Alberta Press, 2002), 11.
60 Howell, "TIFF Strategically Trades."
61 Academy of Canadian Cinema & Television, "Canadian Screen Awards 2020. Film Rules & Regulations," accessed 31 August 2022, https://www.academy.ca/wp-content/uploads/2019/08/2020-Canadian-Screen-Awards-Film-Rules-Regulations-ENGLISH.pdf.
62 Radheyan Simonpillai, "TIFF Scraps Popular Canada's Top Ten Film Festival," *Now Magazine*, 7 November 2018, https://nowtoronto.com/movies/features/tiff-scraps-canadas-top-ten-film-festival/.
63 Howell, "TIFF Strategically Trades." Howell suggests that the Top Ten Festival had been struggling, citing Bailey's observation about attendance.
64 Simonpillai, "TIFF Scraps."
65 Reid, "TIFF Drops Top 10."
66 As cited in Barry Hertz and Molly Hayes, "Losing Focus," *Globe and Mail*, 27 September 2017, online edition.
67 "TIFF Lays Off 15 Employees 'Across All Departments,'" The Canadian Press, Toronto, 20 November 2019, ProQuest (2316919154).
68 Peter Debruge, "Film Review: 'Firecrackers,'" *Variety*, 13 July 2019, https://variety.com/2019/film/reviews/firecrackers-review-1203266888/.
69 Janet Harbord, "Contingency, Time, and Event: An Archaeological Approach to the Film Festival," in de Valck, Kredell, and Loist, *Film Festivals*, 80.
70 Ibid., 79.
71 Ibid., 72, 79.
72 Ibid., 76.
73 National Canadian Film Day, "National Canadian Film Day is Back by Popular Demand, Featuring More Than 700 Screenings across the Country and around the World," Press Release, 28 March 2018, https://canadianfilmday.ca/about-ncfd/press-releases/more-than-700-screenings/.
74 National Canadian Film Day website, accessed 31 August 2022, https://canadianfilmday.ca.
75 Harbord, "Contingency," 79.
76 National Canadian Film Day, "NCFD World Tour: Taking Over Film Festivals in Austria, China and the USA," 16 April 2017, https://canadianfilmday.ca/ncfd-world-tour-taking-over-film-festivals-in-austria-china-and-the-usa/.
77 Harbord, "Contingency," 80.
78 Kate Taylor, "Toward a National Cinema: How this Non-Profit Brings Canada to the Silver Screen," *Globe and Mail*, 17 April 2018, https://www.

theglobeandmail.com/arts/film/article-toward-a-national-cinema-how-this-non-profit-brings-canada-to-the/.
79 National Canadian Film Day, *National Canadian Film Day 2020*: National Canadian Film Day 2020 Highlights, https://cdn.canadianfilmday.ca/wp-content/uploads/2020-NCFD-Report.pdf, 3.
80 Reel Canada, "About Us," accessed 31 August 2022, https://www.reelcanada.ca/about-us/.
81 Czach, "Film Festivals," 83.
82 Kevan Funk, "There Is an Incentivized Path to Mediocrity," 21 February 2017, https://www.tiff.net/the-review/there-is-an-incentivized-path-to-mediocrity/.
83 Amalia Córdova, "Towards an Indigenous Film Festival Circuit," in *Film Festival Yearbook 4: Film Festivals and Activism*, ed. Dina Iordanova and Leshu Torchin (St Andrews: St Andrews Film Studies, 2012), 75.
84 Aida Vallejo, "Rethinking the Canon: The Role of Film Festivals in Shaping Film History," *Studies in European Cinema* 17, no. 2 (2020): 167.
85 Antoine Damiens, LGBTQ *Film Festivals: Curating Queerness* (Amsterdam: Amsterdam University Press, 2020), 27.
86 Ibid.
87 Ibid.
88 André Dudemaine, Gabrielle Marcoux, and Isabelle St-Amand (trans. S.E. Stewart), "Indigenous Cinema and Media in the Americas: Storytelling, Communities, and Sovereignties," *Canadian Journal of Film Studies / Revue Canadienne d'études cinématographiques* 29, no. 1 (spring 2020): 32.
89 Caroline Klimek, "From Programmer to Curator: How Film Festivals are Pushing the Boundaries of New Media and Expanded Cinema," *Canadian Journal of Film Studies / Revue Canadienne d'études cinématographiques* 27, no. 1 (spring 2018), 73–87.
90 As cited in Burgess, "Negotiating Value," 146.
91 Fiona Morrow, "How VIFF Is Reinventing Itself for a New Audience," *Vancouver Magazine*, 7 September 2016, http://vanmag.com/city/viff-2016-changes/.
92 Burgess, "Negotiating Value," 113.
93 Adrian Mack, "B.C.'s Kevan Funk and a Mob of Inspired Young Filmmakers Are Destroying at VIFF," *The Georgia Straight*, 28 September 2016, https://www.straight.com/movies/797041/bcs-kevan-funk-and-mob-inspired-young-filmmakers-are-destroying-viff.

Contributors

CHARLES ACLAND is distinguished university research professor in communication studies at Concordia University, Montreal. His most recent book is *American Blockbuster: Movies, Technology, and Wonder* (Duke University Press, 2020) and he is a former editor of the *Canadian Journal of Film Studies*.

KARINE BERTRAND is associate professor in the film and media department of Queen's University and co-director (with F. Grandena, University of Ottawa) of the inter-university research group EPIC (Esthétique et Politique de l'Image Cinématographique). She is also a member of the Maniwaki Aboriginal Community. Her research interests are centred around Indigenous cinema and poetry, Quebec cinema, road movies, transnational cinemas, and oral practices of cinema. Her latest publications include book chapters on the rock group U2 (*Mapping the Rockumentary: Images of Sound and Fury*, Mackenzie and Iversen, 2021), and on the exploration of Indigenous lands (*Cinema of Exploration: Essays on an Adventurous Film Practice*, Cahill and Caminati, 2020), as well as an article on Indigenous women and testimonies (*Canadian Journal of Film Studies*, 2020) and an article on Québécois cinema and Americanité (*American Review of Canadian Studies*, 2019).

DAN BROWNE is a filmmaker, multimedia artist, and scholar based in Toronto. He holds a PhD in communication and culture from York/Toronto Metropolitan (formerly Ryerson) Universities, his dissertation exploring themes of technology, environment, and the Anthropocene in recent Canadian cinema. His writings on filmmaking have been published in *Incite Journal of Experimental Media*, *Found Footage Magazine*, *Hors Champ*, *Millennium Film Journal*, and *Process Cinema: Handmade Film in the Digital Age* (2019).

DIANE BURGESS teaches in the School of Journalism, Writing, and Media at the University of British Columbia. Her research explores value creation in the film festival sector, cultural policy, and national cinema. Her work appears in *Film Festivals: History, Theory, Method, Practice* (Routledge) and *Self Portraits: The Cinemas of Canada Since Telefilm* (The Canadian Film Institute), and also has appeared in *Canadian Journal of Film Studies*, NECSUS *European Journal of Media Studies*, and *Media Industries*.

LEE CARRUTHERS is associate professor of film studies at the University of Calgary. Her book *Doing Time: Temporality, Hermeneutics, and Contemporary Cinema* (SUNY Press, 2016) blends philosophy with film analysis to theorize the temporal experience that cinema offers to viewers. Her current research focuses on contemporary directors and the phenomenon of late style in recent cinema.

AMANDA COLES is a senior lecturer in employment relations in the Faculty of Business and Law at Deakin University in Melbourne, Australia. Amanda's research examines the political economy of labour markets and workforce development in the creative and cultural industries with a focus on public policy, collective representation, and intersectional inequality. She is a co-researcher with the SSHRC-funded Interuniversity Research Centre on Globalisation and Work (CRIMT) in Montreal, Canada. Her academic career is informed by her professional history in the Canadian independent film and television production sector.

DAVID DAVIDSON is a PhD student at the University of Toronto. His dissertation is on the post-1980 history of *Cahiers du cinéma*. His film writing has appeared in the *Globe and Mail* and he has a regular Canadian screening series, Toronto Film Review Presents.

SETH FELDMAN is an author, broadcaster, film programmer, and professor emeritus/senior scholar at York University in Toronto. A founder and past president of the Film Studies Association of Canada, he has published widely on Canadian cinema, documentary film, and media. In addition to his numerous publications he is an author and broadcaster of twenty-six radio documentary series for the CBC program *Ideas*, as well as two short documentary films. Professor Feldman is a former dean of the Faculty of Fine Arts. In recognition of his teaching and administrative work, he holds the honorific title of university professor, one of twenty such positions at York. He is a fellow of the Royal Society of Canada.

TANYA HORECK is associate professor of film, media, and communication at Anglia Ruskin University in Cambridge, England. She is the author of *Public Rape: Representing Violation in Fiction and Film* and *Justice on Demand: True Crime in the Digital Streaming Era*. Her current research projects include a UK Research and Innovation/Arts and Humanities Research Council–funded study on online sexual risks for young people during COVID-19, and a British Academy–funded study on the rise of consent culture and intimacy coordination.

CHARLIE KEIL is professor in the Cinema Studies Institute and the Department of History, and principal of Innis College at the University of Toronto. His research has consistently focused on early and silent American cinema, though he has also published on later periods and on topics as diverse as documentary, stardom, and modernism/modernity.

MURRAY LEEDER is an adjunct professor in the Department of English, Film, Theatre, and Media at the University of Manitoba. He is the author of *Horror Film: A Critical Introduction* (Bloomsbury, 2018), *The Modern Supernatural and the Beginnings of Cinema* (Palgrave Macmillan, 2017), and *Halloween* (Auteur, 2014), and editor of *Cinematic Ghosts: Haunting and Spectrality from Silent Cinema to the Digital Era* (Bloomsbury, 2015) and *ReFocus: The Films of William Castle* (Edinburgh University Press, 2018). He has published in such journals as *Horror Studies*, *The Canadian Journal of Film Studies*, *The Journal of Popular Culture*, and *The Journal of Popular Film and Television*.

PETER LESTER is an associate professor in the Department of Communication, Popular Culture, and Film at Brock University. His work has appeared in such journals as the *Journal of Cinema and Media Studies*, *The Moving Image*, *Film History*, and the *Canadian Journal of Film Studies*. He is a former president of the Film Studies Association of Canada.

MIKE MENEGHETTI is the author of *Martin Scorsese's Documentary Histories: Migrations, Movies, Music* (Bloomsbury Academic, 2021). His work has been published in *New Review of Film and Television Studies*, *Film-Philosophy*, *Studies in Documentary Film*, and *Canadian Journal of Film Studies*. He is a sessional lecturer at the University of Toronto.

AIMÉE MITCHELL (she/her) is currently the research officer for the School of Art, Media, Performance, and Design at York University. She holds a PhD in communication and culture from York–Toronto Metropolitan University. Mitchell is an independent media art programmer and a current board member of the Liaison of Independent Filmmakers of Toronto and the8fest small-gauge film festival, and she was a founding member for the Toronto Queer Film Festival. She is an advocate for audiovisual media makers across formats and gauges big and small.

GILLIAN ROBERTS is professor of contemporary literature and culture in the Department of American and Canadian Studies at the University of Nottingham. She is the author of *Prizing Literature: The Celebration and Circulation of National Culture* (2011) and *Discrepant Parallels: Cultural Implications of the Canada-US Border* (2015); co-editor with David Stirrup of *Parallel Encounters: Culture at the Canada-US Border* (2013); and editor of *Reading between the Borderlines: Cultural Production and Consumption across the 49th Parallel* (2018).

IAN ROBINSON is a film and media scholar whose research specializes in areas of national and transnational cinemas, film festivals and exhibition cultures, and topics related to the intermediality of cinema. His research has been published in several journals including the *Canadian Journal of Film Studies*, *Public: Art, Ideas and Culture*, *Cinema & Cie*, and multiple anthologies in film and media studies. He completed his PhD at York University and teaches in the Department of Film and Media at Queen's University.

MIRIAM SIEGEL is a PhD candidate in cinema studies at the University of Toronto, where she also completed her master's and bachelor's degrees. Her primary research interests include theories of narration and genre with a particular focus on the relationship between storytelling and style in popular American cinema.

Contributors

JEAN-PIERRE SIROIS-TRAHAN is a film studies professor in the Département de littérature, théâtre et cinéma at Université Laval. He is interested in particular in the beginnings of moving pictures, about which he has published several articles and co-edited two books, *Au pays des ennemis du cinéma ...* (Nuit blanche, 1996) and *La Vie ou du moins ses apparences* (Cinémathèque québécoise/GRAFICS, 2002). With Sophie-Jan Arrien he co-edited the volume *Le Montage des identités* (PUL, 2008). He co-edited a special issue (fall 2003) of the journal *Cinémas* on cinematic "dispositifs," and an issue of *Nouvelles Vues* on new Quebec cinema (2011).

CHARLES TEPPERMAN is associate professor in the Department of Communication, Media, and Film at the University of Calgary. He is the author of *Amateur Cinema: The Rise of North American Moviemaking, 1923–1960*, and director of the Amateur Movie Database project. His work on Canadian cinema, film history, and amateur media has appeared in *Screen*, *Film History*, *Media Industries Journal*, *The Moving Image*, and the *Canadian Journal of Film Studies*.

JENNIFER VANDERBURGH is associate professor in the Department of English Language and Literature at Saint Mary's University in Halifax, Canada, where she teaches courses on film, television, and media. Her research interests include Canadian film and television, national media discourses, formal and informal media archives (VHS collections and YouTube), and film/television and the city.

MELANIE WILMINK is a Banting Postdoctoral Fellow at Yonsei University (Seoul, South Korea) where she investigates the art of the Korean smart-city. She holds a PhD in visual art and art history from York University (Toronto), with honours such as the 2014 Elia Scholars Award and a 2015 SSHRC Doctoral Fellowship. Specializing in the spectatorial dynamics of media art environments and art as embodied knowledge-production, her ongoing research emerged through her independent curating practice. Past exhibitions include the *Situated Cinema* project (Pleasure Dome, 2015), *Winter Warmer* (Sidewalk Labs Toronto, 2019), and *Re[new]All* (Sensorium: Centre for Digital Arts and Technology, 2021). She is the co-editor of the anthologies *Sculpting Cinema* (2018) and *Landscapes of Moving Image* (2021) with Solomon Nagler.

Index

Aboriginal Peoples Television Network (APTN), 88, 92, 98, 101
Abrahamson, Lenny, 17, 321, 329; *Room* (2015), 321–4, 328–36
Academy Awards, 27, 67, 275–6, 321–2, 335
Adele, 14, 32, 39
Ahmed, Sarah, 70, 74–7, 80
Åkervall, Lisa, 217–18
Alexander, Shannon, 99
Alias Grace (Polley, 2017), 67–8, 382
Alliance of Canadian Cinema Television and Radio Artists (ACTRA), 301–3, 310–14
Allison, Leane, 222–3; *Bear 71* (Allison and Mendes, 2012), 16, 220, 221–6
American Mary (Soska and Soska, 2012), 158, 159
American Movie (Smith and Price, 1999), 171, 179–80, 185n21
amours imaginaires, Les / Heartbeats (Dolan, 2010), 30, 33, 35–6, 109
Anthropocene, 235, 248
Appadurai, Arjun, 121

Araneda, Cecilia, 16, 246–9; *The Space Shuttle Challenger* (2017), 246; *What Comes Between* (2009), 246–8
Arcand, Denys, 3, 12, 33, 61
Arnait Video Productions, 95
Arrival (Villeneuve, 2016), 43, 46, 49–54, 57–60, 62
art gallery–based cinema, 16, 256–9, 264–6, 270. See also skoltz, dominique t.
arte povera, 105
Assault (Radwanski, 2007), 138, 139, 143
Atanarjuat: The Fast Runner (Kunuk, 2001), 3, 8, 95, 327; and New Wave of Indigenous filmmaking, 12; representation of water, 123, 130
Atwood, Margaret, 67–8, 152–3, 225; adaptation of *Alias Grace* (1996), 67–8; *Survival* (1972), 152–3, 225
auteur, 3–4, 13, 14; American auteurism, 44–5; auteur-star, 25; auteur theory (*Cahiers du Cinéma*), 44, 62; auteurist frameworks,

43–4, 57, 61–2, 63n2; commerce of auteurism, 29–30; Denis Côté as auteur, 116; critiques of, 43; Xavier Dolan as auteur-star, 25–41; and film festivals, 370, 376; horror auteur, 157–60; Sarah Polley as auteur, 68; Denis Villeneuve as equivocal auteur, 42–66. *See also* Sarris, Andrew
Awashish, Eruoma, 91
Away from Her (Polley, 2006), 67–8, 71, 74–5

Backcountry (MacDonald, 2014), 153–5, 157, 163
Bacon, Joséphine, 87, 91
Bahrani, Ramin, 136
Bailey, Cameron, 381, 382, 383, 386
Baltruschat, Doris, 330, 332
Banff World Media Festival, 372, 387
Barlow, Maude, 129
Barnaby, Jeff, 12, 16, 95; *Blood Quantum* (2019), 155; *Etlinisigu'niet (Bleed Down / Vidés de leur sang)* (2015), 203–6; *File Under Miscellaneous* (2010), 155–6; and horror films, 151, 155, 158; *Rhymes for Young Ghouls* (2013), 95, 155; *Souvenir* (NFB, 2015) film series, 203–6, 208, 213
Barthes, Roland, 106, 262, 268–9
Battle, Christina, 347–8, 354, 363
Bazin, André, 55, 62, 64n4, 106, 109
Bear 71 (Allison and Mendes, 2012), 16, 220, 221–6
Beard, William, 7, 197
Bearwalker (Cheechoo, 2000), 327
Beauty Day (Cheel, 2011), 169–85
Bell Lightbox. *See* Toronto International Film Festival
Bellemare, Sylvain, 43

Berlant, Lauren, 70, 81
Berlin Film Festival, 26, 111, 139, 145, 374
Bernadet, Henry, 106, 107
Bestiary (Côté, 2012), 112, 114, 115, 116
Beyond the Black Rainbow (Cosmatos, 2010), 162
BIPOC TV and Film, 284
Black Screen Office, 6
Blade Runner 2049 (Villeneuve, 2017), 43, 46–7, 49–51, 53–4, 62, 382
Blood Quantum (Barnaby, 2019), 155
Body Remembers When the World Broke Open, The (Hepburn and Tailfeathers, 2019), 327–8
Boileau, Sonia Bonspille, 8, 12, 14, 87–103; and APTN, 88, 92, 98, 101; community involvement, 100–1; creative process, 96–7; cultural identity, 91–3; *Le Dep* (2014), 88–9, 92, 95–8, 100; *Last Call Indien* (2010), 88, 91; and missing and murdered Indigenous women, 88, 99–100; *The Oka Legacy* (2015), 88, 91–2, 100; *Princesses* (A. O'Bomsawin, 2016), 88, 92–3, 98–9; representation of women, 97–9; *Rustic Oracle* (2019), 88, 96–7, 99–100; *Skindigenous* (2018), 88, 92–3, 96, 98; storytelling tradition, 95; and visual sovereignty, 88
Bon Cop, Bad Cop (Canuel, 2006), 163, 333
Bordwell, David, 47
Borgias, The (Showtime, 2011–13), 329, 332
Boris sans Béatrice / Boris without Béatrice (Côté, 2016)
Bouchard, Serge, 90
Bourdieu, Pierre, 280, 352

Index 403

Bourgeois, Louise: *Maman* (1999), 54
Bourges, Antoine, 139–40
Breadwinner, The (Twomey, 2017), 329, 335, 382
Breathing Light (Turrell, 2013), 51, 52, 64n10
Brennan, Jason, 93
British Columbia, 10, 151, 276, 285; film and television unions, 301, 308, 311; film festivals, 370–2
Bronstein, Ronald, 136
Brooklyn (Crowley, 2015), 321, 329, 331, 333, 335
Burgess, Marilyn, 290–1

Cahiers du Cinéma, 44, 62, 108, 135–6
Canada Council for the Arts, 121, 132, 140, 348
Canada's Top Ten Film Festival, 137, 376–83
Canadian Audio-Visual Certification Office (CAVCO), 281, 319n24, 322, 326
Canadian Broadcasting Corporation (CBC), 67, 205, 312, 314, 368n64, 384
Canadian Film Development Corporation. *See* Telefilm Canada
Canadian Film or Video Production Tax Credit (CPTC), 281–5, 290–1, 335
Canadian Filmmakers Distribution Centre (CFMDC), 341–3
Canadian Media Producers Association (CMPA), 278, 304
Canadian Screen Awards, 321. *See also* Genie Awards
Cannes Film Festival, 3, 8, 14, 32, 370, 384; Directors Fortnight, 140, 275; and industry festivals, 371–2; and international festival circuit, 25, 32, 38, 371; women directors, 276. *See also* Dolan, Xavier; film festivals; Toronto International Film Festival (TIFF); Villeneuve, Denis
Cap'n Video Show, The (Zavadil, 1990–95), 170–6, 179–83
Carcasses (Côté, 2009), 107, 110, 114, 140, 148n16
Cariou, Warren, 203, 213
Carmody, Don, 275–6
Carrey, Jim, 173–4
Carson, Anne, 235
Caruth, Cathy, 237
César et son canôt d'écorce / César's Bark Canoe (Gosselin, 1971), 212
Chartrand, Rhéanne, 212
Cheel, Jay, 15, 169–71, 181–3; *Beauty Day* (2011), 169–85. *See also* documentary film
Chiang, Ted: "Story of Your Life," 57, 58, 60
Chicago (Marshall, 2002), 275–6
Circle of the Sun (Low, 1960), 204–5
Cividino, Andrew, 15, 122, 382; *Sleeping Giant* (2015), 15, 122–3, 126–32, 135, 382
Cizek, Katerina, 16, 219–20, 227–32; *Highrise: The Towers in the World, the World in the Towers* (2010–15), 16, 219–20, 226–31
climate change, 13, 129–30, 234, 248–9
Cockburn, Daniel, 138–9; *You Are Here* (2010), 138
Continental, un film sans fusil / Continental, a Film without Guns (Lafleur, 2007), 107
co-productions. *See* international co-productions
Corneil, Marit Kathryn, 226–7
Corner, John, 217, 218

Côté, Denis, 11, 14, 55, 138, 140; *Bestiary* (2012), 112, 114, 115, 116; *Boris sans Béatrice / Boris without Béatrice* (2016), 112, 114; *Carcasses* (2009), 107, 110, 114, 140, 148n16; and community, 109–11; *Curling* (2010), 106–8, 108–14, 138; *Elle veut le chaos / All That She Wants* (2008), 108, 110, 114; *Les États nordiques / Drifting States* (2004), 104–6, 107–10, 114; *Lignes ennemis / Enemy Lines* (2010), 111, 114; *Maïté* (2007), 117; and nihilism, 111, 118; *Nos vies privées / Our Private Lives* (2007), 107, 108, 109, 110, 114; and Quebec, 108–9; *Que ta joie demeure / Joy of Man's Desiring* (2014), 14, 15; and *renouveau*, 26–7, 104–19, 136; *Répertoire des villes disparues / Ghost Town Anthology* (2019), 107, 113, 114; *Ta peau si lisse / A Skin So Soft* (2017), 114, 116; *Vic + Flo ont vu un ours / Vic + Flo Saw a Bear* (2013), 26, 107, 111, 114; *Wilcox*, 105, 114 (2019)

Counting Past 2: Performance-Film-Video-Spoken Word with Transsexual Nerve! festival, 350–3

Cousineau, Marie-Hélène, 95

Cowards Bend the Knee (Maddin, 2003), 186, 188

C.R.A.Z.Y. (Vallée, 2005), 27

Cree Hunters of Mistassini (Richardson and Ianzelo, 1974), 208, 211

Cronenberg, Brandon, 139, 158; *Antiviral* (2012), 139, 158; *Possessor* (2020), 158

Cronenberg, David, 57, 136, 146, 275, 336n6; as established auteur, 3, 42, 61; and horror film, 150, 152, 158–60

Curling (Côté, 2010), 106–8, 108–14, 138

Cyr, Louis, 116

Czach, Liz, 376, 377, 379, 380, 386

de Rosa, Maria, 290–1

de Valck, Marijke, 32

Deakins, Roger, 43, 50, 52, 53

Death of a Ladies' Man (Bissonnette, 2021), 331–2

Deer, Tracey, 12

del Toro, Guillermo, 17, 152, 159–60, 162, 276

Delluc, Louis, 44

Delorme, Stéphane, 135

Denis, Mathieu, 106

Dep, Le (Boileau, 2014), 88–9, 92, 95–8, 100

Deraspe, Sophie, 11, 26, 105–6; *Rechercher Victor Pellerin / Missing Victor Pellerin* (2005), 105

Derrida, Jacques, 210

diaspora and cinema, 13, 16, 18, 40n8, 234–55

direct cinema, 104–5, 177–9, 182, 226–31

Directors Guild of Canada (DGC), 18, 301–3, 310–14

Dirties, The (Johnson, 2013), 135, 141, 143–4, 145

diversity in Canadian cinema, 4, 5, 18, 120, 279; and film festivals, 342, 347, 354, 377, 386; measures for achieving, 5–6, 284; and policy, 5–6, 289, 317n12; and queer cinema, 345–6

DIY cinema, 13, 15, 105, 134–49, 352, 355

documentary film, 15–16, 88, 90, 284; archival material, 16, 192–4, 201, 203–16, 221–2, 229; autobiographical, 188–92, 240; *Bear 71* (Allison and Mendes, 2012), 16, 220, 221–6; *Beauty Day* (Cheel, 2011), 169–85; and Sonia Bonspille Boileau, 91–4, 96–7, 100–1; and Denis Côté, 114, 117; direct cinema, 104–5, 177–9, 182, 226–31; experimental, 240; *Highrise* (Cizek, 2010–15), 16, 219–20, 226–31; interactive documentary (i-doc), 217–32; and Sarah Polley, 67, 72–3; post-documentary, 217–18; rockumentary, 178; and self-realization, 182–3; *Souvenir* (NFB, 2015) film series, 16, 203–16; and Toronto DIY filmmakers, 134, 138, 140, 145; and Denis Villeneuve, 46, 63. *See also* Cheel, Jay; Maddin, Guy; *My Winnipeg* (Maddin, 2007); National Film Board

Dolan, Xavier, 5, 14, 25–41, 136; *Les amours imaginaires / Heartbeats* (2010), 30, 33, 35–6, 109; as auteur-star, 29–32, 38; and film festivals, 26, 32–4; international co-productions, 33–4; international reputation, 12, 14; *J'ai tué ma mère / I Killed My Mother* (2009), 30–3, 35–6, 109; *Juste la fin du monde / It's Only the End of the World* (2016), 30–1, 33, 35–6; *Laurence Anyways* (2012), 28–9, 31, 33, 35–7; *The Life and Death of John F. Donovan* (2018), 30, 34; *Matthias & Maxime* (2019), 31; *Mommy* (2014), 14, 28, 30, 33, 35–9; and popular music, 37–9; and Quebec culture, 25–9, 31, 34–9; and *renouveau*, 26–9, 106–7, 109, 111, 117; sense of place, 34–9; *Tom à la ferme* (2013), 31, 33, 35, 111; transnational culture, 34–9

Donnan, Wendy, 378
Donoghue, Emma, 329, 334
Dont Look Back (Pennebaker, 1967), 178
Dorland, Michael, 293
Drake, 64n10
Drljača, Igor, 140
Druick, Zoë, 204, 209, 210, 211
Dune (Villeneuve, 2021), 62
Duran, Francisca, 16, 246–9; *Cuentos de mi niñez (Tales from My Childhood)* (1991), 248; *8401* (2017), 248; *Even if my hands were full of truths* (2012), 248; *It Matters What* (2019), 248; *Retrato Oficial (Official Portrait)* (2003, 2009), 247–8; *Traje de Luces* (2018), 248
DuVernay, Ava, 328

Echaquan Dubé, Jemmy, 88
Echo (Pruska-Oldenhof, 2007), 242–4
Édouin, Guy, 106
Egoyan, Atom, 84n32, 136, 138, 146, 239, 386; and Canadian identity, 120–1; as established auteur, 3, 61, 370; and international co-productions, 322–3, 336n6
Elder, R. Bruce, "The Cinema We Need," 235, 254n28, 277
Elliot, Nicholas, 135
En terrains connus / Familiar Grounds (Lafleur, 2011), 107
Émond, Anne, 26, 333; *Our Loved Ones* (2015), 333

Enemy (Villeneuve, 2013), 43, 47, 49–54, 56, 58
Ennis, Simon, 138; *Lunarcy!* (2012), 138; *You Might as Well Live* (2009), 138
États nordiques, Les / Drifting States (Côté, 2004), 104–6, 107–10, 114
Etlinisigu'niet (Bleed Down / Vidés de leur sang) (Barnaby, 2015), 203–6
Eurimages, 322, 329
experimental film, 15–16, 88, 143; and Denis Côté, 114; and diaspora, 234–55; and gallery exhibition, 256–9; queer and trans, 341–3, 345, 355, 363–4. *See also* Araneda, Cecilia; Duran, Francisca; McIntyre, Lindsay; Nagler, Solomon; Pruska-Oldenhof, Izabella; skoltz, dominique t.; Torossian, Gariné; Toronto Queer Film Festival

F Word, The (Dowse, 2013), 329, 331
Falardeau, Philippe, 27, 332, 333; *The Good Lie* (2013), 27; *Monsieur Lazhar* (2011), 27; *My Internship in Canada?* (2015), 333; *My Salinger Year* (2020), 332
feminist cinema, 14, 68–9, 76–7, 82, 98, 353. *See also* Polley, Sarah
Ferguson, Scott, 361
Festival du nouveau cinéma, 26, 374
Fido (Currie, 2006), 151, 161
File Under Miscellaneous (Barnaby, 2010), 155–6
Film Farm (Rural Imaging Retreat), 249, 254n30
film festivals, 17, 26; circuit in Canada, 370–94; industry festivals, 371–3, 377, 386, 389nn5–6; queer film festivals, 340–69. *See also* Banff World Media Festival; Berlin Film Festival; Canada's Top Ten Film Festival; Cannes Film Festival; Festival du nouveau cinéma; Inside Out LGBT Film Festival; Montreal World Film Festival; National Canadian Film Day (NCFD); Sundance Film Festival; Toronto International Film Festival (TIFF); Toronto Queer Film Festival (TQFF); Vancouver International Film Festival (VIFF)
film production in Canada, 9–13; English-language production, 10–11; foreign service (runaway) production, 10–11, 275–97; Indigenous production, 12–13; international co-productions, 321–39; Quebec, 11–12; and unions, 298–320. *See also* foreign service (runaway) production; Indigenous filmmaking; international co-productions; National Film Board; policy, government film; Quebec; Telefilm Canada
Film or Video Production Service Tax Credit (PSTC), 285–6, 288–91
Fioret, Cameron, 130
Flahive, Gerry, 219, 227–8
Flanders, Elle, 360–1
foreign service (runaway) production, 10–11, 17, 275–97, 305–6
Fortin, Marc André, 203–4
Fournier, Yves Christian, 106; *Tout est parfait / Everything Is Fine* (2008), 109
Fraser, Crystal, 212–13
Funk, Kevan, 386

Genie Awards, 67, 70, 157. *See also* Canadian Screen Awards
Ghosh, Amitav, 234–5
Ginger Snaps (Fawcett, 2000), 150, 153, 159
Girl from Moush (Torossian, 1993), 238–40
Giroux, Maxime, 106, 107
Gittings, Christopher, 19n9, 20n13
Globerman, Steve, 287–90
Godard, Jean-Luc, 30, 53, 64n4, 106
Good Lie, The (Falardeau, 2013), 27
Goulet, Danis, 102, 157, 328; *Night Raiders* (2021), 328; *Wakening* (2013), 157
Gracq, Julien, 118, 119
Grbovic, Yvan, 106
Grierson, John, 218–19
Gross, David, 328
Gross, Paul, 333

Habib, André, 55
Handling, Piers, 61, 383
Harron, Mary, 83n3, 160
Hartman, Saidiya, 206, 208
Heisserer, Eric, 57
her silent life (McIntyre, 2011), 249–51
Hey Lady! (Polley, 2020), 67
Highrise: The Towers in the World, the World in the Towers (Cizek, 2010–15), 16, 219–20, 226–31
Hjort, Mette, 27–8
Hoffman, Philip, 249, 254n30
Hollywood, 11, 98, 373; big budget productions, 14, 15; career trajectory, 27–8; and Xavier Dolan, 30, 32–3; and horror film, 152, 157; and international co-productions, 322, 324; LGBT cinema, 361; and tax credits, 281, 290; and unions, 299, 312; and Denis Villeneuve, 42–4, 50, 54, 56–8, 61
Hopkins, Zoe, 88, 101
horror films, 15, 35, 95, 113–14, 150–66; auteurs, 157–60; comedy, 160–1; *giallo*, 161; Indigenous horror filmmakers, 152, 155–7; international co-productions, 152–3; subgenres, 152, 160–2; theorizing Canadian horror, 152–3; and wilderness, 152–5
Howell, Peter, 382
How Heavy This Hammer (Radwanski, 2015), 135, 143, 145
Hubbard, Tasha, 12
Hudecki, Sam, 43
Hunt, Dallas, 204, 213

I Shout Love (Polley, 2001), 14, 70–5
Idle No More movement, 88, 91, 207
imagineNATIVE Film + Media Arts Festival, 12, 101, 387–8
Incendies (Villeneuve, 2010), 27, 43, 47–51, 54, 56, 322
Indian Memento (Régnier, 1967), 209, 210–11, 212
Indigenous filmmaking, 7–10, 12–13, 284, 291, 300; and data sovereignty, 300; and horror films, 152, 155–7; Indigenous women filmmakers, 87–103; and international co-productions, 327–8; narrative sovereignty, 12; *Souvenir*, 203–16; and Quebec, 89–91; and visual sovereignty, 88; Wapikoni Mobile, 88. *See also* Barnaby, Jeff; Boileau, Sonia Bonspille; Goulet, Danis; imagineNATIVE Film + Media Arts Festival; Indigenous Screen Office; Kunuk, Zacharais; Monkman,

Kent; Monnet, Caroline; National Film Board
Indigenous Screen Office, 6, 12, 284, 291
industry. *See* film production in Canada
Inside Out LGBT Film Festival, 17, 340–1, 346–64; and censorship, 355–8; commercialization of, 360–2; founding of, 353–5; funding controversy, 356–60. *See also* Counting Past 2; film festivals; queer Canadian cinema; Toronto Queer Film Festival
International Alliance of Theatrical Stage Employees, Moving Picture Technicians, Artists and Allied Crafts of the United States, Its Territories and Canada (IATSE), 301–3, 310–14
international co-productions, 4, 17, 121, 321–39; Canadian-Irish co-productions, 283, 322, 328–9, 331–3, 337n18, 338n19; criticism of, 104, 146, 322–4; and cultural policy, 275, 283–6, 290; history in Canada, 324–8; horror films, 152; and unions, 313–14; and United States, 296n17; and Xavier Dolan, 28, 30, 33, 38. *See also* film production in Canada; foreign service (runaway) production; policy, government film; *Room* (Abrahamson, 2015); Telefilm Canada; tax credits
Inuit. *See* Indigenous filmmaking
Iordanova, Dina, 32, 373

Jack Brooks: Monster Slayer (Knautz, 2007), 161, 162
Jackson, Lisa, 12, 88, 101, 156; *Savage* (2009), 156–7

J'ai tué ma mère / I Killed My Mother (Dolan, 2009), 30–3, 35–6, 109
Jameson, Fredric, 41n23, 173–4
Jóhannsson, Jóhann, 43
Johnson, Matt, 15, 134–7, 140–1, 143–7; *The Dirties* (2013), 135, 141, 143–4, 145; *nirvanna the band the show* (2017–18), 134, 141, 144–5; 145; *Operation Avalanche* (2016), 135, 137, 141, 144, 145; Zapruder Films, 141, 146–7
Joly, Mélanie, 277, 322
Journals of Knud Rasmussen, The (Cohn and Kunuk, 2006), 327
Juno (Reitman, 2007), 281
Juste la fin du monde / It's Only the End of the World (Dolan, 2016), 30–1, 33, 35–6

Kahana, Jonathan, 177
Kanapé Fontaine, Natasha, 87
Kanata: Legacy of the Children of Aataentsic (Labelle, 1999), 211
Kanehsatake: 270 Years of Resistance (Obomsawin, 1993), 90–2, 94
Kaplan, E. Ann, 237
Kelly, Randy, 93
Kennedy, Rosanne, 204
King, Graham, 27
Kirshner, Mia, 223, 292
Kunuk, Zacharais, 5, 12, 95; *Atanarjuat: The Fast Runner* (2001), 3, 8, 12, 95, 123, 130, 327; *The Journals of Knud Rasmussen* (Cohn and Kunuk, 2006), 327; *Maliglutit (Searchers)* (2016), 385

labour market, film and television. *See* film production in Canada; unions, Canadian film and television
LaBruce, Bruce, 112, 151

Lafleur, Stéphane, 26–7, 32, 105, 107, 117; *Continental, un film sans fusil / Continental, a Film without Guns* (2007), 107; *En terrains connus / Familiar Grounds* (2011), 107; *Tu dors Nicole* (2014), 32
Lanser, Susan, 188
Lantos, Robert, 146
Last Call Indien (Boileau, 2010), 88, 91
Laurence Anyways (Dolan, 2012), 28–9, 31, 33, 35–7
Lavin, Sylvia, 265
Lavoie, Simon, 26, 106
Leach, Jim, 7
L'empreinte (Poliquin, 2014), 90
Lester, John, 288–90
Life and Death of John F. Donovan, The (Dolan, 2018), 30, 34
Lignes ennemis / Enemy Lines (Côté, 2010), 111, 114
Litz, Nadia, 138–9; *Hotel Congress* (2014), 139
Locarno International Film Festival, 26, 105, 106, 110, 148
Loiselle, André, 7, 35, 153
Loist, Skadi, 343, 371
Longfellow, Brenda, 64n9, 370
Low, Colin, 204, 225, 226, 230; *Circle of the Sun* (1960), 204–5
Lübecker, Nikolaj, 78
Lubezki, Emmanuel, 59

MacDonald, Adam, 163; *Backcountry* (2014), 153–5, 157
MacKay, Lindsay, 15, 122, 141; *Wet Bum* (2014), 15, 122–6, 129–32
MacKenzie, Scott, 8, 65n14
Maddin, Guy, 5, 15, 151, 186–202; and autobiographical fiction, 188–92; *Brand upon the Brain!* (2006), 188; *Cowards Bend the Knee* (2003), 186, 188; and documentary, 186–202; "Me Trilogy," 186, 188; *My Winnipeg* (2007), 186–202; *Saddest Music in the World, The* (2003), 186
Maelström (Villeneuve, 2000), 47, 50, 52–3, 56, 61
Magder, Ted, 312
Malick, Terrence, 45, 59
Maliglutit (Searchers) (Kunuk, 2016), 385
Manuel, George, 210
Maracle, Lee, 87
Marchessault, Janine, 7–8
Marks, Laura U., 237–8
Marshall, Bill, 90
Martel, Jean-François, 93
Matthias & Maxime (Dolan, 2019), 31
Maudie (Walsh, 2017), 329, 332, 338n27
Mayer, So, 82
McCarrol, Jay, 141, 144
McDonald, Bruce, 138, 169; *Hard Core Logo* (1996), 169; *Pontypool* (2008), 150, 153
McIntyre, Lindsay, 249–51; *her silent life* (2011), 249–51
McLuhan, Marshall, 235–6, 254n33
McSorley, Tom, 7, 121
Medium Density Fibreboard Films (MDFF), 134, 139, 142, 147
Mehta, Deepa, 3, 123, 131, 380; *Water* (2006), 131
Mendes, Jeremy, 222–3; *Bear 71* (Allison and Mendes, 2012), 16, 220, 221–6
Merleau-Ponty, Maurice, 174, 237
Messier-Rheault, Francois, 113
#MeToo movement, 68, 83n8, 292
Miller, Matthew, 137, 141
Mills, Jacquelyn, 139

Mobilize / Mobiliser (Monnet, 2015), 203, 208–12
Mollen Dupuis, Mélissa, 88, 91
Mommy (Dolan, 2014), 14, 28, 30, 33, 35–9
Monk, Katherine, 77, 150, 380
Monkman, Kent, 16, 203–4, 206–8, 213; *Sisters & Brothers / Soeurs et frères* (2015), 203, 206–8. See also *Souvenir* (NFB, 2015) film series
Monnet, Caroline, 16, 88, 203–4; *Mobilize / Mobiliser* (2015), 203, 208–12; *Portrait of an Indigenous Woman* (2014), 88. See also *Souvenir* (NFB, 2015) film series
Monsieur Lazhar (Falardeau, 2011), 27
Montgomery, Dan, 139–40, 142–3
Montpellier, Luc, 69
Montreal World Film Festival, 371, 374, 389n5
Mother of Many Children (Obomsawin, 1977), 93
Mouawad, Wajdi, 48
Moussinac, Léon, 44
Mulvey, Laura, 69
Muñoz, José Esteban, 345–6, 348, 364
Munro, Alice, 68
My Internship in Canada? (Falardeau, 2015), 333
my I's (Pruska-Oldenhof, 1997), 242
My Salinger Year (Falardeau, 2020), 332
My Winnipeg (Maddin, 2007), 186–202

Nabokov, Vladimir, 49, 54
Nagler, Solomon, 16, 244–6, 249; *perhaps/We* (2003), 244–6
Namaste, Viviane, 351, 353
Natali, Vincenzo, 151, 158–9; *Splice* (2009), 150, 158
National Canadian Film Day (NCFD), 375, 380, 383–8
national cinema, 9, 42, 61, 120–1, 169, 276; and film festivals, 370–94; and international co-productions, 321–39; Quebec national cinema, 28, 31, 34. See also Canada's Top Ten Film Festival; film production in Canada; National Canadian Film Day; national identity; Reel Canada; transnational cinema; Toronto International Film Festival (TIFF)
National Film Board (NFB), 4, 10, 16, 138, 368n64; archive, 16, 203–16, 220; Challenge for Change, 225, 226–7; Digital Studios, 220; and Indigenous filmmakers, 8, 16, 203–16; interactive documentary (i-doc), 217–26, 231–2; John Spotton Cinema, 361; *Souvenir* (2015) film series, 16, 203–16; and Denis Villeneuve, 42, 46, 63n1. See also documentary film; Grierson, John; Low, Colin; Perlmutter, Tom
national identity, 7–9, 25, 37, 103, 120–1; and cultural policy, 287, 333. See also Indigenous filmmaking; Quebec; transnational cinema
Netflix, 6, 67, 159, 304, 362; and Canadian film policy, 277; and co-productions, 328
New Wave of Quebec Cinema. See *renouveau*.
NFB. See National Film Board
Nichols, Bill, 34, 73
Night Raiders (Goulet, 2021), 328

Niro, Shelley, 101
nirvanna the band the show (Johnson, 2017–18), 134, 141, 144–5
Nguyen, Kim, 11, 27, 334; *Rebelle / War Witch* (2012), 334–5
Nolin, Manon, 87
Nos vies privées / Our Private Lives (Côté, 2007), 107, 108, 109, 110, 114
Nova Scotia, 151, 293, 302, 332, 338n27

Obomsawin, Alanis, 12, 14, 88–94, 101, 211; *Kanehsatake: 270 Years of Resistance* (1993), 90–2, 94; *Mother of Many Children* (1977), 93
O'Bomsawin, Angie-Pepper, 92, 98; *Princesses* (2016), 92–3
O'Bomsawin, Kim, 88, 93, 101; *Quiet Killing* (2017), 88
Odjick, Maisie, 99
Odobasic, Ajla, 139
O'Doherty, Brian, 257–8, 264–5, 269
Oka Legacy, The (Boileau, 2015), 88, 91–2, 100
Ontario, 7, 10; coming-of-age films in, 120–33; film classification and censorship, 355, 357–8; film industry, 10, 276–7, 285, 308, 322, 360; and horror films, 153–4, 159; and low-budget filmmaking, 136, 169, 249
Operation Avalanche (Johnson, 2016), 135, 137, 141, 144, 145
Oscars. *See* Academy Awards
Ouellet, Rafaël, 106, 109
Our Loved Ones (Émond, 2015), 333
Owen, Don, 146, 208–9; *High Steel* (1965), 208–9

Papamichael, Stella, 77
Parker, Maureen, 11
Pereda, Nicolás, 140
perhaps/We (Nagler, 2003), 244–6
Perlmutter, Tom, 219–20, 226–7
Perry, Alex Ross, 136
Petrychyn, Jonathan, 343
Picasso, Pablo: *Guernica* (1937), 50, 54
Pike, David, 7, 132n4
Pilote, Sébastien, 106, 113
Piotrowska, Agnieszka, 73
poetic cinema. *See* experimental film
policy, government film, 3–6, 11–13, 17; Canada Media Fund, 284, 291, 312–14, 326, 385; and film festivals, 370, 372–5, 387–8; and Indigenous filmmaking, 12–13; international co-productions, 321–39; and low-budget filmmaking, 105; Quebec, 12; tax credits, 275–97; and unions, 299–300, 311–15. *See also* Black Screen Office; Canada Council for the Arts; Canadian Audio-Visual Certification Office (CAVCO); Indigenous Screen Office; international co-productions; National Film Board; Quebec; Telefilm Canada
Polley, Sarah, 5, 14, 67–86, 382; adaptations of literary work, 67–8; *Alias Grace* (2017), 67–8, 382; *Away from Her* (2006), 67–8, 71, 74–5; and feminist cinema, 68–70, 76–7, 80, 82; *Hey Lady!* (2020), 67; *I Shout Love* (2001), 70–5; and melancholy, 70, 74–5, 77–9, 82; and #MeToo movement, 68, 83n8; *Stories We Tell* (2012), 67–8, 72–4, 84n24; *Take This Waltz* (2011), 75–82

Polytechnique (Villeneuve, 2009), 27, 32, 47, 50–6, 275
Pompeii (Anderson, 2014), 275, 291n2, 325
Pontypool (McDonald, 2008), 150, 153
Princesses (A. O'Bomsawin, 2016), 88, 92–3, 98–9
Prisoners (Villeneuve, 2013), 27, 43, 47–54, 56
Pruska-Oldenhof, Izabella, 16, 242–4; *Echo* (2007), 242–4; *my I's* (1997), 242
PSTC. *See* Film or Video Production Service Tax Credit

Que ta joie demeure / Joy of Man's Desiring (Côté, 2014), 14, 15
Quebec, 3–4, 7, 218, 277, 380, 389n5; film production in, 10–13, 285, 300, 308, 312; Indigenous women's cinema, 87–103; international co-productions, 322–3, 325, 331; Loi sur le cinema, 12; *renouveau*, 13, 104–19, 136; transnational auteur cinema, 25–41; and Denis Villeneuve, 42, 54, 63. *See also* Dolan, Xavier; film production in Canada; Indigenous filmmaking; national identity; policy, government film; Société de développement des entreprises culturelles (SODEC); transnational cinema
Québékoisie (Huggins and Carrier, 2013), 90
queer Canadian cinema, 14, 17, 121, 340–69; queer futurity, 346–8, 364; re-defined, 345–6; and transgender identities, 350–3. *See also* Counting Past 2; Dolan, Xavier; Inside Out LGBT Film Festival; Toronto Queer Film Festival (TQFF)

Raab, Jared, 137, 141, 144
Radwanski, Kazik, 15, 134–5, 138–40, 142–7; *Anne at 13,000 ft* (2019), 143; *Assault* (2007), 138, 139, 143; *How Heavy This Hammer* (2015), 135, 143, 145; Medium Density Fibreboard Films (MDFF), 134–5, 139, 142, 147, 149n21; *Tower* (2012), 135, 139, 143, 145
Rastegar, Roya, 376, 379
Rathbone, Marjorie, 93
Rebelle / War Witch (Nguyen, 2012), 334–5
reconciliation. *See* Truth and Reconciliation Commission
Reel Canada, 384–6
renouveau, 13, 104–19, 136. *See also* Côté, Denis; Deraspe, Sophie; Dolan, Xavier; Émond, Anne; Lafleur, Stéphane; Lavoie, Simon
Répertoire des villes disparues / Ghost Town Anthology (Côté, 2019), 107, 113, 114
Resident Evil: Afterlife (Anderson, 2010), 17, 275, 277, 279, 325
Retrato Oficial (Official Portrait) (Duran, 2003, 2009), 247–8
REW-FFWD (Villeneuve, 1994), 46, 63n1
Rhymes for Young Ghouls (Barnaby, 2013), 95, 155
Ringuette, Eve, 89, 92, 96
Roby, Daniel, 157
Rogers, Anna Backman, 74
Room (Abrahamson, 2015), 321–4, 328–36
Ross, Mirha-Soleil, 350–3

Royal Commission on Aboriginal Peoples, 90, 92
Rozema, Patricia, 3, 370
runaway film production. *See* foreign service (runaway) production
Rustic Oracle (Boileau, 2019), 88, 96–7, 99–100

Saddest Music in the World, The (Maddin, 2003), 186
Safdie, Josh and Benny, 136
Salah, Trish, 352–3
Salesman (Maysles, Maysles, and Zwerin, 1969), 178
Samian, 88
Saramago, José 42, 49, 53, 56, 58
Sarris, Andrew, 44–5, 55, 60, 61; interior meaning, 45, 55, 60, 64n8. *See also* auteur
Savage (Jackson, 2009), 156–7
Scarry, Elaine, 237
Scorsese, Martin, 27
Shape of Water, The (del Toro, 2017), 17, 276–7, 279
Shields, Carol, 82n1, 331
Shin, Albert, 140
Sicario (Villeneuve, 2015), 32, 47, 49–54, 56, 60
Sicondolfo, Claudia, 378
Simpson, Leanne, 87
Sinclair, Murray, 207–8
Sirois-Trahan, Jean-Pierre, 55, 136
Sisters & Brothers / Soeurs et frères (Monkman, 2015), 203, 206–8
Skindigenous (Boileau, 2018), 88, 92–3, 96, 98
skoltz, dominique t., 16, 256–72; *Face à Face* (2015), 267–8, 270; *y2o* (2013–15), 257–70; *y2o dualités_*, 259–60, 263, 266, 270; *y2o Huis clos* (2015), 261–2, 266, 268

Sleeping Giant (Cividino, 2015), 15, 122–3, 126–32, 135, 382
Sobchack, Vivian, 173
Société de développement des entreprises culturelles (SODEC), 12, 30–1, 42; and international co-productions, 322, 332
Song of Granite (Collins, 2017), 332
Soska, Jen, 151, 159; *American Mary* (Soska and Soska, 2012), 158, 159
Soska, Sylvia, 151, 159, *American Mary* (Soska and Soska, 2012), 158, 159
Souvenir (NFB, 2015) film series, 16, 203–16. See also *Etlinisigu'niet (Bleed Down / Vidés de leur sang)* (Barnaby, 2015); *Mobilize / Mobiliser* (Monnet, 2015); *Sisters & Brothers / Soeurs et frères* (Monkman, 2015)
sovereignty: data, 300; narrative, 12; visual, 88
Sparling, Gordon, 218
Splice (Natali, 2009), 150, 158
Stahl, Matt, 178–9, 184n11
Stalker (Tarkovsky, 1979), 53
Stay (von Carolsfeld, 2013), 331–2
Stone Time Touch (Torossian, 2007), 240–2
Stories We Tell (Polley, 2012), 67–8, 72–4, 84n24
Straw, Will, 7–8
Strong, Amanda, 88, 101
Sundance Film Festival, 26, 145, 221
Surviving Crooked Lake (Drews, Krybus, and Miller, 2008), 141

Ta peau si lisse / A Skin So Soft (Côté, 2017), 114, 116
Tagaq, Tanya, 204, 207, 210, 212
Tailfeathers, Elle-Máijá, 12, 88, 101, 327–8; *The Body Remembers When*

the World Broke Open (Hepburn and Tailfeathers, 2019), 327–8
Take This Waltz (Polley, 2011), 14, 75–82
tax credits, 3, 11, 12, 17, 33, 121; Canadian Film or Video Production Tax Credit (CPTC), 281–5, 290–1, 335; Capital Cost Allowance, 281, 313, 325, 334; and cultural policy, 275–97; and co-productions, 322–36; European, 290–1; Film or Video Production Service Tax Credit (PSTC), 285–6, 288–9, 335; provincial tax credits, 285–6; and unions, 312–14. *See also* Canadian Audio-Visual Certification Office (CAVCO); film production in Canada; foreign service (runaway) production; international co-productions; policy, government film; Telefilm Canada
Taylor, Diana, 204, 210
Telefilm Canada, 4, 10, 18, 121, 143, 291; Canada Feature Film Fund, 373, 375; Canada Showcase Program, 374, 390n9, 391n25; Canadian Film Development Corporation, 281, 313, 372; and cultural policy, 312, 313, 370; definition of Canadian production, 283, 296n17, 297n27; and Xavier Dolan, 30–1; and film festivals, 362, 270, 373, 374, 377, 387; funding envelopes, 105, 146; and gender parity, 6; international co-productions, 321–2, 325–6, 332–3, 335, 337n10; microbudget funding, 15; Talent to Watch program, 146–7, 381; Theatrical Exhibition Program, 375. *See also* film production in Canada; foreign service (runaway) production; international co-productions; policy, government film; tax credits
television, 13, 17, 18, 176; directors, 88, 136, 141–2, 159; industry, 275–8, 280–7, 301, 305, 329–32. *See also* Aboriginal Peoples Television Network (APTN), Canadian Broadcasting Corporation (CBC), Netflix
Tessier, Albert, 218
Tierney, Kevin, 333, 335
TIFF. *See* Toronto International Film Festival
Todd, Loretta, 101
Tom à la ferme (Dolan, 2013), 31, 33, 35, 111
Tony Robbins: I Am Not Your Guru (Berlinger, 2016), 182
Toronto DIY filmmakers movement, 15, 134–49
Toronto International Film Festival (TIFF), 3, 30, 34, 102; Bell Lightbox, 18, 138, 370, 376–8, 382–3, 386–8; best Canadian films poll, 67, 377; in Canadian festival landscape, 370–94; Festival of Festivals, 363, 370; Film Circuit, 378; Film Reference Library, 146; and Indigenous filmmaking, 12, 102, 103n9; Perspective Canada program, 4, 370, 376–7, 380–2, 386, 391n25; Student Showcase, 139. *See also* Canada's Top Ten Film Festival; film festivals
Toronto New Wave, 136, 138
Toronto Queer Film Festival (TQFF), 17, 340–50, 362–4; established, 341, 345, 348; and queer futurity,

345–6; and radical queer and trans art, 341–2, 343–5, 347–9; Toronto Queer Media Arts Centre, 348. *See also* film festivals; queer Canadian cinema

Torossian, Gariné, 238–42, 244; *Girl from Moush* (1993), 238–40; *Stone Time Touch* (2007), 240–2

Tower (Radwanski, 2012), 135, 139, 143, 145

transnational cinema, 6, 9, 13–14, 61, 69–70; and Xavier Dolan, 25–41; and film festivals, 388; and international co-productions, 121, 321–39; opportunistic transnationalism, 27–8

trauma and cinema, 16, 65n14, 83n8, 206, 234–55; and haptic visuality, 237–8

Tree of Life (Malick, 2011), 59

32 août sur terre, Un (Villeneuve, 1998), 32, 47, 50–3, 60

Tribe Called Red, A, 204, 207, 212, 214n6

Trimble, Nakkita, 93

Truffaut, François, 113, 116

Truth and Reconciliation Commission, 9, 90, 92, 203, 207

Tu dors Nicole (Lafleur, 2014), 32

Turrell, James, 52, 54, 60; *Breathing Light* (2013), 51, 64n10

unions, Canadian film and television, 17, 292, 298–319; and independent production, 304–9; policy development, 312–14; and training, 310–11. *See also* Alliance of Canadian Cinema Television and Radio Artists (ACTRA); Directors Guild of Canada (DGC); film production in Canada; International Alliance of Theatrical Stage Employees, Moving Picture Technicians, Artists and Allied Crafts of the United States, Its Territories and Canada (IATSE); Writers Guild of Canada (WGC)

Unless (Gilsenan, 2016), 331

Urquhart, Peter, 281

Vallée, Jean-Marc, 12, 26–7, 136, 382; C.R.A.Z.Y. (2005), 27; *Young Victoria* (2009), 27

van Belkom, Edo, 150, 163

Vancouver International Film Festival (VIFF), 370–2

VanderBurgh, Jennifer, 281, 293

Vermette, Patrice, 43, 52

Verreault, Myriam, 106, 107

Vic + Flo ont vu un ours / Vic + Flo Saw a Bear (Côté, 2013), 26, 107, 111, 114

Vikings (History, 2013), 329, 332

Villeneuve, Denis, 5, 14, 42–66, 322, 382; *Arrival* (2016), 43, 46, 49–54, 57–60, 62; as auteur, 42–4, 61–2; *Blade Runner 2049* (2017), 43, 46–7, 49–51, 53–4, 62, 382; *Dune* (2021), 62; *Enemy* (2013), 43, 47, 49–54, 56, 58; *Incendies* (2010), 27, 43, 47–51, 54, 56, 322; international success, 26–7, 32; *Maelström* (2000), 47, 50, 52–3, 56, 61; *Polytechnique* (2009), 27, 32, 47, 50–6, 275; *Prisoners* (2013), 27, 43, 47–54, 56; REW-FFWD (1994), 46, 63n1; and Quebec cinema, 12, 14; *Sicario* (2015), 32, 47, 49–54, 56, 60; *Un 32 août sur terre* (1998), 32, 47, 50–3, 60

Void, The (Kostanski and Gillespie, 2016), 158, 162

Voshart, Daniel, 139
Vuckovic, Jovanka, 151, 159–60

Waititi, Taika, 328
Wakening (Goulet, 2013), 157
Wang, Ban, 237
Wapikoni Mobile, 88
Water (Mehta, 2006), 131
water, imagery and thematics of, 28, 87, 120–33, 259–63, 267–70
Waugh, Tom, 340–1, 346
Weerasethakul, Apichatpong, 106
Weinstein, Harvey, 68, 292
Wente, Jesse, 12, 102
Wet Bum (MacKay, 2014), 15, 122–6, 129–32
What Comes Between (Araneda, 2009), 246–8
White, Jerry, 7, 120
White, Patricia, 62, 362

Wilcox (Côté, 2019), 105, 114
Williams, Owen, 137, 144
Williams, Paul, 204–5
Wilner, Norm, 333, 335
Wintonick, Peter, 219; *Seeing Is Believing: Handicams, Human Rights and the News* (2006), 219
Women in Film and Television, 284, 317n12
Writers Guild of Canada (WGC), 11, 301–3, 312–14

Young Victoria (Vallée, 2009), 27
y2o (skoltz, 2013–15), 257–70

Zapruder Films, 141, 146, 147
Zavadil, Ralph, 170–6, 179–83; *The Cap'n Video Show* (1990–95), 170–6, 179–83. See also *Beauty Day* (Cheel, 2011)